Macroeconomics for Managers

J. R. CLARK
University of Tennessee at Martin

CLIFFORD F. THIES
University of Baltimore

J. HOLTON WILSON
Central Michigan University

SAUL Z. BARR
University of Tennessee at Martin

ALLYN AND BACON
Boston   London   Sydney   Toronto

This book is dedicated to

TOM E. HENDRIX

An Entrepreneur and Philanthropist,
Whose Positive Attitude
and Belief in the Potential of Every Human Being
Is an Inspiration

Copyright © 1990 by Allyn and Bacon
A Division of Simon & Schuster, Inc.
160 Gould Street
Needham Heights, Massachusetts 02194

Cover administrator: Linda Dickinson
Production administrator: Lorraine Perrotta
Series editor: Rich Wohl
Series editorial assistant: Kelley Saunders-Butcher

Library of Congress Cataloging-in-Publication Data

Macroeconomics for managers / [edited by] J.R. Clark . . . [et al.].
   p. cm.
  Includes index.
  ISBN 0-205-12210-8
  1. Managerial economics.   2. Macroeconomics.   I. Clark, J. R.
(Jeff R.)
HD30.22.M23   1990
339'.024658—dc20   89-35099
                                        CIP

Printed in the United States of America.
10 9 8 7 6 5 4 3 2 1   94 93 92 91 90

Contents

═ Preface ═══════════════════

Macroeconomics for Managers is designed for intermediate- and advanced-level courses in macroeconomics. It teaches the basic theory of macroeconomics in a pragmatic and usable fashion to decision makers in business, finance, and related areas. It is an applied text that provides real-world case studies, as well as problems and projects, to illustrate the conduct of business in the contemporary, dynamic, and international macroeconomy. Every chapter begins and, in many cases, ends with specific illustrations of how the theory is used by the manager. In many areas of the text, the discipline of finance has actively been integrated into macroeconomic theory so that the state of the art in both fields is represented.

As the economy becomes more complex, the number of factors corporate managers must take into account increases substantially. The growth of multinational corporations and increasing world trade make international considerations a larger part of corporate decision making than ever before.

Accordingly, Part I of the text stresses the uses of macroeconomics in business planning and forecasting. Coverage is also afforded the increasing role played by the public sector and its impact on the corporate decision-making process.

Part II concentrates on economic policy and the influence of government institutions on both the development and implementation of economic policy.

In Part III, Chapters 8 and 13 stress the significant role of interest rates in corporate capital expansions and the term structure of interest rates. Asset pricing, capital budgeting, loanable funds, and the effects of inflation are covered in these chapters as well. We present an in-depth understanding of consumption concentrating on views that transcend the traditional Keynesian approach to include more recent contributions involving the effects of policy changes in taxes, budget deficits, social security, wealth, and liquidity. The material again is presented in a fashion that illustrates its relevance to business managers.

Part IV addresses several major economic problem areas including inflation, unemployment, interest rates, and growth and productivity. Part V focuses on business conditions analysis providing the managerial decision maker with the tools and techniques of forecasting. This section of the text is designed to stand alone or it can be a reference tool for managers who use forecasting information produced by others. Part V serves as an interpretive as well as explanatory section and may be used with varying levels of intensity depending upon student and faculty interest.

The overall goal of *Macroeconomics for Managers* is to provide a quick, efficient, and useful means of integrating macro theory into the manager's corporate tool kit. The text can easily be used both to learn the theory and to serve as an ongoing reference volume when future need arises. To this end, each chapter provides current references, which are suggested to further the user's scope of understanding.

A full complement of ancillary support materials are available to the student and instructor including a student study guide, instructor's manual, and computerized problem sets. The software package offers an applied, user-friendly set of problems with solutions to guide the student and faculty through the use of macro theory in solving real-world problems.

Acknowledgments. This volume, like all others, benefited from the contributions of many individuals. The usual broad spectrum of economists who reviewed the manuscript and a large group of technical, clerical, and support staff helped to convert the project from a collection of ideas into a finished, professional product.

There are several individuals whose contributions were of such significance that they should be acknowledged individually. First and perhaps foremost, Dr. Fred McKara of East Tennessee University contributed a painstaking review, which served to improve the content significantly. Additional insightful reviews of the manuscript were provided by Stuart Allen, University of North Carolina at Greensboro; Ziad Keilany, University of Tennessee at Chattanooga; Thomas O. Wisley, Western Kentucky University; Sayez A. Elayon, Northwest Louisiana State University; Willis Peterson, University of Minnesota; and Michael Cook, William Jewell College. In addition, Christopher F. Baum of Boston College, Robert Crawford of Brigham Young University, and Thomas Sturrock of Federal National Mortgage Corporation contributed to several professional conversations on topics that eventually found prominent places in the text.

We appreciate the outstanding clerical and research support provided by Fonda Barnhart, Debbie Martin, Kelly Taylor, DoRann Killebrew, and Ron Barbati, who assisted a great deal in the background research for the volume.

We are also indebted to our mentors Charles Goetz of the University of Virginia and James Buchanan of George Mason University and our colleagues Philip R. Manger of York College and J. Huston McCulloch of Ohio State University.

We must also acknowledge the support of Dr. Gary Young, Dean of the School of Business, University of Tennessee at Martin, as well as support by the schools of business administration at Central Michigan University and the University of Baltimore.

Finally, having acknowledged the contributions of others, it is traditional to accept responsibility for any errors that might remain. This we do out of tradition and a sense of professional responsibility. Macroeconomics, like all sciences, is a continuously evolving set of working hypotheses. It is based not so much on proof from authority but on a handful of basic insights into human behavior and on our best rationalization of history and statistics. We are grateful for our inheritance of knowledge but mindful of the need for prudence in employing it unquestioned in our decision making. We urge you to share this view.

For any errors of omission or commission that may remain, we actively encourage students and faculty alike to drop us a note so that we can continually improve the text to best meet their needs.

J. R. Clark
J. H. Wilson
C. Thies
S. Z. Barr

PART ONE

Introduction and Basic Models

_1_
An Introduction
to Macroeconomics

1.1 INTRODUCTION

Economics is the study of how society allocates its scarce resources among
its unlimited wants and needs. Since resources have some finite limit, we
are forced to make choices. We must choose which needs to fulfill and which
needs to let go unfulfilled. Therefore, economics in its most basic form is
the study of choice making. The economic science has traditionally been
divided into microeconomics and macroeconomics. *Microeconomics* is the
study of choices made on the individual level, with the unit of analysis being
one producing or consuming unit. *Macroeconomics* has traditionally examined the choice process from the viewpoint of the entire economy. For example, macroeconomics would be concerned with the levels of inflation,
unemployment, and interest rates that prevail in an economy at any particular
point in time.

In recent years, however, the distinction between micro and macro has
been blurred by the rising popularity of what some economists refer to as
the "microeconomic foundations of macroeconomics." Such economists
argue that, in reality, only individuals make choices, and therefore, these
economists place much greater emphasis on the role of the individual in the
macro economy. While a variety of viewpoints exist, there are three key
ingredients to gaining a meaningful understanding of contemporary macroeconomics. The study of macroeconomics must be based on (1) an understanding of the individual as choice maker and (2) a consideration of the role

played by government and social institutions in (3) the pursuit of society's economic goals. Subsequent sections of this chapter develop each of these key ingredients more fully.

This text is devoted to the study of applied contemporary macroeconomics for managerial decision making. In brief, this is a book about macroeconomics for managers with an emphasis on the growing importance of finance and international transactions. It considers the individual as the primary choice-making unit but also traces out the increasing influence of social institutions such as government, the courts, and the Federal Reserve System on the outcomes of the choice process.

1.2 MACROECONOMICS IN PRIVATE-SECTOR DECISIONS

The importance of macroeconomics for managerial decision making is increasing rapidly from two directions. First, the complexity of corporate decision making is increasing. As the economy itself becomes more complex, the number of factors corporate managers must take into account grows. Second, the growth of multinational corporations and increasing world trade make international considerations a larger part of corporate decision making than ever before. For these reasons, corporate financial executives have a growing need to understand and be able to apply macroeconomics to their decision process. Specifically, macroeconomics has an impact on two major areas of corporate decision making: forecasting and planning.

Forecasting   In a world where change is the creator of opportunity and the destroyer of those too slow to react, forecasting is an essential tool. A firm must be able to forecast with some accuracy the future demand for its product. Failure to do so could result in either insufficient inventory and lost sales or excessive inventory levels and significantly increased costs and reduced profits. Accurate demand forecasts also enable the producer to plan production schedules, acquire sufficient raw materials, and build the most efficient size of plant. Demand for a product usually depends on consumer income, employment, interest rates, consumer tastes and preferences, tax rates, and a host of other variables. Much of this information is clearly economic in nature and increases the dependency of managerial decision making on an understanding of economics.

Planning   The corporate planning function takes on two dimensions, both of which involve economics-based decision making. First, financial planning requires decisions on capital budgeting. The firm must decide in which projects to invest scarce capital and which projects should be avoided. Choices about when to invest in capital expansions are frequently as important as which projects to undertake. Both the ''which'' and ''when'' questions in capital budgeting require an understanding of interest rates, product demand, the time value of money, and the effects government policies might have on any of these economic variables. The financial planner will be engaged in estimating the cash flow of the firm and choosing among alternative uses for the cash the firm is expected to produce. At the same time, estimates must be made of the firm's future borrowing needs. All such estimates will be influenced not only by the demand for the firm's products, but also by general economic conditions and government economic policy.

The second aspect of planning is more strategic in nature and is concerned with much longer-run questions such as what industries the firm wants to be involved in over the next decade. For example, given the current wave of antismoking legislation and popular sentiment, R. J. Reynolds–Nabisco might want to consider whether they will emphasize the food-products aspect of the corporation and phase out their involvement in tobacco products in the next decade. Alternatively, their strategic planning might consider efforts to develop and market tobacco substitutes. Such decisions will obviously require demand forecasts and considerations of consumer income, employment, tastes and preferences, costs of capital conversion from tobacco production to alternatives, and so on. As we can see, all these decisions have a very large economic component.

Other strategic planning might require an assessment of not only the current and future economic climate but also political influences on that economic climate. For example, during the last 2 months of 1980, Ronald Reagan had been elected to, but not yet sworn in as, President of the United States. Reagan ran on a platform of rebuilding America's military strength. During this same time period, interest rates were very high, with the prime rate reaching 20 percent, and much of private-sector corporate investment was choked off. Reagan's election, however, prompted firms in the aerospace and defense-related industries to begin very large capital expansions even in the face of such high interest rates. Obviously, the political influence of Mr. Reagan's election had significantly affected the future demand for military products. Firms in these industries frequently had both military and nonmilitary product lines, but they made strategic decisions to emphasize military production and in many instances reduce their nonmilitary production. The point here is that an understanding of the economic consequences of changes in the political and institutional environment also contributes to the quality of managerial decision making.

1.3 MACROECONOMICS AND PUBLIC-SECTOR DECISIONS: POLITICAL ECONOMY AND THE ROLE OF GOVERNMENT

The choices that take place in the government and institutional sector have very large impacts on the private sector. Government and the social institutions we have created provide the overall framework in which private-sector economic transactions take place. Accordingly, an understanding of the macro economy is incomplete without consideration being given to political economy. Government affects the economy most directly through the three means of fiscal policy, monetary policy, and regulation. We will discuss each of these functions in more detail.

1.3.1 Fiscal Policy

Fiscal policy is the taxation and spending aspects of government. In its taxing and spending behavior, the government creates incentives that significantly affect the choices of both producers and consumers. For example, if income tax rates are increased, the incentives for workers to work more hours, producers to produce more goods, and savers and investors to save and invest more are significantly reduced. A tax reduction would have the opposite effect. On the expenditure side, government spends approximately 20 percent of the nation's gross national product and is the largest single employer in the economy. Spending of such magnitude can obviously affect overall demand in the economy as well as the levels of employment.

1.3.2 Monetary Policy

Monetary policy concerns the expansion and/or contraction of monetary aggregates to control the money supply in an attempt to provide a more stable economy. Federal Reserve control of the money supply can affect the prevailing level of interest rates. Changes in interest rates affect the incentives faced by savers and investors as well as the willingness of firms to engage in direct capital expansion. Rapid fluctuations in interest rates also affect the risk levels in investing and the level of business optimism and/or pessimism. In addition, many economists argue that the expansion and contraction of the money supply can have a direct effect on the level of spending in the private sector. For these reasons, the monetary behavior of government exerts considerable influence on the choice making of households and firms. The details of this relationship are explored more fully in Chapters 6 and 7.

1.3.3 Regulation

The *regulatory function* of government establishes and enforces laws in an attempt to encourage competition, protect the public, and generally assist markets to function more efficiently. The regulatory function of government is perhaps its most pervasive. Government sets the rules of the economic game, and the rules, to a large extent, can determine who the winners and losers are. Choice makers operating within a given set of rules and property rights will strive to maximize their well-being within the constraints of those rules. However, as James Buchanan pointed out as early as 1962 in *The Calculus of Consent,* there may be even greater gains to be made by individuals in attempting to influence the structure of the rules themselves. By defining and enforcing property rights through a system of laws and courts, government provides the environment in which private-sector transactions take place. Government defines nonpermissible forms of business behavior, such as prohibiting coercion, fraud, theft, collusion, and certain types of environmental pollution. It encourages permissible forms of business behavior such as marketplace competition. Just how effective government has been at achieving its goals in the regulatory function has been and will continue to be the subject of much controversy. However, it is safe to say that in total the fiscal, monetary, and regulatory activities of government do exert significant influence on private-sector decision making.

1.4 NORMATIVE ECONOMICS AND SOCIETY'S ECONOMIC GOALS

1.4.1 Positive and Normative Economics

Economists are frequently called on both to identify the alternative solutions to an economic problem and to suggest which is the superior alternative. This dual responsibility involves both the positive and normative aspects of the economic science. *Positive economics* is that branch of economics which deals with what is or what will be. It concerns objective factual matters that are measurable or verifiable in nature. A positive economic statement would be, ''If the price of gasoline rises rapidly, consumers will reduce their consumption of gasoline.'' *Normative economics,* on the other hand, deals with value judgments and is not verifiable or measurable. An example of a normative economic statement would be something like, ''Taxes in the United States are too high or corporate profits are unfair.'' Positive economics can establish the alternative choices in a given situation and identify the cost and benefits of each. Determining which choice should be made requires value judgments and is clearly in the realm of normative economics. In the area of economic goals and government policy, normative economics has been a growing and, in many cases, dominant force, as illustrated in James Buchanan's 1986 Nobel address. He stated, ''The constructivist urge to assume a role as social engineer, to suggest policy reforms that 'should' or 'should not' be made, independently of any revelation of individual's preferences through the political process, has simply proved too strong for many to resist.''

1.4.2 Economic Goals

All economies face the basic economic problem of limited resources and unlimited wants and needs. Therefore, there is always a need to establish economic goals that identify the priorities of the economy. While these economic goals may vary from nation to nation, there appears to be a prevailing desire to maximize employment, output, and economic growth while maintaining a relatively stable price level. Since 1946, the United States has had a formal statement of at least part of its economic goals in the form of the Employment Act. The act set out useful employment opportunities for those able to and seeking work as well as the promotion of maximum production and purchasing power as key economic goals.

1.4.2.1 Employment and Output

The level of goods and services an economy produces is a direct function of its level of resource use. Therefore, maximizing output tends to support the goal of full employment. With the great depression of the 1930s, output fell by approximately 30 percent, and as much as one-quarter of the labor force was unemployed. Today, with much higher levels of output, unemployment rates exceeding 6 percent focus a great deal of political attention on the issue. In an economy as complex and changing as that of the United States, it is highly unlikely that 100 percent of the labor force will be fully employed at any one time. At least some portion of the work force will be between jobs or in the search process all the time. While there is little debate on the merits of full employment as a major economic goal, just what constitutes full employment and how it might be attained are controversial questions subject to political, as well as economic, considerations, and these will be discussed in detail in Chapter 12.

1.4.2.2 Economic Growth

Economic growth is a key goal for three reasons. First, as population grows and larger segments of that population enter the labor force, economic growth provides increasing employment opportunities. The absence of growth under an expanding population or at least an increasing work force usually means increasing unemployment. Second, since wants and needs are unlimited, the economy always desires to produce more goods and services to meet those needs. Third, efforts to promote economic equality and stability through income redistribution are accepted more readily by the population in periods of growth. It is politically easier to redistribute the fruits of a growing economy than one that is contracting.

1.4.2.3 Price Stability

Rapidly fluctuating prices increase the risks of capital expansion and therefore reduce the level of business investment. Production planning is greatly complicated by frequent changes in the prices of raw materials. Labor contracts, interest rates, and many other expectations-based agreements are adversely affected by rapid price changes. For these reasons, price stability is an important goal. Stability does not necessarily imply constant prices as much as it does prices that fluctuate with less magnitude and frequency. Also, it is difficult to quantify how large or how frequent price changes must be before they affect expectations.

The specific means by which different economies pursue their economic goals vary a great deal, as does their degree of success in attaining them. However, since these are national goals, there is always some degree of political influence involved in their selection as well as their pursuit. It is in the interplay of economics and politics that normative economics is most pervasive. In the setting of economic goals and the selection among various means to achieve them, normative economics and political considerations frequently play as large a role as positive economics.

1.5 ECONOMIC THEORY AND WHY ECONOMISTS DISAGREE

1.5.1 Economic Theory

All economies make choices guided by economic theory. An economic theory is a simplified view of reality. Economic theory creates descriptive rules of human choice behavior based on real-world observation. For example, by observing the fluid-consumption habits of large numbers of people, we can formulate a single descriptive rule that says people consume more fluids in summer than in winter. More specifically, we might observe a positive relationship between the ambient temperature and fluid consumption. Our descriptive rule or "theory" might be that fluid consumption rises with temperature. Knowing this general behavioral rule is more helpful to us than attempting to continually assimilate and understand all the individual data on fluid consumption. The manager in a beverage manufacturing firm does not need to know exactly how much fluid you or I consume and when, but he or she does want to know if production should be expanded in the summer months or whether the product will be consumed more in warmer climates. Such a manager is more interested in a useful descriptive behavioral rule than in a collection of specific consumption data. The theory itself does have limits and is not necessarily accurate for each and every consumer all the time. For example, the behavioral rule might not hold beyond a certain temperature or level of fluid consumption. We may consume more fluids as the temperature rises up to some maximum, say, four quarts a day. Beyond this point, however, we may not be able to consume more fluid, and the limits of the theory have been exceeded. The managerial decision maker must be concerned with the limitations as well as the usefulness of the theory. The real goal of economics is to produce useful models that accurately predict the choices people make. Macro for managers centers around the use of these predictions to plan, organize, and produce more efficiently.

1.5.2 Why Economists Disagree

All economic models are built on some basic assumptions and limitations regarding market structure, institutional interactions, and human motivations and are, at least in part, subject to normative interpretations. For example, the theory of temperature and fluid consumption may be quite accurate for Western economies, while drawing conclusions from it for Middle Eastern nations might be quite erroneous. A beer producer might find that his or her product has higher per capita consumption in the Deep South, where temperatures are higher, than in the northern United States. Realizing that the mean temperature of Saudi Arabia is higher than that of the southern United States, the beer producer might want to believe that potential sales in Saudi Arabia would be very large. However, this nation has somewhat severe religious sanctions against the consumption of alcohol that invalidate the theory in this particular application. Since models are usually assumed to be correct unless sufficient evidence has been compiled to refute their validity, a wide variety of economic opinion may exist on any given issue.

Economic theory is also based on the observed behavior of human beings, and human beings learn from experience and modify their behaviors over time. For example, John Maynard Keynes revolutionized economic thinking in the 1940s when he disputed the older classical model of the economy. Keynes may have more accurately modeled the choice process of people of his time than his classical predecessors. However, over the following 45 years, human beings lived and learned from their economic experiences, and their choice-making process is probably quite different today. It is not surprising then that Keynesian theory has done a relatively poor job in recent years of predicting current economic behavior. Economic theory is a dynamic and evolving science, and as such, it will always be the subject of varying opinions based on differing assumptions and changing behaviors. This is why, by nature, economists and economic theory must disagree if the science is to progress.

1.6 HOW MACRO FOR MANAGERS IS ORGANIZED

To be supportive of managerial decision making, macro for managers must have an applied approach. It must place emphasis on the financial and international aspects of macroeconomics and demonstrate their usefulness. This book has been designed specifically for that purpose. Part I of the text lays out the basic macroeconomic concepts and models, beginning in Chapter 1 with an introduction. In Chapter 2, the circular-flow model is used to illustrate the sources and uses of macroeconomic measurements to support managerial decision making. Much of this material is related to the managerial functions of forecasting and planning previously discussed in this chapter. Chapter 3 traces out several approaches to the concept of equilibrium and lays the foundation for understanding the contemporary aggregate demand − aggregate supply model in Chapter 4.

Part II concentrates on economic policy and the influence of government and institutions in the choice process. Chapter 5 examines fiscal policy and the impact of taxes, the government deficit, the crowding out of private investment, and investment tax credits on private-sector choices. Chapter 6 explains the basic monetary institutional structure in the economy and sets the foundation for Chapter 7, on monetary policy. In Chapter 7, the impact of monetary policy on interest rates and expectations is explained, as well as the implications of changes in these variables for consumption, investment, output, employment, and income in the private sector.

Part III analyzes the investment, consumption, and international sectors of the economy in more detail. In Chapter 8, on investment, the term structure of interest rates is explained, as well as asset pricing, capital budgeting, loanable funds, and inflation effects. This chapter may well be the single most useful chapter in the text to support financial decision making. Chapter 9 presents an indepth look at consumption, considering the Keynesian view as well as alternatives such as the life-cycle approach and both the permanent and absolute income hypotheses. Chapter 10 details the role of international transactions in both trade and finance. Here balance of trade and balance of payments are discussed along with exchange-rate analysis and the effects of inflation and interest-rate fluctuations. This chapter is also very applied in nature and is likely to be quite valuable to the corporate decision maker.

Part IV concentrates on the analysis and possible solutions to various economic problems, including inflation, unemployment, interest rates, and growth and productivity. Chapter 11, on inflation, considers current views on the causes and possible cures of inflation and its effects on expectations. Chapter 12 explains the types and causes of unemployment as well as potential policy to deal with the problem. The political considerations involved in unemployment policy are also discussed along with the role played by expectations. Chapter 13 traces out the effects of interest-rate changes as well as taxes and tax policy on growth and productivity.

Part V focuses on business-conditions analysis, providing the managerial decision maker with the tools and techniques of forecasting. These techniques are especially helpful in fulfilling the managerial functions of demand forecasting and financial and strategic planning. Chapter 14 presents an overview of the basic sources of forecasting information and illustrates the use of forecasts at several different levels. Chapter 15 explains in some detail the actual techniques of forecasting in a fashion useful to the manager. Chapter 16 includes a brief presentation of how managers can analyze the business cycle and also presents specific applications of forecasting to GNP and to such industries as automobile manufacturing and housing construction. Part V is designed to stand alone as a continuing guide to forecasting for the manager who must actually perform the techniques. However, some managers will rely on a staff to perform the actual forecasting techniques. Realizing this, Part V is also written in such a fashion that it may be used as a reference and aid to interpreting the forecasts of others.

Throughout the text, the financial and international aspects of macroeconomics are stressed to give the manager maximum exposure to pragmatic information. Many of the chapters feature applied cases and examples taken directly from corporate situations and explain how macroeconomic analysis and techniques were used to solve them.

1.7 SUMMARY

1. Macroeconomics has traditionally examined the choice process from the viewpoint of the entire economy. The three key ingredients to gaining a meaningful understanding of macroeconomics are (1) an understanding of the individual as choice maker and (2) a consideration of the role played by government and social institutions in (3) the pursuit of society's economic goals.

2. Macroeconomics has an impact on two major areas of corporate decision making: forecasting and planning.

3. Government affects the economy most directly through the three means of fiscal policy, monetary policy, and regulation.

4. Positive economics is that branch of economics which deals with what is or what will be. It concerns objective factual matters that are measurable or verifiable in nature. Normative economics, on the other hand, deals with value judgments and is not verifiable or measurable. Positive economics can establish the alternative choices in a given situation and identify the costs and benefits of each. Determining which choice should be made requires value judgments and is clearly in the realm of normative economics.

5. Economic goals may vary from nation to nation. However, four that appear most frequently are the maximization of (1) employment, (2) output, and (3) economic growth while maintaining a relatively (4) stable price level.

6. An economic theory is a simplified view of reality that creates descriptive rules of human choice behavior based on real-world observation. Knowing the general behavioral rule is frequently more helpful than attempting to assimilate all the individual data on a given behavior.

7. All economic models are built on some basic assumptions and limitations regarding market structure, institutional interactions, and human motivations and are at least in part subject to normative interpretations. Also, economic theory is based on the observed behavior of human beings, and human beings learn from experience and change their behaviors over time.

1.8 EXERCISES

1. What are the three key ingredients to gaining a meaningful understanding of macroeconomics?

2. Why should the study of macroeconomics proceed from its microeconomic foundations? What is the major difference between microeconomics and macroeconomics? Is there any difference between choices in the private sector and choices in the public sector?

3. Discuss two major areas in which macroeconomics has an impact on effective managerial decisions in the private sector and how it affects each area.

4. Explain the three areas in which public-sector decisions affect the private sector.

5. Compare and contrast positive and normative economics. Which form of economics might play a larger role in political economy?

6. Discuss at least four major economic goals of most market-type economies.

7. Explain what a theory is and how it may be useful. Discuss several reasons why two economists might use the same theory and produce two quite different sets of conclusions from that theory.

1.9 REFERENCES

Blaug, M. *The Methodology of Economics: Or How Economists Explain*. New York: Cambridge University Press, 1980.

Brookings Institution, The. *Setting National Priorities*. Washington, D.C., 1982.

Buchanan, J. M., and Tullock, G. *The Calculus of Consent*. Ann Arbor, Mich.: University of Michigan Press, 1962.

Buchanan, J. M. "The Constitution of Economic Policy," 1986 Nobel Address. Reprinted with permission in *The American Economic Review*, June 1987, pp. 243–250.

Carincross, Sir Alec. "Economics in Theory and Practice," *American Economic Review,* May 1985, pp. 1–14.

McCloskey, D. N. "The Rhetoric of Economics," *Journal of Economic Literature,* June 1983, pp. 481–515.

_2_
Measuring the Macro Economy

2.1 INTRODUCTION

This chapter is concerned with aggregate statistical measurements of the economy. These measurements provide a statistical description of the macro economy and quantify such key economic variables as income, employment, production, inflation, interest rates, and international transactions. While the media frequently quotes such statistics, a great deal of confusion exists among the general population and those engaged in management decisions regarding their use. In this chapter we will consider what is being measured and why. We will also examine the sources and managerial uses of aggregate measurements as well as problems inherent in their interpretation.

2.2 WHY MEASURE ECONOMIC AGGREGATES?

Market conditions for most individual goods and services are significantly affected by the general condition of the macro economy. Therefore, managerial decision making frequently requires not only a thorough understanding of the individual market in which a product or service is sold but also an ability to gauge the current state of the entire economy and its impact on the individual market. For example, managers in the construction industry must be aware of current national conditions regarding housing demand, interest rates, and government spending. Banking and financial managers must keep abreast of such aggregates as interest rates, government borrowing, income, and employment, just to name a few. These aggregate measures are important because causal relationships exist between the overall production of goods and services and the levels of employment and income that occur at any one time in the economy. The levels of employment and income strongly affect spending in all sectors.

2.3 AN OVERVIEW OF THE MACRO ECONOMY

It is possible to gain an overall view of the macro economy by considering Figure 2.1, which illustrates the circular flow of economic activity, where production by firms and consumption by households are simply two sides of the same transaction. One dollar's worth of goods exchanged in the marketplace produces one dollar of income. This is true because the receipts of business are paid out in the form of wages, interest, profits, and rents to the owners of productive resources such as land, labor, capital, and management. Through the upper loop of Figure 2.1, known as the *product flow,* goods and services flow from firms to households and a stream of receipts flows from households to firms. In order to produce goods and services, firms must acquire productive resources through the lower loop, known as *income flow.* Here resources (land, labor, capital, and management) flow from households

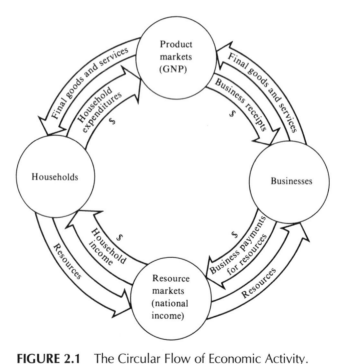

FIGURE 2.1   The Circular Flow of Economic Activity.
The circular flow of economic activity implies that production by firms and consumption by households are two sides of the same transaction. Therefore, production and household income are closely related.
Source: Derived from Clark, J.R., and Veseth, Michael, *Economics: Cost and Choice* (San Diego, Calif.: Harcourt Brace Jovanovich, 1987), p. 186.

to firms and a stream of receipts, or income in the form of rents, wages, interest, and profits, goes from firms to households. These payments by firms for the productive resources controlled by households form the basis of household income. From this circular flow it is easy to see that production, employment, and income are interrelated and that when we measure production we are also gaining valuable information about income, employment, and several other macro variables at the same time. Early in the 1940s, Simon Kuznets realized the importance of measuring these flows to provide guidelines for both economic policy and managerial decision making and developed the national income accounting system in use today.

2.4 WHAT IS AND WHAT IS NOT BEING MEASURED IN THE NATIONAL INCOME ACCOUNTS

Gross national product (GNP) and numerous other macro statistics are frequently quoted in the popular media as if minute variances could exactly predict both the direction and magnitude of future economic changes. The astute manager should keep in mind that all macro statistics are really estimates in nature and that their longer-run trends are of more importance than month-to-month or other short-term variations. These statistics are subject to invalid sampling, reporting and collection problems, and all the other possibilities of error that befall large statistical samples. As presented in the popular press, a month-to-month or even quarter-to-quarter change in, for example, the level of employment could be completely accounted for by statistical error. Accordingly, economic aggregates are probably best viewed as possible ranges of values rather than exact point estimates.

When national income statistics are used as a basis for managerial decisions, it is important to keep in mind just what is and is not being measured. As indicated earlier, GNP is nothing more than a measure of production calculated in current prices that could be considered comparable over time. It is not an all-inclusive measure, and it does not reflect the quality of life or standard of living within an economy. For example, GNP includes only final goods and services that pass through a market. It does not include transactions that occur in the underground economy, such as people working for unreported cash, illicit drug sales, and other illegal transactions. Domestic services of a spouse, such as child rearing, food preparation, laundry, and housekeeping, contribute a great deal to the quality of life, but since they are not monetary transactions, they are excluded from the calculation of GNP. The specific merit of any good or service also cannot be measured, since each dollar spent, for example, on entertainment has the exact same weight in the GNP statistics as one spent for a smallpox vaccination. In addition, the GNP of a specific country says nothing about the size of its population. Two countries could have identical GNP measures and yet one could have several times as large a population and therefore much lower income per capita. Comparisons of GNP between and among countries can be very misleading because of differences in populations, working conditions, accounting methods, and nonmeasurable factors.

2.5 MEASURING PRODUCTION THROUGH GNP ACCOUNTING

2.5.1 Gross National Product

Gross national product (GNP) is the sum of the market value of all final goods and services produced in an economy over an accounting period, such as one year. It is calculated in two ways: either as total expenditures (in the upper loop of Figure 2.1) or as total income paid to the factors of production (in the lower loop). It is calculated quarterly but reported as an annualized rate by the U.S. Department of Commerce in its *Survey of Current Business.*

In the expenditure (or upper-loop) approach, the total spending on goods and services is divided among the four major sectors of the economy into consumption, investment, government, and net exports. Table 2.1 displays these accounts for 1984. Utilizing the expenditure approach, gross national product is equal to the sum of consumption, investment, and government expenditures:

$$\text{GNP} = C + I + G \tag{2.1}$$

Figure 2.2 traces out the value of the GNP measure as well as several other aggregate income measures over a 30-year period.

2.5.1.1 Consumption

Consumption (C) represents spending by households on three types of consumable items: durables, nondurables, and services. Consumer *durables* are goods that render productive use to consumers for longer than one year and include such items as houses, cars, and major appliances. *Nondurables* are normal consumption items such as food and clothing that are frequently used up faster than their durable counterparts. *Services* include expenditures on labor to provide items such as health care, haircuts, or home repair. Many other highly detailed subcategories of consumption statistics are also available from the Department of Commerce that help to illustrate allocation patterns by consumers between and among various goods and services. Such statistics

TABLE 2.1   Actual GNP Accounting Figures for 1984

Expenditure Type	Amount (billions)	Percent of Total
Personal consumption	2342.1	64
Durables	318.4	
Nondurables	858.3	
Services	1165.7	
Gross investment	637.3	17
Fixed	580.4	
Inventory change	56.8	
Government spending	748.0	20
Net exports	− 66.3	− 2
Exports	363.7	
Imports	429.9	
GNP	3661.3	100

Source: Economic Report of the President.
Note: Totals do not agree due to revised GNP data released in 1986.

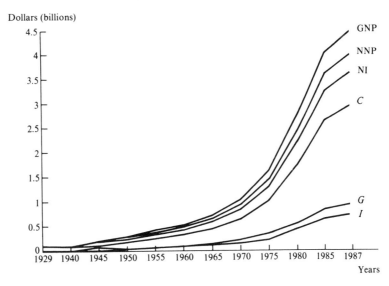

FIGURE 2.2   GNP, NNP, NI, C, I, and G over Time.
Various income and expenditure measures in the national income
accounts over time.
Source: Derived from Clark, J.R., and Veseth, Michael, *Economics: Cost and Choice*
(San Diego, Calif.: Harcourt Brace Jovanovich, 1987), p. 205.

often provide key support to managerial decision making in specific industries, since over 50 percent of total spending in the economy is some form of consumption.

2.5.1.2 Government

Government expenditures (G) comprise the second largest component of GNP. This account includes expenditures by government at all levels — federal, state, and local — to provide public goods and services. Included are salaries of government workers and the military, expenses for police and fire protection, and the costs of roads and schools and all other public goods and services. Since it is currently impossible to place a dollar valuation on the "output" of government, its purchases of goods and services have traditionally been considered final goods in the national income accounting system.

2.5.1.3 Investment

Investment (I), in the economic sense of the word, is the process by which resources are allocated away from current consumption to the production of a good or service that will increase future productive ability. It creates some new productive capacity. Investment in the financial sense is another matter, and there is an important likeness between economic investment and financial investment that will be explored in more detail in Chapter 8. In the national income accounting system, only economic investment is considered.

Gross private domestic investment includes three major subcategories: new plant and equipment, new residential housing, and changes in inventory valuations. *New plant and equipment* is usually referred to as fixed investment. It is expenditures by business on new industrial and commercial buildings as well as new machines. *New residential housing* includes only structures completed and purchased for the first time regardless of whether they are owner-occupied or for rent. The resale of an existing structure creates no new investment, since only ownership changes hands but nothing new is created. *Inventory investment* represents goods held by businesses as a buffer against the lack of synchronization between their productive capacity and the demand for their goods. While plant capacity may be 100 units of output per day, certain days may see consumer demand for 1000 units and other days may see demand for 1 unit. By maintaining an inventory, producers can meet high-demand days and rebuild inventory during low-demand days while operating their plant at relatively smooth output rates. Inventory investment fluctuates a great deal at times and has a significant effect on the overall economy. This is one reason why inventory expenditures receive so much attention in the business media. The Department of Commerce regularly publishes data on manufacturers' inventories. The levels of inventory businesses hold are affected by consumer demand, production and inventory costs, and general macroeconomic conditions. Inventory values can increase by two means: (1) the actual number of total units held in inventory can go up, or (2) the prices of a constant number of inventory units can rise. The national income accounting system does not consider changes in inventory valuations based only on price increases, since, again, nothing new is produced.

2.5.1.4 Net Exports

Our foreign trade consists of domestic goods sold abroad *(exports)* and foreign goods bought by us *(imports)*. The value of imports is already included in the consumption, investment, and government expenditure accounts previously discussed. The difference between exports and imports is the *net exports figure* (X_n). As we can see from Table 2.1, we are currently importing more than we are exporting, and therefore, we are running a trade deficit.

2.5.2 Depreciation and Net National Product

The GNP figure provides an approximate measure of current production in the economy. The fixed-investment component of GNP measures the new capital goods produced each year. What it overlooks, however, is the fact that a portion of the capital stock is used up each year. Wear and tear as well as obsolescence of machinery and buildings occur all the time, and these serve to reduce the net additions to the capital stock. To adjust GNP for this wearing out of the capital stock, a depreciation component or capital-consumption adjustment (C_{ca}) is subtracted to arrive at *net national product* (NNP):

$$\text{GNP} - C_{ca} = \text{NNP} \qquad\qquad (2.2)$$

Figure 2.2 illustrates the net national product account over time.

The capital-consumption adjustment is the difference between gross and net investment. The term *capital-consumption adjustment* is more appropriate here than *depreciation* because of the confusion between depreciation in the accounting sense and depreciation in the economic sense. Accounting depreciation is based on some arbitrary life selected for capital equipment. It does not accurately reflect the true functional life of equipment and machinery. The capital-consumption allowance attempts to more accurately portray this life cycle. However, it too is subject to some degree of error in estimate and assumption. Obsolescence is a difficult concept to truly measure, and therefore, the estimates of net national product are also of limited value.

2.5.3 Other Derivative Income Measures

2.5.3.1 National Income

National income (NI) is the total income received by the factors of production for their role in producing goods and services. It represents the total of payments by businesses to resource owners. These payments take the form of wages (W), profits (P), interest (i), and rents (R). Largest among the factor payments is the wage account or compensation to employees. Over time, approximately 60 percent of GNP has been paid out to wage earners in this form. Profits are the second largest account, representing compensation to incorporated businesses for supplying entrepreneurial talent and risk taking to the production process. A second type of profit exists in the proprietors income account, and it represents compensation to unincorporated businesses such as proprietorships and partnerships. The interest account represents payments to those who supply capital to firms, and it has been growing as a percentage of total income over the last few years. Rental income is paid to those who supply land and other private property to firms. The total of the wages, profits, interest, and rents accounts indicates the total earning of the factors of production:

$$NI = W + P + i + R \qquad (2.3)$$

2.5.3.2 Personal Income and Personal Disposable Income

While the national income account indicates the total gross earnings of households, there is a more accurate picture of household income. *Personal income* (PI) is determined by subtracting social security (SS) taxes and corporate profits not paid out in dividends (UDCP) from national income and adding in government transfer payments (T_g) and interest paid by government (i_g). *Personal disposable income* (PDI) is a measure of what consumers actually have left over to spend or save after paying their taxes. It is equal to personal income (PI) minus personal income taxes (PYT):

$$PI = NI - SS - UDCP + T_g + i_g \qquad (2.4)$$

$$PDI = PI - PYT \qquad (2.5)$$

2.6 ADJUSTING THE NATIONAL INCOME ACCOUNTS

In order for the national income accounts to more accurately reflect the levels of production and income, several adjustments are necessary. These adjustments exclude certain types of market activity from the calculation of GNP and include imputations for some other nonmarket activities.

2.6.1 Exclusions

Individuals may receive income that is not included in GNP from several sources either because the income is not reported or because it is not closely related to the production process. Unreported income from illegal transactions and/or people working ''off the books'' is not included because there is no effective way to measure it. Estimates of activity in the underground economy range from as little as 3 percent to as much as 20 percent of GNP. However, since criminals and tax evaders do not report this income, it is impossible at this time to have an accurate measurement. Government transfer payments such as social security benefits, interest paid by government, and capital gains on property do not arise from private-sector production of current goods and services and therefore are not included in GNP.

2.6.2 Included Adjustments

In addition, the calculation of GNP does include imputations for several activities that do not pass through a market but do contribute significantly to the circular flow of income. For example, owner-occupied dwellings are treated as if their owners rent the homes to themselves. The owner is consuming the home even though he or she is not making rental payments. This keeps GNP from being understated as the percentage of owner-occupied dwellings increases over time. In addition, many employees also receive some of their income in kind in the form of meals, housing, or other company benefits. Such imputations are included because they are, in reality, current goods and services being consumed, and they assist the GNP calculation in providing a more realistic view of the current level of production and consumption.

2.7 REAL AND NOMINAL GNP

The price level plays a major role in the calculation of the GNP statistic. GNP could be envisioned as the multiplication of two vectors, one for price and one for quantity. The price vector P would be the array of prices for all goods in the economy:

$$P = <P_1, P_2, \ldots, P_n> \tag{2.6}$$

The quantity vector Q would be the respective quantity produced of each good in the economy:

$$Q = <Q_1, Q_2, \ldots, Q_n> \tag{2.7}$$

GNP would then be the dot product of these two vectors:

$$\text{GNP} = <P_1Q_1 + P_2Q_2 + \ldots + P_nQ_n> \tag{2.8}$$

or the price of good 1 times its quantity plus the price of good 2 times its quantity all the way out to the nth good in the economy. GNP calculated in current prices in this way is referred to as *nominal GNP*. From this view of GNP, it is easy to see that nominal GNP can increase just by an increase in the price level. If P increases, so does nominal GNP, but no additional goods or services are produced. To adjust for this shortcoming in the nominal GNP measure, price indexes have come into common use. Price indexes are an attempt to separate increases in GNP due to the actual production of additional goods and services from those which arise solely from increases in price. Such indexes usually compare the total price of a given group or "market basket" of goods in the current time period to its price in some arbitrary base time period. For ease of calculation, the base-year price index is assumed to be 100. For example, the GNP deflator price index would be calculated as follows:

$$\text{GNP deflator index} = \frac{\Sigma Q_b \times P_c}{\Sigma Q_b \times P_b} \times 100 \tag{2.9}$$

Here the subscript b denotes the base year and the subscript c denotes the current year. Therefore, if we sum the base-year quantities times the current prices of each good and divide by the sum of the base-year quantities times the base-year prices and multiply this number by 100, we get the GNP deflator. The numerator is really the cost of the market basket in the current year, and the denominator is the cost of that same basket of goods in the base year. If the market basket "costs" $100 in the base year and $200 today, then prices have increased 100 percent from the base year to now. The price index in this case would be $(200/100) \times 100 = 200$.

To adjust GNP for the effects of price changes using this price index, we simply divide nominal GNP by the ratio of current prices to base-year prices. If nominal GNP was $3000 billion, then real GNP would be $3000/($200/$100) = 1500 billion. As we can see from Figure 2.3, while nominal GNP has continued to grow over the last 25 years, real GNP has grown at a much slower rate and has actually declined in some time periods.

2.7.1 Types of Price Indexes

Several different types of price indexes have been developed to isolate different types of price increases in the economy. For example, the *consumer*

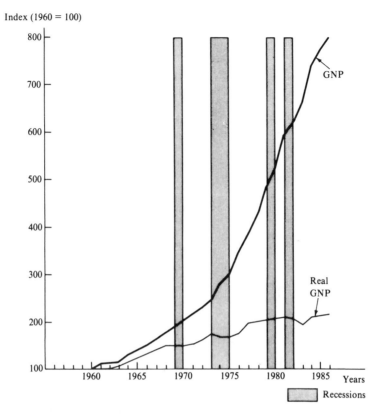

FIGURE 2.3   Real and Nominal GNP over Time.
While nominal GNP has continued to grow over time, real GNP has
grown at a much slower pace and has actually declined in some
time periods.
Source: Economic Report of the President, 1988. Tables B–1, B–2, B–30, and B–44.

price index (CPI) has been developed to measure price changes that affect
the average urban blue-collar worker. The market basket of goods examined
here is representative of those goods consumed by such a subgroup of the
population. The *producer price index* (PPI) measures the impact of price
changes on producers by examining a market basket more representative of
the buying of business firms. The *GNP implicit price deflator* is a more general
index concerned with goods that compose the GNP measure. Figure 2.4
illustrates each of the CPI and deflator indices over the last 30 years. As we
can see, the price level was subject to significant increases in the late seventies
and early eighties, which, while increasing nominal GNP, did not indicate
an increase in real GNP or income.

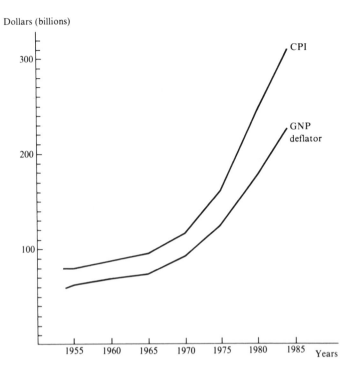

FIGURE 2.4   CPI and GNP Deflator over Time.
The price level in the late seventies and early eighties rose quickly
and pushed up nominal GNP, but this did not necessarily indicate
an increase in real GNP. (Data for 1984 was a preliminary estimate.)
Source: Based on data from *Economic Report of the President*, *1985*. Tables B–3, B–
52, B–56, B–61, and B–66.

2.7.2 How the Weighted Price Index Is Constructed

Specific goods and services that compose a given market basket are weighted
with regard to their importance in the hierarchy of the basket. Table 2.2
illustrates the actual construction technique of a weighted price index such
as the CPI. Column 1 indicates the specific good, while column 2 displays
the weight attached to that good in the market basket. Column 3 displays
price in the base year, and column 4 multiplies the weight times that price.
Column 5 is the price of the good in the current year, and column 6 multiplies
the current price times the weight. The ratio of the respective totals of columns 4 and 6 multiplied by 100 yields the price index.

TABLE 2.2 An Applied Example of Price Index Construction

1	2	3	4	5	6
Good	Weight	Price (b)	Cost	Price (c)	Weighted Cost
X	0.20	$1.00	$0.20	$ 2.0	$0.40
Y	0.50	$2.00	$1.00	$ 4.0	$2.00
Z	0.30	$5.00	$1.50	$10.0	$3.00
		Total	$2.70		$5.40

The price index is ($5.40/$2.70) × 100 = $200

2.7.3 Problems with Price Indexes

Price indexes make meaningful corrections to the national income accounts, but like all statistical techniques, they do have limitations of their own. Changes in quality, price-related substitutions, and new and different goods all create problems with price indexes. First, because of price-related substitutions, the specific market basket of an index may not continue over time to accurately reflect the buying pattern of those it was designed to represent. For example, the CPI basket in 1962 might have contained 100 gallons of gasoline. With the very large price increases in gasoline in the 1970s and 1980s, consumers have significantly reduced their gasoline consumption by substituting more fuel-efficient automobiles, walking, and the use of public transportation. However, the weight that is afforded to gasoline in the current market basket may not have been changed at all. Also, there are many new and higher-quality goods such as personal computers bought by the average consumer that did not even exist when the last base-year and market-basket composition changes were made. With millions of wage and price agreements, federal salaries, and other financial instruments affected by the CPI, it is not surprising that changes in its composition and base come infrequently. All such changes create both winners and losers on a large scale and are subject to political as well as economic considerations.

2.8 EMPLOYMENT AND GNP

As mentioned earlier in this chapter, GNP measures production, and labor resources are required in the production process. Therefore, there is at least some degree of correlation between the level of goods and services an economy is producing and the number of workers it is employing. Measuring the level of employment can contribute valuable detail to the economic picture produced through GNP accounting and can provide at least partial insight into the plight of workers in the labor force. Employment statistics provide information about the size and composition of the labor force, the portion of the labor force that is employed, and the portion that is not. Like many statistical measures, however, employment statistics are frequently misunderstood when reported in the popular press and there is a strong incentive to look to a single summary measure when much more detailed analysis is necessary to draw meaningful conclusions. In this section of the chapter we discuss the sources and availability of employment statistics as well as what they do and do not mean.

2.8.1 The Employment Statistics Series

The popular press most frequently reports what they refer to as "the unemployment rate." This is really one of a series of employment-related statistics composed of three separate measures. First among this series is the labor force. The *civilian labor force statistic* indicates the number of nonmilitary personnel ready and available for work. It omits full-time students, prison inmates, hospital patients, and other institutionalized persons. The *total labor force* includes U.S. resident military personnel. The *employment rate* is the percentage of the total labor force currently working for pay. An interesting caution in considering the employment rate is that it can actually fall while the number of employed persons is rising. The statistic itself is the ratio of the number of employed persons to the total labor force. If the number of new entrants into the labor force exceeds the increase in the number of employed workers, the employment statistic falls. During the last decade, as increasing percentages of the female population have entered the work force, the employment rate has had periods of decline even while record numbers of persons were being employed. A similar problem befalls the unemployment rate as well. Figure 2.5 illustrates the labor force, employment, and unemployment figures for the last 25 years.

The third component of the employment series is the *unemployment rate*. This is the ratio of unemployed persons to the total labor force. Since there is zero unemployment in the military population, the inclusion of military personnel in the labor force base of this statistic tends to make the unemployment rate somewhat optimistic. If more workers leave the work force, say, to return to school, than are laid off or lose their jobs for other reasons, the unemployment rate can fall at the very time employment is falling. A second problem with the unemployment statistic is that it aggregates all unemployment into a single number. While the average level of unemployment in the United States might be reported as 6 percent, the rate among

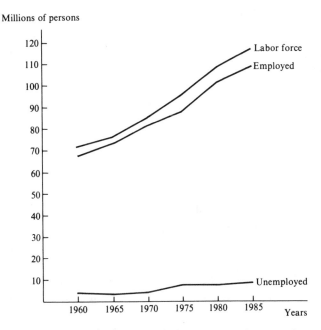

FIGURE 2.5 Labor Force, Employment, and Unemployment over Time.
Due to changes in the size of the labor force, both the employment rate and the unemployment rate can increase at the same time.
Source: Based on data from *Economic Report of the President, 1986.* Table B–31.

black teenagers might be 50 percent and the rate among white male heads of households might be less than 1 percent. Here the statistic tells us nothing about how the burden of unemployment is distributed among various segments of the population. A further consideration of the burden issue involves the length of unemployment. As the economy turns downward and unemployment rises, the average length of unemployment increases. This serves to increase the existing burden of unemployment disproportionately among different segments of the population.

Finally, many economists subscribe to the notion that a natural rate of unemployment exists. The *natural rate* is that level of unemployment that results when labor markets have found their long-run equilibrium. This rate was estimated to be around 7 percent in the 1970s and has been a source of substantial controversy between economists and political policymakers. It is for these reasons that the single summary statistic of "the unemployment rate" as quoted in the popular press requires much more detailed analysis than is obvious to the casual observer.

2.8.2 Classifications of Unemployment

Within the ranks of the unemployed are four basic types of unemployment: frictional, cyclical and seasonal, structural, and hidden. *Frictional unemployment* is composed of those workers who do have employable skills, have worked in the past, and are currently between jobs. Some level of frictional unemployment is always present in the economy, since skilled workers can frequently change jobs and there is seldom a perfect time correlation between the end of one job and the beginning of the next. Indeed, if frictional unemployment falls below a certain level, there is no pool of readily available skilled workers for employers to choose from. Then firms must bid workers away from each other with higher wages, causing an acceleration in the rate of inflation. This wage/inflation phenomenon is discussed in more detail in Chapter 11. *Structural unemployment* occurs when workers in the available employment pool do not possess the necessary skills required by current employers. For example, the newspaper industry might have openings for 100 operators to control computerized typesetting machines when the only experienced newspaper workers available are those familiar with the old method of setting hot-metal type. There is just no demand for the skills possessed by the available labor pool. With the current growth rate of industrial technology increasing rapidly, the structural component of unemployment will probably be subject to significant increases.

Cyclical unemployment represents those workers who are laid off as a result of cyclical changes in their industry. For example, the housing industry experiences periods of expansion and contraction due to general economic conditions and/or swings in interest rates as a part of the longer-run business cycle. Seasonal unemployment occurs in industries subject to seasonal swings in demand. For example, the housing industry experiences marked increases in demand during the spring and summer months, but the winter months show periods of decline.

Hidden unemployment takes two separate forms. First, there are many workers who are at least temporarily underemployed. These are workers who have substantial job skills that are not being utilized by their current employment. For example, many college graduates might take clerical jobs in the hopes of working their way into a position that fully utilizes their college training. During this period, they are technically employed and do not appear in the unemployment statistics even though their skills are not being fully utilized. A second form of hidden unemployment exists in the case of workers who search for a job for so long that they become discouraged and simply stop looking. This discouraged-worker phenomenon increases during periods of recession because it is more difficult for all workers to find jobs during recessions, especially those who have a marginal work history.

2.8.3 Using Employment Measures

While employment statistics have limitations, they do reveal valuable information about the performance of an economy. When the full range of these statistics is carefully analyzed, we also learn a great deal about the role played by labor resources in the overall productive process. The use of employment statistics in managerial decision making can contribute significantly to expansion and hiring decisions, wage and salary negotiations, and many other fields. The key to their use, however, lies in understanding what they do and do not tell us and in considering the full range of available information.

2.9 HIGH-EMPLOYMENT GNP AND POTENTIAL GNP

While GNP accounting measures the actual production of goods and services, it does not consider what could be produced if the economy fully utilized its productive resources. It says little, if anything, about how the economy is producing relative to its productive capacity. To have a more accurate picture of what could be produced, economists have developed the concepts of high-employment GNP and potential GNP. *High-employment GNP* is a measure of the real output of goods and services possible if the economy were operating at full employment. The exact definition of *full employment* and the types and causes of unemployment are discussed in more detail later in this chapter, but the high-employment GNP calculation is based on a natural rate of unemployment with about 94 percent of the labor force working. The gap between the actual and high-employment GNP figures might be viewed as loss of goods and services resulting from underutilizing the economy's resource base, and one major goal of economic policy is to minimize that gap.

Potential GNP attempts to quantify essentially the same concept as high-employment GNP, but it uses a different methodology. Calculating the potential GNP requires several key assumptions about employment and growth rates that lend themselves to criticism. Changes in the composition of the work force are also having an increasing impact on these measures. For these and other reasons, some controversy surrounds both the high-employment and potential GNP measurements; however, they have provided an approximation of where the economy stands relative to its potential and will continue to do so.

2.10 OTHER MEASUREMENTS OF THE MACRO ECONOMY

2.10.1 Interest Rates

In addition to measurements of income and employment, there are several other statistical series available to support managerial decision making. First among these are interest rates. An *interest rate* reflects the price a borrower pays to a lender for the privilege of using money. The magnitude of the interest rate depends primarily on the duration of the loan, the default risk involved, and the expectations held by both the borrower and lender with regard to future interest and tax rates. Longer-term loans of equal risk usually require higher interest rates. Riskier loans and loans in periods where borrowers and lenders have expectations of increasing future prices and interest rates usually carry larger interest rates as well. Many managerial decisions are affected by prevailing interest rates. For example, the cost of carrying inventory investment is heavily dependent on interest rates. Businesses considering large fixed capital expansions must be concerned not only with current interest rates, which would affect the cost and therefore the overall profitability of a project, but also what future interest rates might be. The timing of a capital expansion is very important, since a decision to borrow now or later will most likely affect the interest rate paid on the project. It is also important to keep in mind that the interest rate is a key consideration regardless of whether a firm must borrow for capital expansion or has its own internal expansion funds. Even if the firm has its own internal funds, the market interest rate represents the opportunity cost to that firm of borrowing. This is true because, in lieu of the project, the firm could loan out its own funds on the market and earn the market interest rate.

Several types of interest rates are reported in the financial media. The *prime rate* is probably the most widely quoted statistic, and it represents the rate banks charge their most creditworthy commercial borrowers for short-term loans. While few borrowers are fortunate enough to borrow at the prime rate, it is a benchmark rate upon which lenders add on risk, duration, and expectations premiums for their more risky and longer-term borrowers. The *Federal Reserve discount rate* is the rate the various Federal Reserve district banks charge on funds they loan to their members. This rate can and does vary from district to district and in addition to other considerations is affected by the current monetary policy being pursued by the Federal Reserve System. A third key interest rate available is the *federal funds rate*. Commercial banks who hold excess reserves loan them out indirectly to other commercial banks in need of reserves for very short periods of time in the federal funds market. The interest rate on these loans is the federal funds rate. Taken together, the three key interest rates—prime, discount, and federal funds—can paint a somewhat accurate picture of the conditions of the money markets. These are published daily in *The Wall Street Journal* and the business sections of many major metropolitan newspapers. As with almost all macro measurements, for managerial decision making purposes, the current range and direction of these rates are really more important than a particular point value.

2.10.2 Capacity-Utilization Rates

Capacity-utilization rates indicate current production as a percentage of the economy's maximum use of factories and equipment. These numbers are compiled and published by the Federal Reserve System and, in effect, show how much of our current productive capacity is being used. This number is subject to wide ranges of interpretation and has at least one surprising characteristic. Lower utilization rates do not always imply the lack of a need for capital expansion. A lower utilization rate might mean that existing capital is so obsolete or frequently in need of repair that it is not fully utilized.

2.10.3 International Statistics

With the spread of multinational firms and the growing trade deficit since the early 1970s, international statistics have become much more widely used in managerial decision making. While there are many measures available, the two primary statistics are the balance of payments and the balance of trade. The *balance of payments* records a nation's monetary flows and consists of money inflows minus money outflows for investment. The *balance of trade* measures the value of exports minus the value of imports. Earlier in this chapter we referred to this as net exports in the GNP accounts. Both the trade and payments balances are affected by government controls, such as tariffs, quotas, taxes, and subsidies, as well as the current monetary exchange rates between trading partners. Changes in any of these controls or exchange rates can change the payments figures. However, with these conditions held relatively constant, changes in the payments account usually reflect changes in direction of trade flows, international price advantages, or movements of investment capital. Both the trade and payments accounts as well as the role played by exchange rates and government controls are developed more fully in Chapter 10. The effects of these international transactions on both foreign and domestic investments are explained in Chapter 8.

Finally, a wide variety of industry-specific macro measures is available. The U.S. Department of Commerce publishes both the *Survey of Current Business* and the *Business Conditions Digest* on a regular basis. The U.S. Department of Labor and the Bureau of Labor Statistics provide ongoing data on employment, earnings, and prices. The Federal Reserve publishes a monthly bulletin with industrial production statistics. The details of these and many other sources of macro measurements are covered in Chapters 14 to 16, and the successful manager may well benefit from a familiarization with them.

2.11 SUMMARY

1. This chapter is concerned primarily with aggregate statistical measures that attempt to quantify such key economic variables as income, employment, production, inflation, interest rates, and international transactions.

2. These aggregate measures are beneficial in managerial decision making on several different levels because the market conditions for most individual goods and services are significantly affected by the general condition of the macro economy.

3. The circular flow of economic activity implies that production by firms and consumption by households are two sides of the same transaction. Therefore, production, employment, and household income are closely related.

4. The GNP is the sum of the market value of all final goods and services produced in the economy within one year. GNP can be calculated by either the expenditure or income approach. The expenditure approach measures what was spent by all sectors in the economy to buy the goods and services that were produced. The key equations for the expenditure approach are

$$\text{GNP} = C + I + G + X_n$$

$$\text{NNP} = \text{GNP} - C_{ca}$$

The income approach measures GNP by what was paid out by firms to the factors of production in order for them to produce goods and services. The key equations of the income approach are

$$\text{NI} = W + P + i + R$$

$$\text{PI} = \text{NI} - \text{SS} - \text{UDCP} + T_g + i_g$$

$$\text{PDI} = \text{PI} - \text{PYT}$$

5. The national income accounts are only a measure of current production and do not reflect the quality of life or general standard of living within the economy. Several shortcomings of the national income measures are that nonmarket production is not measured, inflation can significantly affect nominal GNP, new and better-quality goods can develop over time, and international comparisons are not accurate owing to differences in population, tastes, customs, and working conditions.

6. Real GNP is nominal GNP adjusted by price index to reflect changes in the actual production of goods and services.

7. Potential GNP and high-employment GNP are estimates of the real goods and services possible if the economy were operating at full employment.

8. Output and employment are closely related. Three key employment statistics available are the labor force, the employment rate, and the unemployment rate. The civilian labor force statistic indicates the number of non-military personnel ready and available for work. The total labor force includes U.S. resident military personnel. The employment rate is the percentage of the total labor force currently working for pay. The unemployment rate is the ratio of unemployed persons to the total labor force.

9. There are four major categories of unemployment. Frictional unemployment consists of those workers who have employable skills and are currently between jobs. Structural unemployment occurs when workers in the available employment pool do not possess the necessary skills required by current employers. Cyclical unemployment represents those workers who are laid off as a result of cyclical changes in their industry. Hidden unemployment consists of those who are under-employed and those who have become discouraged and stopped looking for work.

10. Interest rates significantly affect the cost of carrying inventory, fixed capital expansions, and numerous other business costs. The magnitude of the interest rate depends primarily on the duration of the loan, the risk involved, and the expectations held by both the borrower and lender with regard to future interest and tax rates. The prime rate represents the rate banks charge their most creditworthy commercial borrowers for short-term loans. The Federal Reserve discount rate is the rate the various Federal Reserve district banks charge on funds they loan to their members. The federal funds rate is the rate paid on short-term loans of reserves between and among commercial banks in the federal funds market.

11. Capacity-utilization rates indicate current production as a percentage of the economy's maximum use of factories and equipment.

12. The balance of payments records a nation's monetary flows and consists of money inflows minus money outflows for investment. The balance of trade measures the value of exports minus the value of imports.

2.12 EXERCISES

1. Why are aggregate measurements of production important enough to warrant their collection and analysis?

2. If the GNP of the United States and the GNP of the Soviet Union were both $3 trillion, why then could we not say that the Soviets and the Americans had equal standards of living?

3. Goodyear Tire and Rubber Company sells identical tires to you and to Ford Motor Company. Explain the difference in how the GNP accounting system deals with these two transactions.

4. Drug traffic is believed to be one of the very largest dollar volume industries in the state of Florida. How does this affect GNP?

5. Explain the differences between nominal, real, high-employment, and potential GNP.

6. What are the major types of unemployment, and how is the employment statistic series measured?

7. Why are interest rates important to managerial decision making, and what are the key interest rates?

8. Compare and contrast the balance of payments with the balance of trade accounts.

2.13 REFERENCES

Adams, F. G. *National Income Accounts and the Structure of the U.S. Economy.* New York: General Learning Press, 1973.

Economic Report of the President, 1988. Washington, D.C.: U.S. Government Printing Office, 1989.

Federal Reserve System Bulletin. Washington, D.C.: Federal Reserve Board. Published monthly.

Kendrick, J. W. *Economic Accounts and Their Uses.* New York: McGraw-Hill, 1972.

Ruggles, R., and Ruggles, R. *The Design of Economic Accounts.* Washington, D.C.: National Bureau of Economic Research, 1970.

United States Department of Commerce, *Business Conditions Digest.* Washington, D.C.: Bureau of Economic Analysis, March 1989.

United States Department of Commerce, *Survey of Current Business.* Washington, D.C.: Bureau of Economic Analysis, February 1989.

3

Equilibrium in the Macro Economy

3.1 INTRODUCTION

In the preceding chapter we began an overview of the macro economy, and building on the circular-flow concept, we examined some of the most common macro measurements. In this chapter we begin the construction of basic analytical economic models and examine the concept of macro equilibrium. *Equilibrium* in the general scientific sense implies a state where there is no tendency for change. In economics, this is true because it occurs when aggregate demand is equal to aggregate supply. At the current price level, the amount of goods and services producers are both willing and able to produce is equal to the total amount demanded by consumers, investors, government, and the foreign sector. More formally stated, the first equilibrium condition is that

Aggregate demand (AD) = aggregate supply (AS)

Since aggregate demand is equal to aggregate supply, inventories consist only of those levels of goods firms have planned to hold as a buffer against fluctuations in demand. No unplanned inventory exists. Therefore, the second equilibrium condition is that

Savings (S) = planned investment (I_p)

Each of these equilibrium conditions has several specific implications that will be discussed in greater detail.

3.2 AGGREGATE DEMAND AND AGGREGATE SUPPLY

Aggregate demand *AD* is the sum of all planned expenditures in the economy by consumers, investors, government, and the foreign sector:

$$AD = C + I_p + G + X_n \tag{3.1}$$

This can be represented as a downward-sloping function with respect to the existing price level, as in Figure 3.1, with output on the horizontal axis and the price level on the vertical axis. With all other things held constant, as prices rise, the planned expenditures of these sectors tend to fall. Anything other than the price level that affects aggregate demand would determine the location and slope of the aggregate demand function. An increase in tax rates would, for example, decrease income and spending and cause the aggregate demand function to shift inward and to the left, resulting in fewer goods and services being demanded at every price level.

Similar to the computation of GNP in the previous chapter, aggregate supply *AS* is a measurement of the total output of real goods and services in the economy. It can be graphed as a positively sloped function with regard to the current price level for a given capital stock. With all other things held constant, as the price level increases, the total quantity of goods and services firms are willing to produce also increases. While there is significant professional debate about the shape and location of the aggregate supply function, for our analytical purposes in this chapter, we can plot it as an upward-sloping function with regard to price, as in Figure 3.1. Chapter 4 more closely examines the aggregate supply function and explains both the content and implications of the professional debate that surrounds it.

The intersection of the aggregate supply and aggregate demand functions illustrates the current equilibrium output and price level, such as P_e and O_e in Figure 3.1. At P_e and O_e, the real quantity of goods and services produced is equal to the total demanded by all sectors of the economy.

3.3 THE CLASSICAL VIEW OF EQUILIBRIUM: SUPPLY DOMINATES

The classical economists viewed macro equilibrium primarily as a self-attaining and self-correcting mechanism that in the long run always produced full employment. They believed that the economy was driven primarily by aggregate supply and that flexible prices and wages would quickly act to restore full employment of resources even when aggregate supply and/or aggregate demand were fluctuating. Much of the essence of classical economics revolved around what Jean Baptiste Say called his law of markets,

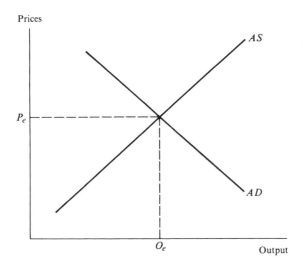

FIGURE 3.1   The Basic Aggregate Demand – Aggregate Supply
Diagram.
Both aggregate supply and aggregate demand can be envisioned as
functions of the existing price level. All else being held constant, increases in the price level could be expected to reduce total spending
by consumers, government, investors, and the foreign sector. Increases in the price level could, all else being equal, increase the
quantity of goods and services firms are willing and able to supply to
the economy.

in which "supply creates its own demand." Figure 3.2 illustrates the classical
concept of equilibrium, with the supply curve assumed to be vertical at the
full-employment level of output for simplification. If, for example, aggregate
demand were to fall from AD_1 to AD_2, inventories held by firms would increase. As inventories increase, firms attempt to decrease output and lay off
workers. This shifts the aggregate supply curve inward and to the left from
AS_1 to AS_2, and the short-run equilibrium occurs at point B. In response to
reduced employment opportunities, workers bid down their wage demands,
reducing production costs and causing firms to increase production back to
the full-employment level, but at lower prices and wages (point C). A symmetrical scenario would occur with an increase in aggregate demand. Since
the economy was, by definition, already operating at full employment (say,
point C), an increase in aggregate demand (from AD_2 to AD_1) would simply
bid up the wages of existing workers. In the short run this would increase
producer costs, and firms would eventually increase prices (from P_2 to P_1).
The long-run equilibrium would occur at the same level of output (O_1), but
with higher wages and prices (P_2).

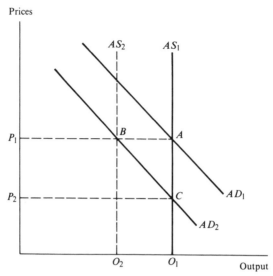

FIGURE 3.2   The Classical View of Macro Equilibrium.
The classical concept of equilibrium with the supply curve assumed
to be vertical at the full-employment level of output. If aggregate demand falls from AD_1 to AD_2, inventories held by firms would increase. Firms attempt to decrease output and lay off workers. The
aggregate supply curve shifts inward and to the left from AS_1 to AS_2
and short-run equilibrium occurs at point B. With fewer jobs available, workers bid down wage demands, reducing production costs,
and firms increase production back to the full-employment level, but
at lower prices and wages (point C).

    The most important feature of this classical approach to equilibrium
was that government interference in the economy was believed to be unneeded and unwanted. Stabilization policy was considered to interfere with
the natural self-correcting forces that would return the economy to full-
employment equilibrium on its own. Any unemployment that did exist was
considered to be short term in nature and would be eliminated in the long
run as wages and prices adjusted and the economy corrected itself. Classical
doctrine was well accepted in its time; however, beginning in the late 1920s,
continuing high levels of unemployment fueled academic criticism of the
theory. Some economists began to rethink their analytical approach to equilibrium, and the ideas of John Maynard Keynes began to gain significant
popularity.

3.4 THE KEYNESIAN APPROACH: DEMAND DOMINATES

During the late 1920s and well into the 1930s, the Great Depression produced significant long-term declines in aggregate supply and continuing periods of unemployment. The classical view that in the long run flexible wages and prices would return the economy to full-employment equilibrium did not appear to accurately predict current economic behavior. The value of any economic theory is only as great as its ability to predict. Realizing the difference between economic theory and current observed reality, John Maynard Keynes began to fashion new theories that would more accurately describe the economic behavior of the time. Keynes' work was published in 1936 as *The General Theory of Employment, Interest, and Money* and set out both a revised view of macro equilibrium and the appropriate role of government. The Keynesian view was that wages and prices were "sticky downward" due to less than perfectly competitive markets for both goods and labor, and while there may be natural forces operating in the economy that bring about equilibrium, that equilibrium need not be at the full-employment level of output. Keynes contended that active government intervention to stimulate or dampen aggregate demand was necessary to bring about stable equilibrium at full employment. In the following pages we will examine the Keynesian model both in graphic and mathematical form.

Contrary to his classical predecessors, Keynes began to believe that aggregate demand was the driving force behind the economy and that insufficient levels of aggregate demand produced long periods of unemployment and low levels of output or aggregate supply. As supply fell, producers would lay off workers and income in the economy would fall, further reducing spending by consumers and investors and, therefore, further reducing aggregate demand. In the Keynesian model, since aggregate supply is the source of all income produced in the economy, the dollar value of income and the dollar value of all the goods and services produced are the same. In other words, aggregate supply is equal to income, or $AS = Y$. Earlier we defined aggregate demand as the sum of all planned expenditures by consumers, investors, government, and the foreign sector, or $AD = C + I_p + G + X_n$. Consumption is composed of autonomous and induced elements with an equational structure of $C = a + B(Y_d)$. The term a equals autonomous consumption, and B is the marginal propensity to consume (MPC) or the percentage of each incremental dollar of income which is spent on consumption. Yd is disposable income or income minus taxes $(Y - T)$. Investment is assumed to be fixed for the time being, and government is the exogenous policy variable determined outside the model. At equilibrium, aggregate supply is equal to aggregate demand, or alternatively stated, total income is equal to total spending. We can substitute the preceding identities to algebraically determine equilibrium output and income:

At equilibrium,

$$AD = AS \tag{3.2}$$

$$AS = Y \tag{3.3}$$

$$AD = C + I_p + G + X_n \tag{3.1}$$

$$C = a + B(Y_d) \tag{3.4}$$

$$Y_d = Y - T \tag{3.5}$$

$$AD = a + B(Y - T) + I_p + G + X_n \tag{3.6}$$

At equilibrium,

$$Y = a + B(Y - T) + I_p + G + X_n \tag{3.7}$$

If, for example, autonomous consumption were \$30 billion, the MPC were 0.80, planned investment were \$150 billion, government spending were \$100 billion, net exports were \$50 billion, and taxes were \$100 billion, then the equilibrium level of income would be

$$Y = 30 + 0.80(Y - 100) + 150 + 100 + 50$$
$$= \$1250 \text{ billion} \tag{3.8}$$

As is evident from the equations, the Keynesian system is driven by changes in aggregate demand that are believed to call forth changes in aggregate supply. Supply is assumed to accommodate any changes in aggregate demand. Thus, Keynes theorized that when the economy attained equilibrium at less than the full-employment level of output, changes in fiscal policy such as direct increases in government expenditures or reductions in taxes could increase the aggregate demand and stimulate the economy to the full-employment output level. A graphic explanation of the Keynesian system and the use of fiscal policy to produce full-employment equilibrium appears in Figure 3.3.

In the Keynesian cross diagram, the vertical axis represents consumption, planned investment, government spending, and net foreign spending, while the horizontal axis is total output. The 45-degree line is the locus of points where total spending equals total income and is assumed to be synonymous with aggregate supply. The aggregate demand function AD_1 intersects the 45-degree line at a total spending and total output level of \$1250 billion. The full-employment level of output, however, is \$1300 billion, and the economy is experiencing significant levels of unemployment. Keynesian doctrine would suggest fiscal policy changes such as an increase in govern-

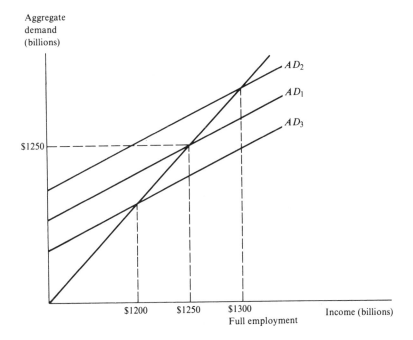

FIGURE 3.3 The Keynesian View of Macro Equilibrium.
The aggregate demand function AD_1 intersects the 45-degree line at
a total spending and total output level of $1250 billion, which is
below the full-employment level of $1300 billion. The economy is
experiencing unemployment. Government spending is increased,
which would increase aggregate demand to the AD_2 level. As demand increases, inventories would decline, producers would step
up production, output and employment would rise, and income
would increase to the $1300 billion level, producing equilibrium at
full employment.

ment spending, which would increase aggregate demand to the AD_2 level.
As demand increased, inventories would decline, producers would step up
production, output and employment would rise, and income would increase
to the $1300 billion level, producing equilibrium at full employment.

We also could relax the assumption of fixed levels of investment for a
moment to trace out a financial parallel. Investment consists of both planned
and unplanned components. Businesses plan, for example, to either expand,
contract, or hold constant their levels of inventories. If, because of increased
demand, inventories fall below planned levels, firms find themselves holding
less investment than they desire. Planned investment is greater than actual
investment. In the Keynesian system, firms would step up production to return
inventories to their planned levels. However, the planned level of investment

also can increase. From a purely financial viewpoint, as aggregate demand increased, producers could take a more optimistic view of investment opportunities. As expected income streams from potential investments increased, more investment projects could now produce positive net present values even in the face of higher interest rates. Increased investment costs could be overshadowed by greater potential income, and in addition to replacing depleted inventories, planned investment would expand and reinforce the existing expansion in demand.

In another approach to fiscal policy, government could stimulate aggregate demand by reducing taxes. This tax reduction would increase disposable income and therefore consumption expenditures, as can be seen from Equations (3.4) and (3.5). The effects of changes in government spending and taxation are symmetrical to both increase and decrease aggregate demand. If, for example, full-employment output was $1200 billion in the economy and, through inflation, current output was $1250 billion, then government spending could be decreased or taxes increased to reduce aggregate demand to the D_3 level in Figure 3.3. Inventories would increase above planned levels, producers would cut back production and lay off workers, and equilibrium income would decline to $1200 billion. The financial parallel view of this scenario implies reductions in projected income streams that would reduce the number of available investment projects with positive net present values even if lower interest rates were available. Reduced projected revenues could overshadow reduced investment costs, producing a decline in investment. The decline in planned investment could aggravate the existing decline in demand even further.

The specific differences between changes in taxation and direct changes in government spending will be addressed later in this chapter. However, it is important to note for now that both techniques were integral parts of established Keynesian doctrine. In addition, the role played by the net-exports component of aggregate demand has become so much larger over the past two decades that it warrants a separate discussion of its own and will be presented in detail in Chapter 10. For simplicity of explanation here, the foreign sector will be excluded from further discussion in the development of the Keynesian example.

3.4.1 The Expenditure Multiplier

From the Keynesian algebra of Equation (3.7), equilibrium income is equal to total planned expenditures. We can distribute the B term over the $(Y - T)$ term in Equation (3.7) to become $BY - BT$ and then subtract BY from both sides of the equation to get Equation (3.9):

$$Y - BY = a - BT + I_p + G \tag{3.9}$$

Dividing both sides of Equation (3.9) by the term $1 - B$, we get

$$Y - \frac{a - BT + I_p + G}{1 - B} \tag{3.10}$$

It is interesting to note what happens to equilibrium income in the Keynesian model when government expenditures change. If, for example, G was increased by \$10 billion in Equation (3.10), Y would increase by much more than \$10 billion. Substituting all the assumed values of Equation (3.8) into Equation (3.10) but increasing government spending from \$100 billion to \$110 billion, equilibrium income increases from \$1250 billion to \$1300 billion:

$$Y = 30 + 0.80(Y - 100) + 150 + 110 + 50$$
$$= \$1300 \text{ billion} \tag{3.11}$$

Here, a \$10 billion increase in government spending produced a \$50 billion increase in equilibrium income. In the more general algebraic sense, we can rewrite Equation (3.10) as follows:

$$Y = \frac{a - BT + I_p + G + 10}{1 - B} \tag{3.12}$$

Breaking the right side of Equation (3.12) into two terms, we get

$$Y = \left(\frac{a - BT + I_p + G}{1 - B}\right) + \left(\frac{10}{1 - B}\right) \tag{3.13}$$

The first term is the old equilibrium income, and the second bracketed term to the right is really the change in equilibrium income that comes about through the increase in G. Here it is easy to see that $\Delta Y = (\Delta G / 1 - B)$. If we substitute 0.80 for B, we get

$$\Delta Y = \frac{\Delta G}{1 - 0.80}$$
$$= \frac{\Delta G}{0.2}$$
$$= 5 (\Delta G)$$

Each $1 increase in government spending would produce $5 in additional equilibrium income. In effect, the Keynesian expenditure multiplier was $1/(1-0.8)$, or 5. The general equation for the expenditure multiplier is

$$M_e = \frac{1}{(1-B)} \tag{3.14}$$

The multiple expansion of equilibrium income occurs because each additional $1 injected into the economy through government spending is first received as income by its recipients, who then spend part (as indicated by the MPC) and save part. The part that is respent becomes income for those who receive it. These second-round recipients then in turn respend part and save part. This spending and respending chain continues; however, since the MPC is less than 1, each subsequent round produces less additional income than its predecessor. The term $1-B$ really indicates the MPS or the percentage of each dollar received as income that is saved (not respent). Realizing that B is constant, the total income produced by an increase in government spending would be a simple declining geometric series, as illustrated in Table 3.1

3.4.2 The Tax Multiplier

The Keynesian model suggests changes in fiscal policy through government expenditures and taxes to effect changes in aggregate demand and alter equilibrium output. Both government spending and taxation are subject to a multiplier process. However, there are marked differences in the outcomes of these processes. From Equations (3.4), (3.5), and (3.6) it is clear that changes in taxation affect equilibrium income by changing disposable income, which then changes consumption expenditures, which in turn affects aggregate demand. This roundabout process does not have as large a total effect on aggregate demand as do direct changes in government expenditures. This is true because as taxes are reduced, there is no direct first-round injection of spending, as there was in the case of an increase in government spending. Tax reductions increase disposable income, which triggers off the equivalent of the second round and all subsequent rounds of spending in Table 3.1, but no first round of buying goods and services takes place. This means that the total effect of a change in taxation is one less than the total effect of a change in government spending, and therefore, the tax multiplier is one less than the expenditure multiplier. We also should keep in mind that income moves in the opposite direction of the change in taxation. When taxes

TABLE 3.1 How the Multiplier Works

Spending (Round)	Incremental Income	Change in Spending	Change in Saving
0	—	10	0
1	10	8	2
2	8	6.4	1.6
3	6.4	5.1	1.3
4	5.1	4.08	1.02
5	4.08	3.264	.816
6	3.264	2.611	.653
7	2.611	2.080	.522
8	2.080	1.664	.416
All other rounds	8.465	6.081	1.673
Total*	50.00	50.00	10.00

Note: All values in billions; MPC assumed to be 0.80.
*Total without first round injection as in a tax reduction $40.00.

are reduced, disposable income is increased, and vice versa. If we recalculate Equation (3.11) with government at the original level of 100 and reduce taxes by $10 billion to $90 billion, we get

$$Y = 30 + 0.80(Y - 90) + 150 + 100 + 50$$
$$= \$1290 \text{ billion} \tag{3.15}$$

Here, reducing taxes by $10 billion increased equilibrium income from $1250 billion to $1290 billion, for a net change of $40 billion. The earlier expenditure multiplier example produced a $50 billion increase in income by increasing government expenditures by $10 billion.

We can derive the tax multiplier by rewriting Equation (3.10) as two terms:

$$Y = \frac{(a - BT + I_p + G)}{1 - B}$$
$$= \left[(a + I_p + G)\frac{1}{1 - B}\right] - \frac{B}{(1 - B)T} \tag{3.16}$$

The tax multiplier would therefore equal the change in income divided by the change in taxes:

$$M_t = \frac{-B}{1-B}$$

$$= \frac{-0.8}{1-0.8} = -4 \tag{3.17}$$

Comparing Equations (3.14) and (3.17), we find that the tax multiplier is one less than the expenditure multiplier.

3.4.3 The Balanced-Budget Multiplier

The most important aspect of the numerical difference between the expenditure multiplier and the tax multiplier is the policy implications it produces. For example, if government expenditures and taxes were increased by an equal amount, the two policy changes would not equally offset each other. Equilibrium income would expand by the amount of the initial increase in spending. Alternatively, if equal reductions in government expenditures and taxes were implemented, equilibrium income would contract by the amount of the original reduction. This is true because the tax multiplier is always one less than the expenditure multiplier. With the MPC of 0.8 that we have been using, an increase in government spending of $100 billion expands equilibrium income by $500 billion, and the accompanying increase in taxes of $100 billion contracts equilibrium income by $400 billion for a net change of a positive $100 billion. Algebraically,

$$\Delta Y = \Delta G\left(\frac{1}{1-B}\right) + \Delta T\left(\frac{-B}{1-B}\right) \tag{3.18}$$

If $\Delta G = \Delta T$, then

$$\Delta Y = \frac{1-B}{1-B}$$

$$= 1$$

The sizes of both the expenditure and tax multipliers have significant policy implications in the Keynesian system because they determine the magnitude of needed changes in taxes and spending to achieve full-employment equilibrium income. Given these policy implications, the balanced-budget multiplier concept has produced one of the more controversial conclusions arising from Keynesian economics. Based on this idea, Keynes believed that at less than full-employment output, equal increases in both taxes and government spending could simultaneously balance the budget and restore full employment. While this theory may have accurately predicted economic behavior in the 1930s and 1940s, it has been less successful in current years. A more complete discussion of alternative views on this appears in Chapter 5.

3.5 SAVINGS, PLANNED INVESTMENT, AND THE ROLE OF INVENTORIES

In the introduction to this chapter, two equilibrium conditions were stated: first, that aggregate demand was equal to aggregate supply, and second, that savings was equal to planned investment. Here we will take a closer look at the second condition and examine the role played by the inventory component of investment.

We can illustrate the proof of our second equilibrium condition as follows: At equilibrium,

$$Y = C + I_p + G + X_n \qquad (3.19)$$

and

$$S = Y - C \qquad (3.20)$$

Holding G and X_n constant at zero for simplification and subtracting C from both sides of Equation (3.19), we get:

$$Y - C = I_p \qquad (3.21)$$

From Equation (3.20) we can see that $Y - C = S$; therefore, we can rewrite Equation (3.21) as follows: At equilibrium,

$$S = I_p \qquad (3.22)$$

The common sense of this proof is that the level of unplanned inventories that exist at any one time depends to a large extent on consumer spending and saving behavior. Firms determine the level of inventory they plan to hold based on some estimate of consumer sales. If consumers spend less, i.e., save more than firms had expected them to, inventory exceeds planned levels. If consumers spend more than expected, inventories fall below planned levels. There is, therefore, a distinct link between consumer savings and the equilibrium level of investment. At equilibrium, savings is equal to planned investment.

Business investment consists of fixed expenditures on new plant and equipment and changes in inventory valuations. It is the inventory component that has particular significance in macro equilibrium. Total inventory values are made up of both planned and unplanned expenditures. For example, if firms in the aggregate plan to carry $200 billion worth of inventory throughout the year, planned inventory investment is $200 billion. However, sales could fall below expected levels, and firms could find that they now hold $250 billion worth of inventory. Total inventory investment would now consist of $200 billion in planned investment and $50 billion in unplanned investment. With excess inventory, firms would begin to cut back production in the hope that sales would soon reduce inventory to its planned level. When production is cut back, firms employ fewer workers and income paid to workers falls. A symmetrical scenario occurs when total investment falls below planned levels. If firms had planned to hold $200 billion in inventory and sales exceeded expected levels so that current inventory was $150 billion, then there would be a negative unplanned investment of $50 billion. Firms would step up production to rebuild inventories to planned levels. In doing so, they would hire more workers and total income paid out to workers would increase.

Inventories are really a valuable indication of the direction in which the economy will be moving. If they exceed planned levels, we can expect, all else being equal, that equilibrium income will decline, and if they fall below planned levels, we can expect equilibrium income to increase. If inventories are at the planned expenditure levels, we are in equilibrium, since there is no tendency for change in the economy. We could say that one identity of equilibrium is that actual or total investment is equal to planned investment, since unplanned investment is zero:

Total investment = planned + unplanned investment
At equilibrium, unplanned investment = 0
Therefore, total investment = planned investment
At equilibrium, savings = planned investment

3.6 THE PARADOX OF THRIFT

The required equality between savings and planned investment at equilibrium income produces one of the more interesting paradoxes in Keynesian economics. Traditionally, saving has been viewed as a positive and beneficial form of economic behavior. On an individual level, saving more today provides the ability to have greater future consumption. On the aggregate level, however, greater savings by everyone can produce the *paradox of thrift*, where reduced consumption expenditures can have negative effects on aggregate income, consumption, and savings. When consumers in mass increase their savings, they reduce their cunsumption. As consumption falls, inventories rise above planned levels. With positive unplanned inventory investment, firms cut back production. The reduction in consumer demand triggers off the expenditure multiplier. When the multiplier comes into play, equilibrium income falls by a much larger amount than the original decline in consumption. Since both savings and consumption are functions of the level of income, the resulting decline in equilibrium income ends up reducing consumption and savings.

Paradoxically, when everyone tries to save more, they may trigger off a chain of events that ends up reducing income, consumption, and savings. The specifics of this process are illustrated in Figure 3.4. The economy is initially in equilibrium at the $1300 billion income level, with $AD = Y$ and savings = planned investment. Consumption at the $1300 billion income level

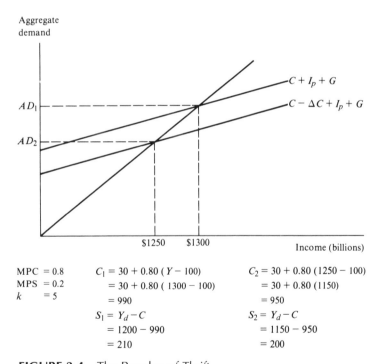

FIGURE 3.4 The Paradox of Thrift.
Initial equilibrium occurs at the $1300 billion income level with $AD_1 = Y$ and savings = planned investment. Consumption at $1300 billion income = 990; savings = 210. If consumers suddenly increase savings by $10 billion, with an MPC of 0.8 and a multiplier of 5, equilibrium income will fall by $50 billion. The new consumption equals 950. The new savings equals 200.

is equal to $a + B(Y - T)$, or $30 + 0.8(1300 - 100) = 990$. Savings $= Y_d - C$, or $1200 - 990 = 210$. If consumers suddenly increase savings by \$10 billion, with an MPC of 0.8 and a multiplier of 5, equilibrium income will fall by \$50 billion (5×10). The new level of consumption is equal to $30 + 0.8(1250 - 100)$, or 950. The new level of savings is equal to $Y_d - C$, or $1150 - 950 = 200$. The paradox of thrift does not say anything about the increase in savings being rechanneled back into the economy through increased availability of investment funds and therefore is not completely realistic. The general process, however, is a possibility even if the exact magnitudes of its effects are not exactly what the model would imply.

3.7 THE *IS–LM* MODEL OF EQUILIBRIUM

The simplified Keynesian model presented earlier relied on changes in aggregate demand to determine equilibrium income. It did not examine the effects that interest rates or changes in financial markets might exert on the economy. The *IS-LM* model presented here incorporates both a market for goods and services and a market for money in determining equilibrium. The model is useful both to explain the effects of changes in fiscal policy and to introduce monetary aggregates and the role played by monetary policy.

Fiscal policy has dealt with the spending and taxing functions of government. Monetary policy deals with changes in the supply of money and terms of credit that are controlled by the Federal Reserve System. Changes in the money supply can exert influences on interest rates and the level of investment that exists in the economy as well as on the spending and saving behaviors of consumers. While both money and monetary policy are discussed in greater detail in Chapters 6 and 7, the introduction of monetary changes in the model here adds another dimension to our current discussion of macro equilibrium.

3.7.1 Building the *IS* Curve

In building the basic *IS-LM* model, the economy is divided into a goods market and a money market. The goods market attains equilibrium, as in the Keynesian model, at the intersection of aggregate supply and aggregate demand. The level of aggregate demand depends on consumption, investment, and government spending; however, it is affected by the level of prevailing interest rates as well. An inverse relationship exists between the level of aggregate demand and interest rates. As interest rates rise, aggregate demand is expected to decline. Incorporating our previous equilibrium numbers into this construct, we can develop the *IS* curve of Figure 3.5 and the *LM* curve of Figure 3.6.

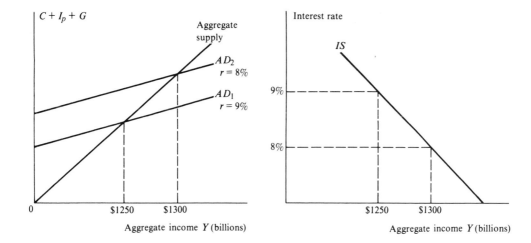

FIGURE 3.5 Derivation of the *IS* Curve.
From the left panel, the original equilibrium income is $1250 billion where aggregate supply intersects AD_1. AD_2 is predicated upon the levels of consumption, investment, and government expenditures that would be forthcoming if the interest rate were 9 percent. When the interest rate falls to 8 percent, aggregate demand would expand to AD_2, producing an increase in equilibrium income to $1300 billion. The right panel depicts the *IS* curve with interest rates on the vertical axis and aggregate income on the horizontal axis. As the interest rate declines from 9 to 8 percent, aggregate income expands to $1300 billion.

From the left panel of Figure 3.5 we can see that the original equilibrium income is $1250 billion, where aggregate supply interesects the first aggregate demand function. AD_1 is predicated upon the levels of consumption, investment, and government expenditures that would be forthcoming if interest rates were 9 percent. If interest rates were to fall to, say, 8 percent, then aggregate demand would expand to AD_2, producing an increase in equilibrium income to $1300 billion. In the right panel of Figure 3.5 we can see the *IS* curve, with interest rates on the vertical axis and aggregate income on the horizontal axis. As interest rates decline from 9 to 8 percent, aggregate income expands to $1300 billion. The *IS* curve is really various combinations of interest rates and income levels that produce equilibrium in the goods market.

Changes other than interest rates in any of the components of aggregate demand will affect the location of the *IS* curve. For example, an increase in consumption or government spending would shift the entire *IS* curve outward and to the right of the existing curve, implying that higher levels of income would be needed at every interest rate to bring the goods market into equilibrium.

3.7.2 Building the *LM* Curve

3.7.2.1 Money Demand

Equilibrium in the money market occurs where the demand to hold money is equal to the supply of money available. The total demand to hold money consists of two components: transactions demand and speculative demand.

Transactions demand is just what the name implies; it is that portion of the total amount of money we all hold for transactions purposes. On an individual basis, it is the cash or checking account balances people hold to be able to buy things with from day to day. In general, our transactions demand is a positive function of income. As income increases, so does our transactions demand:

$$MD_t = f(Y)$$

Speculative demand is that portion of total money demand we all hold with an eye toward profit. Liquid cash for investment purposes held in money-market accounts is an example of speculative demand. It is money held in order to take advantage of an opportunity for profit when it presents itself. The interest rate represents the opportunity cost of holding money balances. It is, in effect, what is given up by holding money instead of having it invested in some form that earns the market rate of interest. For example, if the market rate of interest on passbook savings is 5 percent, each dollar kept in your pocket or in a non-interest-bearing checking account "costs" you the nickel you could have earned by keeping it in savings. If the market rate of interest were 10 percent, the opportunity cost of holding money would be higher. Therefore, speculative demand is a negative function of the interest rate:

$$MD_s = -f(i)$$

As interest rates rise, consumers hold fewer speculative balances, and as interest rates fall, they hold larger speculative balances.

3.7.2.2 Money Supply

The supply of money is constant at any one time, but it can be changed with varying economic conditions, the willingness of banks to lend, and Federal

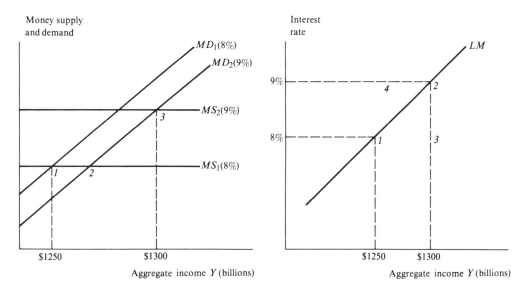

FIGURE 3.6   Derivation of the *LM* Curve.
In the left panel, money supply and money demand are plotted on
the vertical axis and aggregate income is plotted on the horizontal
axis. The original equilibrium occurs at $1250 billion income with
MD_1 at a market interest rate of 8 percent. If interest rates increase,
money demand falls to MD_2. Banks, on the other hand, desire to
lend more money at the current higher interest rates. This serves to
increase the money supply to MS_2. At the $1250 billion income
level (point *1*), money supply is now greater than money demand.
Spending in the economy begins to increase, producing additional
income and moving the economy along the horizontal axis until the
new money demand and supply functions MD_2 and MS_2 now intersect at the income level of $1300 billion (point *3*). In the right panel,
the *LM* curve represents various combinations of interest rates and
income levels that produce equilibrium in the money market. The
combination of 8 percent and $1250 billion will bring the money
market into equilibrium. Increasing the interest rate to 9 percent
would require an income level of $1300 billion to clear the money
market.

Reserve System policy. In the left panel of Figure 3.6, money supply and
money demand are plotted on the vertical axis and aggregate income is plotted
on the horizontal axis. The original equilibrium occurs at $1250 billion in-
come with MD_1 at a market interest rate of 8 percent. The combination of
$1250 billion aggregate income and an 8 percent interest rate will bring the
money market into equilibrium. If the interest rate was 9 percent, the cost

of holding speculative balances would be higher and consumers would decrease their speculative holdings. This would reduce money demand to MD_2. Banks, on the other hand, would desire to lend more money at the current higher interest rates. This serves to increase the money supply to MS_2. At the $1250 billion income level (point *1*), money supply would now be greater than money demand. For the money market to reach equilibrium, transactions demand must increase. Since transactions demand is a positive function of income, only higher levels of income (i.e., $1300 billion) will produce the transactions demand necessary to clear the money market at the 9 percent interest rate. Spending in the economy begins to increase, producing additional income and moving the economy along the horizontal axis until the new money demand and supply functions MD_2 and MS_2 now intersect at the income level of $1300 billion (point *3*).

In the right panel the resulting *LM* curve has been traced out. The *LM* curve represents various combinations of interest rates and income levels that produce equilibrium in the money market. The combination of 8 percent and $1250 billion will bring the money market into equilibrium. Increasing the interest rate to 9 percent would require an income level of $1300 billion to clear the money market. Any interest rate — income combination to the right and or below the *LM* function, such as point *3*, would indicate that money demand exceeded money supply. If this were the case, consumers would attempt to rebuild their money balances by spending less. This would trigger off a reduction in production, and income would fall. At the new lower income, transactions balances would decline and the money market would move back into equilibrium toward the 8 percent and $1250 billion income level. Alternatively, any point to the left and/or above the *LM* schedule, such as point *4*, would be where money supply exceeded money demand. Consumers would begin to spend off the excess supply. Production and income would rise, increasing transactions demand and moving the money market back toward equilibrium at the 9 percent and $1300 billion income level.

3.7.3 Equilibrium in the *IS–LM* Model

This *IS-LM* model of the economy indicates the combinations of interest rate and income that will simultaneously produce equilibrium in both the goods and money markets. The only interest rate and income pair that will achieve this appears at the intersection of the *IS* and *LM* functions. In Figure 3.7, this occurs at an interest rate of 9 percent and $1300 billion in income. Anything that affects the location or slope of either function will change the market-clearing pair. For example, if any of the components of aggregate demand in the goods market, such as autonomous consumption, were to

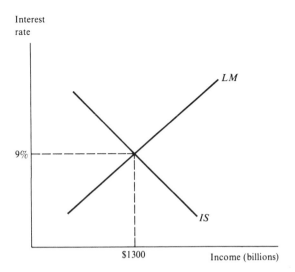

FIGURE 3.7. Equilibrium in the *IS-LM* Model.
The *IS-LM* model of the economy indicates the combination of interest rate and income that will simultaneously produce equilibrium in
both the goods and money markets. The only rate and income pair
that will achieve this is at the intersection of the *IS* and *LM* functions.

increase, the *IS* curve would shift to the right. As a result, income and interest
rates would rise to the new market-clearing pair, as depicted in Figure 3.8.

Alternatively, changes in monetary policy by the Federal Reserve
System would relocate the *LM* curve. An increase in the supply of money
would shift the *LM* curve outward and to the right, as depicted in Figure 3.9,
yielding a reduction in equilibrium interest rates and an increase in equilibrium income.

3.7.4 The Effects of Government Policy

Tracing out the effects of changes in fiscal and monetary policy by government is a relatively simple matter with the *IS-LM* model. The decision maker
must first determine whether the policy change would primarily affect the
goods market (*IS*) or the money market (*LM*). Since fiscal policy is concerned
with government spending and taxation, it is a goods-market phenomenon,
while changes in monetary policy affect the supply of money and accordingly
influence interest rates and income through the money market. Having determined whether a policy change is goods- or money-related, the only remaining task is to trace out the direction and magnitude of the change and
its effect on equilibrium interest rates and income.

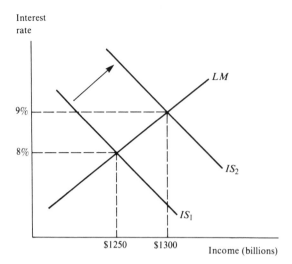

FIGURE 3.8 The Effects of Changes in Aggregate Demand.
If any of the components of aggregate demand in the goods market
were to increase, the *IS* curve would shift to the right, and income
and interest rates would rise to the new market-clearing pair.

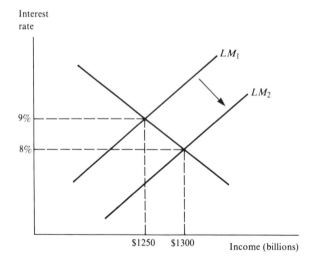

FIGURE 3.9 The Effects of Changes in the Money Supply.
An increase in the money supply by the Federal Reserve System
would shift the *LM* curve outward and to the right, yielding a reduction in the equilibrium interest rate and an increase in equilibrium
income.

3.7.4.1 Fiscal Policy Effects

In general, any change in fiscal policy will alter aggregate demand either directly through changes in government spending or indirectly through changes in taxation that alter disposable income and therefore any portions of the consumption and investment functions that depend on disposable income. Looking back at Figure 3.8, we can trace out each of these scenarios.

First, consider the case of an increase in government spending. All else being equal, this would be a direct exogenous increase in aggregate demand and would shift the *IS* function outward and to the right, increasing equilibrium income and interest rates. In Figure 3.8, the equilibrium would move from IS_1 to IS_2, with interest rates increasing to 9 percent and income expanding to $1300 billion. A contraction in government spending would have the reverse effect of reducing aggregate demand, shifting the *IS* curve inward and to the left, and producing lower equilibrium interest rates and income.

A change in taxation also would alter aggregate demand, shifting the *IS* curve. It is important to keep in mind, however, that the change in aggregate demand would be indirect through the alteration of disposable income and therefore would not have as large an effect as an equal change in government spending. The reasons for this were detailed in the earlier section of this chapter dealing with the balanced-budget multiplier. If, for example, taxes were increased by $10 billion, aggregate demand would decline in our earlier model by 8 (10 billion times the MPC of 0.8). This would shift the *IS* function of Figure 3.8 inward and to the left, but by less than the previous example of direct government spending. The result would be a decline in the equilibrium interest rate below 9 percent but above 8 percent and a $40 billion decline in equilibrium income (10 times the tax multiplier of 4). Symmetrically, if taxes were reduced by $10 billion, aggregate demand would increase by $8 billion and equilibrium income and the interest rate would rise.

3.7.4.2 Monetary Policy Effects

A change in the supply of money will directly influence the location of the *LM* curve and alter equilibrium income and interest rates. If the Federal Reserve System were to expand the money supply, all else being equal, the *LM* function would shift outward and to the right from LM_1 to LM_2 in Figure 3.9 producing a decline in the equilibrium interest rate from 9 to 8 percent and an increase in equilibrium income from $1250 billion to $1300 billion. Alternatively, a contraction in the money supply would shift the *LM* curve inward and to the left, producing an increase in the interest rate and a decline in equilibrium income.

3.7.4.3 Combined Policy Effects

While it is instructional to consider the individual effects of monetary and fiscal policy separately, it is not very realistic. Both forms of policy exist simultaneously and are continually subject to change. For example, government may increase spending to stimulate the economy and reduce unemployment at the same time that the Federal Reserve System is expanding the money supply. In such a case, both the *IS* and *LM* functions shift outward and to the right, as illustrated in Figure 3.10. The result could be an increase in equilibrium income without an increase in the interest rate. This coordination of monetary and fiscal policy may appear to create the more desired outcomes in both the goods and money markets, but it does in fact have numerous problems associated with it. Frequently, such coordination overstimulates the economy and produces inflationary pressures as full employment approaches.

Combined policy effects also can trace out a scenario where monetary and fiscal policy may move in opposite directions at the same time. The Federal Reserve may be contracting the money supply at the same time that government spending is on the rise. Here we would see an outward shift of the *IS* function and an inward shift of the *LM* function. Depending on the relative magnitudes of each of the policy changes, it is at least possible that

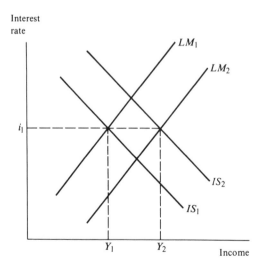

FIGURE 3.10   Combined Policy Effects.
Increases in both government spending and the money supply could produce an expansion in equilibrium income without necessarily increasing the equilibrium interest rate.

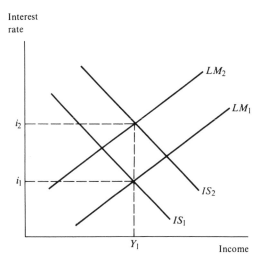

FIGURE 3.11 Combined Policy Effects: Uncoordinated Policy. Increases in government spending with a contraction of the money supply could produce an increase in the equilibrium interest rate while leaving income unchanged.

the new equilibrium could produce increased interest rates and the same level of income as illustrated in Figure 3.11. The key to understanding the combined effects of monetary and fiscal policy lies in the realization that the final outcome depends on the relative magnitudes of each of the changes, as well as the direction of the change.

3.8 SUMMARY

1. Equilibrium implies a state where there is no tendency for change. In economics, this occurs when aggregate demand AD equals aggregate supply AS. Inventories consist only of those levels of goods firms have planned to hold as a buffer against fluctuations in demand. Therefore, the second equilibrium condition is that savings S equals planned investment I_p.

2. Aggregate demand AD is the sum of all planned expenditures in the economy by consumers, investors, government, and the foreign sector:

$$AD = C + I_p + G + X_n$$

3. Aggregate supply AS is a measurement of the total output of real goods and services in the economy.

4. The intersection of the aggregate supply and aggregate demand functions illustrates the current equilibrium output and price level.

5. The classical economists believed that the economy was driven primarily by aggregate supply and that flexible prices and wages would quickly act to restore full employment of resources even when aggregate supply and/or aggregate demand were fluctuating.

6. The classical approach held that government interference in the economy was unneeded and unwanted. Stabilization policy was considered to interfere with the natural self-correcting forces that would return the economy to full-employment equilibrium on its own. Any unemployment that did exist was considered to be short term in nature and would be eliminated in the long run as wages and prices adjusted and the economy corrected itself.

7. The Keynesian view was that wages and prices were ''sticky downward'' because of less than perfectly competitive markets for both goods and labor and that while there may be natural forces operating in the economy that bring about equilibrium, the equilibrium need not be at the full-employment level of output. Keynes contended that active government intervention to stimulate or dampen aggregate demand was necessary to bring about stable equilibrium at full employment.

8. Keynes believed that aggregate demand was the driving force behind the economy and that insufficient levels of aggregate demand produced long periods of unemployment and low levels of output or aggregate supply. As supply fell, producers would lay off workers and income in the economy would fall, further reducing spending by consumers and investors and, therefore, further reducing aggregate demand.

9. The Keynesian model incorporates the following relationships. At equilibrium,

$$AD = AS$$
$$AS = Y$$
$$AD = C + I_p + G + X_n$$
$$C = a + B(Y_d)$$
$$Y_d = Y - T$$
$$AD = a + B(Y - T) + I_p + G + X_n$$
$$Y = a + B(Y - T) + I_p + G + X_n$$

10. The Keynesian system is driven by changes in aggregate demand that are believed to call forth changes in aggregate supply. Supply is assumed to accommodate any changes in aggregate demand.

11. Whenever the full-employment level of output is higher than the current equilibrium level, Keynesian doctrine would suggest fiscal policy changes such as an increase in government spending that would increase aggregate demand. As demand increases, inventories will decline, producers will step up production, output and employment will rise, and income will increase, producing equilibrium at full employment.

12. The expenditure multiplier is a small change in any of the components of aggregate demand resulting in a much larger change in equilibrium income. The equation for the expenditure multiplier is $M_e = 1/(1 - \text{MPC})$.

13. The multiple expansion of equilibrium income occurs because each additional \$1 injected into the economy through government spending is first received as income by its recipients, who then spend part (as indicated by the MPC) and save part. The part that is respent becomes income for those who receive it. These second-round recipients then in turn respend part and save part. This spending and respending chain continues. However, since the MPC is less than 1, each subsequent round produces less additional income than its predecessor. The total expansion of income resulting from the multiplier process is therefore set by the size of the MPC.

14. Changes in taxation affect equilibrium income by changing disposable income, which then changes consumption expenditures, which in turn affect aggregate demand. This roundabout process does not have as large a total effect on aggregate demand as do direct changes in government expenditures because, as taxes are reduced, there is no direct first-round injection of spending. The total effect of a change in taxation is one less than the total effect of a change in government spending, and therefore, the tax multiplier is one less than the expenditure multiplier. The equation for the tax multiplier is $M_t = (1/1 - B)B$.

15. If government expenditures and taxes were increased by equal amounts, the two policy changes would not equally offset each other. Equilibrium income would expand by the amount of the initial increase in spending. This is true because the tax multiplier is always one less than the expenditure multiplier. The value of the balanced-budget multiplier is therefore 1.

16. If consumers spend less, i.e., save more, than firms had expected them to, inventory exceeds planned levels. If consumers spend more than expected, inventories fall below planned levels. There is therefore a distinct link between consumer savings and the equilibrium level of investment. At equilibrium, savings are equal to planned investment.

17. Inventories are really a valuable indication of the direction in which the economy will be moving. If they exceed planned levels, equilibrium income will decline, and if they fall below planned levels, equilibrium income will increase. One identity of equilibrium is that actual or total investment is equal to planned investment, since unplanned investment is zero:

Total investment = planned + unplanned investment
At equilibrium, unplanned investment = 0
Therefore, total investment = planned investment
At equilibrium, savings = planned investment

18. The paradox of thrift contends that when consumers in mass attempt to increase their savings, they reduce their consumption, inventories rise above planned levels, and firms cut back production and trigger off the expenditure multiplier. The resulting decline in equilibrium income ends up reducing consumption and savings. Paradoxically, when everyone tries to save more, they may trigger off a chain of events that ends up reducing income, consumption, and savings.

19. The *IS* curve represents various combinations of interest rates and income levels that produce equilibrium in the goods market.

20. Equilibrium in the money market occurs where the demand to hold money is equal to the supply of money available. The total demand to hold money consists of transactions and speculative demands. Transactions demand is that portion of the total amount of money we all hold for transactions purposes. Speculative demand is that portion of total money we all hold with an eye toward profit.

21. The *LM* curve represents various combinations of interest rates and income levels that produce equilibrium in the money market.

22. Equilibrium in the *IS-LM* model of the economy indicates that combination of interest rates and income that will simultaneously produce equilibrium in both the goods and money markets. The only interest rate and income pair that will achieve this is at the intersection of the *IS* and *LM* functions. Anything that affects the location or slope of either function will change the market-clearing pair.

23. In general, any change in fiscal policy will alter aggregate demand either directly through changes in government spending or indirectly through changes in taxation. Tax changes alter disposable income and therefore any portions of the consumption and investment functions that depend on disposable income.

24. An increase in government spending would be a direct exogenous increase in aggregate demand and would shift the *IS* function outward and to the right, increasing equilibrium income and the interest rate.

25. A change in taxation also would alter aggregate demand, shifting the *IS* curve. An increase in taxes would shift the *IS* function inward and to the left.

26. A change in the supply of money would directly influence the location of the *LM* curve and alter equilibrium income and the interest rate. With an expansion in the money supply, the *LM* function would shift outward and to the right, producing a decline in the equilibrium interest rate and an increase in equilibrium income. Alternatively, a contraction in the money supply would shift the *LM* curve inward and to the left, producing an increase in the interest rate and a decline in equilibrium income.

27. The key to understanding the combined effects of monetary and fiscal policy lies in the realization that the final outcome depends on the relative magnitudes of each of the changes as well as the direction of the change.

3.9 EXERCISES

1. Explain the expected results regarding the equilibrium interest rate and income for each of the following:
   a. An expansion in monetary policy, all else held constant
   b. An expansionary fiscal policy, all else held constant
   c. Relatively equal contractions in both monetary and fiscal policy
   d. Contractionary fiscal policy accompanied by relatively equal expansionary monetary policy

2. Compare and contrast the basic views of the classical economists with those of John Maynard Keynes.

3. The Keynesian model consists of an aggregate demand function and an aggregate supply function. The aggregate demand function is composed of functions for consumption, investment, and government spending. Write out the basic equations that make up this system, assign hypothetical values to each of the variables in the system except equilibrium income, and solve for equilibrium income, consumption, and savings.

4. State the two conditions for macro equilibrium in the Keynesian system and explain why savings is equal to planned investment.

5. Compare and contrast the expenditure and tax multipliers and explain why the balanced-budget multiplier has a value of 1.

6. Explain the paradox of thrift.

7. Compare and contrast the *IS* with the *LM* curve. Explain the importance of the intersection of these two functions in the *IS-LM* model.

8. Trace out the effects of an increase in the autonomous component of consumption on the equilibrium interest rate and income through the *IS-LM* model.

9. *The Case of the Government Policy Expert and the Corporate Planner*. The following exercise requires that you assume two different roles. First, you are appointed to the President's Council of Economic Advisors. Through existing research, you know the following parameters:

> Autonomous consumption = $60 billion
> Consumers spend about 75 cents of each additional dollar of income on consumption.
> Government spending and taxes are balanced at $400 billion.
> Planned investment spending is currently $600 billion.
> The full-employment level of income in the economy is $3240 billion.

Now you must assume that you are a corporate decision maker. Your corporation produces luxury automobiles and contracts fleets of utility vehicles such as delivery jeeps for the Postal Service and agency automobiles for the U.S. government. Through corporate research you know that total dollar sales of your automobiles in the United States has historically been about $0.02 times total income in the economy. Planned inventory levels for your firm are currently at $200 million. Current total inventory is about $210 million. You have just read in *The Wall Street Journal* that the fiscal policy suggestions that you prepared for the President in part (a) of this case have been approved by the Congress and will be implemented over the next 2 years. You must make recommendations to your board about the following issues:

b. What should be done about the existing excess inventory?

c. The firm presently operates both a brand new and an older assembly facility. The new facility is operated 16 hours a day, and the older factory operates one 8-hour shift. Some board members have suggested that the new facility be operated 24 hours per day now and the older factory sold and the work force either transferred or laid off. Where do you stand on this issue?

d. Would it make any difference to you whether the fiscal policy recommendations were in the form of changes in taxes or changes in government spending? If so, why?

3.10 REFERENCES

Keynes, J. M. *The General Theory of Employment, Interest, and Money*. New York: Harcourt, Brace, and World, 1965.

Leijonhufvud, A. *On Keynesian Economics and the Economics of Keynes*. New York: Oxford University Press, 1968.

Samuelson, P. ''The Simple Mathematics of Income Determination,'' in *Income Employment and Public Policy: Essays in Honor of Alvin H. Hansen*. New York: Norton, 1948.

_4_
The Contemporary Aggregate Demand – Aggregate Supply Model

4.1 INTRODUCTION

"You can't fool all of the people all of the time."[1]

This chapter takes an approach to macroeconomics that is, at the same time, old and new. The contemporary aggregate demand – aggregate supply model, or *AD-AS* model, is "new" relative to the standard Keynesian macroeconomic model covered in the preceding chapter. The *AD-AS* model also is "old" because it can be considered a restatement of the *preclassical* quantity theory of money, a theory of inflation and the business cycle that predates the so-called classical school.

In addition to being both old and new, the *AD-AS* model is both simple and complex. The *AD-AS* model is simplicity itself, being no more than the most basic concept of economics, supply and demand curves, elevated to the macroeconomic level. Still, the *AD-AS* model is complex, because, at a fundamental level, there is no such thing as a true macroeconomic price. Macroprices, such as the GNP deflator and the CPI, are indexes representing the price level or the average price. These are not the prices of some *things* in terms of other *things*. Rather, these are the money prices of things in

[1]Abraham Lincoln

general—how much money it takes to buy a market basket of goods and services.

The *AD-AS* model is simple, in the sense described above, and yet it is very powerful. The model is able to explain the cycle of inflationary-boom and recessionary-bust that has characterized macroeconomies for centuries. More than that, it easily couples the political economy with the macroeconomy, explaining the inflation-unemployment spiral and the series of government policy responses of recent years. For these reasons, the *AD-AS* model is an extremely useful device to business executives attempting to understand the macroeconomic environment in which they conduct their business.

4.2 THE AGGREGATE DEMAND – AGGREGATE SUPPLY MODEL

The aggregate demand – aggregate supply model can be used to analyze movements of the *price and quantity* components of the macroeconomy. In this model, the aggregate demand curve—analogous to a microeconomic demand curve—results from macroeconomic spending, including consumer, business, government, and foreign spending. The location of the aggregate demand curve is affected by consumer and business confidence, liquidity, interest rates, and exchange rates, as well as by government monetary and fiscal policies.

The aggregate supply curve—analogous to a microeconomic supply curve—results from macroeconomic costs of production, including wages, raw materials prices, and the prices of intermediate goods such as business plant and equipment. The location of the aggregate supply curve is affected by supplies of raw materials, technological progress, taxes on productive effort, and expectations.

An aggregate demand – aggregate supply model is illustrated in Figure 4.1. Note that the axes of the *AD-AS* curve are (1) on the horizontal, macroeconomic quantities, such as real GNP, production, employment, or income, and (2) on the vertical, macroeconomic prices, that is, an index of the general price level, such as the GNP deflator and the CPI.

Just as with microeconomic demand and supply curves, the *AD* curve represents the ability and willingness to buy at various prices. This curve is downward-sloping, so that at higher macroprices, macrobuying would be lower. The *AS* curve represents the ability and willingness to sell at various prices. This curve is upward-sloping, so that at higher macroprices, macroselling would be higher. Each of these two curves is hypothetical, representing the amounts that would be bought or sold at different prices and not just the amount that is bought and sold at the observed price. Short-run

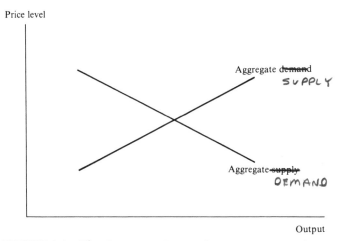

FIGURE 4.1   The Aggregate Demand – Aggregate Supply Model.

equilibrium is obtained when macrobuying is equal to macroselling. This determines the macroquantity measured on the horizontal axis and the macroprice measured on the vertical axis.

4.2.1 Real Prices vs. Macroprices

It is important to point out a fundamental indeterminacy in the aggregate demand – aggregate supply model. In microeconomic demand and supply models, price—the vertical axis—is the price of a particular good or service *relative to the prices of other goods and services*. If the particular good or service being considered is apples, it is the price of apples relative to the prices of oranges and other things. That is, it is the *real price* of apples, the price of apples *in terms of* other goods and services.

Getting back to the aggregate demand – aggregate supply model, the price on the vertical axis is a macroprice, such as the GNP deflator. The question is, To what, if anything, does this price relate? One thing is for sure, the price in the aggregate demand – aggregate supply model is not the price of apples, or anything else, relative to the prices of other goods and services. Changes in the GNP deflator and other general price indexes are representations of changes in *all* prices, not of some prices relative to others.

There are two related ways to interpret the price variable in the aggregate demand – aggregate supply model: First, the macroprice can be viewed as the price of final output *relative to* the prices of labor, raw materials, and intermediate goods. And second, the macroprice can be viewed as the actual purchasing power of money *relative to* the perceived purchasing power of money, i.e., the actual GNP deflator relative to the expected GNP deflator. The purchasing power of money is what $1 will buy in terms of goods and services. Objectively, it is measured by the inverse of the GNP deflator. Subjectively, it depends on what people *think* money is worth—what it will be able to buy when spent—which is usually based on their *past experience* with spending money.

4.2.2 The Purchasing Power of Money

The *purchasing power of money* is what $1 will buy in terms of goods and services. If prices double, then the purchasing power of money halves. For example, if the GNP deflator goes from 100 to 200, then the purchasing power of money goes from 1/1 to 1/2. In general, the purchasing power of money, relative to its purchasing power during the base year, is $1/P$, where P is the macroprice index.

What people think money will buy can differ from what money will actually buy because no price index is perfect and because it takes time to gather and tabulate the required data to compute a price index. More important, people's expectations for the purchasing power of money can be wrong because their knowledge for forming their expectations is usually restricted to their own past purchases and those of their friends. That is, usually people adapt their expectations for the purchasing power of money to their experience.

The first interpretation, that the macroprice index is the price of final output relative to the prices of labor, raw materials, and intermediate goods, indicates that the *AD-AS* model depends on *differential* changes between output prices and input prices, i.e., an increase in the prices of (final) goods and services relative to wages.

The second interpretation, that the macroprice index is measuring the actual purchasing power of money relative to money's expected purchasing power, indicates that the *AD-AS* model depends on *differences* between the actual and the expected purchasing power of money. Both of these interpretations have important implications for *long-run* analysis using the aggregate demand—aggregate supply model. These implications will be developed later in this chapter.

4.2.3 Static vs. Dynamic Analysis

Depending on their scientific methodology, economists either emphasize the short run versus the long run or the static versus the dynamic. *Short-run* versus *long-run analysis* refers, loosely, to the time lapse following an initial change. The short run includes more nearly immediate effects, while the long run includes more distant effects. The period of time it takes to get from the short run to the long run, however, is not constant, but varies according to such factors as the flexibility of prices, especially the flexibility of wages.

More precisely, the short run refers to the period of time during which the aggregate demand and aggregate supply curves are fixed (except for the initial change being studied). In the short run, it is often reasonable to assume that wages do not immediately adjust to changes in prices. Given this assumption, a shift in the aggregate demand curve that raises prices does not immediately cause a shift in the aggregate supply curve. However, in the long run, it is usually reasonable to assume that wages do adjust to changes in prices. Therefore, after an increase in prices from an initial shift in the aggregate demand curve, it is reasonable to expect that wages will adjust to this increase in prices, i.e., that wages will also increase, and that this increase in wages will shift the aggregate supply curve.

Static analysis refers to analysis of the long run. In a sense, this type of analysis ignores the process by which a macroeconomy adjusts from an initial change to the new long-run equilibrium. In another sense, this type of analysis assumes that this process is short and does not itself affect the new long-run equilibrium. While these are strong assumptions, static analysis is often useful for determining the long-run implications of initial changes. Of course, to the extent that the process of adjustment is long and affects the new long-run equilibrium, the predictions of static analysis will only be approximately correct. On the other hand, there are cases in which the process of adjustment is short and has little effect on the new long-run equilibrium. In these cases, the predictions of static analysis are completely correct.

Dynamic analysis tracks the macroeconomy through the process of adjustment from an initial change to the new long-run equilibrium. While potentially more precise than static analysis, this type of analysis requires detailed knowledge of the structure of the macroeconomy. For example, dynamic analysis requires detailed knowledge about the process by which wages are adjusted to changes in prices and the process by which expectations are formed.

4.2.4 Keynesian vs. Classical Economics

While any brief description of economists is bound to be simplistic, it is useful at this point to make some broad generalizations about scientific methodologies. On the one hand, classical economists such as David Ricardo stressed long-run and static analyses. On the other hand, the early Keynesian economists stressed short-run analysis. John Maynard Keynes is, in fact, well known for saying, ''In the long run, we are all dead.'' In contrast to the Keynesian-classical dichotomy, most economists today conduct analysis that

TABLE 4.1   Keynesian versus Monetarist Economics

KEYNESIAN ECONOMICS	*MONETARISM*
1. Emphasizes the short run	1. Emphasizes the long run
2. Presumes that wages and expectations are fixed in the short run	2. Presumes that the degree of flexibility in wages and expectations depends on the commitment of the monetary authority to maintain the value of money
3. That is, presumes that the aggregate supply curve is fixed in the short run	3. That is, does not necessarily presume that the aggregate supply curve is fixed in the short run
4. Presumes that wages, loans, and other financial agreements are essentially arbitrary and often should be redone by macroeconomic policy	4. Believes that wages, loans, and other financial agreements are very important for macroeconomic coordination and that coordination is disrupted by changes in macroeconomic policy, with the result of inefficiency and unemployment
5. Not necessarily opposed to wage-and-price controls, which are referred to as "incomes policy"	5. Opposes wage-and-price controls (some monetarists favor widespread indexation so that wages will automatically be adjusted for inflation)
6. Favors discretionary monetary and fiscal policies to "manage" the macroeconomy	6. Opposes use of discretionary monetary and fiscal policies to "manage" the macroeconomy
7. Believes that, without "management," the macroeconomy will feature slow growth, underemployment, instability, and inequitable income distribution	7. Favors "automatic" macroeconomic policies. Sometimes, this is described as favoring "rules" versus "discretion."
8. Believes that macroeconomies are complex and different, requiring detailed knowledge for analysis and macroeconomic policy based on case-by-case analysis as opposed to rules	8. Believes that the macroeconomy best governs itself and will spontaneously generate socially optimal growth, employment, stability, and income distribution
	9. Believes that macroeconomies are much too complex to analyze in detail and so conducts analysis at a highly theoretical and simplified level
	10. Believes that macroeconomies are fundamentally similar, so that macroeconomies of different countries and different time periods can be analyzed for understanding how all macroeconomies function

includes elements of short-run, dynamic, and long-run analysis. The emerging consensus in macroeconomics may be described as Keynesian in the short run, classical in the long run, and featuring a process of adjustment from the short to the long run that can be described as neo-Keynesian or monetarist, depending on one's economic ''roots.''

4.3 THE KEYNESIAN SHORT RUN

In short-run Keynesian economics, illustrated in Figure 4.2, an increase in spending corresponds to an outward shift of the aggregate demand curve. This, in turn, affects macroprices and quantities according to supply conditions. If there is widespread unemployment, the aggregate supply curve will be flat. In this case, an increase in spending results only in increased employment and output and not at all in an increase in prices. This is shown in Figure 4.2*a*.

If there is little unemployment, the aggregate supply curve will be vertical. In this case, an increase in spending results only in higher prices and not at all in an increase in employment and output. This is shown in Figure 4.2*b*. If there is some, but not widespread, unemployment, the aggregate supply curve will be positively sloped. In this case, an increase in spending results in both increased employment and output and higher prices. This is shown in Figure 4.2*c*. Thus the mix of higher prices versus higher employment and output that results from an increase in spending depends on the extent of unemployment.

FIGURE 4.2   The Short-Run Keynesian Model.   ────────▶
(a) The flat portion is the "pure" Keynesian portion of the aggregate supply curve. Here there is massive unemployment, e.g., the Great Depression. Expansionary policy that shifts out the aggregate demand curve only increases output and employment and does not increase prices. (b) The vertical portion is the "pure" classical portion of the aggregate supply curve. Here there is full employment. Expansionary policy that shifts out the aggregate demand curve only increases prices and does not increase output or employment. (c) The sloped portion is the "normal" economy. Here there is moderate unemployment. Expansionary policy that shifts out the aggregate demand curve increases both output and employment as well as prices.

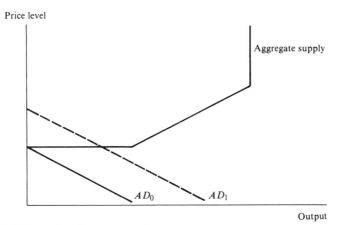

(a) **Flat portion of aggregate supply curve**

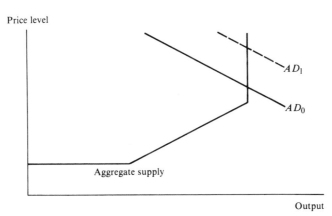

(b) **Vertical portion of aggregate supply curve**

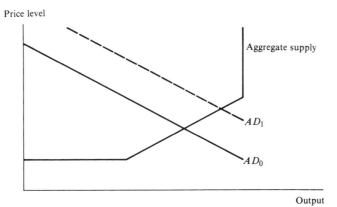

(c) **Sloped portion of aggregate supply curve**

To early Keynesian economists, the classical school's conclusion that an increase in the money supply only causes changes in prices resulted from an assumption of full employment. In the more general case, a combination of higher prices *and* higher employment and output results. And, in a world featuring massive unemployment such as characterized the 1930s, it is conceivable that only higher employment and output—and no inflation—result.

4.3.1 Demand-Pull Inflation

Contemporary Keynesian economists usually distinguish between two types of inflation. The first type, *demand-pull inflation*, refers to the inflation that results from an outward shift of the aggregate demand curve. When there is moderate unemployment (Fig. 4.2c), demand-pull inflation is associated with an increase in employment and output. Only in the special case of a vertical supply curve (Fig. 4.2b) does demand-pull inflation result only in higher prices. This is the Keynesian version of the classical school.

Outward shifts of the aggregate demand curve can be due to a number of causes: (1) increased *autonomous* spending of consumers, businesses, governments, and foreigners; (2) increased spending on consumer durables, housing, and fixed business investment induced by increased liquidity and lower interest rates as a result of expansionary monetary policy; and (3) increased government spending and increased consumption spending as a result of reduced taxes and increased transfers, i.e., expansionary fiscal policy.

4.3.2 Cost-Push Inflation

The second type of inflation, *cost-push inflation*, refers to an upward shift of the aggregate supply curve and is associated with a decrease in employment and output. Cost-push inflation can result from increases in wages and other input prices that raise the cost of production.

4.4 THE DYNAMIC KEYNESIAN MODEL

At this time it is appropriate to consider the economic forces set into motion from a shift of one or both of the aggregate demand and aggregate supply curves. First to be considered is *a sequence of shifts* in the aggregate demand and aggregate supply curves that can follow expansionary monetary policy. This will be followed by consideration of the possibility of *simultaneous shifts* of the aggregate demand and aggregate supply curves that can follow expansionary monetary policy.

4.4.1 Sequential Shifts

The specific expansionary monetary policy to be examined is an increase in the Federal Reserve's purchases of Treasury securities that increases the money supply and lowers interest rates. The sequence of shifts is illustrated in Figure 4.3. The expansionary monetary policy will induce increased spending by consumers and businesses on consumer durables, housing, and fixed business investments and so shift the aggregate demand curve out. This shift of the aggregate demand curve results in a new short-run equilibrium featuring higher prices and increased employment and output. This first round is shown in Figure 4.3*a*. Note its similarity to Figure 4.2*c*.

At this time, wages have lost ground to inflation, and they are raised in order to regain their lost purchasing power. (Wages can be raised by union bargaining or by intensified bidding for labor services in free markets.) In a second round, increases in wages result in an upward shift of the aggregate supply curve. This second round is shown in Figure 4.3*b*.

This second-round shift of the aggregate supply curve reduces output and employment—we shall presume back to their original levels—while increasing prices still further. Because of this further increase in prices, wages *again* lose ground to inflation and so are again raised. In a third round, the additional increase in wages results in an additional upward shift of the aggregate supply curve. This third round is shown in Figure 4.3*c*. Notice that this third round features continuing inflation in conjunction with output and employment below their initial (normal?) levels. *Stagflation*—or an inflationary recession—and a boom-bust business cycle are clearly forecast as part of the sequence of effects following an expansion of the money supply.

After all the shifts are concluded, what results *in the long run* is simply a higher level of prices at the initial level of employment and output. This is shown as the fourth round in Figure 4.3*d*. However, just as with a roller coaster, even though you may wind up in real terms back at where you started, the trip can be quite exciting.

4.4.2 Simultaneous Shifts

Contemporary monetarists include ''new classicalists'' such as Robert Barro who emphasize the long-run equilibrium effects of policy. New classicalists also emphasize *rational expectations*, which —simply stated—is the idea that people cannot be systematically fooled, or that people learn from their mistakes. A particular implication of rational expectations is that if it is known that expansionary monetary policy will lead eventually to higher prices, then workers will raise their wages immediately in anticipation of the higher prices. In this case, both the aggregate demand curve and the aggregate

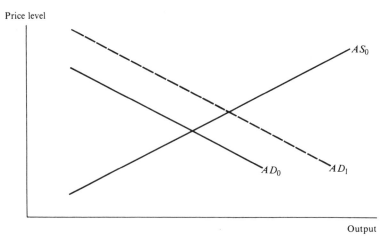

(a) First round

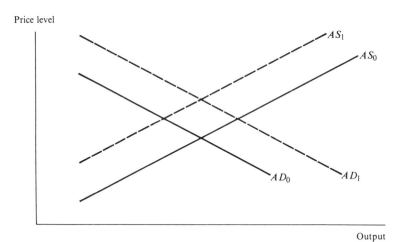

(b) Second round

FIGURE 4.3 The Dynamic Keynesian Model.
(a) In the short run, or first round, an increase in the money supply shifts out the aggregate demand curve and increases both output and employment, as well as prices. (b) In the second round, workers realize they have lost purchasing power to inflation and so increase their wages. This shifts the aggregate supply curve up, reducing output and employment—we shall say to their initial levels—and further increasing prices. (c) In the third round, workers again realize they have lost purchasing power to inflation and so again increase their wages. This again shifts the aggregate supply curve up, further

supply curve will shift simultaneously, and the economy "jumps" to its new long-run equilibrium. The simultaneous shifting of both the aggregate demand and aggregate supply curves is illustrated in Figure 4.4. This is the monetarist version of the classical school.

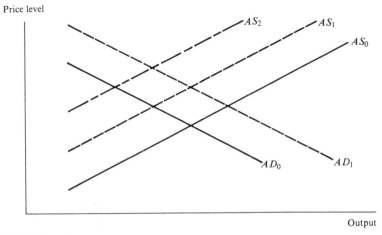

(c) Third round

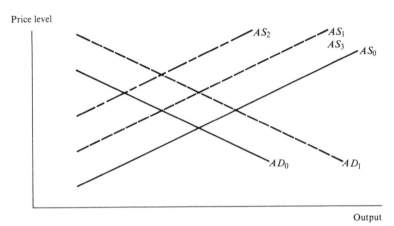

(d) Fourth round

FIGURE 4.3 Continued

reducing output and employment—now to below their initial levels
—and further increasing prices. This combination of below-normal
output and employment and continuing inflation is an inflationary
recession and is referred to as *stagflation*. (d) In the fourth, or final,
round, more than usual unemployment among workers creates competition among workers for available jobs. This forces workers to reduce their wages, shifting the aggregate supply curve down. This
results in an increase in output and employment—we shall say back
to their initial levels—and reduces prices. This combination is a
noninflationary recovery.

4.4.3 Adaptive vs. Rational Expectations

Adaptive expectations are expectations that adapt to actual experience. When
expectations are adaptive, workers react to inflation only *after* it occurs,

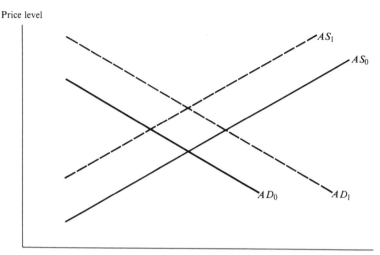

FIGURE 4.4   The New Classical Model.
The announcement of an expansion of the money supply causes
workers—who are assumed to understand macroeconomics—to
raise their wages in anticipation of inflation. Therefore, even as the
aggregate demand curve is shifted out, the aggregate supply curve is
shifted up. All that happens is that prices are raised; output and employment are not affected. (Similar results are obtained if wages are
indexed to prices, except that — in this case—managers and not
workers track monetary policy.)

wages lag changes in prices, and the aggregate supply curve is fixed in the
short run. The concept of adaptive expectations implies that when inflation
accelerates, it will be underestimated, and when it decelerates, it will be
overestimated.

Rational expectations are expectations that are based on all "available"
information, including monetary policy if this is a precursor of inflation, so
wages need not lag changes in prices. The aggregate supply curve can move
simultaneously with movements of the aggregate demand curve. If expectations are rational, inflation is not systematically underestimated or
overestimated.

It is important to note that rational expectations are not necessarily
more correct than adaptive expectations. The difference is not so much pre-
dictive ability as it is the flexibility of rational expectations to quickly react
to changes in monetary policy instead of being tied to the history of inflation.
If expectations are adaptive, policymakers can depend on expectations—
and wages—responding slowly to changes in inflation. Monetary and fiscal

policies can therefore have powerful effects. If expectations are rational, policymakers cannot depend on a slow response, and monetary and fiscal policies are less effective.

During a period of price stability, it is difficult to imagine that workers would follow monetary policy and speculate on its implications for inflation. With price stability, adaptive expectations and the dynamic Keynesian model may be more appropriate than rational expectations and the new classical model. However, with a high degree of inflation uncertainty, it is plausible that workers—at least through their unions—would track inflationary trends more closely. In particular, it is plausible that wages would come to be *indexed* to inflation, which would have the effect of shifting the tracking of monetary policy to business executives. Therefore, the higher the degree of inflation uncertainty, the more appropriate is rational expectations and the new classical model.

4.4.4 Indexation

Indexation involves automatically adjusting wages for inflation. For example, setting the money wage W equal to $(P/P_0)W_0$, where P is currently the GNP deflator or the CPI, P_0 is the GNP deflator or the CPI at the time of the wage bargain, and W_0 is the money wage at the time of the wage bargain. In practice, cost-of-living adjustments (COLAs) in most union contracts in the United States provide only rough adjustments for inflation.

Many financial securities today are effectively indexed by specifying interest rates that "float" with market interest rates; e.g., every quarter the interest rate will be reset at the bank's "prime" interest rate plus 1 percent.

4.5 INFLATION AND UNEMPLOYMENT

As the 1950s came to a conclusion, naggingly persistent unemployment of about 6 percent raised political concerns. On the one hand, Keynesian economists argued that expansionary monetary and fiscal policies were needed to move the economy "up" the Phillips curve to full employment. On the other hand, certain conservative economists (premonetarists?) advised against such policies—and the inflation they would cause—for fear of the potential long-run consequences.

The expression *Phillips curve* refers to the statistical relation developed by Australian economist A. W. Phillips, studying a long history of wages and unemployment rates in Great Britain over the period 1861 – 1957. Amazingly, the same statistical relationship appeared to fit the United States! To Keynesian economists, this relationship represented a "menu of policy choices." It was the government's job to use monetary and fiscal policies to, in effect, pick the "right" combination of inflation and unemployment off the Phillips curve.

4.5.1 Relation to *AD-AS* Model

The Phillips curve is, in a sense, a twist on the aggregate demand – aggregate supply model. Instead of real GNP or employment, the horizontal axis of the Phillips curve is the *unemployment rate*. And instead of the price level, the vertical axis is inflation, or the rate of price *change*. In the short-run Keynesian model, the aggregate supply curve is considered to be constant, to be nonshifting. Movements of the aggregate demand curve therefore determine real GNP and employment as well as the price level according to where the aggregate demand curve intersects the aggregate supply curve. This corresponds, roughly, to movements along the Phillips curve; i.e., expansionary monetary and fiscal policies result in low unemployment and high inflation. Restrictive monetary and fiscal policies result in high unemployment and low inflation.

Examining the movements of the Phillips curve from the 1960s to the present will prove an effective way of seeing the aggregate demand – aggregate supply model in action. It also will be useful for seeing the interconnections between the political economy and the macroeconomy.

4.5.2 The Keynesian Side of the Phillips Curve Debate

To Keynesian economists, the Phillips curve represented a tradeoff between inflation and unemployment. The "cost" of lowering unemployment was higher inflation, and vice versa. Even during the early 1960s, Keynesians recognized that the Phillips curve represented the *short-run tradeoff* between inflation and unemployment. However, Keynesians argued that shifts of the Phillips curve were difficult to predict. Expansionary policies could, by affecting expectations, cause the Phillips curve to shift up. Alternatively, expansionary policies could, by increasing stability and efficient utilization of resources, cause the Phillips curve to shift down. The only really predictable thing was that in the short run, inflation and unemployment were negatively correlated.

To Keynesian economists, unemployment was considered a much worse problem than inflation. First, unemployment was unfair, affecting a few in a devastating way, while inflation affected many in a moderate way. Second, output lost to unemployment was output lost forever, while inflation basically was a zero-sum game, redistributing purchasing power from some (creditors) to others (debtors).

More important, the *kind of inflation* that Keynesians were advocating

—a steady, moderate pace of rising prices—was altogether different from the kind of inflation that conservative economists feared. Keynesians were *not* advocating hyperinflation; they were advocating only a few percent per year, just enough to keep the economy going at a fast pace, employing its available resources and growing at its maximum sustainable rate.

The effects of the expansionary policies of the Kennedy-Johnson administrations are easy to see in Figure 4.5. Unemployment that began at around 6 percent was progressively lowered to around 4 percent, and inflation that was near zero was progressively increased to around 4 percent. This appeared to verify Keynesian economics. The Phillips curve made its way into the college textbooks and even into the 1969 *Economic Report of the President*.

4.5.3 The Monetarist Side of the Phillips Curve Debate

As the Kennedy-Johnson administrations moved the economy "up" the Phillips curve, an emerging group of economists known as *monetarists* clarified their criticism. Instead of merely expressing unquantified fears of inflation, monetarists argued that the Phillips curve was a temporary and possibly even illusionary tradeoff. Attempting to exploit the apparent tradeoff between inflation and unemployment would result in shifts of the Phillips curve that would return unemployment to its "natural rate." In addition, attempting to keep unemployment below its natural level would require offsetting the shifts

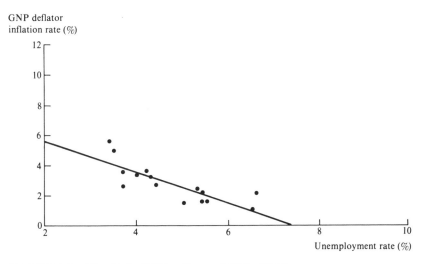

FIGURE 4.5   The U.S. Phillips Curve, 1954–1969.
Source: Adapted from *Economic Report of the President, 1969*, p. 95.

of the Phillips curve with ever more inflation. This argument became known as the *accelerationist hypothesis*.

The *natural rate of unemployment* is the unemployment rate that will emerge if the macroeconomy features a steady rate of inflation. The assumption is that the unemployment rate that would emerge from a macroeconomy with stable prices, i.e., with no inflation, would be the same unemployment rate that would emerge at any steady rate of inflation.

Estimates of the natural rate of unemployment vary. These estimates vary first because of the changing composition of the labor force. A useful working assumption is that because of changes in the composition of the labor force, a 6 percent unemployment rate during the early 1980s was equivalent to a 4 percent unemployment rate during the early 1960s. Whether these rates of 4 and 6 percent were the natural rates of unemployment for their time periods is a matter of debate.

If these were the natural rates of unemployment, then inflation would have tended to accelerate only if unemployment was pushed below 4 percent during the early 1960s and would have tended to decelerate if unemployment was pushed to only above 6 percent during the early 1980s. Keynesian economists tend to accept these rates of 4 and 6 percent as the natural rates of unemployment for their time periods. Monetarist economists tend to estimate higher rates.

The accelerationist hypothesis is that to keep the unemployment rate below the natural rate, inflation must be continually increased so that it will always be at a faster rate than expected.

To monetarists, the Phillips curve resulted from surprise inflation, not from inflation itself. When inflation is faster than expected, wages lag inflation and so firms find that workers are cheap to hire. This is why firms hire so many workers and the unemployment rate falls. When inflation is slower than expected, wages lead inflation and so firms find that workers are expensive to hire. This is why firms do not hire very many workers and the unemployment rate increases.

The reason why the historical Phillips curve appeared to be a stable statistical relationship was that until recently inflation was a episodic event, associated only with wars and their aftermath. Inflation was not persistent and therefore was not incorporated into expectations. Once inflation became persistent, monetarists argued, it would come to be expected to continue, and the Phillips curve would shift. The statistical Phillips curve would break down. Instead, a series of Phillips curves, each one at a level higher than the previous one, would appear.

Monetarists argued that attempting to move ''up'' the Phillips curve would result in inflation that would become incorporated into expectations.

This would shift the Phillips curve up and return unemployment to its natural level. The long-run Phillips curve would simply be a vertical line at the natural rate of unemployment.

Monetarists eventually also argued that inflation would affect the slope as well as the level of the Phillips curve. Once the economy learned that prices could vary unexpectedly, it would develop more flexible arrangements including indexation of wages. Accordingly, unexpected inflation would have a reduced effect on employment. Eventually, even the short-run Phillips curve would become a vertical line.

To monetarists, the 1970s constituted a great experiment to see which theory—the Keynesian tradeoff theory or the monetarist natural rate theory —was correct. That the 1970s were years in which the Phillips curve appeared to shift verified the monetarist theory. Said Robert Lucas of the University of Chicago in 1981, "Proponents of a class of models which promised 3 1/2 to 4 1/2 percent unemployment to a society willing to tolerate annual inflation of 4 to 5 percent have some explaining to do after a decade as we have just come through."[2] The long-run Phillips curve made its way into textbooks and even into the 1982 *Economic Report of the President*. This shifting Phillips curve is shown in Figure 4.6.

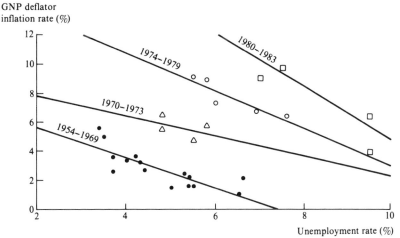

FIGURE 4.6   The U.S. Phillips Curve, 1954–1983.
As inflation accelerated, the short-run Phillips curve appeared to shift up. Note that the datum for 1975 is not included because it seems to be "off" the 1974–1979 short-run Phillips curve.
Source: Adapted from *Economic Report of the President, 1982*, p. 51.

[2]"Tobin and Monetarism: A Review Article," *Journal of Economic Literature*, 29, June 1981, pp. 558–585.

To monetarists, inflation is harmful because it *distorts* prices and *disrupts* economic plans and coordination. Relationships among prices, wages, rents, and so forth, determined by competition and bargaining, are overturned. Long-term financial arrangements, including loans, insurance policies, and pensions, are rearranged. Tax rates, determined by the democratic process, are changed. Inflation is, in a word, inefficient. It undermines planning, reduces saving and economic growth, and leads in the long run to higher—not lower—unemployment. In this view, the long-run Phillips curve is not exactly a vertical line but has a positive slope. Thus, in the long run, there is a positive, not a negative, correlation between inflation and unemployment.

4.5.4 The Stop-Go Political Economy

Looking back to the 1970s, an inflation-unemployment spiral appears obvious. During the ''go'' phase of this spiral, expansionary monetary and fiscal policies were used to lower unemployment at the expense of accelerating rates of inflation. When inflation reached a politically unacceptable level, a ''stop'' phase followed, during which restrictive monetary and fiscal policies were used to try to arrest the accelerating inflation.

During the ''stop'' phase, however, prices continued to rise as a result of the upward shift of the Philips curve as expectations caught up to the actual rate of inflation. The restrictive policies therefore did not appear to work. Inflation appeared unresponsive. Inflation seemed to have a life of its own; ''inflation psychology'' appeared to have settled into the economy. Moreover, at the same time, unemployment was increasing.

It was predictable that during this stagflation phase pressure would have been brought onto democratic governments to ''do something'' about the dual problem of inflation and unemployment. Since restricting money supply growth and government spending did not appear to work, wage-and-price controls were urged onto the government. Indeed, wage-and-price controls are often employed at this juncture of the inflation-unemployment spiral. They were instituted by the Republican administration of President Nixon in the United States as well as by the Conservative administration of Prime Minister Heath in England during the early 1970s. All the wage-and-price controls succeeded in doing, however, was further distorting economies already suffering from inflation.

Because of the increase in unemployment to politically unacceptable levels, a new ''go'' phase of inflation, which can be termed *reinflation*, was instituted. By this time, the politically acceptable level of inflation had been increased, so that this cycle of the inflation-unemployment spiral took place

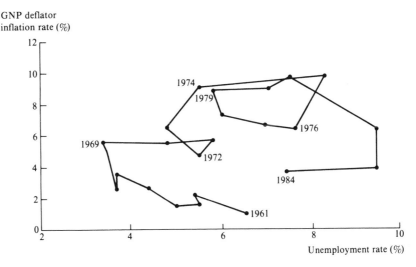

FIGURE 4.7   The U.S. Stop-Go Economy, 1961–1984.
During the first "go" phase, 1961 – 1969, the Kennedy- Johnson administration used expansionary monetary and fiscal policies to
"trade off" higher inflation for reduced unemployment. In the second "stop" phase, 1969 – 1972, President Nixon attempted to lower
inflation with restrictive monetary and fiscal policies. However,
these policies appear to have been ineffective because "inflation
psychology" appears to have set into the economy. Therefore,
wage-and-price controls were resorted to. In the third "go" phase,
1972 – 1974, President Nixon, with wage-and-price controls breaking down and under pressure from the brewing Watergate investigation, attempted to restimulate the economy with expansionary
monetary and fiscal policies. In the fourth "stop" phase, 1974–
1976, President Ford again attempted to lower inflation, at the cost
of unemployment, including his own. In the fifth "go" phase,
1976 – 1979, President Carter lowered unemployment at the cost of
reinflation. In the sixth "stop" phase, which began in 1979, President Carter's newly appointed chairman of the Federal Reserve, Paul
Volcker, slams the brakes on the money supply.

at a higher level of inflation. However, because of increasing inefficiency
and uncertainty, the short-run Phillips curve was shifting outward instead of
straight up and becoming more steeply sloped. It was taking more and more
inflation to temporarily lower unemployment, and all the while unemployment was hitting record post-World War II highs. The stop-go inflationary
spiral is illustrated in Figure 4.7.

4.5.5 Disinflation

As the 1970s neared their conclusion, the United States faced a difficult choice: either it would have to muster the political resolve to end inflation or it would have to accept the next phase of the inflation-unemployment spiral. The problem with ending inflation was that, with expectations of inflation deeply ingrained into the economy, the probable result was a severe recession.

James Tobin, a leading Keynesian economist, warned that attempting to reduce inflation would result in a *very* long recession, with double-digit unemployment lasting until the end of the 1980s. See Figure 4.8 for Tobin's forecast of what would be the cost of disinflating the U.S. economy. Milton Friedman, a leading monetarist economist, advocated a slow and steady reduction in money supply growth in order to mitigate the adverse impact of disinflation.

Contrary to the analyses of Tobin and Friedman, rational expectationist or new classicalist economists conjectured that disinflation could be painless if prefaced by a "credible announcement." A *credible announcement* is an announcement that — without a change in actual experience — causes a change in expectations. A credible announcement presumably would cause a shift in the Phillips curve so as to allow disinflation without recession. In addition, "supply side" economists theorized that tax cuts could cause the economy to grow rapidly and so offset disinflationary pressure.

The problem with a credible announcement of disinflation, causing re-negotiation of wages, loans, rents, and so forth and allowing painless disinflation, is that politicians had been claiming to be "fighting inflation" while inflation was, in fact, rising. Would President Ronald Reagan's "announcement" be any different, any more credible? In addition, the exact ways in which inflation expectations are embedded into the economy are numerous, dispersed, subtle, and nonsynchronous. Even if President Reagan's announcement was believed, the change in expectations could not have been completely acted on.

Disinflation was actually begun while President Jimmy Carter was in office, by his appointed chairman of the Federal Reserve Board, Paul A. Volcker. One of the first effects of Volcker's tightening of monetary policy was a recession. (Among the people who lost their jobs because of this recession was President Carter.) A second recession followed in quick order that drove the unemployment rate up to double digits. It looked very much as though the predictions of Tobin were going to come true.

Fortunately, a number of factors combined to break the back of the inflation-unemployment spiral. Prominent among these factors was the breakup of the international oil cartel and fall in energy prices following deregulation of oil prices in the United States. Also, early in his adminis-

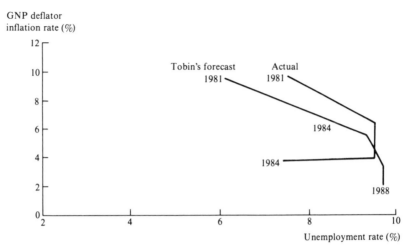

FIGURE 4.8 Wringing Out U.S. Inflation, 1981–1984.
Source: Adapted from Tobin, J., "Stabilization Policy Ten Years After," *Brookings Papers on Economic Activity*, 1:1980, pp. 19–71.

tration, President Reagan was given an opportunity to convincingly demonstrate his resolve—i.e., to make a credible announcement—when the federally employed air traffic controllers went on strike. By firing the air traffic controllers and "decertifying" their union, President Reagan signaled that wage bargaining as usual was no longer appropriate. Finally, it must be admitted that the tax rate cuts passed in 1981 and phased in over several years may have contributed to a growing GNP after the cuts were completely phased in.

However, it easily could have been worse. In western Europe, disinflation resulted in the kind of long recession that Tobin predicted for the United States. See Figure 4.9a for the British experience. Even though disinflation was less severe in the United States, it still resulted in massive unemployment, as well as many personal and business bankruptcies and a great deal of social distress that strained the public- and private-sector safety net. Keynesian economists were quick to advocate reinflation. Said Alan Blinder of Princeton University in 1986, when the economy was on a path of steady, noninflationary recovery, "A more permissive monetary policy, less paralyzed by fears of inflation, is the surest route to faster growth."[3]

The monetarist analysis was to relate the socioeconomic duress of the 1980s to the expansionary macroeconomic policies of the 1960s and 1970s

[3]"A 7% Jobless Rate Is Just Not Good Enough," *Business Week*, February 3, 1986, p.16.

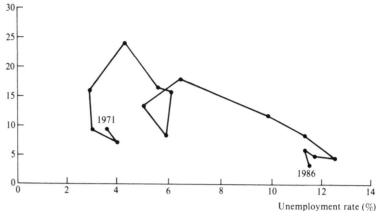

(a) United Kingdom

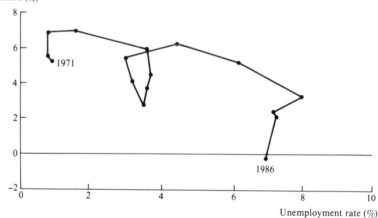

(b) West Germany

FIGURE 4.9 The Phillips Curves for the United Kingdom and West Germany, 1971 – 1986.

Trends in these two countries are similar in pattern to those in the United States over the same time period with one important difference. During the mid-1980s, when the United States began a noninflationary recovery, these two countries and western Europe as a whole languished in high unemployment. Possible reasons for the persistence of high unemployment in western Europe include (1) more militant trade unions and more regulated and socialized industry in western Europe, (2) more liberal unemployment compensation benefits in western Europe, (3) greater credibility of commitment to disinflation in the United States, and (4) more vigorous tax cutting and deregulation in the United States.

Source: Data from OECD *Economic Outlook*, June 1987, pp. 165, 167.

and the accelerations of inflation they fueled. Said Robert Hall of Stanford University, ''To say in 1982 that unemployment is a major social problem is precisely to say that the decision to inflate the economy in the late 1960s and early 1970s was a costly one.''[4]

4.6 SUMMARY

1. The *AD-AS* model is simple, being little more than demand and supply raised to the macro level.

2. The *AD-AS* model is complex because macroprices are not real prices, but are measures of the purchasing power of money and are ''real'' only insofar as the actual purchasing power of money may differ from the subjective purchasing power of money and insofar as some prices—in particular, wages—lag behind other prices when inflation accelerates.

3. The simple Keynesian model assumes that the aggregate supply curve is fixed in the short run, so that variations in aggregate demand cause a mix of price and quantity effects depending on aggregate supply conditions.

4. The dynamic Keynesian model explains the series of effects following an initial shift in either aggregate demand or aggregate supply by considering how expectations and wages adapt to actual experience.

5. The new classical model assumes that with rational expectations and immediate adjustment of aggregate supply, an initial shift in aggregate demand causes the economy to ''jump'' to its new long-run equilibrium. This model may be appropriate after a period of monetary instability.

6. The Phillips curve refers to the short-run negative relationship between inflation and unemployment.

7. In the long run, as an approximation, the Phillips curve appears to shift vertically as expectations adapt to changes in the rate of inflation. Thus in the long-run, the unemployment rate is independent of the rate of inflation.

8. The unemployment rate that is forthcoming with a constant rate of inflation is called the natural rate of unemployment.

9. Actually, because of inefficiencies resulting from high and varying rates of inflation, the Phillips curve appears to shift outward after a period of inflation, so that there is a long-run positive relationship between inflation and unemployment.

[4]''Is Unemployment a Macroeconomic Problem?'' *American Economic Review*, 73, May 1983, pp. 219–222.

10. The Phillips curve, combined with responses of democratic governments to the problems of inflation and unemployment, has resulted in an unemployment-inflation spiral, sometimes referred to as a "stop-go" economy.

11. A predictable part of the stop-go economy is a call for wage-and-price controls. These controls succeed in further distorting macroeconomies already suffering from inefficiencies due to inflation.

12. At some point on the unemployment-inflation spiral, the political resolve must be found to disinflate. This almost inevitably involves a severe recession, including massive unemployment, bankruptcies, and other socioeconomic distress.

13. The severity and duration of the disinflationary recession depend on the flexibility of money wages and the credibility of the announcement of disinflation. The less flexible are money wages and the less credible is the announcement of disinflation, the more severe and longer is the recession.

4.7 EXERCISES

1. Why is Keynesian economics sometimes referred to as "depression economics," and why is monetarist economics sometimes referred to as "full-employment economics?" What macromodel underlies these characterizations of Keynesian and monetarist economics?

2. Discuss three conditions under which expansionary monetary policy does not affect output or employment but only affects prices.

3. Predict the short- and long-run effects on output and employment, as well as on macroprices, of the following:

   (a) After a long period of price stability, the government increases the rate of growth of the money supply.

   (b) After a long period of high and varying rates of inflation, the government increases the rate of growth of the money supply.

4. Predict the short-run and long-run effects on output and employment, as well as on macroprices, of the following:

   (a) The government announces that on January 1 of next year it will give everyone an extra dollar for every dollar they possess.

   (b) The government surprises everyone on January 1 of next year by giving everyone an extra dollar for every dollar they possess.

5. Predict the short- and long-run effects on output and employment, as well as on macroprices, of the following:

(a) The government retires its entire national debt via a special one-time printing of new money and, in conjunction with this, adopts a balanced-budget constitutional amendment and, furthermore, actually balances its budget.

(b) The government retires its entire national debt via a special printing of new money and, in conjunction with this, announces that in the future all deficits will be paid for via this same expedient.

6. What does the 1969 *Economic Report of the President* say about the contributions of labor market conditions, competition in industry, and wage-and-price controls to the short-run Phillips curve?

7. In light of experience, compare, contrast, and evaluate Milton Friedman's and James Tobin's American Economic Association presidential addresses on the subject of inflation and unemployment (see References).

8. Plot the data for 1985 – 1988 onto Figure 4.7, and discuss what appears to have happened to the U.S. Phillips curve during these years.

9. Using *Historical Statistics of the United States*, construct a figure like Figure 4.7 for the period 1928 – 1942, and discuss your findings in light of the short-run and the dynamic Keynesian models presented in this chapter.

10. Using Organization for Economic Cooperation and Development (OECD) data, construct Phillips curves for Japan and for Italy for the period 1971 – 1986. Comment on your findings.

4.8 REFERENCES

Economic Report of the President, 1969. Washington, D.C.: U.S. Government Printing Office, 1969, pp. 94 – 122.

Economic Report of the President, 1982. Washington, D.C.: U.S. Government Printing Office, 1982, pp. 47 – 77.

Fisher, I. "I Discovered the Phillips Curve," *Journal of Political Economy*, 81, March/April 1973, pp. 496 – 502. A reprint of a 1926 article entitled "A Statistical Relation Between Unemployment and Price Changes."

Friedman, M. "The Role of Monetary Policy," *American Economic Review*, 58, March 1968, pp. 1 – 17.

Friedman, M. "Nobel Lecture: Inflation and Unemployment," *Journal of Political Economy*, 85, June 1977, pp. 451 – 472.

Phelps, E. S. *Microeconomic Foundations of Employment and Inflation Theory*. New York: Norton, 1970.

Phillips, A. W. "The Relation Between Unemployment and the Rate of Change of Money Wage Rates in the United Kingdom, 1861 – 1957," *Economica*, 50, November 1958, pp. 283 – 299.

Samuelson, P. A., and Solow, R. "Analytical Aspects of Anti-Inflationary Policy," *American Economic Review*, 50, May 1960, pp. 177 – 194.

Tobin, J. "Inflation and Unemployment," *American Economic Review*, 62, March 1972, pp. 1 – 18.

PART TWO

Policy

5
Fiscal Policy

5.1 INTRODUCTION

In earlier chapters both fiscal and monetary policy were briefly mentioned in regard to their effects on the economy. In this chapter we fully develop the analysis of fiscal policy by examining the appropriations process and the sources and uses of government funds at the federal, state, and local levels. The effects that federal deficits and surpluses have on the economy are analyzed in the context of previous models as well as the political considerations that produce them. We conclude with a careful consideration of the pros and cons of government debt and the impact fiscal policy has on managerial decision making.

Fiscal policy is concerned with the spending and taxing powers of government. Over the last 50 years, government has played an increasingly important role in the economy. Currently, over 40 percent of GNP passes through the public sector and about 20 percent of GNP arises from government spending. Such figures serve to illustrate that government spending and the taxing and borrowing powers that support it have a major impact on aggregate demand, interest rates, equilibrium income, and the composition of output produced in the economy.

5.1.1 The Public Goods Rationale

The major justification offered for government spending in general and the growth of the public sector in particular has been the public goods rationale. Economists for over 200 years have acknowledged the need for at least limited government spending to provide roads, national defense, and a system of courts and laws that the private sector would be unwilling to produce because of their public goods nature. The nature of a public good is such that it is difficult or impossible to exclude nonpayers from their benefit and that they produce externalities that can only be captured by an overall taxing authority with the power of law to compel payment.

National defense is an example of a public good. It would be effectively impossible to defend a nation and exclude nonpayers from that defense. The same MX missile that deters an enemy from attacking New York also deters that enemy from attacking Kansas regardless of who pays the bill. The positive externality produced in national defense can only be captured by a federal taxing authority. Other forms of government expenditures for welfare, health maintenance, manpower training, and a system of courts and laws also may offer significant positive externalities capturable by a taxing authority. If so, the same basic justification for these and other public-sector expenditures may well apply; however, the appropriate magnitude of such expenditures, as well as questions regarding their effectiveness, has been the point of much debate in both the political and economic arenas.

5.1.2 Types of Government Expenditures

There are a large number of specific account titles for government expenditures at all levels. However, most of these accounts can be grouped into the three main categories of goods and services, transfers, and stabilization. The largest single category of fiscal expense is *government purchases of goods and services*. This represents expenditures by federal, state, and local governments to produce national defense, roads, schools, police and fire protection, and other public goods. Since the late 1960s, state government purchases of goods and services have exceeded federal expenditures in this area, but the overall percentage of GNP represented by combined federal and state and local accounts in this category has not experienced marked increases.

The second category consists of *federal government transfer payments* in the form of social security, Medicare, and Medicaid and local and state spending on such accounts as welfare and unemployment compensation that provide a financial "safety net" for the population. Transfers have experienced substantial growth over the last 20 years both in real terms and as a percentage of GNP. Transfers are not accounted for in the aggregate demand portion of GNP accounting even though they influence aggregate demand indirectly by changing the level of disposable income. In addition, when transfers are spent by their recipients, they serve to influence the specific composition of GNP in a manner quite different from what would occur if the government itself had spent the funds on public goods and services.

The third category is composed of *government spending to stabilize the economy* and attempt to smooth out the peaks and troughs of the business cycle. Accounts that fund job-training programs, as well as youth summer employment and the Job Corps, fall under this heading and have expanded since the 1970s. These stabilization expenditures to stimulate the economy during recession should in theory also be expected to decline significantly during periods of economic growth and expansion. Unfortunately, over the last two decades there has been less than perfect symmetry between expansionary and contractionary stabilization policy. Once instituted, expenditure programs appear difficult to curtail.

5.2 SOURCES AND USES OF GOVERNMENT FUNDS

We can gain a more complete picture of fiscal policy by examining both the sources and uses of government revenues. Taxes, borrowing, and grants from other levels of government provide the majority of total government revenues. Figures 5.1 and 5.2 compare the sources of federal and state funds. Figure 5.1 shows estimated sources of federal funds in fiscal year 1987. Personal income tax is the largest federal revenue source, followed by the social security tax and borrowed funds. Borrowing is the third largest federal source. It is similar to a ''tax'' in the sense that the government acquires use of private-sector resources through borrowing just as it acquires the use of private-sector resources through taxes. The corporate income tax provides relatively little revenue to the federal government. The items listed as ''Other taxes'' are mostly sales and excise taxes imposed on items such as liquor, automobile tires, and gasoline.

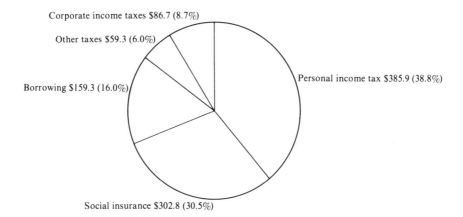

FIGURE 5.1   Federal Revenue Sources (In Billions).
The majority of federal revenues come from personal income taxes, followed by social insurance taxes, such as social security. Borrowing comprises the third largest source, with corporate and other taxes representing the remainder.

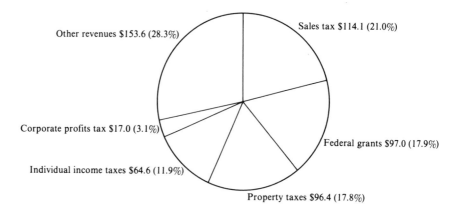

FIGURE 5.2   State-Local Revenue Sources (In Billions).
States and localities raise funds from sales and excise taxes, property
taxes, federal grants, individual income taxes, corporate profits
taxes, and other miscellaneous sources.

Revenues for the state-local government sector come primarily from
taxes on property, sales, and incomes and federal grants (Fig. 5.2). These
grants are an important tool of fiscal coordination. The federal government
uses these grants to provide incentives for state and local governments to
allocate resources in ways they might not otherwise choose to without federal
support. Table 5.1 displays the uses of revenues by government at both the
federal and state-local levels.

TABLE 5.1   Uses of Government Revenues

Use Category	Federal Government, 1985 ($ billions)	State-Local Government, 1985 ($ billions)
Purchases of goods and services	353.9	460.7
(national defense)	(262.0)	—
Transfer payments	366.4	98.8
Grants to state-local government	98.9	—
Interest payments (receipts)	129.0	(31.0)
Total Outlays (including items not listed)	983.0	517.1

Source: *Economic Report of the President, 1986*, Tables B-78 and B-79.
Note: Figures are for calendar years, using national income and product account definition.

State and local governments currently purchase more goods and services than does the federal government because state and local governments deliver the majority of direct government services. Part of these state and local expenditures is supported by federal intergovernmental grants. State and local governments play relatively small roles in transfers and incur very little, if any, debt.

Most of the goods and services that the federal government purchases go toward national defense and transfer payments. Payments of interest on the national debt are also a major budget item for the federal government because it has borrowed heavily in the past to fight wars and to stabilize the economy. State-local governments, on the other hand, actually receive interest payments instead of paying them. Many states and localities are forbidden by state constitutions from borrowing to pay for current services. Thus states and localities have run budgetary surpluses in recent years, making them net recipients of interest payments.

Table 5.2 shows selected details of federal government outlays for fiscal year 1987. National defense and social security are the two largest federal government expenses; however, the large net-interest item in Table 5.2 is noteworthy and will be discussed later in this chapter.

Table 5.3 illustrates the uses of state-local government funds. State and local governments finance the delivery of education, highways, and public welfare partly through state-local taxes and partly through federal intergovernmental grants.

5.3 THE APPROPRIATIONS PROCESS

All categories of government spending are subject to the appropriations process. However, there are differences in how and when various expenditure decisions can be made. At the federal level, the President has the power both to propose expenditure and tax programs and to veto those budgets prepared by Congress of which he disapproves. The Congress can enact or modify the President's proposals and also has the power to override a presidential veto with a sufficient majority of votes. There appears to be a widely held public perception that at the federal level the President makes the budget and Congress approves it. The process is, of course, much more complicated than the public perception, and in fact, very few of the total appropriations of any given year are truly subject to change during that time period. Approximately one-fifth of the total appropriations could be called *discretionary* during any individual Congress, and the remaining four-fifths have already been committed by law given certain economic conditions and are considered *automatic appropriations*.

TABLE 5.2 Estimates of Selected Federal Government Outlays, Fiscal Year 1987–1988

Type of Outlay		Amount ($ billions)
National defense		282.2
International affairs		18.6
General science, space, technology		9.1
Energy		4.0
National resources and environment		11.9
Agriculture		9.5
Commerce and housing credit		1.3
Transportation		25.5
Community and regional development		6.5
Education, training, social services		27.4
Health		34.9
Social security and Medicare		282.4
Social security	212.2	
Medicare	70.2	
Income security		118.3
Veterans benefits and services		26.4
Administration of justice		6.9
General government		6.0
General purpose fiscal assistance		1.7
Net interest		147.9
Total Outlays (including items not listed)		994.0

Source: *Economic Report of the President, 1987*, Table B–74.

5.3.1 Automatic Appropriations

Built into the transfer and stabilization portions of the budget are certain appropriations that automatically expand during periods when the economy is contracting and, in theory, contract when the economy expands. A portion of the total automatic appropriations budget is made up of what are termed *automatic stabilizers*. These types of expenditures tend to dampen the overall effects of the business cycle. For example, during an economic recession, unemployment increases and unemployment benefits automatically expand.

TABLE 5.3   Major State-Local Government Outlays, Fiscal Year
1983–1984

Outlay Type	Amount ($ billions)	Percent of Total
Education	176.1	35%
Highways	39.5	8%
Public welfare	66.4	13%
All other items	222.9	44%
Total Outlays	505.0	100%

Source: *Economic Report of the President, 1986*, Table B–78.

The increased benefits reduce the decline in spending and aggregate demand
that would normally accompany a recession. During an economic expansion,
unemployment decreases and unemployment benefits fall, reducing the magnitude and speed of the expansion and in some cases serving to reduce
inflationary pressure as the economy approaches full employment.

Other parts of the automatic appropriations budget do not have effects
that are as symmetrical as do the automatic stabilizers. During inflationary
periods, social security benefits increase automatically. This serves to further
increase both spending by recipients and aggregate demand when countercyclical fiscal policy would normally call for just the opposite prescription.
At least in theory, such fiscal policy actions serve to aggravate existing economic conditions. Automatic stabilization policy is therefore developed not
only by the current state of the economy, but also by the past legislation that
established such entitlements. While the Congress and/or the President have
the power to enact legislation to change such automatic provisions, this occurs
quite infrequently and is almost always phased in over a lengthy period of
time rather than taking full effect during the year of its enactment.

5.3.2 Discretionary Appropriations

The remaining one-fifth of the budget is composed of items that are subject
to change by the current administration and Congress and generally represent
new programs, as well as planned future advances or declines in existing
programs. New federal programs to rebuild the nation's bridges and interstate
highways or perhaps the Reagan administration-sponsored tax cuts of the
mid-1980s would be examples of discretionary appropriations and fiscal
policies.

5.4 THE EFFECTS OF FISCAL ACTIONS, DEFICITS, AND SURPLUSES

In Chapters 3 and 4 we developed several general models of the economy that incorporated government spending and taxation into the analysis. In this chapter we want to take a closer look at how fiscal actions, as well as the surpluses and deficits they create, affect output, employment, and income in the economy. We can recall from Chapter 3 [Equation (3.1)] that aggregate demand was equal to the sum of consumption, planned investment, net exports, and government spending:

$$AD = C + I_p + G + X_n \tag{3.1}$$

Government spending, unlike any of the other components of aggregate demand, is a completely exogenous variable. It is determined from outside the model and does not necessarily depend on any of the other forms of spending. Government can change its level of spending to achieve social goals regardless of the prevailing levels of consumption, investment, exports, or even the tax level. If, for example, full employment were the primary social goal, government has the ability to stimulate the economy through its spending. An increase in government spending is a direct expansion of aggregate demand, which, in turn, causes producers to increase output, employment, and income. The process is subject to the expenditure multiplier, and therefore, an increase in government spending results in a much larger increase in equilibrium income. As we can see from Figure 5.3, an increase in government spending increased aggregate demand from AD_1 to AD_2, increasing equilibrium income from Y_1 to Y_2. In the right panel, this shifts the IS curve outward from IS_1 to IS_2, increasing interest rates from i_1 to i_2 and income from Y_1 to Y_2.

Changes in taxation affect equilibrium output, employment, and income indirectly and are subject to the tax multiplier. To visualize this, recall the consumption and disposable income equations of Chapter 3:

$$C = a + B(Y_d) \tag{3.4}$$

$$Y_d = Y - T \tag{3.5}$$

If fiscal policy calls for an increase in taxes (T), disposable income (Y_d) will fall by the amount of the tax. From Equation (3.4) we can see that this will reduce consumption expenditures by less than the total amount of the tax, since the marginal propensity to consume (B) has a value of less than unity. This will reduce aggregate demand and trigger off the tax multiplier, leading to a multiple decline in equilibrium income. The tax multiplier is one less

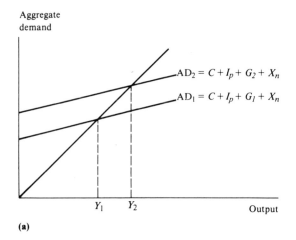
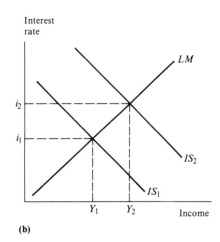

(a)   **(b)**

FIGURE 5.3   Graphical Analysis of the Impact of an Increase in Government Spending on the *IS-LM* Model.
An increase in government spending from G_1 to G_2 increases aggregate demand, increasing equilibrium income from Y_1 to Y_2. In panel (b), the *IS* curve shifts out from IS_1 to IS_2, increasing interest rates from i_1 to i_2 and income from Y_1 to Y_2.

than the expenditure multiplier, so equal increases in government expenditures and taxes still produce an expansion in equilibrium income equal to the initial increase in government spending.

The model of fiscal policy now needs to be modified to include the fact that tax collections by government are a function of the level of income and some constant, as shown in Equation (5.1):

$$T = t + r(Y) \tag{5.1}$$

Here T represents taxes collected by government, t is some constant, r is the tax rate, and Y is the level of income in the economy. Whenever T is greater than government spending (G), the government is running a surplus, and when $T - G$ is negative, the government is running a deficit. This addition to the model provides the insight that when government spending expands to reduce the effects of a recession, the likelihood of a deficit is increased. For example, in a recession, employment falls and income falls as well. Automatic appropriations increase as unemployment and other "safety net" social programs kick in. This, of course, increases government expenditures. At the same time, income in the economy is falling, and as we can see from Equation (5.1), this serves to reduce tax receipts by government. With a decline in tax receipts and an increase in outlays, deficits are the most likely outcome. In such cases, the social good attained by the reduction in human suffering through deficit spending does, in the eyes of government, outweigh the costs of incurring the deficit. Stimulating aggregate demand and producing higher levels of equilibrium income would in this case be considered a social good. Deficit spending, however, has effects that extend beyond the mere stimulation of demand and equilibrium income.

5.4.1 Deficit Financing and the Market for Government Securities

There are a number of ways in which the federal government can finance its deficit. First, the Treasury can sell U.S. Treasury securities to the public through its agent the Federal Reserve. In this case, the Treasury is a risk-free borrower of private funds because government has the power to tax and/ or to print money to pay off its debts. The loan is without risk, but it still absorbs funds from the private loanable funds market. Another means of financing the debt is for the Treasury to sell securities to government agencies and Federal Reserve banks. Such actions do not absorb private loanable funds but do in some cases have effects on market interest rates, especially if the Federal Reserve is already engaged in efforts to alter the money supply. This aspect will be covered in more detail in Chapter 7, on monetary policy. In summary, however, we can say that whenever the government must finance its debt, there can be significant increases in interest rates and reductions in the availability of loanable funds. In time periods where the government runs a surplus, it would appear logical that interest-rate effects and the absorption of private capital would be reversed. However, federal surpluses have occurred so infrequently in the recent past that it is really hard to say whether any real symmetry exists here.

5.4.2 The Crowding-Out Effect

When government sells Treasury securities to the public, each dollar raised is a dollar that could have gone into investment by private-sector borrowers. Government borrowing demands tend to push up interest rates in the loanable funds market. When this happens, private-industry borrowers are crowded out of the market as the higher rates reduce the number of investment projects that can successfully pass the positive net present value test. Government borrowing, however, is not very interest-rate-sensitive. Government spending projects are not evaluated in a net present value context, so that when interest rates rise, government simply sells more debt to cover its larger costs of borrowing. This crowding-out effect appears to have occurred at an increasing pace over the last 15 years. The record indicates that from the mid-1940s to the mid-1960s, Treasury borrowing from private sources increased by $11 billion. From the mid-1960s to the mid-1980s, this same figure increased by over $400 billion. In the earlier 20-year period, less than 1 percent of funds borrowed from the domestic loanable funds market were used to finance the government deficit. In the latter 20 years, over 15 percent of these funds were allocated to the deficit. Clearly, government debt is attracting larger portions of the domestic loanable funds market and crowding out private investment.

5.4.3 Investment Tax Credits

Another means of stimulating the economy involves the use of *investment tax credits*. To encourage private-sector investment, government allows firms to deduct a percentage of the cost of a current investment from their current federal tax liabilities. This amounts to a government subsidy of private investment and may be directed toward specific areas, industries, or technologies. Credits reduce the final cost of investments, enabling more private-sector projects to pass the positive net present value test. When greater private-sector investment takes place, the I_p term in Equation (3.1) increases, expanding aggregate demand, output, and equilibrium income. Such a means of stimulating the economy does not absorb private-sector capital, but no fiscal policy action is without its costs. Investment tax credits do reduce tax revenues collected by government and contribute to the deficit, which must be financed in some manner.

From a historical viewpoint, the investment tax credit programs of the Kennedy and Reagan administrations did produce marked increases in private-sector investment. However, the other side of this issue involves the special-interest effect. Many investment tax credit programs, once begun, are very difficult to curtail when economic conditions improve. When termination is considered, the affected industries have strong incentives to devote substantial resources to influence politicians' votes in favor of continuation and are frequently successful in doing so.

5.5 GOVERNMENT SPENDING AND POLITICAL ECONOMY

Both fiscal policy in general and the appropriations process explained earlier do indeed have noble goals. Unfortunately, the structure of our political economy contains at least three major areas of conflict between good economics and good politics that provide us with a clearer understanding of why fiscal policy does not always achieve its goals. An understanding of these conflicts also can go a long way in explaining why politicians cannot or will not deal effectively with many major economic problems, such as the large and growing government deficit. For example, in 1986, Congress passed the Gramm-Rudman-Hollings Deficit-Reduction Act to force the federal government to live within its means, and yet the deficit continued to grow. The economic solution was to either reduce spending or raise tax revenues, or both. The political solution, however, was to do neither and to continue to increase the deficit. Just why this is the case is a classic example of the *economics of politics* built on the rational ignorance of voters, special-interest effects, and the shortsightedness effect.

5.5.1 The Rational Ignorance of Voters

First, consider the problem of the rationally ignorant voter and its effect on a politician's choices. Less than half the American electorate can correctly identify their congressperson, much less know where he or she stands on various government spending issues. This is not a conviction of the intellect of voters, but simply an illustration that they, like everyone else, make rational choices in allocating their time and effort. Each voter realizes that his or her individual vote is unlikely to greatly influence the outcome of a given election. Therefore, voters have very little incentive to devote costly time and effort to finding out and using detailed political information about how a candidate votes to spend public money. Most voters rely primarily on information provided to them by the media and the candidates themselves. Earners, however, are seldom ignorant of tax increases. Everyone gets a very direct notice in their paycheck or bank account whenever taxes are increased. The importance of the rational ignorance of voters and the awareness of earners is that it gives politicians stronger incentives to oppose tax increases than to control government spending. Increased spending without increased taxes obviously increases the deficit.

5.5.2 The Special-Interest Effect

Consider the incentive structure of the political economy regarding special-interest groups. *Special-interest legislation* is any bill that produces concentrated personal benefits for a small portion of the population, such as the special-interest group itself, by passing on a small disbursed personal cost to each individual in the entire population. A hypothetical example might be a bill to provide a federal subsidy of 5 cents per quart to milk producers. A few people (the milk producers) gain a large amount individually (5 cents per quart times the millions of quarts they produce annually), while almost everyone else loses a small amount individually. The cost of the federal subsidy is spread over the entire taxpaying public. Such special-interest legislation strongly affects the incentives faced by the special-interest group and the successful politician. Members of the special-interest group stand to gain a great deal by having such legislation passed. Therefore, it is rational for them to devote large amounts of time, money, and personal effort to influence the vote of the politician on that issue. The milk lobby will legally and justifiably support the campaigns of candidates favorable to their position and oppose those who do not. The individual voter, however, has a very weak incentive to oppose such legislation because it passes on a very small and unclear individual cost to him or her. Such a voter will not spend much time, effort, and money writing to his or her congressperson or organizing a campaign against the bill or even trying to find out how his or her congressperson voted on the issue because the individual costs of such efforts outweigh the potential benefits. Remember, in most cases the voter is rationally ignorant. The politician, on the other hand, has a strong incentive to listen carefully to the views of special-interest groups. Members of the special-interest group hold in their hands the concentrated benefits the politician seeks. They can provide campaign support not only in money, but also in political endorsements, personnel, and numerous other benefits, such as the actual votes of their members. By supporting special-interest legislation, the candidate stands to gain a great deal and the general voting population will not offer much opposition because they are both rationally ignorant and have little incentive to resist even if they oppose the vote on the issue. Politicians therefore have strong incentives to support special-interest legislation that places upward pressure on federal spending.

5.5.3 The Shortsightedness Effect

Four-year or shorter terms of office also exercise effects on the political economy of the appropriations process. They create strong incentives for politicians to support legislation that produces clear, identifiable short-term (before the next election) benefits with unclear future costs. Since increased government spending can frequently produce short-term visible benefits, such as increased employment, larger social security checks, or more public housing, such bills are quite popular with officeholders. For example, in every past administration, the incumbent has begun a significant expansion in government spending 6 to 8 months prior to the next presidential election. This is an effort to reduce unemployment and get the economy primed up for election day. Of course, this increase in government spending must be paid for someday, either in higher taxes or increases in the deficit, but that day is after the election. To really understand this shortsightedness effect, one need only consider which situation any rational politician would prefer, being a reelected officeholder explaining why the deficit has increased or a defeated candidate trying to tell the population his program was better. Successful politicians must pursue shortsighted goals if they wish to gain or remain in office.

Finally, the conflicts between economics and politics are constraints of the system itself and do not necessarily reflect negatively on human character. Those who seek public office may indeed be quite selfless and public minded. Regardless of their selfless nature, however, politicians who wish to get elected or reelected to office are constrained by the economics of politics. There is no greater a percentage of saints or sinners in the public sector than there are in the private sector. Human beings make the decisions in both sectors, and they are influenced by the individual benefits and costs of those decisions. Until the incentive structure of the political economy is changed, voters will continue to be rationally ignorant, special interests will dominate, and politicians will be shortsighted. As long as we have the current incentive structure, good politics will frequently make for bad economics and many economic problems, such as the deficit, are likely to continue.

5.6 THE PROS AND CONS OF GOVERNMENT DEBT

Over the last decade, increasing government deficits have focused much debate on the public debt. Opponents have contended that current deficits mortgage the future of our economy and place exceptional financial burdens on future generations. Proponents have countered that the debt is one that, as a nation, we only owe to ourselves. In addition, they point out that future generations will inherit the assets that were purchased with the debt, such as interest-bearing U.S. Treasury securities and the infrastructure that government spending has provided. Both these positions are of such a sweeping summary nature that neither could be considered fully correct. We will consider the components of each argument here and attempt to separate economic reality from political rhetoric.

5.6.1 The Growth Issue

The first task here is to place the growth issue in perspective. The absolute magnitude of public debt has experienced significant growth in the last 10 years and, by all appearances, will continue to grow both in absolute and percentage terms for the next decade unless spending is curtailed or the economy grows much faster than it has in the past. It is important to note, however, that the size of the public debt as a percentage of GNP has increased only slightly since the late 1970s. During the postwar period of the late 1940s, debt actually exceeded GNP, while in the early 1980s, the ratio of debt to GNP was slightly over one-third. Another key perspective regarding the growth of public debt is its comparison to the growth in private debt. Since the 1950s, public debt has expanded over 200 percent. During the same time period, private debt holdings have grown over 1000 percent.

Projections of increasing future public debt, as well as growth in the interest-rate burden produced by the current debt, appear to be the major current concern. The interest-rate burden has increased in very real terms over the last 30 years. In the mid-1950s, interest payments on the debt represented only about 1.5 percent of GNP, while that number has grown to almost 3 percent today. The historically high real interest rates of the 1980s have contributed significantly to this problem and could, in fact, continue to be a major source of future concern.

5.6.2 The Inheritance Issue

Future generations will inherit both the debt and its assets. However, there is not necessarily a symmetry between the two. Not all government borrowing is used to build the economy's infrastructure or to invest in future productive capital goods. Government transfer payments and social programs, in general, consume current spending without producing significant future productive assets. To the extent that current government spending falls into the transfer and social programs categories, future generations inherit liabilities without commensurate supporting assets. The record indicates that in recent years transfers and social programs have received increasing portions of total government spending, while government expenditures in support of capital formation have posted marked declines. Also, when expansionary fiscal policy is used by government to stimulate the economy toward full employment, more capital goods are produced and a positive contribution to the welfare of future generations occurs.

5.6.3 The Crowding-Out Issue

As mentioned earlier, large expansions in government debt have a tendency to crowd out private-sector investment. The record indicates that from the mid-1940s to the mid-1980s, Treasury borrowing from private sources increased from $11 billion in the first 20 years to over $400 billion in the last 15 years. Clearly, government debt is attracting larger and larger portions of the domestic loanable funds market. This has a distinct tendency to curtail private investment and reduce the future growth rate of the private sector.

5.7 THE IMPACT OF FISCAL POLICY ON MANAGERIAL DECISION MAKING

Fiscal policy has far-reaching and sometimes quite subtle effects on business at almost every level. While it has a direct impact on managerial decision making in at least eight areas, the existence of the expenditure multiplier and abstract secondary effects imply that very few businesses function without feeling the effects of government actions. The discussion that follows therefore should by no means be considered a comprehensive list of how fiscal policy affects business but merely a sampling of the most obvious area to be considered in formulating managerial decisions.

5.7.1 Taxes and Subsidies

Since its inception, our government has taxed the production and sale of certain goods primarily to generate tax revenues, but also in an increasing number of cases to discourage the production of those goods. Current proposals to increase excise taxes on the sale of alcohol and tobacco would clearly fit into this category. At the same time, subsidies are paid to encourage the production of other goods that government has deemed of benefit to the economy. Both tax and subsidy decisions are subject to very large special-interest effects. Understanding the economics of politics, it is not surprising to find the paradox that government currently subsidizes the growing of tobacco and yet places increasing levels of excise taxes on its sale. In effect, the existing tax system simultaneously encourages and then discourages the same product.

Taxes and subsidies also have a foreign-sector counterpart in the form of tariffs and quotas. While both tariffs and quotas will be discussed in much greater detail in Chapter 10, it is important to point out here that they have the same basic effect as taxes and subsidies on individual products. They increase the cost of producing and selling certain imported goods while, on a relative basis, reducing the relative costs incurred by domestic producers of those same goods. Managers working in industries subject to taxes and subsidies and/or tariffs and quotas would benefit substantially from both an understanding of the fiscal policy impacts on their industry and the economics of politics.

5.7.2 Reporting and Compliance Costs

All industries must bear the normal cost burden of record keeping and reporting required data to the Internal Revenue Service. Changes in the complexity and reporting requirements of the tax code do in fact affect business costs, as can be readily seen from the Tax Revision Act of 1986. Reporting and compliance costs are much more pronounced in industries that are subject to significant government regulation. In fact, the costs of regulation alone are staggering. For example, on January 5, 1981, Ronald Reagan reported to the nation that in 1980 government regulation had added over $100 billion to the costs of goods and services purchased by consumers. Since the early 1980s, government regulation has declined slightly; however, it is important to note that regulation appears to exhibit cyclical effects, rising and falling over time with changes in administrations and public attitudes. This implies that the cost structure incurred by business also will be subject to accompanying cyclical changes as regulation and the complexity of the tax code change.

5.7.3 Locational Effects

Business frequently "votes with its feet." By this we mean that rate differences in state and local corporate income taxes and property taxes have noticeable effects on corporate location decisions. In addition, government expenditure at all levels to provide infrastructure facilities such as highways, rail and port facilities, and high levels of security through police and fire protection all serve to attract corporate locations. Higher rates and lower government expenditures serve to lessen the attractiveness of specific locations to business. These effects are of such magnitude that many state and local governments often find themselves in competition with one another to offer the tax structure and expenditure patterns needed to attract the most desirable industries.

5.7.4 Educational and Training Expenditures

Educational expenditures also serve as not only locational incentives but also overall subsidies to business. For example, a state educational system might provide not only vocationally trained workers but also a more educated public and a pool of highly educated professionals, such as engineers, physicists, research chemists, and so forth, who will clearly serve to reduce the labor-development costs incurred by the business community. The specific lack of these kinds of fiscal policy expenditures will serve to increase the costs of business production.

5.7.5 Composition Effects

Government expenditures for goods and services also will greatly affect the specific composition of business output and the projects in which businesses choose to invest. As government spending changes its emphasis from, for example, the Reagan administration military buildup to new federal construction projects in the space program, interindustry demand is subject to large fluctuations. Aerospace, electronics, shipbuilding, and armaments might well find large declines in demand, while producers of structural steel, roads, and concrete would experience increased demand for their output. Both types of industries also would focus their attention on planned future fiscal policy actions in determining which investment projects they would be willing to undertake and which they would pass up.

5.7.6 Interest-Rate Effects

Whenever fiscal policy requires government borrowing of such magnitude and timing that it affects market interest rates, business decision making is affected. Higher rates reduce the number of business investment projects that can pass the positive net present value test and lower the level of investment that business will undertake. Investment tax credits also serve to alter the hurdle rate of interest required by business to produce positive net present values. Whenever the government is an active player in the financial markets, successful managers will be assessing the direction and magnitude of government borrowing and the current climate of tax incentives.

5.7.7 Stabilization-Spending Effects

A corollary to interest-rate effects occurs in business investment when government engages in stabilization spending. Countercyclical fiscal policy is an attempt to reduce the magnitude of economic cycles. Some economists contend that to the extent that they might improve the stability of the economy, these expenditures serve to increase the level of business investment, since greater stability reduces risk and increases the willingness of businesses to invest. The contention is that effective stabilization spending improves the overall investment climate. It is also important to note, however, that a great deal of debate revolves around whether government actions contribute to or detract from overall economic stability.

5.7.8 Government-Supported Research and Development

The late 1980s have been marked by many technological breakthroughs in such fields as gene splitting, medical, chemical, and information technologies that show tremendous profit potential for the coming decade. Many of these breakthroughs, however, were specific applications of more basic research done in universities supported by government research grants. The expenditures by government to develop the basic technologies upon which these breakthroughs were based constitute government subsidization of the research and development costs of business. The more basic forms of research are not attractive to business investment because such research is very much like a public good. There is little ability to capture its monetary value because basic research cannot be patented. When breakthroughs do occur, the developer's own competitors may be able to apply the basic research in a specific way that produces profits, and yet they do not have to share in the original costs of research and development. Many large government efforts such as the space program have produced technologies that have spilled over into the private sector free of charge. Increases in such government research and development programs tend to increase business investment in future time periods.

5.8 SUMMARY

1. Fiscal policy is concerned with the spending and taxing powers of government and has a major impact on aggregate demand, interest rates, equilibrium income, and the composition of output produced in the economy. One justification offered for government spending is the public goods rationale.

2. Government expenditures can be grouped into the three main categories of goods and services, transfers, and stabilization. Taxes, borrowing, and grants from other levels of government provide the majority of total government funds. Personal income tax is the largest federal source. Most of the goods and services that the federal government purchases go toward national defense and transfer payments. Payments of interest on the national debt are also a major budget item for the federal government. State-local revenues come primarily from taxes on property, sales, and incomes and federal grants. State-local governments, on the other hand, actually receive interest payments instead of paying them.

3. Approximately one-fifth of the total appropriations could be called discretionary during any individual Congress, and the remaining four-fifths have already been committed by law given certain economic conditions and are considered automatic appropriations.

4. Automatic stabilizers expand during periods when the economy is contracting and, in theory, contract when the economy expands. Other parts of the automatic appropriations budget do not have effects as symmetrical as do automatic stabilizers. Automatic stabilization policy is therefore developed not only by the current state of the economy, but also by the past legislation that established such entitlements. The remaining one-fifth of the budget is composed of items that are subject to change by the current Congress and generally represent new programs as well as planned future advances or declines in existing programs.

5. Government spending, unlike any other component of aggregate demand, is an exogenous variable. It is determined from outside the model and does not necessarily depend on any of the other forms of spending. An increase in government spending is a direct expansion of aggregate demand, which, in turn, causes producers to increase output, employment, and income. The process is subject to the expenditure multiplier. Changes in taxation indirectly affect equilibrium output, employment, and income and are subject to the tax multiplier.

6. Whenever the government must finance its debt, there can be significant effects on interest rates and the availability of loanable funds. When government sells Treasury securities to the public, each dollar that is raised is a dollar that could have gone into investment by private-sector borrowers. Government borrowing tends to push up interest rates in the loanable funds market. Private-industry borrowers are crowded out of the market as the higher rates reduce the number of investment projects that can successfully pass the positive net present value test. Another means of stimulating the economy involves the use of investment tax credits.

7. The structure of our political economy contains at least three major areas of conflict between good economics and good politics. First, voters are rationally ignorant. Less than half the American electorate can correctly identify their congressperson, much less know where he or she stands on various government spending issues. Earners, however, are seldom ignorant of tax increases. The rational ignorance of voters and the awareness of earners gives politicians stronger incentives to oppose tax increases than to control government spending.

8. Special-interest legislation produces concentrated personal benefits for a small portion of the population by passing on a small, disbursed personal cost to each individual in the entire population. Special-interest groups hold in their hands the concentrated benefits politicians seek. By supporting special-interest legislation, politicians stand to gain a great deal and the general voting population will not offer much opposition because they are both rationally ignorant and have little incentive to resist.

9. Four-year or shorter terms of office create strong incentives for politicians to support legislation that produces clear, identifiable short-term (before the next election) benefits with unclear future costs.

10. The absolute magnitude of public debt has experienced significant growth in the last 10 years and by all appearances will continue to grow both in absolute and percentage terms for the next decade. The size of the public debt as a percentage of GNP has increased only slightly since the late 1970s. Since the 1950s, public debt has expanded over 200 percent, while private debt holdings have grown over 1000 percent. The interest-rate burden has increased in very real terms over the last 30 years. In the mid-1950s, interest payments on the debt represented only about 1.5 percent of GNP, while that number has grown to almost 3 percent today.

11. Future generations will inherit both the debt and its assets. However, there is not necessarily a symmetry between the two. Transfer payments consume current spending without producing significant future productive assets.

12. The managerial implications of fiscal policy include the effects of taxes and subsidies, reporting and compliance costs, locational effects, educational and training expenditures, composition effects, interest-rate effects, stabilization-spending effects, and the benefits of government-supported research and development.

5.9 EXERCISES

1. The current federal deficit is expected to increase substantially over the next 5 to 7 years. Assume you are a financial manager in a firm that is very capital-intensive. You are considering the possibility of a large capital expansion in the next 3 years. What are your major concerns regarding the national debt?

2. You are currently the chief financial officer of a firm that produces highly advanced semiconductors. Several major business issues are looming on the horizon. Your firm is considering relocation to a facility either in "Silicon Valley" in California or the high-tech corridor in the Baltimore – Washington, D.C. area. Federal tariffs on Japanese semiconductors are being debated on the floor of Congress. Your firm also will expand its technical research work force significantly after the relocation. Explain the major issues in government spending covered in this chapter that affect each of the business issues before you.

3. President Eisenhower once said that the federal debt was like a burden on the future of our grandchildren. Offer arguments that both support and oppose this position.

4. Discuss the major differences between the federal and state and local governments with regard to both their sources and uses of revenues.

5. Explain at least three reasons why there are conflicts between the economic solutions to economic problems and the acceptable political solutions to those problems.

6. When government borrowing crowds out private-sector borrowing, the net effect on the economy is positive because government invests its funds in activities that build productive capital for the future. Comment.

7. Why are investment tax credits really a government subsidy to private investments, and why does the federal government undertake such actions?

8. Compare and contrast automatic and discretionary appropriations.

9. Government transfer payments contribute to the future capital stock of the economy. Comment.

5.10 REFERENCES

Blinder, A. *Fiscal Policy in Theory and Practice*. New York: General Learning Press, 1973.

Blinder, A., and Solow, R. "Analytical Foundations of Fiscal Policy." Reprinted in *The Economics of Public Finance*. Washington, D.C.: The Brookings Institution, 1974.

Buchanan, J. N., and Tullock, G. *The Calculus of Consent*. Ann Arbor, Mich.: University of Michigan Press, 1962.

Carlson, K., and Spencer, R. "Crowding Out and Its Critics," *Federal Reserve Bank of St. Louis Review*, December 1975.

Tullock, G. *Toward a Mathematics of Politics*. Ann Arbor, Mich.: University of Michigan Press, 1967.

6
Money in the Macro Economy

6.1 INTRODUCTION

Part I of the text introduced the basic models managers might use to analyze and understand the macro economy. Part II explains the effects government policy has on the basic models and the determination of output, employment, and income. Chapter 5 began the policy section with an explanation of fiscal policy. This chapter will introduce a basic understanding of money as a foundation upon which to build the analysis of monetary policy in Chapter 7.

This chapter begins with an explanation of what money is and how it exerts influence in the macro economy. The primary goal of this chapter is to develop an explanation of how the money market works. First, the concept of money demand and its components will be examined. Then the supply of money will be examined, as well as banking mechanisms that both facilitate its flow and control its supply. The concepts of money demand and money supply will then be overlapped to explain equilibrium in the money market. A discussion of the alternate views of the money mechanism held by Keynesians and monetarists will follow. Finally, the chapter concludes with an overview of the managerial implications of monetary policy and how financial managers might use such information to improve their decision making.

6.2 WHAT IS MONEY?

Throughout history, many things have served as money, including sea shells, cattle, stones, woodpecker scalps, and even wives. Today, money also takes many forms, such as currency, checkable deposits, and other monetary instruments. The obvious question would seem to be what do all these money forms have in common and what makes them money? The answer is relatively simple: *Money* is anything that can act as a medium of exchange, a measure of value, and a store of value. As a medium of exchange, money need only be acceptable to both trading parties in lieu of goods or services. As a medium of exchange, money speeds up the transactions process and reduces the costs of exchange. As a measure and store of value, money must provide a relatively uniform measuring stick by which to compare the values of differing goods and also be able to preserve the current value of goods into some future time period. For example, a fisherman must be able to convert the day's catch into money to spend in the future, since he cannot simply keep his fish and hope to trade them for other goods weeks or months later. The fish would spoil and be worthless over time, while hopefully a money would hold its value better over time. As a measure of value, money would rank the value of fish relative to all other goods, such as one fish is worth $2 while one pair of shoes might be worth $20. Obviously, in terms of money, one pair of shoes has an equivalent money value of 10 fish.

The time value of money also plays a role in monetary policy. A dollar today is preferred to a dollar one year from now. If we are to lend the purchasing power of our money to others, we expect an interest payment to compensate us both for the potential decline in our money's purchasing power over time and the service we provide to the borrower. Today people can hold money in several forms simultaneously. Just how much of their money people choose to hold in each form is determined not only by their preferences, but also by how effectively each money form fulfills the functions of money and the interest they might receive from holding their money in that form.

The money supply as we know it today has many different definitions. These definitions are all an attempt to isolate the different components of the money supply by the function of money that it fulfills. For example, currency, traveler's checks, demand deposits (checking accounts), and all other checkable deposits are used primarily by people to transact exchanges. This is obviously money used as a medium of exchange and currently is referred to as *M1*. Another current measure of the money supply is *M2*, which includes *M1* and both time deposits (savings accounts) and money-market account balances. Time deposits and money-market balances are money that people usually hold as a store of value. Many other measures of the money supply include such items as large-denomination certificates of deposit. These are usually held by wealthy investors, businesses, and institutions as stores of value.

The primary reason why the money supply is divided by function is in the hope that more effective predictions can be made about changes in the components of the money supply with regard to their effect on the economy.

For example, if *MI* (transactions money) was increasing quickly, it would not be unreasonable to suspect that people were preparing to engage in a higher level of transactions than in the recent past. Alternatively, if the store of value component of *M2* was increasing, we might conclude that people were attempting to save more and therefore spend less. Both scenarios have significant implications for changes in the level of future output, employment, and income in the economy. Monetary policy, which will be discussed in detail in Chapter 7, can alter the money supply and affect the future level of spending.

6.3 AN OVERVIEW OF HOW MONEY AFFECTS THE ECONOMY

The effects of changes in the market for goods and services on the equilibrium level of output, income, and employment have been the focus of most of the preceding chapters. Transactions in the goods market are, however, facilitated by money. Money oils the wheels of exchange and reduces the transactions costs of engaging in exchange. Therefore, the volume of money in the economy can affect the number of transactions going on in the goods market.

Economists have voiced widely differing views about the mechanism by which the volume of money transmits effects to the goods market. This section will present the classical view of money and the equation of exchange as an overview of the effects of money and monetary policy. In a later section of the chapter a presentation of the Keynesian and monetarist views of the monetary transmission mechanism will be presented.

The equation of exchange evolved from the idea that at equilibrium, total spending in the economy is equal to total production (see Chapter 2 for a review of this concept):

$$\$ \text{ Value of total spending } = \$ \text{ value of total production} \qquad (6.1)$$

Both total spending and total production can be further subdivided into their components. The total level of spending in the economy is done with the existing money supply. Therefore, total spending is equal to the money supply (M) multiplied by velocity (V), which is the number of times it turns over (changes hands) during the accounting period. The total dollar value of production is equal to the average price of each output (P) times the average quantity (Q) of each output produced. In equation form, this means that

$$\$ \text{ Value of total spending } = \$ \text{ value of total production}$$

Thus we have the *equation of exchange*:

$$\text{Money supply } (M) \times \text{velocity } (V) = \text{price } (P) \times \text{quantity } (Q)$$
$$MV = PQ \tag{6.2}$$

From the equation of exchange it is easy to see that increases in the money supply would increase the value of the term on the left-hand side of the equation. If the value of total spending were to remain equal to the value of total production, either some change in velocity would have to occur or one or both terms on the right-hand side of the equation would have to increase to offset the increase in money supply. The classical economists contended that velocity and output did not change much in the short run, so that an increase in the money supply would produce more dollars chasing the current level of goods being produced. This would serve to push prices up and decrease the purchasing power of the larger money stock. The right-hand side of the equation would then fall back into equality with the left side. Decreases in the money supply were thought to produce the opposite effect. There would be fewer dollars chasing the current level of goods. Prices would fall, increasing the purchasing power of consumers and bringing the right-hand side of the equation back into line with the left. In this fashion, classical economists believed that price changes were the result of monetary changes.

6.4 THE DEMAND FOR MONEY

Both firms and individuals desire to hold money balances for a variety of reasons, the most prominent of which are to transact exchange, take advantage of potential profitable situations that present themselves, and to make allowances for unexpected expenses. We can therefore divide the total demand for money into transactions, speculative, and precautionary balances. We will discuss each of these individually.

6.4.1 Transactions Demand

Transactions demand is just what the name implies. It is money held to transact exchange. There is almost always a lack of synchronization between the instant when income is received and the time period when expenditures must be made. Those money balances held to act as a buffer between receipts and expenditures by both firms and individuals are considered transactions demand. The optimum level of such balances is a positive function of income and a negative function of the interest rate. Theoretically, the optimization of transactions balances is highly similar to the standard cash-management equations of the firm.

The cash-management problem is best explained using an example in which an individual can choose between cash and interest-bearing bonds as forms in which to hold money. The time horizon is a pay period of 30 days. The individual is assumed to receive a single paycheck of $3000 and spend an average of $100 per day. In the first scenario, the individual might cash the check, holding all $3000 as cash. Spending $100 per day, the entire fund is exhausted at the end of 30 days.

Alternatively, a portion of the original $3000 income could have been used to buy short-term bonds that would be cashed in some time during the 30-day period and would have produced interest income over the ownership life of the bond. For example, the individual could have held $1500 in cash and bought $1500 in bonds. Spending $100 per day, the individual cashes in the bonds on the fifteenth day as cash runs out. At the end of the 30-day period, the original $3000 has been exhausted, but the interest earned on the bonds for 15 days remains. The average amount of cash held by the individual is equal to the $3000 in income divided by 2 times the number of transactions. Since there were two transactions (cashing the check and buying the bonds), the average cash balance was $3000/2(2) = $750. In equation form, the average cash balance is

$$C_b = \frac{Y}{2T} \tag{6.3}$$

where Y is the economists symbol for income, and T is the number of transactions involved. By holding cash, the individual forgoes the interest income the bonds would have generated. The opportunity cost (O) of holding cash is illustrated by the following equation:

$$O = i(C_b) \tag{6.4}$$

where i is the interest rate on the bonds, and C_b is the $750 average cash balance from Equation (6.3). If the market rate of interest is 10 percent, then the opportunity cost of holding the $750 cash balance is $75 × (15/360). The individual also incurs another cost, that of the transactions into bonds. If each transaction has a cost of X, then total transactions (C_t) costs are XT:

$$C_t = XT \tag{6.5}$$

The goal of the individual is to minimize the total costs incurred by holding cash. The equation for this is as follows:

$$\text{Minimize cost of } T \text{ transactions} = XT + \frac{iY}{2T} \tag{6.6}$$

The optimal number of transactions for the individual to conduct is found by taking the first derivative of Equation (6.6) and setting it equal to zero and solving for T. This works out to

$$T = \sqrt{\frac{iY}{2X}} \tag{6.7}$$

Once the optimal number of transactions is determined, it can be substituted back into the average cash balance equation to find how much cash should be held. In equation form, this is equal to

$$\text{Optimal } C_b = \sqrt{\frac{XY}{2i}} \tag{6.8}$$

The most important conclusions to draw from the cash-management analogy are the relationships between cash balances, interest rates, income, and transactions costs. Other things being equal, transactions cash balances are negatively related to the interest rate on bonds and transactions costs and positively related to income. To verify this conclusion, all the reader need do is visualize what happens to C_b as i, XT, or Y doubles in Equations (6.3) to (6.8).

Several important events have altered the total level of transactions balances that consumers have chosen to hold over the last two decades. First and perhaps foremost, the advent of mass ownership of credit cards has made it possible for a significant majority of the population to delay payments for goods and services at least to the end of a billing cycle when income is expected. It is obvious that cash or highly liquid balances are not necessary when payments can be delayed until income is received. Second, since the late 1970s, interest rates have remained at much higher levels than in prior periods. This increase in the cost of holding cash balances has served to reduce the quantities held. Finally, with the new generation of financial instruments and services available from institutions, such as interest-bearing checking accounts, cash-management accounts from brokerage houses, and negotiated order of withdrawal accounts (NOWs), the alternatives to cash transactions balances are both frequent and in most cases more attractive. Given these alternatives, it is not surprising that consumers have chosen to significantly reduce their cash transactions balances.

6.4.2 Speculative Demand

Speculative balances are held in the hope of taking advantage of potential profitable opportunities that may present themselves. In the individual's or firm's portfolio, funds are allocated between several assets, which could include stocks, bonds, real estate, and cash or non-interest-bearing assets. The specific allocation of funds among these assets will depend on several factors, including the market interest rate and the relative degrees of risk and potential return involved in the specific forms in which the funds are held. At higher rates of return and lower levels of risk, each asset becomes more attractive. At lower interest rates and higher levels of risk, each asset becomes less attractive relative to its cash alternative. Figure 6.1 illustrates the relationship between the desire for cash (speculative liquidity) and the interest rate on alternative wealth forms. When interest rates on alternative wealth forms are low, the opportunity cost of increasing speculative liquidity (holding more cash) falls and greater portions of an individual's wealth portfolio are allocated to cash. When rates are high, the opportunity cost of holding cash rises and larger portions of the portfolio tend to be allocated away from cash and into interest-bearing assets.

It is important to note, however, that while market interest rates have a general inverse relationship to speculative cash balances, they are not the only determinant of that liquidity. The degree of speculative optimism and/ or pessimism also plays a major role. There are time periods when interest rates can be very high, implying a large opportunity cost of holding cash and low levels of expected liquidity when actual speculative cash balances are very high. For example, in the final months of 1980, the prime interest rate

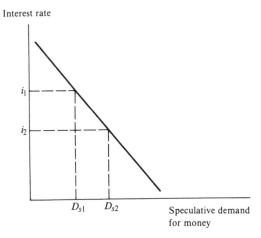

FIGURE 6.1   The Speculative Demand for Money.
The speculative demand for money is an inverse function of the interest rate, and it also depends on the degree of optimism and pessimism that exists in the economy.

stood at around 20 percent; however, economic pessimism was abundant and speculative balances were very high. Alternatively, there have been periods when interest rates were very low and yet optimism was very high, and speculative balances fell. Indeed, the advent of money-market checkable accounts produced remarkable growth rates in speculative-type balances several times in the late 1970s to late 1980s during periods of both high optimism and high interest rates. Such data at least suggest that the interplay of market interest rates and the degree of speculative optimism and pessimism exercises large effects on the level of speculative balances people choose to hold.

6.4.3 Precautionary Demand

Precautionary demand represents the desire to hold money balances as a precaution against unforeseen expenditures, such as emergency automobile repairs or sickness and accidents. A portion of our precautionary demand has been significantly reduced through the advent of precautionary pooling, as in the insurance industry. Increasing liquidity in interest-bearing assets such as money-market funds and interest-bearing checking accounts also has reduced the need for this cash-like holding. However, the human trait of setting aside precautionary cash still exists and constitutes a portion of overall money demand. Many mature adult earners have at least some portion of their wealth portfolio in the form of precautionary cash balances. The level of these balances individuals and firms choose to hold is inversely related to the market rate of interest and also is influenced by the individual and firm preferences with regard to risk. While risk aversion is the expected form of behavior, just how strong this aversion is will certainly vary from person to person and firm to firm, and intertemporally as well. Graphically, the precautionary demand to hold money would have the same general appearance as the speculative demand illustrated in Figure 6.1

6.5 THE SUPPLY OF MONEY

To fully understand the concept of money, it is necessary to differentiate between the concept of stocks and flows. A *flow* is a measure of rate, such as the rate at which water can flow through a pipe or the rate at which a car can travel a given distance over a road. A *stock* is a total accumulated amount. For example, the capital stock of the United States is the total amount of capital the United States has accumulated over our history. The stock of money would, for example, be the total dollar amounts of any of the various measures previously discussed, such as *M1* or *M2*. The supply of money is a flow concept. The *supply of money* is defined as the relationship between

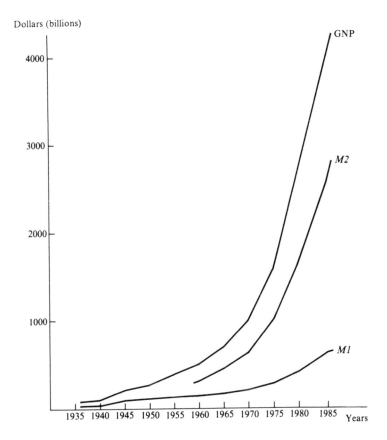

FIGURE 6.2   The Money Stock and GNP over Time.
The money stock is the means by which transactions are carried out.
As one would expect, the money stock and GNP have both risen at
similar rates over time. Note that prior to 1958, separate statistics
were not collected for the M2 money supply measure.
Source: Economic Report of the President, 1987.

the various levels of interest rates and the stock of money available at each
rate. Figure 6.2 illustrates the stock of money and GNP for the last 20 years.

6.5.1 Fractional-Reserve Banking

The supply of money is both facilitated and controlled by the financial system.
The type of banking and monetary control system in use in the United States
is a fractional-reserve system. Under such a system, only a fraction of all
deposits are kept in the bank or in other allowable forms as required reserves.

The required reserve ratio is determined by the Federal Reserve Board of Governors, and all commercial banks subject to Federal Reserve direction must hold that level of reserves against the possible withdrawal needs of depositors. The remainder of all deposits takes the form of excess reserves and can legally be loaned out to borrowers, hopefully at profit. When banks take in deposits, they hold a portion as required reserves and then loan out the remainder. By this process, they convert a liability (the deposit) into an asset (the loan).

The banking system is composed of the network of commercial banks that facilitate the flow of money to support exchange and the Federal Reserve System, which acts as the bankers' bank and exercises control over the banking system. The Fed, as the Federal Reserve System is called, has several tools to control the money supply, including changes in the required reserve ratio, changes in the discount rate, and open-market operations. Each of these tools of monetary policy affects the process by which commercial banks can convert the liability of their deposits into the assets of their loans. The Federal Reserve System and monetary policy will be discussed in greater detail in Chapter 7.

6.5.2 The Money Multiplier

The ability to convert liabilities into assets also creates an interesting money-multiplier process similar to the expenditure multiplier discussed in Chapter 3. Suppose, for example, that a new deposit of $1000 from outside the banking system is made at any commercial bank. For simplicity, we also will assume that before this deposit, the money supply was zero dollars. If the required reserve ratio is 20 percent, then the bank must hold $200 in required reserves and has $800 as excess reserves available to be loaned out. So far the money supply is $1000 in deposits. The bank now makes a loan of the $800. The borrower then spends the $800 loan, and the recipient deposits the $800 back into the banking system. It makes no difference which bank the loan is redeposited into, since all banks are part of the same banking system and all are part of the same money supply. The total money supply now is $1800 in total deposits. When the $800 is redeposited, $160 (20 percent of $800) is held as required reserves, and $640 is available for loan as excess reserves. When the $640 is loaned, spent, and redeposited, it creates $128 (20 percent of $640) in required reserves and $512 in excess reserves. The total money supply is now $2440. Two key points in this process are (1) that each time a loan is redeposited into the banking system, the money supply increases, and (2) because of the required reserve ratio, each loan that is made is 20 percent less than the loan that preceded it. This loan-making, redeposit, and loan-making cycle continues until there are no further funds left to be deposited. Table 6.1 illustrates the increase in money supply and decline in loanable funds arising from each round of the redeposit and loan-making process.

As we can see from Table 6.1 an initial deposit of $1000 with a required reserve ratio of 20 percent produces a total expansion in the money supply of $5000. In this case, the value of the money multiplier would be 5. The formula for the money multiplier is $K_m = 1/r$, where the total expansion due to an initial deposit is equal to the initial deposit (K_m) multiplied by the reciprocal of the reserve requirement (r). The reserve requirement is the key element in the process, since it indicates what portion of each deposit must be withdrawn from the redeposit chain and held as required reserves. The required reserve ratio not only affects the money multiplier, but also the profitability of banks, since it represents the percentage of each deposit that the banks cannot reloan at a profit.

The money-multiplier process itself is dependent on several assumptions if it is to attain the full potential expansion or contraction indicated by the formula. First, there can be no leakages of funds from the system. All loans must be redeposited to the system. This is not always the case, since people sometimes use the proceeds of a loan to save or hold as transactions, speculative, or precautionary cash balances. Second, banks must be willing to loan out all their excess reserves. This also is not always the case. During inflationary periods, bankers believe that future interest rates will rise and frequently hold their excess reserves in the expectation of lending at higher rates in the future. Also, there are periods when the potential borrowers available to a bank represent risks higher than the bank is willing to bear at the going market interest rates. During such periods, banks simply choose to hold excess reserves.

The multiplier process is symmetrical in magnitude but asymmetrical in its temporal effects. If, for example, the money multiplier is 5, a new

TABLE 6.1   The Money-Multiplier Process

Round of Deposit	Amount Deposited	Loanable Funds	Required Reserves
1	$1000	$ 800	$ 200
2.	$ 800	$ 640	$ 160
3	$ 640	$ 512	$ 128
4	$ 512	$ 409.60	$ 102.40
All other rounds	$2048	$1638.40	$ 409.60
Total	$5000	$4000	$1000

deposit of $1000 from beyond the commercial banking system can expand the money supply by $5000. A withdrawal that is not redeposited into the banking system can contract the money supply by $5000. The money multiplier therefore has the same magnitude for both expansions and contractions of the money supply.

The time period required for the multiplier process to take effect is not so symmetrical. The multiplier process takes considerable time to work its way through the economy. The time period from an initial new deposit to the point when the loan-making and redeposit process expands the money supply to its maximum potential has been estimated to be up to 2 years. On the contraction side, however, the process has been estimated to occur in a much shorter period of time, sometimes as short as 6 months. The primary explanation for this asymmetry is that it simply takes less time for banks to call in existing loans or shut off the flow of new loans than it does for loan applications to be approved and processed and money to be lent, spent, and redeposited.

6.6 EQUILIBRIUM IN THE MONEY MARKET

This chapter has developed explanations first of the demand for money and then of the supply of money and how it is controlled. In this section we overlap the two concepts to analyze equilibrium in the money market. Equilibrium occurs when the demand for money is equal to the supply of money. In Figure 6.3 this occurs at income level Y_1. The demand for money is the sum of the transactions, speculative, and precautionary functions developed earlier. The supply of money is exogenously controlled by the Federal Reserve System and at any given time is fixed. Changes in either the supply or demand sides of the market can trigger off effects both on the existing levels of market interest rates and directly in the goods market itself. For example, an expansion in the supply of money by the Fed, all other things being held constant, could increase the supply of loanable funds and exert downward pressure on interest rates. Effectively, this would be identical to an outward and to the right shift of the LM curve developed in the equilibrium model of Chapter 3. Figure 6.3b illustrates the effects of such a shift on the LM curve. Interest rates would fall from i_1 to i_2 and income would rise from Y_1 to Y_2. As interest rates fall, the number of investment projects that could now pass the positive net present value test also would increase. This would serve to increase the level of demand in the goods market as well. An increase in the demand side of the money market would reverse the scenario and tend to push interest rates upward and yield reduced equilibrium income in the future.

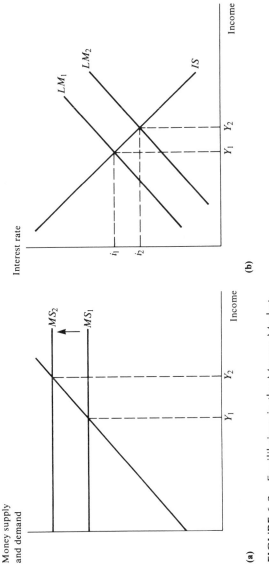

FIGURE 6.3   Equilibrium in the Money Market.
Equilibrium in the money market occurs when money demand, composed of its transactions, speculative, and precautionary elements, is equal to the money supply determined exogenously by the Federal Reserve. An increase in the money supply would shift the *LM* curve of panel (b) outward and to the right, interest rates and income would fall from i_1 to i_2, and Y_1 would rise to Y_2, respectively.

6.7 AN OVERVIEW OF THE KEYNESIAN AND MONETARIST VIEWS OF MONEY

The role played by money in the macro economy has been subject to much debate in the last 40 years, and several schools of thought have evolved. The Keynesian view of money and monetary policy holds that money does not exercise large effects on the economy. Keynes felt that changes in the money supply were transmitted to the economy only through the interest rate – investment mechanism. For example, if the Fed were to increase the money supply, this would drive interest rates downward, increasing investment and causing an increase in aggregate demand and a multiplied increase in equilibrium output, income, and employment. In Keynes view, very large changes in the money supply only bring about small changes in equilibrium income. Keynes also pointed out that in times when significant business pessimism existed, such as during the Great Depression, interest rates can be pushed to very low levels and investment still may not increase much because the potential return on business investment projects is very low.

The monetarists formulated a different view of money and monetary policy but reached conclusions somewhat similar to those of Keynes about the effectiveness of monetary policy. Monetarists believe that changes in the money supply directly alter the relationship between money supply and the demand individuals have to hold money relative to goods and other forms of wealth. When the money supply is expanded, individuals find themselves holding larger money balances than they wish to hold, relative to goods and other forms of wealth, and begin to spend off the excess balances. This increase in the demand for goods and other wealth forms besides money causes the economy to spiral forward, increasing income until money supply again falls back in line with money demand. Alternatively, if the money supply is contracted, individuals find themselves holding less money balances than they wish to hold and reduce their spending and increase their savings to restore those balances to the desired level. This would reduce the demand for goods, reducing income in the economy until money demand and money supply are again equal.

Modern monetarists subscribe to the ''portfolio view'' of money and other wealth forms. They believe that individuals hold wealth in many different forms, such as stocks, bonds, real estate, personal property, and money. Just how much of their total wealth is allocated to each wealth form depends on the rates of return on alternate forms, the price level, expected inflation, income, and the general availability of credit. Changes in any of these factors are believed to alter the specific composition of the individual's portfolio and change the money balances such an individual wishes to hold.

When desired money balances change, this either increases or decreases spending, setting off a series of effects in the goods market.

Monetarists also believe that monetary policy has been ineffective as a stabilizing force in the economy and in many cases has really been the source of increased destabilization as a result of timing problems, bureaucratic incentives, and the role played by adaptive expectations. The Keynesian and monetarist views will be developed in more detail in the next chapter. However, it is important to note here that they differ more in their view of the transmission mechanism whereby money affects the economy than in their conclusions regarding its effectiveness.

6.8 THE MANAGERIAL IMPLICATIONS OF MONEY AND MONETARY ACTIONS

Having just completed a chapter on the basics of money and monetary actions, the pragmatic question is, "How can the financial manager benefit from and use such information?" There are several considerations here. First, different industries have differing dependencies on monetary aggregates. If the manager is employed in an industry that is not very sensitive to monetary aggregates, such as the manufacture of small consumer items like candy, soft drinks, or food, most of the concern will be with the role played by interest rates in possible capital expansions and the optimal holdings of cash. Some industries, however, are much more sensitive to changes in monetary aggregates. For example, demand in the housing industry, automobile manufacturing, and industries producing other "big-ticket items" is very sensitive to changes in the money supply. As interest rates rise, the overall cost to the consumer of these items increases dramatically. Financial managers in big-ticket industries need to evaluate not only the current state of affairs regarding interest rates, but also the effects of increases or decreases on the rate of monetary expansion announced by the Federal Reserve. Monetary conditions also can vary from district to district in the Federal Reserve System, since discount rates are determined by the district banks and are approved by the Board of Governors. When considering the location of, for example, a new automobile dealership, the financial manager would benefit from knowing and understanding the local availability of loanable funds. Monetary expansions and contractions also affect the interest rates available to corporate cash managers on alternative forms of wealth holdings. Increases in interest rates tend to drive the optimal corporate cash balance down, while falling interest rates raise the optimal transactions balance.

Financial managers also should give consideration to the time effects involved in monetary changes, realizing that contractions may reach full magnitude through the money-multiplier process much faster than expansions. Finally, the managerial implications of changes in monetary aggregates are somewhat more complicated than the basic introduction in this chapter. Financial managers should avail themselves of the more detailed understanding of monetary policy presented in Chapter 7 before claiming competency in such decisions.

6.9 SUMMARY

1. This chapter has discussed the basic role of money in the macro economy. Money is anything that serves as a medium of exchange, a measure of value, and a store of value. Money itself has time value. The classical economists believed that money affected the economy through a model referred to as the equation of exchange. The equation stated that the money supply times velocity is equal to the average price of all goods times the average quantity, that is, $MV = PQ$. Changes in the supply of money were therefore believed to bring about changes in prices. In this view, inflation was caused by changes in the money supply.

2. The money market is composed of both a demand for and a supply of money. The demand for money has three components: a transactions demand, a speculative demand, and a precautionary demand. Transactions demand represents the desire to hold money to engage in exchange and is believed to be a positive function of income and a negative function of interest rates. The interest rate is the price (opportunity cost) of holding money as opposed to other interest-bearing assets.

3. From a financial viewpoint, transactions demand is optimized by the use of the standard cash-management formula of Equation (6.3): $C_b = Y/2T$, where Y is the economist's symbol for income, and T is the number of transactions involved. By holding money, the individual foregoes the higher interest income the bonds would have generated. The opportunity cost of holding cash is illustrated by Equation (6.4): $O = i(C_b)$, where i is the interest rate on the bonds, and C_b is the average cash balance. The individual also incurs transactions costs. If each transaction has a cost of $\$X$, then total transactions costs are XT, that is, $C_t = XT$. The goal of the individual is to minimize the total costs he or she incurs by holding cash, that is, minimize $XT + (iY/2T)$. The optimal number of transactions for the individual to conduct is found by taking the first derivative of Equation (6.6), setting it equal to zero, and solving for T, which is equal to Equation (6.7): $T = \sqrt{(iY/2X)}$. Once the optimal number of transactions is determined, it can be substituted back into the average cash balance of Equation (6.3) to find how much cash should be held. This works out to be Equation (6.8): $C_b = \sqrt{(XY/2i)}$.

4. Other things being equal, transactions cash balances are negatively related to the interest rate on bonds and transactions costs and positively related to income.

5. The speculative demand for money is the desire to hold money in the hope of capital accumulation or to take advantage of a profitable speculative opportunity. It is a negative function of the rate of interest.

6. Precautionary demand is the desire to hold money balances for unexpected expenditures, such as emergency automobile repairs or medical expenses. It is also a negative function of the rate of interest and the individual's preference with regard to risk bearing.

7. Individuals may choose to hold their wealth in many different forms, such as currency, bonds, real estate, stocks, and personal property, such as automobiles and jewelry, etc. The specific compositon of the portfolio is dependent on the risk-return ratio of each component, the use value of each component, and the individual's preferences.

8. The supply of money is controlled through the banking system. The U.S. economy has a fractional-reserve banking system, in which a portion of total deposits is kept as required reserves and the remainder is available as loanable funds to potential borrowers. Fractional-reserve banking and the loan-making − redeposit mechanism create the money multiplier. The money multiplier is equal to the reciprocal of the reserve requirement: $K_m = 1/r$.

Equilibrium in the money market occurs when money demand is equal to money supply. Whenever the money-market supply or demand conditions change, there are effects on both interest rates and the goods market.

Keynesians believe that changes in the money supply transmit their effect to the economy through changes in the interest rate − investment mechanism. Monetarists believe that changes in the money supply bring about direct changes in the spending behavior of individuals.

The managerial implications of changes in the money supply include considerations of their effect on interest rates, cash balances to be held by the firm, locational decisions of the firm, the sensitivity of demand in the firm's industry to interest-rate changes, and timing differences between expansionary and contractionary policies.

6.10 EXERCISES

1. Today, in the territory of Yapp, in Micronesia (a real place), large round stones are still used as money. In this day and time, one would think that credit cards, checking accounts, and paper currency would have eliminated such forms of money. Explain how the inhabitants of Yapp can use these stones as money.

2. The classical economists believed that changes in the supply of money would bring about changes in the price level. Using the equation of exchange, explain how this process took place?

3. Explain the three major components of the demand of money. Why don't people choose to hold all their money in the form of cash or checkable accounts?

4. Explain the concept of fractional-reserve banking and the role played by public confidence in the banking system?

5. Compare and contrast required and excess reserves. Why would banks choose to hold excess reserves? What effect do increases in the level of required reserves have on the money supply?

6. Explain the process of the money multiplier. Is the effect of the money multiplier symmetrical for both increases and decreases in reserves? Is the effect of monetary changes symmetrical for increases and decreases in reserves with regard to the time period over which they transpire? How are equilibrium interest rates in the money market determined?

7. Compare and contrast the basic views of the Keynesians and monetarists concerning how monetary policy is transmitted to the economy.

8. Discuss at least three of the major managerial implications of monetary policy.

6.11 REFERENCES

Galbraith, J. K. *Money*. Boston: Houghton Mifflin, 1975.

Ritter, L., and Silber, W. *Money*, 4th Ed. New York, Basic Books, 1980.

7

Money Supply and Monetary Policy

7.1 INTRODUCTION

> Irredeemable paper money has almost invariably proved a curse to the country employing it.[1]

Monetary policy includes both the constitution of money and the specific actions taken within this constitutional framework. The *constitution* of money refers to the nature of money itself. When this country and the world were on a gold standard, the value of money was ultimately determined by the supply of and demand for gold. The value of money had a "real anchor." The discretion of monetary authorities was, at that time, significantly limited.

Today, with *fiat money*, the constraints impinging on monetary authorities are essentially political. Fiat money is irredeemable paper money, liabilities of the government made into legal tender by law. Fiat money has no intrinsic value. Its purchasing power—and the rate of inflation—is simply the result of how much of it the monetary authorities choose to print. With money freed of its "real anchor," control over the money supply can be used to pursue such goals as stabilizing prices, lowering unemployment, and fostering economic growth.

This chapter examines the conduct of monetary policy by the Federal Reserve Board. The tools of monetary policy are defined, and the interplay of the tools, targets, and goals, as well as the channels, of monetary policy

[1]Irving Fisher, *The Purchasing Power of Money* (New York: Macmillan, 1911).

137

are identified. The roles played by the Fed, the banking system, and the public in the money-multiplier process are developed. In addition, the important issues in the matter of whether monetary policy should be conducted using rules or discretion are discussed.

7.2 THE FEDERAL RESERVE

The U.S. Constitution grants Congress the power to "coin money and regulate the value thereof." With the Federal Reserve Act of 1913, Congress created the Federal Reserve System and delegated its monetary powers to it. The immediate reason for creating the Federal Reserve System was the panic of 1907, and the specific purpose of the Federal Reserve System was to end bank panics. In fact, the Federal Reserve System did not end bank panics. Nevertheless, the Federal Reserve System was found useful by the federal government for managing its fiscal, debt, and monetary policies during World War I. And during the period from World War I until World War II, the Federal Reserve System discovered the powers implicit in its control over the money supply for influencing the economy.

As presently constituted, the Federal Reserve System consists of the Federal Reserve Board, in Washington, D.C., composed of 7 governors and 12 regional Federal Reserve Banks and their branches, which are located throughout the country. The most important of these regional Federal Reserve Banks is the New York Federal Reserve Bank because it is through this bank that open-market operations, to be explained later, are implemented.

The Federal Reserve—or the Fed—performs a variety of useful functions, such as clearing checks, regulating banks, and carrying out certain fiscal operations for the U.S. Treasury. These activities are considered "housekeeping functions" by macroeconomists and are not usually covered in macroeconomics courses. Instead, the concern of macroeconomics is monetary policy. Monetary policy includes open-market operations and the setting of reserve requirements and the discount rate. Monetary policy consists of using these "tools" to influence certain "targets" for the purpose of achieving certain "goals."

7.3 THE TOOLS OF MONETARY POLICY

The *tools* of the Federal Reserve, sometimes referred to as *instruments*, refer to the specific activities through which the Fed influences the economy. These tools were not all envisioned by the Congress when it created the Federal Reserve System. In fact, open-market operations—which today constitute the Fed's most important tool—were discovered almost by accident by the Fed during the 1920s. For convenience, the tools of the Federal Reserve are categorized as follows:

Open-market operations

Reserve requirements

Discount rate

Selective controls

Moral suasion

7.3.1 Open-Market Operations

Open-market operations are the buying and selling of U.S. Treasury securities by the Federal Reserve. These operations are conducted by the New York Federal Reserve Bank under the direction of the Federal Reserve's Open-Market Committee. This committee consists of the Board of Governors, the president of the New York Fed, and a rotating set of 4 of the other 11 Fed bank presidents. These operations are conducted by the New York Fed because of the location in New York City of the nation's largest financial markets.

Let's say that the Federal Reserve wishes to increase the money supply. This is easily accomplished through open-market operations. The New York Fed buys U.S. Treasury securities—usually Treasury bills or T-bills—from a securities dealer. The New York Fed then pays for the newly purchased securities with brand new money, created by the very act of its buying the securities, through the crediting of the account at the Fed of the commercial bank of the securities dealer.

To avoid any possible confusion about what is happening, Figure 7.1 shows the balance sheets of the Fed, the commercial bank, and the securities dealer before and after the open-market operation. Before the open-market operation, the figure shows that the assets and liabilities and net worth of the Federal Reserve and the commercial bank are all zero and that the securities dealer has $1 million of Treasury bills in assets and $1 million in net worth, all of these figures being selected for convenience.

The open-market operation consists of a transfer of Treasury bills to the Federal Reserve and a corresponding transfer of money—newly created money—to the bank account of the securities dealer. Notice that after the open-market operation there is $1 million in new money in the economy, this being the money of the securities dealer in his or her bank account.

This creation of new money should appear to be magical. How can any

Federal Reserve		Commercial Bank		Securities Dealer	
Treasury bills	Deposit of commercial bank	Reserves	Deposit of securities dealer	Cash	Net worth
				$0M	
$0M	$0M	$0M	$0M	Treasury bills	$1M
				$1M	

(a) Before open-market operation

Federal Reserve		Commercial Bank		Securities Dealer	
Treasury bills	Deposit of commercial bank	Reserves	Deposit of securities dealer	Cash	Net worth
				$1M	
$1M	$1M	$1M	$1M	Treasury bills	$1M
				$0M	

(b) After open-market operation

FIGURE 7.1   Money Creation and Open-Market Operations.

entity—even the Federal Reserve—create money out of nothing? The Federal Reserve can create money out of nothing because that is what the money of the United States is today. Our money is *fiat money*, nothing more than accounting entries in electronic computers or else paper money, not "backed" by anything such as gold or silver but "backed" only by green ink and the expression "In God we trust." Because our money is fiat money, the Federal Reserve can easily increase or decrease its supply. This is big magic, and this big magic has potentially enormous implications for the economy.

7.3.2 Reserve Requirements

Reserve requirements are the amount of vault cash and deposits at the Fed required of commercial banks and other depository institutions. These reserve requirements are expressed as percentages of deposits by type of deposit; i.e., reserves must equal at least x percent of demand deposits plus y percent of savings deposits plus z percent of time deposits.

The purpose of required reserves is not really to increase the safety of bank deposits. (Safety is provided by the totality of assets of the bank, by the bank's net worth, by deposit insurance, and ultimately, by congressional guarantee of deposit insurance agencies.) The purpose, instead, is to make the money supply more controllable by determining the amount of deposits banks will themselves create from an initial creation of money by the Federal

Reserve. The creation of money by the banking system is part of the money-multiplier process, and the Fed, the banking system, and the public all have important roles to play in it.

Although this money-multiplier process is discussed in detail later in this chapter, an abbreviated discussion is appropriate at this point. Conceptually, there are two kinds of banks: *gyros*, or *100 percent reserve banks*, which simply accept money from depositors and store this money in their vaults, and *fractional-reserve banks*.

Gyros would be very safe banks. With gyros, the only possibility of loss to depositors would be from hazards such as fire, theft, and fraud, which are rather conventional hazards and are easily insured. Gyros also would be very expensive banks. Since gyros could not relend money, they could not cover their administrative costs with the interest earned from their loans and investments. Not only would gyros be unable to pay interest to their depositors, they would have to charge all their costs of doing business to their depositors. Since there are no laws against gyro banking, the fact that gyros are so very rare indicates that depositors do not feel the extra safety they offer to be worth the cost.

The alternative to a gyro is a fractional-reserve bank, i.e., a bank that takes in deposits and relends most of the funds so received, keeping only a fraction in vault cash or on deposit at the Fed. In the absence of required reserves, such a bank would determine its own *optimal reserves*. Optimal reserves would probably reflect a variety of factors, including the opportunity cost of maintaining reserves, the probability of a large number of withdrawals on any given day, and the ease with which the bank could sell loans and investments for cash in order to meet such unusual withdrawals.

Optimal reserves would change as the factors affecting them change. This implies that the money multiplier would change over time, loosening the Federal Reserve's control over the money supply. However, by setting required reserves at a level well above optimal reserves, the Fed insulates the money multiplier from changes in the factors that determine optimal reserves. This particular role of required reserves — stabilizing the money multiplier — can be thought of as a passive role.

The Fed is today very cautious about changing required reserve ratios. However, by having required reserve ratios, open-market operations will be translated into more predictable changes in the money supply. The passive role for required reserves and the active role for open-market operations are in large part explained by the facility with which the Fed conducts open-market operations. Changes to reserve requirements can be characterized as a blunt instrument in the conduct of monetary policy. Changes in reserve requirements can have massive, unpredictable effects that are difficult to reverse. Open-market operations, in contrast, are much more fluid, easier to calibrate, and can be easily reversed when this is found to be necessary.

A second reason for the deemphasis of required reserves as an active tool of monetary policy is that financial innovation has effectively removed much money (technically, near money) from reserve requirements. Banks offer their larger customers several ways of avoiding reserve requirements, including Eurodollar deposits and repos. *Eurodollar deposits* are deposit accounts, denominated in U.S. dollars, in overseas banks and overseas branches of U.S. banks. Because the deposit is "booked" in London or Paris or Bermuda or the Cayman Islands, U.S. banking regulations, including reserve requirements, do not apply.

A *repo* is a combination sale and commitment for future repurchase at a fixed price of an asset, usually Treasury bills. At the end of the day, the bank determines the balance in a depositor's account and uses the balance to buy Treasury bills for the depositor with arrangement for resale the morning of the next day. Thus, when the bank tallies up its deposits subject to reserve requirements, which is done after the bank closes, this particular depositor is found to have a zero balance. Because of this zero balance, the bank need not carry reserves against this account.

Because of the ability of larger depositors to escape required reserves, these requirements should be thought of as a special kind of tax. Because of these required reserves, banks have to use a portion of the funds received from small depositors for non-interest-earning vault cash and deposits at the Fed. This means that the return the bank will offer to small depositors will be lower. After all the complications are worked out, the reduced interest earned by depositors as a result of reserve requirements can be shown to be interest earned by the Fed and "reverted" to the U.S. Treasury.

Let's say a small depositor opens an account at a commercial bank in the amount of $1000. While this may sound like a lot of money, it is not enough to justify the costs involved in opening a Eurodollar account or entering into repos. The bank sets $100 aside—we are assuming a required reserve ratio of 10 percent—and lends out the other $900. Assume the bank pays the full amount of interest earnings to its depositors. If the bank earns 6 percent interest on its $900 loan, the bank will earn $54 and pay 5.4 percent on the depositor's $1000. The lower interest rate on deposits vis-à-vis loans is due to reserve requirements.

The $100 that the bank "sets aside," either in the form of Federal Reserve notes in its vault or as a deposit at the Fed, enables the Fed to buy $100 worth of Treasury bills, on which it will earn, we shall continue to assume, 6 percent, or $6. These earnings of the Fed are turned over, or "reverted," to the U.S. Treasury. Thus the reduced interest on deposit accounts subject to required reserves is a special kind of tax. That this tax is borne by small depositors indicates that it is a *regressive tax*.

7.3.3 The Discount Rate

The *discount rate* refers to the interest rate charged by the Fed on loans it makes to commercial banks and other depository institutions subject to reserve requirements. Lending to banks through the "discount window" was the main tool of monetary policy during the Fed's early history. The term *discount* refers to the original practice of lending reserves to banks through the discounting (or "rediscounting") of short-term securities such as bankers' acceptances.

By raising or lowering the discount rate, the Fed was able very directly to affect short-term interest rates and the profitability of bank lending to businesses. With the discount rate low relative to market rates, it was profitable for banks to borrow from the Fed and extend loans to businesses (especially loans eligible for discounting). With a discount rate high relative to market rates, borrowing from the Fed in order to lend to businesses would diminish.

Today the discount window plays several minor, although still important, roles in the conduct of monetary policy. First, the discount window performs the role of "safety valve." When monetary policy as implemented by open-market operations is too tight, banks will line up at the discount window in order to restore their liquidity. Second, the discount window gives the Fed the ability to lend directly to a bank in trouble, which may be considered necessary in certain situations. For example, when a large bank is identified by federal bank regulators to be in immediate danger of insolvency —which insolvency might affect the liquidity of financial markets as a whole —the Fed can use the discount window to be this bank's *lender of last resort*. Through this lending, the Fed hopes to buy the time necessary for bank regulators to arrange a more permanent solution, which solution may simply be an orderly liquidation of the bank.

Today, when the discount rate is low relative to market rates, there is still incentive to banks to utilize the discount window and in so doing to increase the money supply. However, the quantitative impact of lending through the discount window is small. This is mainly due to the Fed's qualitative control of the discount window. The Fed does not automatically lend to bankers upon their application, and it will look at repeated applications to borrow through the discount window as evidence of unsound banking. Given that the Federal Reserve is an important bank regulator, this dissuades many banks from vigorously utilizing the discount window to take advantage of slight differences in interest rates.

Changes in the discount rate have come to be a useful way for the Fed to signal to financial markets its perception of monetary conditions and, therefore, of the future course of monetary policy. Since changes in the discount rate are relatively infrequent, they signal that the Fed perceives that a "permanent" change in interest rates or monetary conditions has taken place. Investors act on this signal, buying and selling securities according to the implications of the signal and enabling the signal to have real effects.

7.3.4 Selective Controls

Selective controls are controls the Federal Reserve exercises over particular aspects of financial markets. Generally, the purpose of selective controls is not to influence the overall amount of money and credit, but rather to shift their supplies from some activities to others. For example, in the past, the Fed has attempted to shift credit from consumer finance to business finance by establishing *minimum down payments* in conjunction with borrowing in order to buy household durable goods such as cars, furniture, and appliances. Also in the past, the Fed has attempted to curtail speculation by establishing minimum "margin" requirements on borrowing in order to invest in stock. *Margin requirements* refer to the percent of money investors have to put up themselves when borrowing to buy stocks. More than just a down payment, this margin has to be maintained so that if the price of the stock declines, the investor will either have to "liquidate his or her position" (i.e., sell) or "post additional margin" (i.e., put up more money).

Margin is the amount, expressed as a percent, of an investor's equity in a stock bought with borrowed money. For example, with a margin requirement (both an initial and a maintenance margin) of 50 percent, an investor may put up $25 and borrow $25 in order to buy a share of a stock selling at $50. This is a *leveraged investment* because, although the investor only put up half the value of the stock, he or she will enjoy (or suffer) all of any increase (or decrease) in its value. That is, the investor's risk per dollar of equity has been doubled.

Note that on a decline in the price of stock bought on margin, the investor must either post additional margin or sell. Continuing with the preceding example, if the stock price falls to $40, then the investor only has $15 in equity in the security (that is, $40 - $25). Current equity of $15 is less than 50 percent of the stock's current value. Therefore, the investor must either post another $5 or sell.

During the stock market crashes of 1929 and 1987, selling forced by margin calls sent stock prices into freefall. In both cases, a not unusual "correction"—or fall in stock prices following a significant rise—caused some margin calls and liquidations. These forced sales caused further declines in stock prices, which, in turn, caused additional margin calls and liquidations. "Downward momentum" developed, including panic selling, and the corrections turned into crashes.[2]

Following the crash of 1929, stock prices fell by about 75 percent over a 3-year period. In 1987, greatly advanced technologies of trading allowed the Dow Jones Industrial Average to fall by 23 percent on one day: Monday, October 19. The effects of the crash of 1987 on the macroeconomy are discussed in Chapter 9.

With deregulation, many of the Fed's former selective controls have been discarded. For example, the prohibition on paying interest on demand deposits and the setting of maximum interest rates on savings and time deposits—which used to be set by Regulation Q—have been ended. In large part, deregulation was necessary to enable U.S. banks to compete with nonbank financial institutions and foreign banks in an environment of high and volatile interest rates. If U.S. banks could not offer competitive interest rates on deposits, then savings would be shifted to other institutions, such as money-market mutual funds. The transfer of savings, which was referred to as *disintermediation*, disrupted the normal flow of funds through banks and to the particular customers to which banks lend.

The process of deregulation poses problems and challenges of its own. From the time of the banking acts of the 1930s through to the 1970s and deregulation, U.S. banks and thrift institutions were highly regulated. Regulations set reserve and capital requirements, restricted certain loans and investments, set interest rates on deposits, and provided deposit insurance, and monetary and fiscal policies stabilized interest rates in money and capital markets. Banks and thrift institutions almost could not help but make money.

Then, during the 1970s, as inflation accelerated and interest rates became volatile, and as emerging computer and communications technologies tied financial markets closer together, many of these regulations were made obsolete. Through the 1970s and into the 1980s, regulations were discarded one at a time, almost always in response to some immediate crisis. The result was a disorderly process of deregulation, with much trial and error. Going into the 1990s, the banking industry can be categorized as "half regulated and half deregulated," with the prospect of continuing change and discovery.

---

[2]Although the Fed did not then have authority to set margin requirements, early in 1929, in order to dampen stock market speculation, it advised member banks that those lending in the stock market on margin would not be able to borrow at the discount window (*Annual Report of the Federal Reserve Board*, 1929, pp. 2−4).

7.3.5 Moral Suasion

Moral suasion refers to attempts by monetary authorities to persuade, cajole, threaten, inform, and misinform. For example, at the time of the crash of 1987, the new chairman of the Federal Reserve, Alan Greenspan, along with other administration officials, argued again and again that the economy was sound, the dollar was sound, U.S. banks and financial markets were sound, and so on, in order to allay growing concerns in the United States and abroad. These announcements, generally, were not credible, and if they had any impact at all, they exacerbated the concerns.

The effectiveness of moral suasion critically depends on the credibility of the monetary authority. Dr. Greenspan's predecessor, Paul Volcker, over the course of his tenure as chairman of the Fed, developed a high level of credibility. The Central Bank of Japan, from the mid-1970s to the early 1980s, likewise developed a high level of credibility. In these two cases, financial markets developed confidence in the commitment of these monetary authorities to follow through on their announcements of monetary policy.

The problem with moral suasion is that it is tempting to use announcements as a substitute—as opposed to a complement—for actual monetary policy. This is similar to the problem of parents who, loving their children, do not wish to punish them but do wish to correct their misbehavior. Instead of actually punishing their children, these parents merely threaten to punish if misbehavior continues. After a while, the threats are no longer credible, and in the long run, these parents—if they are to correct their children's misbehavior—find they have to punish the children severely.

"Talking" monetary restraint is easy, especially compared to implementing a policy of monetary restraint after a period of monetary ease. Actual monetary restraint—which eventually will lower inflation (or strengthen the dollar, or whatever)—will likely result in a recession. Wouldn't it be nicer to use moral suasion and avoid a recession? However, is moral suasion believable in the absence of actual restraint?

In 1979, shortly after he was named chairman of the Federal Reserve Board, Paul Volcker announced that he would adopt a policy of monetary restraint in order to deal with the problem of accelerating inflation. Theoretically (perhaps), if his announcement was credible, business decision makers would have realigned their wage and price policies, eliminating inflation without the economy going through a recession. However, in 1979, Paul Volcker did not enjoy the credibility he later gained, and disinflation was obtained, as usual, at the cost of a period of recession.

Ideally, moral suasion is used as a complement and not a substitute for actual policy. A monetary authority such as the Central Bank of Japan, which gains credibility through years of honestly communicating its monetary policy to financial markets, has a powerful tool. Such a monetary authority can deal with periods of financial stress without raising concerns for the return of inflation, devaluation, or whatever. Such a monetary authority can change monetary policy—going from a high-inflation to a low-inflation policy, for example—with greatly reduced short-run business cycle effects.

7.4 MONEY MULTIPLIERS

Money multipliers refer to the total increase in *M1* or *M2* money for a $1 increase in Federal Reserve money, referred to as the *monetary base* or *base money*.[3] For simplicity, and because the teaching point is unaffected, this section will ignore the distinction between the *M1* and *M2* multipliers. The money multiplier is important because it is the relationship between what the Federal Reserve directly controls—which is the monetary base—and the money supply, which, in turn, affects macroeconomic performance. The money-multiplier process is a complex process involving the Fed, the banks, and the public. Although the money-multiplier process is complex, it is a relatively stable process, so it can be used by the Fed in implementing monetary policy.

7.4.1 A Monopoly Bank (without Currency)

The money multiplier is easily seen in the case of a monopoly bank in an economy without currency. Imagine that, in such a case, the Federal Reserve "injects" the monopoly bank with $1 million in new reserves. That is, the Federal Reserve buys $1 million worth of Treasury bills, paying for them with $1 million in new base money.

The question is, "What is the maximum amount of *M1* money that the bank can create with this injection of $1 million in reserves?" Because of the assumptions that this is a monopoly bank and that there is no currency, the answer is simple: It depends on the required reserve ratio according to the following formula:

$$M1 = \frac{1}{r} M0$$

where *M1* stands for *M1* money, in this case, deposits; *r* stands for the required reserve ratio; and *M0* stands for the monetary base. For example,

---

[3]Sometimes, Federal Reserve money is referred to as *outside money*, and demand deposits and other forms of checkable accounts are referred to as *inside money*.

if the required reserve ratio were 20 percent, then the answer is $5 million. The fractional expression is referred to as the *money multiplier*. With *r* equal to 20 percent, the money multiplier is equal to 1/0.2, or 5.

The way in which the new base money gets multiplied into *M1* money is interesting. The bank creates the new *M1* money (almost) out of thin air in the act of lending. Let's say the bank receives a loan application for a purpose such as financing the construction of a new factory. The bank, if it approves the loan application, can make the loan by opening a checking account with a balance equal to the loan amount. The process is illustrated in Figure 7.2. In a sense, the bank's loan is a trade of *M1* money for a claim on future earnings — in this case, the earnings of the new factory in the future. However, in another sense, the bank is creating new *M1* money.

7.4.2 Multiple Banks (without Currency)

Things get somewhat complicated when there are multiple banks. Let's say there are multiple banks, and an individual bank — we shall call it bank 1 — is injected with new reserves. Because a borrower's check may be deposited at another bank, and because bank 1 will want to be able to make

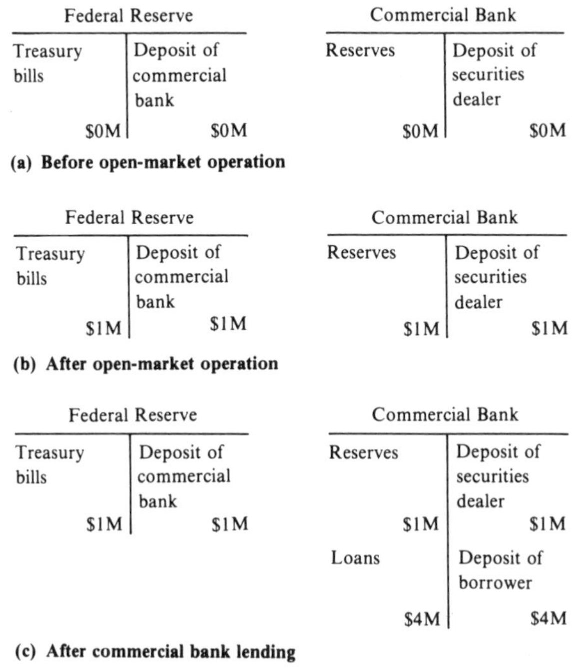

Federal Reserve		Commercial Bank	
Treasury bills	Deposit of commercial bank	Reserves	Deposit of securities dealer
$0M	$0M	$0M	$0M

(a) Before open-market operation

Federal Reserve		Commercial Bank	
Treasury bills	Deposit of commercial bank	Reserves	Deposit of securities dealer
$1M	$1M	$1M	$1M

(b) After open-market operation

Federal Reserve		Commercial Bank	
Treasury bills	Deposit of commercial bank	Reserves	Deposit of securities dealer
$1M	$1M	$1M	$1M
		Loans	Deposit of borrower
		$4M	$4M

(c) After commercial bank lending

FIGURE 7.2 Money Creation through Fractional-Reserve Banking.

good on this check, bank 1 may not want to lend a multiple of its new reserves. Instead, it may want to lend only the amount of its new reserves, i.e., only $1 million. In this case, the full multiple amount of new *M1* money will result from successive rounds of lending.

Bank 1 will lend the first $1 million. Then, after the check clears, some bank—we shall call it bank 2—will find itself with reserves of $1 million and deposits of $1 million. However, because of fractional-reserve banking, this bank only needs to have 20 percent of its deposits, or $200,000, in reserves. This means it can lend $800,000. With the second round of lending, the *M1* money supply will grow to $1.8 million, the $1 million created by bank 1 and the $800,000 created by bank 2. With subsequent rounds of lending and money creation, the full amount of $5 million will eventually come to be created.

Today's banking system is very efficient in redirecting reserves from where they happen to be to where they are most in demand. Therefore, the full multiplication of *M1* money often occurs in one step. Bank 1 finds itself with new reserves of $1 million. Because there are system-wide excess reserves, bank 1 or bank 2 or any other bank can therefore extend more loans. Let's say bank 34 makes a $5 million loan. The borrower draws a check on this $5 million that is deposited in bank 35. Bank 35 will therefore have a deficiency of reserves; it will be short $1 million in reserves. It will have to borrow reserves in what is called the *federal funds market* to cover its deficiency. In the federal funds market, bank 1 will lend $1 million in reserves to bank 35. Thus the full multiple creation of *M1* money from the new monetary base money occurs in one step.

Individual banks do not have to know the amount, if any, of system-wide excess reserves. All individual banks have to do is compare the federal funds rate to lending rates. If the federal funds rate is relatively low, this means there are excess reserves. Simultaneously, if the federal funds rate is relatively low, it will be profitable for banks to increase their lending, which will soak up the excess reserves.

The federal funds market is a large, informal market in which banks are tied in to each other through telephone and other electronic connections. That is, there is no single meeting place where trading takes place, such as is the case with the New York Stock Exchange or the Chicago Board of Trade, where stocks and commodity futures are traded. Banks with excess reserves lend to banks short of reserves for very short terms in this market, usually for 1 day at a time. In this way, the banking system acts as though it were one big monopoly bank, lending money to whoever is most demanding credit and redirecting reserves as necessary to satisfy the reserve requirements of the deposits created by this lending.

7.4.3 Currency and Money Creation

Things get further complicated when there is currency in the economy. This is so because currency represents base money held directly by the public and therefore unavailable to banks for the purpose of supporting deposit creation. If there were no fractional-reserve banks, then the amount of *M1* money would be equal to the amount of base money. This would make the money multiplier 1. If there were no currency, then the money multiplier would be, as given earlier, $1/r$. Because there is both currency and fractional-reserve banking, the money multiplier is kind of an average of 1 and $1/r$.

Let's say the public wishes to hold c cents in currency for every dollar in deposits. Then we can determine the money multiplier with the following formulas:

$$C = cD \qquad \text{(Currency} = c \times \text{deposits)}$$
$$R = rD \qquad \text{(Reserves} = r \times \text{deposits)}$$
$$M1 = C + D \quad (M1 = \text{currency} + \text{deposits)}$$
$$M0 = C + R \quad \text{(Monetary base} = \text{currency} + \text{reserves)}$$
$$M1 = mM0 \qquad (M1 = \text{multiplier} \times \text{monetary base)}$$

By substitution, we get

$$m = \frac{1 + c}{c + r}$$

For example, let r equal 0.20 and c equal 0.10. Then the money multiplier m will equal $[(1 + 0.10)/(0.10 + 0.20)]$, or 3.67. Notice that this is between 5, which is what the multiplier would be equal to in an economy without currency, and 1. The multiplier is lower because some of the monetary base has been withdrawn from the banking system by the public for use as currency. This portion of the monetary base cannot be used to support deposit creation.

The role played by the public in the money-multiplier process complicates monetary policy in two ways not reflected in the preceding mathematics. The first consideration is the timing of currency withdrawals from the banking system. The Fed begins the process of money expansion by injecting banks with new reserves. Almost immediately, banks will increase their lending and, in the process, create new deposit money. Sometime after this, the public will withdraw a portion of these new reserves as currency. Currency will probably be withdrawn *after* the newly created deposit money gives rise to a mix of real and inflationary expansion of the economy and as additional currency is therefore required for transactions purposes. Accordingly, an injection of new bank reserves will lead immediately to expanded lending and money creation followed somewhat later by currency withdrawals.

The second consideration is the changing preference of the public for currency versus deposits. This relationship is usually a stable function of the time of year, currency demand being highest around the Christmas shopping period. Furthermore, the demand for currency has been falling over time because of such financial innovations as credit cards. Historically, a major increase in the public's demand for currency—and a failure of the Fed to respond to the change in the money multiplier—was a significant factor in the collapse of the banking system and the ensuing Great Depression of the 1930s.

7.4.4 Excess Reserves

Excess reserves are the reserves banks maintain over and above their reserve requirements. Today, with an efficient federal funds market, excess reserves are generally very low. Formerly, when reserves could not be so easily transferred from one bank to another, excess reserves were higher and responded to market conditions. When interest rates were low, so that the opportunity cost of carrying excess reserves was low, banks would generally carry additional excess reserves. More important, following periods of financial crisis, banks would generally carry substantial excess reserves in order to be able to meet currency withdrawals by the public.

Excess reserves can be incorporated into the money multiplier in the following way: Replace the preceding equation for reserves with $R = (r + e)D$, where R is total reserves, r is (as before) the required-reserve ratio, e is the desired excess-reserve ratio, and D is (as before) deposits. With excess reserves, the money multiplier becomes $m = (1 + c)/(c + r + e)$. With r equal to 0.20, c equal to 0.10, and e equal to 0.05, then $m = (1 + 0.10)/(0.10 + 0.20 + 0.05) = 3.14$, which is less than the multiplier of 3.67 obtained earlier when, implicitly, e equaled zero.

As with the public's demand for currency, bank demand for excess reserves features some dynamics not captured in the money multiplier. When the Fed injects banks with new reserves, these are, almost necessarily, excess reserves. It will take some time for these new reserves to be transformed into required reserves through the creation of deposits in the process of lending. Today, however, because of an efficient federal funds market, this process no longer takes very much time. Furthermore, over time, because of the development of the federal funds market, the trend of excess reserves has been downward, toward zero. And, because of deposit insurance and the end to bank panics, banks no longer demand excess reserves to allay depositor fears of insolvency.

7.5 THE CONDUCT OF MONETARY POLICY

The policy objectives or goals of the Federal Reserve have included price stability, full employment, economic growth, balance of payments equilibrium, and low interest rates. While creating money out of nothing may be considered to be big magic, it may not be big enough magic to achieve the potentially competing and dynamically inconsistent goals of the Federal Reserve.

In contrast to the expansive list of goals of the Federal Reserve, the original purpose for which Congress created the Fed is well defined. Congress created the Fed to end bank panics. The Fed was to be a lender of last resort. It was to use its magical ability to create new money when runs on banks drained them of reserves and threatened to collapse the money supply. The focus of monetary policy, however, has not been on the Fed's role as lender of last resort. Instead, it has been on more ambitious goals, such as "noninflationary economic growth."[4]

7.5.1 Operating Procedures

To say that the Fed's goal is noninflationary economic growth is not sufficient from the standpoint of the account manager at the New York Fed bank. This person needs to know if he or she is to buy or sell Treasury securities, in what amounts, and at what times.

In the early 1980s, the Federal Reserve adopted operating procedures that entail setting immediate targets for nonborrowed bank reserves. The immediate targets for nonborrowed bank reserves are chosen because they are, according to the Fed's macromodel, consistent with achieving its intermediate targets. The intermediate targets are, in turn, and also according to the Fed's macromodel, consistent with achieving its goals. Once informed of the immediate targets for nonborrowed bank reserves, the account manager at the New York Fed bank has sufficient information to conduct open-market operations.

This operating procedure is illustrated in Figure 7.3. Figure 7.3a graphs the supply and demand for bank reserves or, what is the same thing, the supply and demand for federal funds. The supply curve is initially vertical at the amount of nonborrowed reserves supplied by the Fed's open-market operations.[5] Then, at the point where the federal funds rate equals the Fed's

---

[4]As stated by Fed Governor H. Robert Heller in "Implementing Monetary Policy" (*Federal Reserve Bulletin*, July 1988, pp. 419–429). Nevertheless, Governor Heller shows that from the middle to late 1980s, the expressed concerns of the Federal Reserve's Open Market Committee have varied from inflation to exchange rates to financial market conditions.

[5]Technically, there would also be some borrowed reserves not motivated by the difference between the federal funds rate and the discount rate.

Federal funds rate

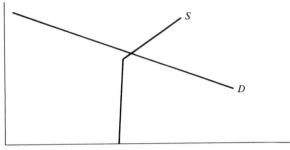

Bank reserves

(a) The supply of and demand for bank reserves

Federal funds rate

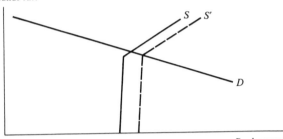

Bank reserves

(b) After open-market operation

Federal funds rate

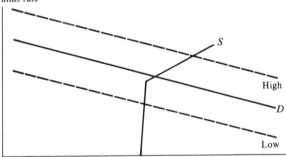

Bank reserves

(c) With shifts in demand curve

FIGURE 7.3 Federal Funds Market.
(a) The amount of nonborrowed reserves, or reserves supplied through open-market operations, is the horizontal intercept of the supply curve. The kink in the curve is at the point where the federal funds rate equals the discount rate. To the extent that the federal funds rate exceeds the discount rate, banks increase their borrowing of reserves through the discount window. (b) Purchase of Treasury securities pushes the supply curve out, resulting in a lower federal funds rate and a greater amount of bank reserves. (c) Shifts in demand affect bank reserves and the federal funds rate assymetrically. If demand falls, most of the adjustment is in the federal funds rate. However, if demand rises, the willingness of the Fed to lend through the discount window moderates the rise in the federal funds rate.

153

discount rate, the supply curve becomes positively sloped because additional reserves are borrowed at the discount window. Additional reserves are borrowed because it is cheaper to borrow at the discount window than to borrow in the federal funds market. The greater the difference between the federal funds rate and the discount rate, the greater is the incentive to borrow reserves at the discount window.

The demand curve for federal funds is, as is usually assumed, negatively sloped. The intersection between the demand and supply curves determines both the quantity of bank reserves (equal to borrowed plus nonborrowed reserves) and their price, the federal funds rate. Figure 7.3b illustrates what happens when the Fed increases nonborrowed reserves through open-market operations. In this case, the supply curve is shifted out, increasing reserves and lowering the federal funds rate.

This particular operating procedure has the result of biasing the federal funds rate downward. This bias is illustrated in Figure 7.3c. Start from a point at which demand equals supply with no borrowed reserves and with the federal funds rate equal to the discount rate. Let the demand for reserves fall. The entire adjustment to this fall in demand will be in the federal funds rate. Alternately, let the demand for reserves increase. Only part of this increase in demand will be in the federal funds rate. The rise in the federal funds rate will be moderated by the willingness of the Fed to extend borrowed reserves at the discount rate. The Fed will "lean against the wind" *if* the "wind" is pushing in the direction of higher interest rates.

7.5.2 Targets

The Fed has, since the 1970s, set targets for money supply growth. These targets are usually stated as ranges such as 6 to 9 percent annual growth in *M2* and initially included target ranges for *M1*, *M2*, and other measures of liquidity. Presumably, the instructions given the Fed's account manager enable these targets to be hit, and the hitting of these targets enables the Fed to accomplish its goals.

Actually, targets for money supply growth are little more than forecasts. Through the course of the year, the Fed continually reassesses its targets in light of developing conditions. If a target range for money supply growth is violated, the Fed decides if it will allow the target range to constrain the course of monetary policy through the remainder of the year. At the end of the year, new targets for money supply growth are set without regard for accumulated undershooting or overshooting.

One reason why the Fed's target ranges for money supply growth are nonbinding is that the Fed sets multiple targets, so there is no clear indicator of monetary policy. Another reason is constantly changing macroeconomic conditions that upset the assumptions underlying the Fed's macromodels and forecasts. To illustrate the discretionary nature of the Fed's targets, during July 1986, the Fed indicated that continued growth of *M1* above its target range would be acceptable and, in fact, suspended the setting of targets for *M1* growth. The explanation for suspension of target setting for *M1* growth was that, with deregulation, many components of *M1* came to offer interest, so that the opportunity cost of holding *M1* decreased and the demand curve for *M1* shifted. Figure 7.4 illustrates recent monetary targets for the United States, West Germany, and the United Kingdom.

7.5.3 The Channels of Monetary Policy

The specific ways in which money affects the economy are referred to as the *channels* of monetary policy. The major channels of monetary policy are or have been through liquidity, credit availability (or credit rationing), wealth, consumer and business confidence, interest rates, and exchange rates. These channels are important for examining the detail of the effects of monetary policy, i.e., how a given increase in the money supply will affect investment versus consumption spending.

The *liquidity effect* of an expansion of the money supply refers to the increase in spending that results from a relaxation of liquidity constraints. Presumably, some number of households and firms are constrained from spending all they would choose to spend if they had easier access to credit. Regarding households, these are typically newly formed households seeking to borrow in order to finance purchases of homes, cars, furniture, and major appliances. Regarding businesses, these are typically small, growing businesses seeking to borrow in order to finance expenditures on plant and equipment.

The liquidity constraints these households and businesses face are not to be confused with their wealth constraints. It is not, for example, that newly formed households are poor from the standpoint of their *lifetime* income. It is that their wealth is in the form of ''human capital'' and is therefore illiquid, not able to be used as collateral in borrowing. An increase in overall liquidity in the economy removes at least some of these households and businesses from their liquidity constraints and enables them to increase their spending.

Related to the liquidity channel is the credit-availability or credit-rationing channel. *Credit rationing* is defined to exist when there is an excess demand for credit at the prevailing interest rate. Credit rationing can result from state usury laws and from Regulation Q restrictions on deposit interest rates. Credit rationing also can result from the bank practice of borrowing

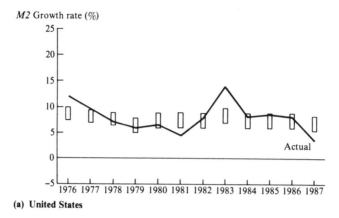

(a) United States

(b) West Germany

FIGURE 7.4 Monetary Policy, 1976–1987.
(a) Target ranges for M2 growth have varied between 5 and 10 percent annual growth. (b) Target ranges for M0 growth have been reduced over the years to a range of 3 to 6 percent annual growth. Notice that the West German central bank sets targets for base money, which is what central banks directly control. Also, the West German central bank sets growth targets that are lower than those set by the Fed and that are arguably consistent with long-run steady prices. Finally, during 1979–1981, the West German central bank tightened money in order to maintain the value of the German mark in the face of rising oil prices and high U.S. interest rates. All these indicate commitment to stable prices as opposed to allowing inflation.

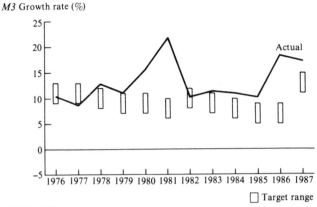

M3 Growth rate (%)

(c) **United Kingdom**

FIGURE 7.4 Continued
(c) Target ranges for *M3*, a monetary aggregate similar to *M2*, have
ranges between 5 and 15 percent annual growth, and actual *M3*
growth has often exceeded its targeted ranges. In particular, during
1979 – 1981, the British central bank loosened money in the face of
rising oil prices and high U.S. interest rates.

short and lending long, i.e., financing long-term fixed-interest-rate loans with
deposits whose interest rates are market-sensitive. Credit rationing can be
thought of as increasing the quality of credit when the price of credit—the
interest rate—is not free to bring the supply and demand for credit into
equilibrium. In fact, credit rationing is usually proxied by such measures as
the loan-to-value ratio, which are regarded as measures of creditworthiness.

As Figure 7.5 demonstrates, prior to the mid-1970s—and financial
innovation and deregulation—credit rationing appeared to be highly correlated with changes in interest rates. However, since the 1970s, credit rationing appears to be greatly reduced. When credit rationing was a significant
channel of monetary policy, monetary tightness would affect certain sectors
of the economy disproportionately. For example, monetary tightness would
choke off the flow of credit into the residential real estate market.

Since the mid-1970s, the major channels of monetary policy appear to
be through interest rates and exchange rates. The implications, therefore, of
monetary tightness are difficult to forecast from macromodels based on prior
experience. Monetary tightness may no longer work through choking off the
flow of credit to certain sectors of the economy, and monetary ease may no

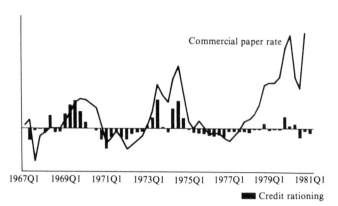

FIGURE 7.5   Changes in Credit Rationing, 1967 – 1981.
Prior to the mid-1970s—and financial innovation and deregulation
—there was a strong correlation between credit rationing and interest rates. (The index of credit rationing illustrated was constructed by
the authors from a periodic survey of commercial bank loan officers
conducted by the Federal Reserve until 1981. In this survey, loan officers were asked about changes in the willingness of their banks to
extend credit to various categories of borrowers.)

longer work by releasing certain households and businesses from liquidity
constraints. Revision of macromodels to determine the specifics of how monetary policy affects the economy today will necessarily await the accumulation of new experience.

7.6 THE CONSTITUTION OF MONEY

The men and women who have served in the Federal Reserve have, through
the years, attempted to responsibly exercise their control over the nation's
money supply. And yet, the years following creation of the Federal Reserve
have been characterized by banking crises, business cycles, the Great Depression, and more recently, persistent inflation. Could things have been worse
had the country remained on the nineteenth-century gold standard?

For a small minority of economists, capitalistic economies are inher-
ently instable, always verging on collapse, and are being continually rescued
from themselves by government intervention. For these economists, the lack
of success of the Fed in bringing stability to the economy is evidence of
capitalism's instability. For a different small minority of economists, capitalism is totally flexible, always in rational-expectations equilibrium, and
monetary policy is neutral in the short run as well as in the long run. For

these economists, the lack of success of the Fed is evidence of the neutrality of money.

The vast majority of economists believe in something between these two extreme views. For most economists, capitalistic economies tend, in the long run, to equilibriums featuring reasonably full employment. However, in the short run, these economies are characterized by a certain degree of fluctuation. In the short run, money is not neutral and can have either positive or negative effects on economic stability depending on how monetary policy is actually implemented.

Within this vast majority of economists, a debate rages on the issues of whether monetary policy has historically contributed to economic stability or not and whether it can be reformed so as to contribute to economic stability in the future. For the 1930s, for example, some economists argue that the Fed allowed the banking system to collapse and so allowed a not unusual recession to turn into the Great Depression. Other economists argue that money was passive during the Great Depression. The chairman of the Federal Reserve Board argued at the time that attempting to use monetary policy to get the country out of the depression would be like ''pushing on a string.''

7.6.1 Rules vs. Discretion

Milton Friedman has made famous the distinction between rules and discretion in monetary policy. *Rules* refer to operating procedures from which the monetary authority cannot deviate (except, perhaps, in an emergency). Friedman's famous rule is his proposal of constant growth of the money supply at a noninflationary rate of, say, 4 percent per year. *Discretion* refers to flexibility in the conduct of monetary policy. Discretion allows the Fed to ''tighten'' or ''loosen'' money as it determines most appropriate.

Rules offer the advantages of being simple and hence enforceable, credible, and automatic. A rule such as Friedman's constant growth rate is simple; it is simple to implement, simple for financial markets to observe, and simple for Congress to oversee. Moreover, because it is easy to administer, observe, and enforce, a rule is credible. Financial markets can believe in monetary policy based on rules. In contrast, discretion offers no guidance as to what the Fed is supposed to do. Officials of the Federal Reserve have to rely on their judgment to determine what to do. Financial markets must learn that they can trust the judgment of these officials.

A rule is automatic. There are no lags in implementing monetary policy. Therefore, a carefully chosen rule for monetary policy becomes an automatic stabilizer. In contrast, discretion requires, first, recognition of the problem in the economy to be addressed by monetary policy and, second, action by the monetary authority to implement the policy. Friedman referred to these as the "inside lag" in monetary policy. A similar inside lag would apply to fiscal policy. The "outside lag" in monetary or fiscal policy is the time from the implementation of the policy to the policy's effects in the economy.

Figure 7.6 presents the periodic ups and downs of an economy characterized by a business cycle. If, in reality, business cycles were as regular as pictured, there would be no lag problem in monetary or fiscal policy. The next up or down in the economy could be forecast, and the appropriate policy changes could be made in anticipation. In reality, however, business cycles are quite irregular, and the next upturn or downturn is always difficult to forecast.

Because of this difficulty in forecasting, it usually takes some time for the accumulation of data *after* a turn in the business cycle for policymakers to confirm the turn. This may take up to 6 months. With monetary policy, the rest of the inside lag is short. This is so because of the makeup of the Federal Reserve, which is a small, concensus-oriented decision-making body that conducts its meetings in private. In contrast, the U.S. Congress is a large, adversarial decision-making body that conducts its business in public. The inside lag of the Congress is only getting started with confirmation of a turn in the business cycle.

With monetary policy, then, the inside lag is relatively short. The outside lag, however, may be quite long. This is so because it takes time for

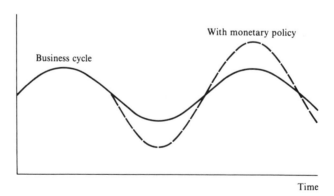

Time

FIGURE 7.6 Lag in Effect of Monetary Policy.
Because of "inside" and "outside" lags in monetary policy, contractionary policies implemented during the expansionary phase of a business cycle may take effect *after* the expansion is concluded and *during* the following recession, and expansionary policies implemented during the recessionary phase may take effect *after* the recession is concluded and *during* the following recovery. As a result, the business cycle is more severe.

changes in monetary policy to induce changes in consumer and business spending. Therefore, while the inside lag of monetary policy is short, its outside lag is long. With fiscal policy, it is just the opposite. It can easily take years for tax or appropriations bills to become enacted in response to a turn in the business cycle. While the inside lag of fiscal policy is long, the outside lag is short because taxes and government spending very directly affect aggregate demand.

Because of lags and the unpredictable periodicity of the business cycle, discretionary policy can increase rather than reduce economic instability. That is, the effect of policy designed to expand the economy during a recession or slow down the economy during an expansion can likely take place during the next phase of the business cycle. Therefore, counterrecessionary policy can likely *add* to inflationary pressures, and counterinflationary policy can likely *add* to recessionary pressures during the next phase in the business cycle.

As a result of concern for the potentially *destabilizing* effects of monetary policy, Friedman prefers rules to discretion. Rules are automatic; they do not suffer the problem of lags. While automaticity is an advantage, it must be remembered that economists such as Friedman believe that, most of the time, the economy fluctuates within tolerable limits. Furthermore, the possibility of suspending rules in order to deal with an emergency is not necessarily denied by those favoring rules.

7.6.2 What Rule?

With a rule, the monetary authority gives up some of its ability to respond precisely to the situation at hand. Since a monetary authority could always choose to do what the rule says to do, not having a rule allows it to do whatever is best. The argument for a rule, then, is not that a rule is optimal in every situation, but rather that an appropriate rule avoids serious mistakes. This suggests that rules should be evaluated on the basis of their *robustness*, their satisfactoriness under a variety of circumstances.

Milton Friedman's constant-growth rule undoubtedly reflects his research into the history of recessions and inflations in this and other countries. Regarding inflation, hardly any economist disagrees with the contention that inflation is impossible with slow and steady growth of the money supply. Regarding recession, there *is* controversy. Friedman accepts that the business cycle is to some extent inevitable in a capitalistic economy. With automatic stabilizers such as unemployment insurance and a money supply growing at a constant rate, these recessions will be of tolerable duration and severity. Most important, disasters such as the Great Depression would be avoided.

Pro-discretion economists, on the other hand, believe that discretion can improve the performance of the economy relative to performance with a rule such as constant money supply growth. These economists tend to deny that inflation has significant social costs, and they argue that the Fed is not likely to make policy blunders in the future as Friedman alleges they made during the 1930s.

The question of rules versus discretion brings us to the issue of the constitution of money. If there is to be a rule, then what rule? Among the rules that have been proposed are (1) a gold standard, (2) a price index rule, and (3) a money supply rule. With a gold standard, the value of money in terms of gold is fixed. This gives money a "real anchor" and keeps fluctuations in the quantity and value of money within certain limits. Economists have differing opinions about the acceptability of the historical fluctuations in the quantity and value of money under the nineteenth-century gold standard.[6]

Early this century, following the creation of the Federal Reserve System, the American economist Irving Fisher proposed a price index rule. The Federal Reserve would stand ready to redeem paper currency for a *variable* amount of gold having a constant purchasing power as measured by a general price index. Fisher's proposal received wide attention and almost led Congress to direct the Federal Reserve to control the money supply so as to keep the producer price level at its 1920s level. However, the Great Depression turned public attention toward the more immediate problem of combatting unemployment and deflation.[7]

Price index rules have recently regained the attention of monetary theorists. A number of academic economists have proposed forms of money that would stabilize its value relative to one or another price index. By the mid-1980s, the Federal Reserve began experimenting with adding a commodity price index to its set of targets, and the Treasury discussed use of commodity prices to help stabilize international exchange rates. Admittedly, these steps are far removed from establishing a price index *rule*.

The search for stable money reflects continuing dissatisfaction with the results of discretionary monetary policy. That the search has not reached a conclusion probably indicates that there is no easy solution. While the idea of a rule may sound simple, implementation may involve subtle complications. For example, the constant-money-growth rule requires an operational definition of the money supply. In a world of continuing financial innovation, either the Fed would lock in a definition for the money supply that would

---

[6]In conjunction with the report of the Gold Commission of 1980, Senator Jesse Helms and Congressman Ron Paul introduced bills to implement (different) gold standards.

[7]Even so, the Goldsborough Bill of 1932, if it had passed, would have required the Fed to restore the predepression price level.

soon become obsolete, or it would periodically redefine the money supply and have the potential to subvert the rule through these changing definitions.

7.6.3 Rules vs. Targets

It is instructive to conclude this chapter on monetary policy by drawing the distinction between rules and targets. The Full Employment Act of 1946 commits the federal government to maintaining full employment. The Humphrey-Hawkins Act of 1978 further commits the federal government to 0 percent inflation and 4 percent unemployment in the long run. The objectives of these laws, obviously, have not been obtained. Even so, officials of the Federal Reserve are in no danger of being arrested for breaking these laws.

While the federal government has established certain *goals* for monetary policy, the Federal Reserve is trusted to use its judgment to achieve these goals. That is, monetary policy is discretionary. The procedure by which the Fed acts on these goals is to use its tools, according to certain operating procedures, in order to affect certain targets which, in turn, are supposed to achieve the goals. Thus the sequence is operating procedures, targets, and goals. These targets are intermediate in the sense of being between what the Fed actually controls through its operating procedures—which is the monetary base—and the goals. Over the years, targets have included interest rates, exchange rates, monetary aggregates, and commodity prices.

These targets are different from rules for the following three reasons: Rules are chosen beforehand, are clearly chosen, and are internally and dynamically consistent. Targets, on the other hand, are often multiple in number, contradictory, expansive, and nonbinding. The Federal Reserve may have targets, simultaneously, for interest rates and monetary aggregates that are inconsistent with each other. These targets may be expressed in terms allowing wide variation, such as a growth rate for the *M1* money supply of between 4 and 10 percent. Actual variation beyond these limits may be allowed and need not be reversed in the future. Targets, as specified in the United States, are clearly part of discretionary policy. Contrariwise, in Japan, one single target, precise to one decimal point, is announced quarterly for growth of the money supply, and this target is invariably attained. In Japan, targets may effectively amount to rules.

The specification of multiple goals and targets serves the purpose of distancing Congress from responsibility for macroeconomic outcomes. Members of Congress can take credit for voting for such goals as lowering inflation and increasing employment while blaming the Federal Reserve for high interest rates, business cycles, trade deficits, and so on. The Federal Reserve is wipsawed from one crisis to another. Control over money and credit is continually used to achieve goals other than stabilizing the value of money.

The political pressure on the Fed to "do something" about whatever is the latest concern may imply that, in reality, there is little discretion to discretionary monetary policy.

7.7 SUMMARY

1. The Federal Reserve uses the tools of monetary policy, according to its operating procedures, in order to influence certain targets. Hitting these targets is, in turn, supposed to achieve certain goals.

2. The tools of monetary policy include (1) open-market operations, (2) reserve requirements, (3) the discount rate, (4) selective controls, and (5) moral suasion.

3. The most important tool is open-market operations, which is the buying and selling of Treasury securities. Through open-market operations, the Fed creates and destroys base money ($M0$).

4. New base money is converted into a multiple amount if $M1$ or $M2$ money through the money-multiplier process. The money multiplier m equals $(1 + c)/(r + c + e)$, where c is the public's demand for currency as a fraction of deposits, r is the required reserve ratio, and e is bank demand for excess reserves as a fraction of deposits. Note that the money multiplier is a function involving decisions of the Fed (r), the banks (e), and the public (c).

5. Because of the unpredictable periodicity of the business cycle and lags in monetary policy, certain economists advocate rules versus discretion, an example of which is Milton Friedman's rule for 4 percent annual growth of the money supply. Advocates of rules believe that appropriately chosen rules would be automatic stabilizers. While not optimal in every situation, they would provide some dampening of the business cycle and avoid policy blunders.

6. Instead of rules, monetary policy is actually conducted with targets that are multiple in number, allow wide latitude, and are nonbinding. Multiple goals and targets allow and may even impel the Federal Reserve to "do something" about macroeconomic problems, whatever they are, as they develop.

7.8 EXERCISES

1. Use Figure 7.3a to illustrate the effects of the Fed decreasing the discount rate.

2. Use Figure 7.3a to examine how a "penalty" discount rate, i.e., a discount rate higher than the federal funds rate, changes the Fed's operating procedure.

3. Why may financial innovation and deregulation have contributed to interest rates rising so high after the Fed tightened money in 1979?

4. Distinguish between rules, discretion, and *laissez faire* in the conduct of monetary policy.

5. Correlate changes in monetary policy during 1986 – 1987 with subsequent changes in economic conditions.

6. According to Friedman and Schwartz, why was monetary policy so inept during the Great Depression? (See *A Monetary History of the United States*, pp. 407 – 419.)

7. According to Arthur Burns, why is monetary policy in the United States biased toward inflation? Given his analysis, why do you think monetary policy in West Germany and Japan is not biased toward inflation?

7.9 REFERENCES

Burns, A. F. "The Anguish of Central Banking," *Federal Reserve Bulletin*, September 1987, pp. 687 – 698.

Dorn, J. A. and Schwartz, A. J. (Eds.). *The Search for Stable Money*. Chicago: University of Chicago Press, 1987.

Fisher, I. *Stable Money: A History of the Movement*. New York: Adelphi, 1934.

Friedman, M. "The Lag in Effect of Monetary Policy," *Journal of Political Economy*, 69, October 1961, pp. 447 – 466. Reprinted in *The Optimum Quantity of Money and Other Essays*. Chicago: Adeline, 1969, pp. 237–260.

Friedman, M. *A Program for Monetary Stability*. New York: Fordham University Press, 1959.

Friedman, M. "A Monetary and Fiscal Framework for Economic Stability," *American Economic Review*, 38, June 1948, pp. 245 – 264. Reprinted in *Essays in Positive Economics*. Chicago: University of Chicago Press, 1953.

Friedman, M., and Schwartz, A. J. "The Great Contraction," in *A Monetary History of the United States*. Princeton: Princeton University Press, 1963, pp. 299 – 419.

Kydland, F. E., and Prescott, E. C. "Rules Rather than Discretion: The Inconsistency of Optimal Plans," *Journal of Political Economy*, 85, June 1977, pp. 473 – 491.

Mayer, T. *Monetary Policy in the United States*. New York: Random House, 1968.

"Monetary Policy and Open-Market Operations During 1986," *Federal Reserve Bank of New York Quarterly Review*, Spring 1987, pp. 35 – 56.

"Monetary Policy and Open-Market Operations During 1987," *Federal Reserve Bank of New York Quarterly Review*, Spring 1988, pp. 41 – 58.

Simons, H. C. "Rules versus Authorities in Monetary Policy" *Journal of Political Economy*, 44, February 1936, pp. 1 – 30. Reprinted in *Readings in Monetary Theory*. Homewood, Ill.: Richard D. Irwin, 1951, pp. 337 – 369.

Tobin, J. "Monetary Policies and the Economy: The Transmission Mechanism," *Southern Economic Journal*, 44, January 1978, pp. 421–431.

Tobin, J. "Stabilization Policy Ten Years After," *Brookings Papers on Economic Activity*, 1:1980, pp. 19–71.

—————— *MANAGERIAL CASE* ————————————————————

MONEY AND THE GREAT DEPRESSION

The Great Depression represents the most serious economic catastrophe the United States has suffered short of war itself. A *short list* of contributing factors identified by economists include stock market speculation, tax increases, wage-and-price controls and regulation of business (i.e., the National Recovery Act), the Smoot-Hawley tariff, and growing concerns for world peace because of the rise of totalitarianism in Europe. There certainly was enough blame to go around. For a long time, however, monetary policy during the depression was considered benign. Then, during the early 1960s, Milton Friedman and Anna J. Schwartz published *A Monetary History of the United States*, the result of a massive historical investigation and one of the most influential books in the history of economics.

Friedman and Schwartz demonstrated that the data of the 1930s correlate well with the quantity theory of money. That is, the movements in real and nominal income and in production, sales, employment, and prices corresponded with movements in the quantity of money. This is illustrated in Exhibit 7.1 by the movements in $M1$, falling from 1929 to 1933, recovering thereafter to 1936, falling again during 1937, and beginning a sustained recovery in 1938. The recessionary periods of the 1930s were precisely 1929 to 1933 and 1937.

Interestingly, the movements in $M1$ are not at all paralleled by movements in the monetary base ($M0$). The monetary base moves rather steadily upward all throughout this turbulent period. The key to the movements in $M1$ is not to be found in the monetary base, but is to be found in the *money multiplier*. From 1930 to 1933, a series of bank panics lead to massive withdrawals of currency from the banking system. This is indicated by the movements of the ratio of currency to deposits c shown in Exhibit 7.2.

Friedman and Schwartz fault the Fed for not replenishing depleted bank reserves with injections of new base money through open-market purchases. Had the Fed done so, Friedman and Schwartz theorize, liquidity would have been maintained, and the banking system would not have collapsed. This may have prevented the downturn in the economy from becoming so severe.

While the Federal Reserve Board was created specifically to end bank panics, the bank panics of the early 1930s were the worst in history. The Fed absolved itself of responsibility for these bank panics, claiming that the newly formed Reconstruction Finance Corporation had responsibility for failing banks and other corporations.

Dollars (billions)

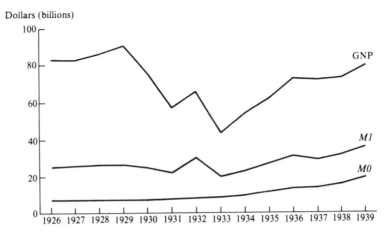

EXHIBIT 7.1   Money, the Money Multiplier, and the Great Depression.
Source: Data from Philip Cagan, *Determinants and Effects of Changes in the Stock of Money, 1875 – 1960* (Washington, D.C.: National Bureau of Economic Research, 1965).

Deposits (%)

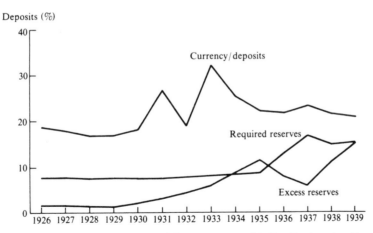

EXHIBIT 7.2   Determinants of the Money Multiplier During the Great Depression.
Source: Currency-to-deposit ratio: Milton Friedman and Anna J. Schwartz, *A Monetary History of the United States, 1867 – 1960* (Washington, D.C.: National Bureau of Economic Research, 1963); required reserve ratio and excess reserve ratio (Federal Reserve Member Banks): Philip Cagan, *Determinants and Effects of Changes in the Stock of Money, 1875 – 1960* (Washington, D.C.: National Bureau of Economic Research, 1965).

Was Money Tight During 1929 – 1933?

Keynesian economists, pointing to the steady growth of the monetary base and to falling short-term interest rates, claim that money was "easy" during the Great Depression. As Exhibit 7.3*a* illustrates, short-term interest rates did, in fact, fall during 1929 – 1933. However, short-term interest rates are only one measure of the "price" of money. Another "price" of money is the spread between short- and long-term interest rates, sometimes referred to as the *liquidity premium*; yet another is the spread between risky and risk-free interest rates, sometimes referred to as the *risk premium*. As Exhibit 7.3*a* also illustrates, these "prices" of money showed money to be tight during the Great Depression. Other measures of monetary tightness include commodity prices, which fell precipituously during the Great Depression, and credit rationing. As Exhibit 7.3*b* shows, the supply of credit was nearly every-where insufficient to meet demand at the prevailing interest rate.

Required Reserves and the Recession of 1937

The fall in *M1* during 1937 is traced to a particularly poor decision by the Fed. Because of reduced opportunity costs of holding excess reserves and increased concern for liquidity following the bank panics of the early 1930s, banks began to increase their reserve holdings. This buildup of excess reserves worried the Federal Reserve, which feared loss of control over the money supply. Therefore, the Fed decided to "sop up" the excess reserves with a two-step increase in required reserve ratios.[1]

Banks, however, wanted to carry excess reserves, and the increase in required reserves simply caused banks to further increase their reserve holdings. This again reduced the money multiplier and precipitated the fall in *M1* in 1937.

---

[1]This two-step increase in required reserve ratios was described as "precautionary" by the Fed (*Annual Report of the Federal Reserve Board*, 1937, p. 4).

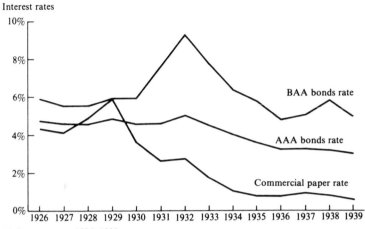

(a) Interest rates, 1926–1939

(b) Excess demand for mortgage credit

EXHIBIT 7.3   The Great Depression.
(a) While short-term interest rates fell during 1929 – 1939, long-term interest rates, especially those on riskier securities, rose. (b) A periodic survey conducted by the National Association of Real Estate Boards showed that credit was tight in most areas of the country during the Great Depression. Shown here is the percent of real estate boards responding "loans seeking money," as opposed to "money seeking loans" or "equilibrium," when asked about the availability of real estate loans at prevailing interest rates in their communities.
Source: Commercial and Financial Chronicle, various issues.

PART THREE

Sectorial Analysis

8

Investment

8.1 INTRODUCTION

Investment is not only a large component of GNP, it is also a highly volatile and procyclic component. Managers in construction and in producers' durable equipment manufacturing are naturally concerned with forecasts of investment demand. Economists debate whether the correlation between investment and the business cycle is due to fluctuations in investment demand *causing* fluctuations in total spending or to fluctuations in total spending *causing* fluctuations in investment demand. Fiscal and monetary authorities are concerned with how their policies affect investment because the amount of investment spending will, in the long run, determine economic growth, productivity, and standards of living. This chapter examines the composition and behavior of investment spending and its connections to economic growth, productivity, and the business cycle.

8.2 SOME DEFINITIONS

By *investment*, economists mean expenditures on productive capacity, or *physical* investment. This definition contrasts with the common use of this word to refer to *financial* investment. The everyday definition focuses on what investment means to an individual. For an individual, activities such as depositing money in a bank account and purchasing shares of stock are considered to be "investments." However, these activities do not themselves add to the economy's productive capacity. These activities rearrange *ownership* of productive capacity but do not add to the economy's productive capacity; they are therefore not themselves investments in the economic sense.

173

8.2.1 Three NIPA Categories

According to the national income and product accounts (NIPA), investment includes three categories of expenditure: fixed business investment, changes in business inventories, and residential construction. *Fixed business investment* includes nonresidential construction and producers' durable equipment, or — in business jargon — plant and equipment. This categorization of investment emphasizes additions to the economy's stock of *physical capital*. Examples of physical capital include factories, warehouses, retail and service outlets, and many other kinds of commercial buildings; machinery, professional instruments, computers, construction and farm equipment, trucks, railroads, and many other kinds of tools and vehicles; raw materials, work in progress and finished inventories; and single and multifamily housing.

Table 8.1 presents the composition of investment during 1986. To be precise, Table 8.1 presents *gross private domestic investment*, which by definition excludes the investment expenditures made by federal, state, and local governments. As can be seen, spending on business plant and equipment constitutes about two-thirds of investment. Because of the magnitude of spending on business plant and equipment, this chapter focuses on these two categories of investment.

8.2.2 Stock of Capital vs. Flow of Investment

Investment represents additions to the stock of productive capacity. The stock of productive capacity includes current and past investment net of their accumulated depreciation. For 1986, fixed private capital, including business plant and equipment and residential structures, but not including business inventories, was estimated to be $7,670.1 billion, which compares to gross private domestic investment of $671.0 billion (see Table 8.2). This illustrates that at any given time productive capacity is determined mainly by *past* as opposed to current investment.

TABLE 8.1   Gross Private Domestic Investment, 1986 ($ Billions)

GNP	$4235.0
Gross private domestic investment	671.0
Nonresidential structures	137.4
Producers' durable equipment	299.5
Change in business inventories	15.7
Residential construction	218.3

Source: Survey of Current Business, March 1988, pp. 4–5.

TABLE 8.2   Fixed Private Capital, 1986 ($ Billions)

	Gross	*Net*[a]
Total	12,798.4	7,670.1
Nonresidential structures	3,565.1	2,045.6
Producers' durable goods	3,439.0	1,876.7
Residential construction	5,794.3	3,747.9

Source: Survey of Current Business, August 1987, pp. 100–103.
[a]Net represents gross less accumulated depreciation. All figures are on a current-cost basis.

8.2.3 Gross vs. Net Investment

Because almost all physical capital wears out with use, gross investment does not indicate the change in the stock of physical capital over a period of time. Instead, the increase in the stock of physical capital is gross investment *less* depreciation. Depreciation is referred to in the national income and product accounts as *capital consumption allowance*. Gross investment less this capital consumption allowance is known as *net investment* (see Table 8.3).

Note that the components of gross investment, other than changes in business inventories, must be positive. However, if investment spending is lower than the capital consumption allowance, net investment will be negative. This actually occurred during the Great Depression when investment spending fell to near zero, hitting a low of $1.0 billion during 1932. During the Great Depression, net investment was negative, and the stock of productive capacity fell.

During the 1970s, net investment, while remaining positive, fell as a fraction of GNP. During this time, productivity lagged, and standards of living among working-class families fell. While productive capacity is at any time mainly a function of past investment, lack of investment eventually takes its toll.

TABLE 8.3   Net Investment, 1986 ($ Billions)

GNP	4,235.0
Gross private domestic investment	671.0
Less capital consumption allowance	456.7
Net private domestic investment	214.3

Source: Survey of Current Business, March 1988, pp. 4–5.

8.2.4 Other Forms of Investment

A number of additional forms of investment—not well represented in the national income and product accounts—should be considered. These include, but are not limited to, research and development, exploration, and education. Even the traditional categories of investment are undergoing change. For example, it is estimated that 20 percent of investment in producers' durable goods involves purchases of computers, and that 1 percent involves purchases of industrial robots.

The traditional view of productive capacity is quite mechanistic, emphasizing labor-saving machinery and nonhuman energy. However, total horsepower in this country, in automobiles, electrical generating plants, factories, and other forms of physical capital, has been relatively stable during the 1980s—estimated at 32.5 billion in 1985. What has been happening is that investments in physical capital have been more energy efficient because of advances in technology. In addition, the industrial mix has shifted from traditional "smokestack" enterprises to new technology-based and service-based enterprises.

In 1986, research and development expenditures totaled $118.6 billion, or 2.8 percent of GNP, an amount rivaling net investment in plant and equipment. As Table 8.4 shows, some industries are more research and development intensive than others.

Generally, research and development expenditures are expensed, even though they are made for the purpose of producing new technologies that will be available for the indefinite future. Regardless of their tax and accounting treatment, and even regardless of their treatment by the national income and product accounts, research and development expenditures have the economic characteristics of investments. That is, research and development expenditures will increase the quality and quantity of products and services that can be produced in the future.

TABLE 8.4 Research and Development Expenditures, 1986 (Selected Industries as a Percent of Sales)

All industries	3.8
Aircraft and missiles	16.9
Professional and scientific instruments	9.3
Electrical equipment	7.2
Machinery	6.0
Chemicals	4.5
Motor vehicles	3.4

Source: Statistical Abstract of the United States, 1987, p. 567.

The difference between research and development and the traditional categories of investment is that research and development adds to the stock of technology, which is difficult to measure, while the traditional categories of investment involve additions to the stock of physical capital, for which market values are more or less available. Conservatism in the valuation of intangible assets may explain why research and development expenditures are not treated as investments but are simply expensed.

8.3 CAPITAL BUDGETING

Capital budgeting refers to the process within companies that leads to investment spending. Capital budgeting usually starts with engineering, marketing, and economic studies that forecast the revenues and expenses of projects under consideration. Then, these forecasts of revenues and expenses are evaluated using one or another investment criteria in order to determine which, if any, of the projects will actually be undertaken.

Interest rates are usually considered to be parameters in this process. *Given* the interest rate, a project will either be found to be profitable and will be undertaken or else it will not. This section, by going through the process of capital budgeting, will demonstrate the negative relation between interest rates and investment demand.

Forecasts of revenues and expenses are necessarily subjective and depend to a large part on business confidence. This section also will demonstrate the positive relation between business confidence and investment demand. Finally, depreciation and tax rules determine how revenues and expenses become translated into cash flows. This section also will demonstrate how depreciation and tax rules can encourage or discourage investment spending.

8.3.1 Net Present Value

Net present value is an investment criterion that takes into account the time value of money. Specifically, the net present value of a project is the value *today* of its present and future cash flows. Usually, a project involves an initial negative cash flow followed by a series of positive cash flows. For example, the initial negative cash flow may be the investment outlays required to construct a factory, and the following series of positive cash flows may be the operating income during each of the years of the factory's economic life. What net present value does is appropriately discount the future cash flows given the required rate of return.

Figure 8.1 illustrates hypothetical sequences of revenues and expenses associated with an investment project that we shall imagine to be a factory.

First, expenses are initially high as a result of construction costs. After the factory is built, expenses fall. Then, some time in the future, expenses rise because of maintenance, repair, and modernization costs. Second, revenues are initially low because until the factory is built, there is no production to sell. After the factory is built, revenue increases. Then, some time in the future, because of competition, technical obsolescence, and the product life cycle, revenue falls.

During the initial, construction phase of the project, cash flows are negative. During the following, operating phase, cash flows are positive. Two points of intersection are noteworthy. The first point of intersection is where the cash flow turns from negative to positive. In business jargon, this is where the project goes from being "in the red" to being "in the black." This is a kind of *break-even point*. The second point of intersection is where the cash flow turns from positive back to negative. This is the *shutdown point*. At this point, the factory will be shut down and the project terminated. At the beginning of the project, when future revenues and expenses are being forecasted, there is probably a lot of uncertainty about when this shutdown point will occur. Only as the future reveals itself will this shutdown point come to be known with any degree of certainty.

For a project to be profitable, it is obvious that the total of the positive cash flows during the operating phase of the project must at least equal the

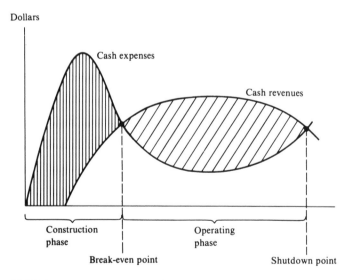

FIGURE 8.1 A Prototypical Investment Project.
Source: Adapted from John R. Hicks, *Capital and Time* (Oxford: Clarendon Press, 1973), p. 15.

total of the negative cash flows during the construction phase. However, mere comparison of these totals is not enough. For a project to be profitable, the future, positive cash flows must be large enough so that when discounted to present value they are still larger than the initial, negative cash flows.

Analysis of a simplified model will help clarify this point. Figure 8.2 presents an investment project with one initial negative cash flow, referred to as the *investment outlay*, followed by a series of constant positive cash flows, referred to as the *operating cash flows*. The investment outlay can be considered to be the total of the initial negative cash flows during the construction phase, the constant operating cash flows can be considered to be an average of the positive cash flows during the operating phase, and the length of the series can be considered to be the time period between the break-even and shutdown points.

Note that the simple sum of the operating cash flows equals $20,000, which is double the initial outlay of $10,000. However, this does not necessarily mean that the net present value of the project is positive. The interest rate must be used to bring the operating cash flows to present value. In Table 8.5 the net present value of this project is calculated using an interest rate of 10 percent. At this interest rate, net present value is positive and the investment is profitable.

An alternative method for calculating net present value for projects that have constant operating cash flows involves use of annuity tables. Use of

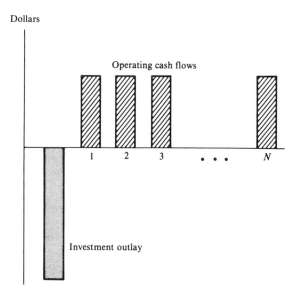

FIGURE 8.2   A Simplified Prototypical Investment Project.

TABLE 8.5   Calculation of Net Present Value

Time Period	Cash Flow	Discount Factor (at 10 percent)	Present Value (Col. 2 × Col. 3)
0	− $10,000	1.0000	− $10,000.00
1	2,000	0.9091	1,818.20
2	2,000	0.8264	1,652.40
3	2,000	0.7513	1,502.60
4	2,000	0.6830	1,366.00
5	2,000	0.6209	1,241.80
6	2,000	0.5645	1,129.00
7	2,000	0.5132	1,026.40
8	2,000	0.4665	933.00
9	2,000	0.4241	848.20
10	2,000	0.3855	771.00
		Net present value	$2,288.60

annuity tables is normally taught in managerial finance. Basically, net present value is calculated using annuity tables in the following manner:

$$NPV = -I + \sum_{t=1}^{N}\left(\frac{1}{1-R}\right)^{t}OCF \tag{8.1}$$

where NPV is net present value, I is investment outlay, N is economic life, R is the required rate of return, and OCF is operating cash flow. A number from the annuity tables corresponding to the interest rate R and the number of periods N is substituted for the summation of discount factors. In the present case, $NPV = -\$10,000 + (6.1446)\$2000 = \$2289.20$. The slight difference between the two answers is attributable to rounding error and, given the uncertainties in forecasts of future cash flows, is inconsequential. Use of annuity tables was important for calculating net present value prior to the widespread availability of computers. Today, spreadsheet software facilitates calculation along the lines illustrated in Table 8.5. Nevertheless, use of annuity tables is still helpful in the classroom for teaching the basics of capital budgeting because of its simplicity.

8.3.2 Tax and Depreciation Rules

Depreciation and tax rules play an important role in determining net present value. Taxes on business profits reduce the level, and depreciation rules affect the timing of cash flows. In 1986, Congress passed a comprehensive tax reform bill that established new depreciation and tax rules. On the one hand, corporate and individual tax rates were reduced, and on the other hand, the investment tax credit and long-term capital tax preference were eliminated and depreciation schedules were stretched out. The net effect somewhat reduced the incentives for investment spending.

To examine how depreciation and tax rules affect investment demand, consider the investment project described in Table 8.5. Let's say that the investment outlay is to be depreciated on a straight-line basis over the project's economic life, that the income generated by the project is to be taxed at a 46 percent rate, that salvage value will be zero, and that the investment qualifies for a 10 percent investment tax credit. This constitutes an approximation of the pre-tax reform rules. Because of the assumption of straight-line depreciation, depreciation will be $\delta = I/N = \$1000$. Operating cash flows, equal to after-tax profits plus depreciation, are given in Table 8.6 as $1540 per year, reduced from $2000. Notice that depreciation is subtracted from operating income in determining taxable income but, not being a cash expense, is added back in determining operating cash flow.

Under the pre-tax reform rules, net present value would be equal to the investment outlay net of the investment tax credit plus the present value of the operating cash flows; that is,

$$NPV = -(1-0.10)\$10{,}000 + (6.1446)\$1540 = \$463$$

To illustrate the effect of tax reform, let the tax rate be reduced to 34 percent and eliminate the investment tax credit. Table 8.7 shows that the revised operating cash flow is $1660. However, offsetting the increase in operating cash flows is elimination of the investment tax credit. With the new

TABLE 8.6   Calculation of Operating Cash Flows: Pre-Tax Reform Rules

Operating income	$2000
− Depreciation	− 1000
= Taxable income	1000
− Taxes (at 46 percent)	460
= After-tax profit	540
+ Depreciation	1000
= Operating cash flow	$1540

TABLE 8.7 Calculation of Operating Cash Flows: Post-Tax Reform Rules

Operating income	$2000
− Depreciation	− 1000
= Taxable income	1000
− Taxes (at 34 percent)	340
= After-tax profits	660
+ Depreciation	1000
= Operating cash flow	$1660

tax rules, this project has a smaller, but still positive net present value; that is,

$$NPV = -\$10,000 + (6.1446)\$1660 = \$200$$

8.3.2.1 Accelerated Depreciation

The Tax Reform Act of 1986 partially returned depreciation schedules to straight line from the greatly accelerated schedules allowed by the ''accelerated capital recovery system'' of the Tax Reform Act of 1981. Depreciation schedules for investments in equipment and vehicles were slightly stretched out and for investments in commercial and residential buildings were significantly stretched out.

Acceleration of depreciation does not affect the total dollars of depreciation that will be allowed over the life of an investment. However, it does affect *when* depreciation will be allowed. With accelerated depreciation, more depreciation will be allowed earlier and less later. Accelerated depreciation can either take the form of depreciation over a shorter period of time or it can take the form of a formula such as double declining balance—as shown in Table 8.8—which front-loads depreciation within a given time period. Because of the time value of money, accelerated depreciation will increase the net present value of an investment.

Table 8.8 contrasts straight-line versus accelerated depreciation of a 5-year investment. Notice that the undiscounted sums of the depreciation charges are the same—$1000—under the straight-line and double declining balance methods. However, because the earlier depreciation charges are higher with accelerated depreciation, their present value is higher. Accelerated depreciation, therefore, increases investment demand.

TABLE 8.8   Straight-Line versus Accelerated Depreciation

Year	Discount Factor (at 10 percent)	Straight Line[a]	Present Value (Col. 2 × Col. 3)	Double Declining Balance[a]	Present Value (Col. 2 × Col. 5)
1	0.9091	$100	$ 90.91	$200	$181.82
2	0.8264	200	165.28	320	264.45
3	0.7513	200	159.26	192	144.25
4	0.6830	200	136.60	115	78.55
5	0.6209	200	124.18	115	71.40
6	0.5645	100	56.45	58	32.74
		Total present value	$732.68		$773.21

[a]Incorporates "half-year convention"; double declining balance switches to straight line at the optimal point.

8.3.2.2 Inflation and Depreciation

Inflation affects investment demand in several ways. Inflation increases interest rates as well as future revenues and costs. Inflation inevitably increases the riskiness of investments. Inflation also erodes the value of depreciation. While cash must be expended right now, in the present, to make an investment, depreciation rules only allow this cost to be written off over a period of time. With inflation, and with nonindexed depreciation, the value of depreciation write-offs to be taken in the future will be reduced. Inflation combined with nonindexed depreciation reduces the investment demand.

To illustrate the effects of inflation on investment demand, the problem discussed in the previous section is modified in the following way: Let inflation increase operating income by 10 percent per year, and let inflation increase interest rates by 10 percentage points, from 10 to 20 percent. The present value of operating income, as calculated in Table 8.9, is $9094, which is less than the investment outlay of $10,000. The net present value of this investment, because of the effects of inflation on the value of future depreciation write-offs, is negative.

It was because of the inflation of the 1970s that Congress, in 1981, greatly accelerated depreciation schedules. Most equipment and vehicles were to be depreciated over 3- or 5-year periods, and buildings were to be depreciated over 15-year periods. By accelerating depreciation, the effect of inflation on reducing the value of depreciation was reduced and the incentive to invest was restored. By 1986, however, inflation was significantly reduced.

TABLE 8.9 Inflation and Depreciation

Year	Operating Income	Depre- ciation	Taxable Income	Income Taxes (at 34 percent)	After-Tax Profit	Operating Cash Flow	Discount Factor (at 20 percent)	Present Value
1	$2000	$1000	$1000	$340	$ 660	$1660	0.8333	$1383
2	2200	1000	1200	408	792	1792	0.6944	1244
3	2420	1000	1420	483	937	1937	0.5787	1121
4	2662	1000	1662	565	1097	2097	0.4823	1011
5	2928	1000	1928	656	1272	2272	0.4019	913
6	3221	1000	2221	755	1466	2466	0.3349	826
7	3543	1000	2543	865	1678	2678	0.2791	747
8	3897	1000	2897	985	1912	2912	0.2326	677
9	4287	1000	3287	1118	2169	3169	0.1938	614
10	4716	1000	3716	1263	2453	3453	0.1615	558
							Total present value	$9094

The need to offset the effect of inflation by accelerating depreciation was gone. Congress, therefore, stretched depreciation schedules back out.

8.3.3 Internal Rate of Return

Net present value is one of several investment criteria. Another criterion, *internal rate of return*, is appealing because it expresses the return on a project in the form of an interest rate. This facilitates comparison of the project's return with the cost of funds used to finance the project. Fortunately, for most investments, internal rate of return is mathematically equivalent to net present value; i.e., the internal rate of return and net present value criteria suggest the same investment decisions.

The *internal rate of return* of a project is that interest rate which sets the project's net present value equal to zero. Using the net present value method, the known quantities are the investment outlay I, operating cash flows OCF, and required rate of return R. These are used to determine net present value NPV. A positive net present value is the signal to undertake the investment. Using the internal rate of return method, the known quantities again are the investment outlay I, operating cash flows OCF, and required rate of return R. The first two are used to determine the internal rate of return IRR. An internal rate of return larger than the required rate of return is the signal to undertake the investment. Equation (8.2) presents the formula for internal rate of return:

$$I = \sum_{t=1}^{N} \left(\frac{1}{1 + IRR} \right)^{t} OCF \tag{8.2}$$

Comparing this to Equation (8.1), notice that if net present value equals zero, then the internal rate of return is the required rate of return. Of course, this derives from the definition of internal rate of return.

For all investments in which there is an initial negative cash flow, i.e., the investment outlay followed by a series of positive cash flows (the operating cash flows), the internal rate of return method is equivalent to the net present value method. For these investments, the relationship between alternative required rates of return and net present value is illustrated in Figure 8.3. Note that if the internal rate of return is greater than the required rate of return, net present value is necessarily positive. Therefore, the two decision rules are equivalent.

While internal rate of return is equivalent to net present value in many cases, there are cases in which the equivalence between these two decision rules breaks down. In these cases, net present value should be relied upon.

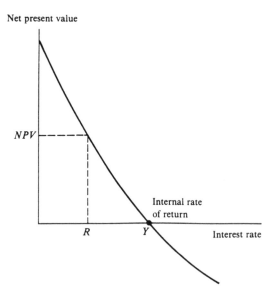

FIGURE 8.3   Net Present Value vs. Internal Rate of Return:
"Normal" Projects.
The internal rate of return of a project is that interest rate which sets
its net present value equal to zero. In the graph, this would be the
point Y, where the curve crosses the horizontal axis. Notice that for
all required rates of return R less than Y, net present value is greater
than zero.

One instance in which the equivalence breaks down is in deciding between
mutually exclusive projects. It is possible for internal rate of return to indicate
that one project is preferred over another when, actually, net present value
indicates otherwise. This usually occurs when a small-scale project featuring
a large percentage return is compared with a large-scale project featuring a
return that is not so large in percentage terms. Sometimes it is better to make
an extra 1 percent on a million dollars than an extra 100 percent on a thousand
dollars.

　　Another instance in which the equivalence between internal rate of
return and net present value breaks down occurs when there are negative
cash flows other than at the beginning of the project. For example, at the
conclusion of a strip-mining project, the land may have to be refilled and
recontoured. In this case, there may be zero, one, or multiple internal rates
of return, and none of them is useful for decision making.

　　The usual equivalence between internal rate of return and net present
value is both an advantage and disadvantage. Because internal rate of return

is usually equivalent to net present value, managers can use it for its appealing similarity to interest rates. However, because managers often use internal rate of return, they may feel that it should somehow be relied on even in those cases where it is not appropriate.

8.4 INVESTMENT AND THE BUSINESS CYCLE

Economists disagree sharply on the role of investment in the business cycle. While it is obvious that investment spending is highly correlated with the business cycle, economists debate whether fluctuations in investment spending *cause* fluctuations in total economic activity or if fluctuations in total economic activity *cause* fluctuations in investment spending. This section reviews the major competing theories of the role of investment in the business cycle.

8.4.1 Neo-Keynesian Theory

Neo-Keynesian economists argue that fluctuations in investment are major causes of the business cycle. Neo-Keynesians analyze the roles of business confidence, interest rates, and the user cost of capital in determining investment spending. Fluctuations in investment spending, in turn, through the multiplier process, lead to magnified fluctuations in total spending.

Neo-Keynesian theory assumes the existence of unemployed resources (at least in the short run). With unemployed resources, additional demand calls forth additional production. (With fully employed resources, additional aggregate demand ''merely'' results in inflation and additional sectoral demand ''merely'' results in changes in relative prices and a shift in production.) This is why neo-Keynesians examine the determinants of investment demand. If stronger business confidence, lower interest rates, or a lower user cost of capital induces increased investment spending, this will result in an increased gross national product. If business confidence weakens, interest rates increase, or the user cost of capital rises, then the gross national product will fall.

Even if resources are fully employed, neo-Keynesian analysis of investment demand is important. As is parenthetically noted above, if resources are fully employed, changes in sectoral demand result in changes in relative prices and a shift in production. Therefore, changes in business confidence, interest rates, and the user cost of capital can shift production from consumption to investment. In the long run, this will have enormous implications for economic growth, productivity, and standards of living. Furthermore, fiscal and monetary policy can—purposefully or not—favor investment in certain industries relative to others. For example, historical cost depreciation during a period of inflation will effectively constitute an "industrial policy" favoring research and development – intensive industries versus physical capital – intensive or "smokestack" industries.

8.4.1.1 Business Confidence

More than 50 years ago, John Maynard Keynes argued that business investment plans were dominated by "animal spirits." Forecasts of future revenue and cost, 10 or more years out, amounted "to little and sometimes to nothing."[1] Instead of being based on sound judgment, business confidence followed the herd. When "bullish," business confidence drove the economy as well as the stock market upward, and when "bearish," it drove the economy and the market downward. Mr. Keynes made an assumption that is almost the opposite of today's rational expectations theory and an assumption that you yourself are contradicting by your study of business and economics.

Today, few economists accept the original Keynesian view of business confidence. Yet, from time to time, "bulls" and "bears" do seem to be stampeding. Moreover, nearly all professional forecasters incorporate the data of surveys of business confidence into their models.

As Equations (8.1) and (8.2) make clear, the net present value and internal rate of return of an investment project depend positively on the forecast of future operating cash flows. Business confidence can affect the subjective profitability of investment in two ways. First, if business confidence is strong, business executives may predict higher operating cash flows. Second, if business confidence is strong, business executives may use a lower required rate of return; i.e., business executives may use a smaller risk premium on top of the risk-free rate of return. Both these effects will increase the net present values of projects under consideration.

8.4.1.2 Interest Rates

Referring again to Equation (8.1), the net present value of a project depends negatively on the required rate of return used to discount future operating cash flows. Higher interest rates, due, for example, to monetary policy, will reduce the present value of the future operating cash flows and may turn the net present value of certain projects negative. Similarly, referring to Equation (8.2), higher interest rates may make the internal rate of return of an investment project insufficient.

Higher interest rates and overall monetary tightness may choke off investment in a different way. Banks and other financial intermediaries may

[1]*The General Theory* (New York: Harcourt, Brace, 1936), pp. 149–150.

simply refuse to lend to businesses, especially to new and small businesses, regardless of the loan rate. This is known as *credit rationing*. The available evidence suggests that prior to bank deregulation, much of the effect of monetary policy was transmitted through credit rationing as opposed to loan rates.

8.4.1.3 User Cost of Capital

The *user cost of capital* is the rental price, as opposed to the purchase price, of capital goods. When the rental price or user cost of capital is high, the optimal capital stock as well as investment spending will fall. If there were rental markets in all capital goods, then the rental price or user cost would be immediately available. However, because capital goods are heterogeneous, rental markets in capital goods are not common. Accordingly, economists estimate the user cost of capital based on what a company would need over the lifetime of capital goods to cover their purchase prices.

Imagine that a firm purchases a capital good, uses it for one period, and then resells it. What would be the cost of having used this capital good (other than transaction costs)? If this capital good was purchased with borrowed funds, it is obvious that part of its cost is the interest paid on the borrowed funds. However, even if this capital good was purchased with a person's or a corporation's own funds, the interest *forgone* is still part of the cost. In addition, the depreciation of this capital good is part of the cost, since depreciation would reduce proceeds on resale. Therefore, two components of the user cost of capital are interest and depreciation.

Measure capital so that its unit price is \$1, let R be the interest rate and N be the capital's economic life, and let capital depreciate straight line over its economic life. Therefore, depreciation δ equals $1/N$. The opportunity cost of purchasing a unit of capital is interest foregone. If you were to lend \$1, after a year you would have \$1 in principal and R in interest. If you were to invest \$1, after a year you would have $1 - \delta$ units of capital and G in earnings before depreciation. For these two returns to be equal, G must equal $R + \delta$; thus, the user cost of capital includes interest and depreciation.

If interest and depreciation were the only components taken into account by the user cost of capital, it would not be a very useful predictor of investment demand. Economists who emphasize user cost go beyond interest and depreciation, carefully considering the effects of tax and depreciation rules, including corporate and individual income taxes and capital gains taxes, depreciation schedules and the effect of inflation on the value of depreciation, and the investment tax credit.

Prior to the Tax Reform Act of 1986 and the disinflation of the 1980s, and mainly because of asymmetrical tax treatment, estimated user costs varied significantly from one industry to another. The 1982 *Economic Report of the President* presents some estimates of the real before-tax rate of return required to provide a 4 percent real after-tax return for several types of depreciable assets. These are shown in Table 8.10. From the 1950s to the 1970s, the user cost of machinery, equipment, and vehicles fell slightly — mainly because of introduction of the investment tax credit during the 1960s — and the user cost of buildings rose slightly.

The 1981 accelerated capital recovery system lowered the user cost of capital. This was supposed to increase investment and productivity growth. However, the accelerated capital recovery system retained variations in user cost across types of investments. Investments would be skewed toward the particular capital goods favored by the tax code. One of the purposes of the Tax Reform Act of 1986 was to more nearly equalize the effective tax rate across industries so as to make investment spending more efficient.

8.4.1.4 Tobin's q

Nobel laureate James Tobin, in 1969, proposed a refreshing, if not entirely new, approach to investment demand. Why would companies purchase *new* productive capacity if *existing* productive capacity could be bought for less? For the same reason there are limited markets in rental capital (heterogeneity), there are limited markets in used capital. Nevertheless, there *is* an ongoing market in ownership of bundles of productive capacity known as the *stock market*. Professor Tobin theorized that if stock prices were low relative to the value of corporate assets, then firms seeking to expand would do so by purchasing other firms instead of by investment. If stock prices were high relative to the value of corporate assets, then firms seeking to expand would do so by investment financed with new stock.

TABLE 8.10 Required Before-Tax Rates of Return (Percent)

Period	Construction Machinery	Industrial Equipment	Trucks, Buses, and Trailers	Industrial Buildings	Commercial Buildings
1955–1959	8.9	9.5	10.8	8.0	8.0
1960–1964	7.4	7.8	8.7	7.9	7.9
1965–1969	6.5	6.9	7.5	7.6	7.6
1970–1974	6.6	6.7	7.6	8.6	8.4
1975–1979	6.1	6.4	7.6	9.0	8.7
1981	3.4	3.5	3.5	6.6	6.2

Source: Economic Report of the President, 1982, Table 5–5, p. 123.
Note: Real before-tax rate of return required to provide a 4 percent real after-tax return.

The ratio of the market value of a firm's debt and equity to the inflation-adjusted book value of its assets is called the *q ratio*. An estimate of the *q* ratio of large manufacturing corporations from 1926 to 1983 is presented in Figure 8.4. As this figure shows, *q* was low during the 1930s and 1970s, during which times investment spending was low. Conversely, *q* was high during the 1920s and 1960s, during which times investment spending was high.

The *q* ratio approach to investment demand is appealing because it relates the market's subjective assessment of value to a more objective, accounting-based measure of value. The *q* ratio contrasts the market's assessment of the present value of future cash flows to the firm's inflation-adjusted

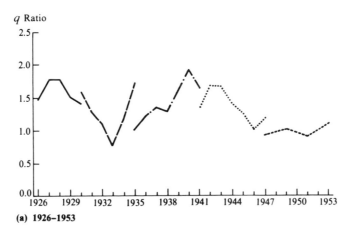

(a) 1926–1953

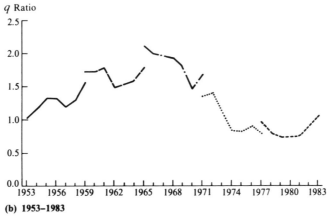

(b) 1953–1983

FIGURE 8.4   Tobin's *q*.

Source: Data from John Ciccolo and Christopher F. Baum, "Changes in the Balance Sheet of the U.S. Manufacturing Sector, 1926 – 1977" (in Benjamin Friedman (Ed.), *Corporate Capital Structure*. Chicago: University of Chicago Press, 1985); updated by Christopher F. Baum and Clifford F. Thies.

cost. If the economy were perfectly competitive, and if all profitable investment opportunities were undertaken and all unprofitable ones avoided, then the q ratio would always be 1. That is, the market price of a firm would equal both the present value of its future cash flows and its inflation-adjusted cost. Therefore, if the q ratio is greater than 1, there are profitable investments to be undertaken, and if it is less than 1, there are not.

At the micro level, there is a growing body of evidence that individual firms' q ratios are a major determinant of investment and merger and acquisition activity.[2] There is less evidence, however, that the economy-wide q has such impacts.

8.4.2 Neoclassical Theory

Neoclassical theory reverses the presumption made by Keynesian economists regarding the direction of causality between investment and gross national product. While Keynesians believe that fluctuations in investment *cause* fluctuations in GNP, neoclassicalists believe that fluctuations in investment are *caused by* fluctuations in GNP. Neoclassical economists view investment as a kind of residual. Investment is what is left over after consumption and government purchases are subtracted from GNP. Therefore, the correlation between investment and GNP is passive and is not something that can be used by fiscal or monetary authorities to manage the macroeconomy.

Let us look at a model of the economy the way a neoclassicalist does:

$$Y^0 = C + I + G^0 \tag{8.3}$$

$$C = f(Y^p) \tag{8.4}$$

Equation (8.3) is the GNP identity. Gross national product Y is the sum of consumption C, investment I, and government purchases G. The zero superscripts on Y and G indicate that neoclassical economists treat GNP and government purchases as predetermined to this model; GNP is determined by supply-side conditions, and government purchases constitute a policy variable. GNP is determined by supply because neoclassicalists presume that full employment exists. Equation (8.4) is the consumption function. According to neoclassicalists, consumption C is a function of permanent income Y^p and is not (directly) a function of current income.

Imagine a random fluctuation in GNP. Perhaps crop yields are high because of weather conditions. This increase in GNP would have little effect on permanent income and hence would have little effect on consumption

---

[2]See, for example, Henry W. Chappell and David Cheng, "Firms' Acquisition Decisions and Tobin's q Ratio," *Journal of Economics and Business*, 36, February 1984, pp. 29–42.

spending because of its presumed randomness. GNP would be high, but C and G would remain normal. Therefore, almost as a residual, investment would be high. When crop yields are randomly high, consumption remains normal and inventories are increased. Conversely, when crop yields are randomly low, consumption is sustained by drawing down inventories. The correlation between GNP and investment is explained by a supply-driven GNP and a permanent income-driven consumption function.

In the neoclassical theory, the way in which fiscal and monetary policies affect investment is by influencing consumption (and, therefore, savings and the aggregate amount of investment) and by favoring one versus another form of investment (through the user cost of capital). Note that the effects of inflation, government deficits, the tax structure, pension policy, and so forth on consumption are examined in Chapter 9.

8.4.3 Neo-Austrian Theory

Neo-Austrian economists propose yet another explanation of the correlation between investment spending and the gross national product. While Keynesians argue that recessions are caused by investment being too low, Austrians argue that recessions are caused by investment being too high!

In the Austrian view, the business cycle is composed of two interconnected parts: the "boom" and the "bust." During the boom, expansionary monetary policy lowers interest rates and induces increased investment spending. However, the boom is not sustainable. Continuing the boom requires faster and faster money growth and spiraling inflation. Eventually, the monetary authority has to tighten monetary policy in order to control inflation. This ushers in the bust.

During the bust, interest rates rise and many investment projects—referred to as "malinvestments"—are forced into liquidation. The economy suffers a recession because of the discovery and liquidation of the malinvestments made during the boom. For business enterprises, this process of liquidation often takes the form of bankruptcy. For workers, it often takes the form of unemployment.

The sequence of boom and bust is illustrated in Figure 8.5. Initially, in Figure 8.5a, the interest rate serves to coordinate the consumption, savings, and investment plans of the individuals in the economy. That is, producers plan to produce (C_0^0, C_1^0), which is what consumers plan to consume. Then, in Figure 8.5b, the monetary authority expands the money supply, lowering interest rates and inducing additional investment. At this time, production plans form about the point (C_0^1, C_1^1), but consumers plan to consume (C_0^2, C_1^2). Notice that the interest rate no longer coordinates savings and investment plans, but is simply a product of monetary policy.

Future consumption

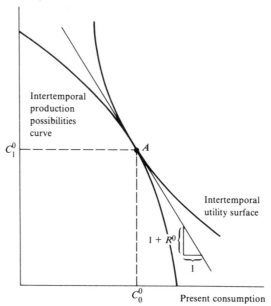

(a) Initial equilibrium

Future consumption

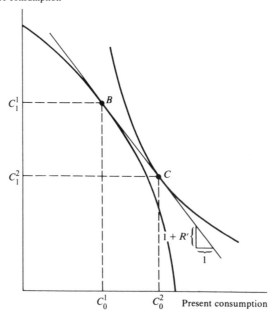

(b) The "boom"

FIGURE 8.5 The Austrian Business Cycle.

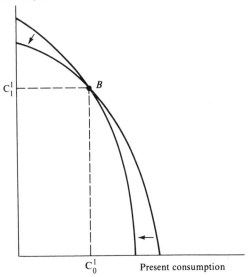

(c) "Hardening" of the intertemporal production possibilities curve

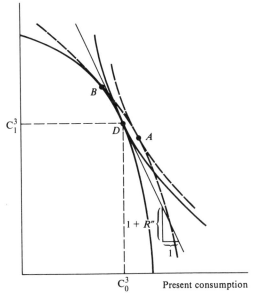

(d) The "bust"

A distinguishing characteristic of Austrian economists is their view of prices, including interest rates, as the traffic signals along the economic highway system. By following these signals, each individual person can drive from wherever he or she finds himself or herself (point A) to a freely chosen destination (point B) with a minimum of traffic jams and accidents. However, when fiscal or monetary policies "distort" these signals, economic activity is no longer coordinated. Expectations prove wrong, plans are disappointed, inventories go unsold, industrial capacity is underutilized, and workers are unemployed.[3]

Because of the heterogeneity of capital, once producers plan to produce (C_0^1, C_1^1), the intertemporal production possibilities curve "firms up" about this point. This is illustrated in Figure 8.5c. The firming up of the production possibilities curve reflects that investment decisions are not easily reversed. Tradeoffs between present and future consumption become more severe. The economy loses some of its former flexibility. In the extreme, the production possibilities curve would become kinked at the point (C_0^1, C_1^1).

Once money is tightened, the new equilibrium is determined by the restricted intertemporal production possibilities curve. Given this restricted curve, the optimum is (C_0^3, C_1^3), illustrated in Figure 8.5d. This equilibrium features higher interest rates, as well as lower consumption and lower investment, and, necessarily, lower GNP relative to the original equilibrium. Surprisingly high interest rates—indeed, inverted term structures of interest rates—*do* presage recessions. Yet, it is difficult for rational expectations-oriented macroeconomists to accept that the economy can be repeatedly fooled into malinvestments by fiscal and monetary policies, and the reluctance of Austrian economists to conduct econometric research leaves the quantitative importance of their analysis in doubt.

8.5 SUMMARY

1. Investment refers to additions to the capital stock. Investment spending increases productive capacity. The national income and product accounts identify three categories of investment: business plant and equipment, changes in inventories, and residential construction. In addition, research and development, exploration, and education have the economic characteristics of investment.

2. Net investment, or the change in the capital stock, equals gross

---

[3]The highway analogy follows the late Austrian economist Fritz Machlup, "Marginal Analysis and Empirical Research," *American Economic Review*, 36, September 1946, pp. 519–554.

investment less depreciation. Depreciation is referred to as capital consumption allowance in the national income and product accounts.

3. Capital budgeting refers to the investment decision-making process in business. Investments with net present values greater than zero are profitable and should be undertaken. For "normal" projects, a mathematically equivalent rule is to undertake investments with internal rates of return greater than their required rates of return.

4. According to neo-Keynesian theory, fluctuations in investment spending are a major cause of the business cycle. Therefore, fiscal and monetary policies that maintain investment spending can increase economic stability as well as sustain economic growth.

5. Neo-Keynesian theory, in addition, investigates how fiscal and monetary policies can affect the composition of investment spending, e.g., how depreciation and tax rules differentially affect the user costs of particular types of capital goods.

6. According to neoclassical theory, the observed positive correlation between investment spending and gross national product is explained by the regularity of consumption and government spending. Investment is viewed as a residual, determined by the difference between a fluctuating GNP and relatively constant consumption and government spending.

7. According to neo-Austrian theory, the observed positive correlation between investment spending and gross national product is a misleading statistical artifact. Much of the investment spending during the "boom" of the business cycle is "malinvestment" induced by artificially low interest rates. During the subsequent "bust" of the business cycle, these malinvestments are liquidated.

8.6 EXERCISES

1. When is higher education investment and when is it consumption?

2. If accelerated depreciation does not affect the total amount to be depreciated over the economic life of an investment, how can it affect the investment's net present value?

3. Using both the net present value and internal rate of return criteria, explain how a lower interest rate affects the quantity of investment demanded.

4. How did the 1981 accelerated capital recovery system affect aggregate investment demand as well as the relative attractiveness of investments in commercial real estate versus investments in business machinery, equipment, and vehicles?

5. How did the Tax Reform Act of 1986 affect aggregate investment demand as well as the relative attractiveness of investments in commercial real estate versus investments in business machinery, equipment, and vehicles?

6. How does inflation affect investment demand?

7. Using the neo-Keynesian, neoclassicalist, and neo-Austrian theories, explain the observed positive correlation between fluctuations in investment spending and gross national product.

8.7 REFERENCES

Kenneth J. Arrow, "The Future and the Present in Economic Life," *Economic Inquiry*, 16, April 1978, pp. 157–170.

Peter K. Clark, "Investment in the 1970s: Theory, Performance and Prediction," *Brookings Papers on Economic Activity*, 1:1979, pp. 73–113.

Martin Feldstein, *The Effects of Taxation on Capital Accumulation.* Chicago: University of Chicago Press, 1987.

Robert J. Gordon and John M. Veitch, "Fixed Investment in the American Business Cycle, 1919–1983," in Robert J. Gordon (Ed.), *The American Business Cycle: Continuity and Change.* Chicago: University of Chicago Press, 1986, pp. 267–335.

Robert E. Hall and Dale W. Jorgenson, "Tax Policy and Investment Behavior," *American Economic Review*, 57, June 1967, pp. 391–414.

John R. Hicks. *Capital and Time: A Neo-Austrian Theory.* Oxford: Clarendon Press, 1973.

J. Huston McCulloch, "Misintermediation and Macroeconomic Fluctuations," *Journal of Monetary Economics*, 8, July 1981, pp. 103–116.

Gerald P. O'Driscoll, *Economics as a Coordination Problem.* Kansas City: Sheed Andrews and McMeel, 1977.

Lawrence H. Summers, "Taxation and Corporate Investment: A *q*-Theory Approach," *Brookings Papers on Economic Activity* 1:1981, pp. 67–127.

——— *APPENDIX 8A* ———

INVESTMENT AND TIME PREFERENCE

This appendix develops a relatively sophisticated model of investment demand one step at a time. It begins with a simple one-person, two-period model. In this introductory model, there is no real difference between savings and investment. Next, a multiple-person, two-period model is developed. In this second model, the role of financial intermediation is made explicit. The savings of those who save in this model are not necessarily invested, but can be borrowed and spent on consumption goods by others. This appendix concludes with some additional considerations in the determination of savings, borrowing, and investment, including heterogeneous capital and agency costs.

8A.1   A Simple Model of Investment

We begin with a simple model. In this model, there is only one person, so there is no financial intermediation (and there is no borrowing and lending) and savings and investment are the same thing. Furthermore, there is no uncertainty; the only criteria determining savings and investment are time preference — or impatience to consume — and the productivity of investment. Savings and investment are determined by the tradeoff between consuming *now* versus consuming *more later*.

Imagine an economy, which we shall describe as a "Robinson Crusoe economy," composed of one person who lives for two periods, the present and the future. This person has a stock of units that he or she can either consume during the present or not consume — i.e., save — and invest. Depending on how many units this person saves, he or she will have units to consume in the future. Every unit saved will increase the number of units available in the future, but at a diminishing rate. (This relationship embodies diminishing marginal productivity of investment.)

The curved line $A B$ in Figure 8A.1 illustrates the resulting relationship between present and future consumption. (This line is a production possibilities curve, with present consumption on the horizontal axis and future consumption on the vertical axis.) Point A represents con-

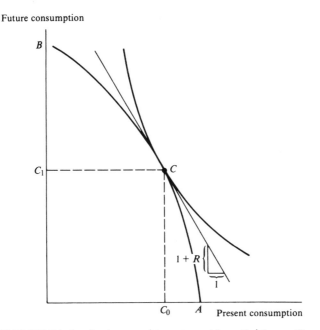

FIGURE 8A.1   Savings and Investment in a Robinson Crusoe Economy.

suming all the stock of units in the present, saving and investing none of them, and having no units to consume in the future. Point B represents consuming none of the stock of units in the present, saving and investing all of them, and maximizing the number of units available for consumption in the future.

It is natural to suppose that a fully informed person would choose to consume *part* of the stock of units in the present and to save and invest the other part. Point C represents one such point. Point C happens to provide an equal number of units for consumption in both the present and the future. It is important to note that while it is entirely possible that a pattern of consumption that is constant over time could emerge in this simple economy, such a pattern is not necessary.

Notice the tangent line at point C. Its slope is negative and is equal to $-1/(1+R)$, where R is naturally defined as the rate of interest (even though, in the context of this model, there is no financial intermediation). R is the rate of interest because another unit not consumed in the present, but saved and invested, will produce another $1+R$ units in the future.

Given the production possibilities curve, R indicates the impatience to consume or time preference of the person in this economy. A high R would indicate a person who is very impatient to consume, and a low R would indicate a person who is less impatient. Without getting too deeply into the psychology involved, reasons cited for differences in time preference among individuals are differences in age, wealth, information, and tastes.

Economists represent a person's preferences, including his or her preferences among present and future consumption, with a *utility function*. The utility function represents the level of utility that combinations of goods deliver. A line showing the combinations of goods that deliver the *same* level of utility is referred to as a *utility surface*. Generally, utility surfaces farther away from the origin represent higher levels of utility (because more is preferred to less), and these utility surfaces are bowed away from the origin (because of diminishing marginal utility).

Given the production possibilities frontier *and* a utility function, determination of consumption, savings, and the interest rate in our Robinson Crusoe economy is straightforward. Present and future consumption is the point of tangency between the production possibilities frontier and the highest attainable utility surface. Furthermore, the interest rate is implicit in the slope at this point of tangency and reflects the (objective) marginal rate of transformation of present into future units available for consumption, as well as the (subjective) marginal rate of substitution of present for future units of consumption in the person's utility function. (Economists are impressed with the harmony of objective and subjective tradeoffs obtained or at least approximated in unfettered markets!)

8A.2 Financial Intermediation

The model just developed represents savings and investment and the determination of interest rates in a Robinson Crusoe economy. However, since this is a one-person economy, interest rates are only *implicit* in the tradeoff between present and future consumption. In this section, a multiple-person economy is developed in which there is borrowing and lending among individuals and in which interest rates are therefore *explicit*.

Let there be N individuals in an economy, numbered $1, 2, ..., N$. Let some of these individuals, those numbered $1, 2, ..., M$, have an income endowment in period 1 (the "present") of Y_1 and in period 2 (the "future") of zero. Let the others, those numbered $M + 1, M + 2, ..., N$, have income endowments in period 1 of zero and in period 2 of Y_2. The obvious problem facing the individuals of this economy is the ability to consume in both periods when each of them has an income endowment in only one of the periods.

While we want to focus on the role of financial intermediation, we cannot ignore the possibility of investment. Persons with income endowments during period 1 can consume in both periods either by lending to persons with income during period 2, to be repaid during period 2, or by investing as in the previous model. Obviously, in the real world, part of (gross) savings is borrowed and part is invested.

Recognize that no one with an income endowment during period 1 would lend to anyone with an income endowment during period 2 unless they were to receive interest at the rate R that they could obtain, at the margin, through investment. Moreover, in a multiperson economy, the interest rate is actually determined through the forces of supply and demand. Each person takes the interest rate as determined in the market as exogenous to his or her savings, investing, and borrowing decisions. Each person, in fact, *uses* the interest rate as found in the market to guide his or her savings, investment, and borrowing decisions.

In a multiperson economy, each person maximizes the utility of present and future consumption in a two-step function. First, given income endowments during periods 1 and 2, investment opportunities, and the interest rate, each person maximizes his or her wealth. *Wealth*, in this model, is defined as the present value of a person's present and future income. [In the real world, wealth includes *both* the present value of present and future (labor) income and the value of a person's stock of real and financial assets.] Then, given wealth and the interest rate, each person maximizes the utility of present and future consumption. This two-step procedure in which individuals separately make their investment and consumption decisions is known, in economics, as the *separation theorem*.

First, maximizing wealth is stated as

$$\underset{z}{\text{Max}} \ W = Y_1 - Z + \frac{1}{1 + R} [Y_2 + F(Z)] \tag{8A.1}$$

where W is wealth and is the present value of present and future income, $Y1$, is income endowment during period t, Z is the amount invested, some or all of which could be borrowed, and F represents a one-period production function. Maximization implies that $F' = 1 + R$, so that each individual invests to the point where the marginal product equals one plus the interest rate (or the gross required rate of return).

Then, given the maximized value of wealth, utility maximazation is stated as

$$\text{Max} \ U(C_1, C_2) \tag{8A.2}$$
$$C_1, C_2$$

subject to

$$C_1 + \frac{1}{1+R} C_2 = W \tag{8A.3}$$

where U represents a person's utility function. Solving this problem delivers the following two sets of conditions:

$$C_1 + \frac{1}{1+R} C_2 = W \tag{8A.4}$$

$$\frac{U_1}{U_2} = \frac{1}{1+R} \tag{8A.5}$$

The first set of conditions is merely a restatement of the wealth constraint. The second set of conditions is that each person brings his or her marginal rate of substitution of present for future consumption into alignment with the economy-wide marginal rate of transformation as embodied in the interest rate (i.e., more harmony). Figure 8A.2 illustrates a particular individual in this multiperson economy with savings, investment, and borrowing. This person begins with income endowments of Y_1 and zero during periods 1 and 2. By investing part of his or her income during period 1, this person increases his or her wealth from Y_1 to W. In addition, given this person's maximized wealth and time preferences, he or she chooses the combination of present and future consumption represented by point D. Amazingly (?), point D represents as much consumption during period 1 alone as this person began with!

Until now the interest rate has been considered fixed. Yet, it is itself determined *within* this fictitious economy. For the first M individuals, i.e., those having income during period 1, the preceding two utility maximizing conditions describe an *implicit function* for C_1 and therefore for (gross) savings. For the last $N - M$ individuals, utility maximization describes an implicit function for borrowings. For all individuals, the condition for wealth maximization describes an implicit function for investment. That is,

$$\text{Gross savings} \; = \; \sum_{i=1}^{M} Y_1 - C_1(R) \tag{8A.6}$$

$$\text{Borrowings} \; = \; \sum_{i=M+1}^{N} C_1(R) \tag{8A.7}$$

$$\text{Investment} \; = \; \sum_{i=1}^{N} Z(R) \tag{8A.8}$$

where C_1 and Z_1 are these implicit functions.

It can be shown that consumption in period 1 is a *negative* function of interest rates. Therefore, (gross) savings are a positive function of interest rates and borrowings are a negative function. It also can be shown that investment is a negative function of interest rates.

Gross savings *as a function* are referred to as the *supply of loanable funds*. Borrowing *plus* investment is referred to as the *demand for loanable funds*. The equilibration of the supply of and demand for loanable funds determines the interest rate, just as in the standard microeconomic analysis of supply and demand. Therefore, the seemingly uncoordinated actions of individuals result in savings, investment, and borrowing that jointly maximize everybody's utility (given their endowments of income and investment opportunities). While seemingly uncoordinated, the interest rate—as determined by these forces of supply and demand—serves to coordinate the otherwise disparate actions of these individuals. For economists, interest rates, like other market-determined prices, are signals to decision makers, economically communicating the relevant information regarding scarcity in a way in which self-interest naturally inclines them to make optimal decisions.

To be sure, real-world markets are much more complicated than we could ever hope to represent mathematically. This does not necessarily mean that real-world markets are "imperfect." What it does mean is that our mathematical representations of real-world markets are simplifications. Hopefully, they are *useful* simplifications, enabling us to see some of the more important characteristics of real-world markets.

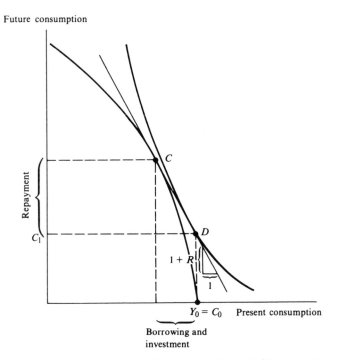

FIGURE 8A.2   Savings and Investment in a Multiperson Economy.

The present model is a useful simplification because it enables us to see the following important characteristics of savings, investment, borrowing, financial intermediation, and interest rates:

1. Interest rates economically communicate to savers, investors, and borrowers the economy-wide marginal rates of substitution *and* transformation of present into future consumption goods.
2. Investments are undertaken when their marginal product is at least as great as their required rate of return.
3. The investment decision is logically separate from and prior to the consumption decision.
4. Saving and borrowing, as distinct from investing, allow individuals to consume according to their lifetime incomes, as opposed to having their consumption being determined by current income.
5. Saving and borrowing also allow individuals to finance investments, as opposed to having investments being determined by each individual's own wealth.

8A.3 Some Other Considerations

The models just developed blur the distinction between the *stock* of capital and the *flow* of investment. In these models, there is only one good—"units"—that can be used with equal facility in either consumption or investment; there are only two time periods—the "present" and the "future"—and there are no transactions costs in the lending and borrowing of money. As a result, the economy immediately jumps from whatever capital stock it inherited from its past to its new optimal capital stock.

In the long run, the optimal capital stock *does* determine the actual stock. However, when a change in the optimal capital stock occurs, the economy *does not* immediately jump from its inherited stock to its new optimal stock. Instead, the economy takes into account the costs of adjustment and adjusts to the new optimal capital stock over a period of time. This section discusses some of the problems of the "transition" from the actual to the optimal capital stock.

Heterogeneous Capital

Capital goods are different from consumption goods. In addition, there are differences among capital goods. Because of these differences, resources cannot be costlessly transferred to the production of particular capital goods. Moreover, because it is costly, an increase in the optimal stock of any particular capital good will be met gradually with higher investment over a period of time.

Consider the case of a large *increase* in the optimal stock of a particular capital good. Assume that, initially, the actual stock equals the optimal stock. Then, because of—let's say —a large decline in interest rates, there is a large increase in the optimal capital stock. If there were no costs of adjustment, investment would be very large in order to immediately increase the actual stock to the new, higher level of the optimal stock. However, because the economy takes costs of adjustment into account, it does not immediately adjust to the new, higher level. Economists hypothesize that investment equals *a certain fraction of* the difference between the new optimal capital stock and the actual stock. Therefore, the actual capital stock does not jump immediately to the new, higher optimal capital stock, but adjusts to this higher level over time. During the period of adjustment, investment spending will be high, but not so high as to complete the adjustment in one period.

Excepting changes in business inventories, gross investment has a natural minimum of zero. Therefore, upon a large decrease in the optimal capital stock, due to —let's say —a large increase in interest rates, the fastest the actual capital stock can adjust to a new, *lower* optimal capital stock is the depreciation rate. During a period of adjustment to a new, lower optimal capital stock, gross investment will be near zero and net investment will be negative.

Because of adjustment costs and the natural floor under gross investment, the stock of capital —as an aggregate —can be viewed as constantly adjusting toward its optimal level. With regard to particular capital goods, it is entirely possible for investment to be strong for some capital goods and near zero for others. This was the case during the 1970s. Changes in energy prices and the emergence of new technologies drove the optimal stock of certain capital goods well below the stocks inherited from the past and, at the same time, drove the optimal stock of other capital goods well above. Gross investment was near zero for certain capital goods, while it was strong for others. The aggregate figure for investment did not adequately convey what was actually happening in the economy.

Agency costs

One of the most important characteristics of a free-market economy is that owners have a natural incentive to employ their resources efficiently. Those who do will be rewarded with profits. Those who do not will suffer losses and will eventually see the resources they had owned transferred to others more capable.

Borrowing and lending—while enabling redistribution of control over resources from those who own them to those who can employ them more efficiently—can compromise the incentives of the profit motive. A person who finances investments with debt, as opposed to using his or her own savings, will have a different incentive structure. With enough debt, such a person would be inclined to undertake more risky projects. With 100 percent debt finance, for example, a person would be inclined to undertake very risky projects because any profit would be his or hers, while any loss would, after he or she declares bankruptcy, be suffered by the lenders.

In the finance literature, the problems associated with separation of ownership and control are referred to as *agency costs*. *Agency* refers to the relationship between the "principal" who owns resources and his "agent" who exercises control over them when it is costly for the principal to supervise the agent. In practice, agency can result from the use of debt and — in the case of corporations — from "public" ownership, i.e., nonmanagement, of equity.

A variety of practices have evolved to enable borrowing and lending to take place while keeping agency costs in check. One of these practices is a limit on debt financing. For example, mortgage lenders typically require home buyers to make down payments of 20 percent (or else require federal or private mortgage insurance). Because home buyers have to make a significant down payment, they are inclined to take only prudent risks. Therefore, the advantages offered by borrowing and lending have to be weighed against the disadvantages of agency costs. That free markets do not ignore agency costs in borrowing and lending is not an "imperfection," but a judicious concern for *all* the costs that are involved.

9
Consumption

9.1 INTRODUCTION

> One of the most dangerous by-products of a period of depression is the crop
> of false economic theories which win popular credence and gain political
> support . . . .As in all previous depressions, the commonest explanation which
> is offered to the mass of thinking people is some form of underconsumption
> theory.[1]

Personal consumption spending is by far the largest component of gross
national product, accounting — in the United States during the post-World
War II period — for somewhat more than 60 percent of GNP and for about
90 percent of personal disposable income. Simply because of its size, consumption spending is an important part of the macroeconomy. However, it
is important for other reasons as well. Some economists view variations in
consumption spending to be major contributors to the business cycle. The
economic historian Peter Temin, for example, argues that a fall in consumption spending was a major cause of the Great Depression.[2] Furthermore,
from time to time, economists have argued that consumption spending has
been too low — threatening the macroeconomy with "secular stagnation"
— or has been too high, with the result of declining productivity growth.

    This chapter presents several competing theories of consumption spend-
ing, including the Keynesian (or "current income") consumption function

---

[1]E. F. M. Durbin, *Purchasing Power and Trade Depression* (London: Jonathan Cape, 1934).
[2]Peter Temin, *Did Monetary Forces Cause the Great Depression?* (New York: W. W. Norton,
1976), pp. 62–82.

and the permanent income and life-cycle consumption functions. It then analyzes the roles of income, wealth, liquidity constraints, temporary tax changes, social security, and deficit spending in determining consumption (and its logical counterpart, saving). It concludes by addressing some implications of consumption spending for inventories, liquid assets, and other managerial policies.

9.2 THE CONSUMPTION FUNCTION

John Maynard Keynes, in *The General Theory*, presented what he called the "fundamental psychological law" governing consumption and saving. Keynes argued that given an additional dollar of income, people would tend to spend part and to save part. That is, he argued that the *marginal propensity to consume*—the amount of an additional dollar of income that is spent—is between zero and 1. In addition, Keynes argued that the proportion of income that is spent, or the *average propensity to consume*, falls as income rises.

When presented, Keynes's theory of consumption, together with its implications for business cycle analysis and stabilization policy, swept the economics profession off its feet. Mathematical economists and econometricians were especially captivated. Politicians and policymakers concluded that deficit spending, inflation, redistribution of wealth, and discretionary monetary and fiscal policies were necessary to maintain full employment and economic growth.

Today, looking back at *The General Theory*, it is possible to argue that Keynes's "fundamental psychological law" was just another restatement of the underconsumption theory of the business cycle, a repeatedly discredited theory that nevertheless resurfaces upon major downturns in the macroeconomy.[3] Alternately, it is possible to argue that Keynes brilliantly, even though unclearly, identified how a break down in liquidity can break down the forces that usually bring about macroequilibrium at a high level of employment and thus usher in massive unemployment and economic stagnation.[4]

---

[3]Probably the most famous underconsumptionist prior to Keynes was Thomas Malthus. His thoroughly pessimistic theories were popular during the early part of the nineteenth century. For a history of these theories, see M. F. Bleaney, *Underconsumption Theories* (New York: International Publishers, 1976).

[4]This thesis has been developed by Axel Leijonhufvud in *On Keynesian Economics and the Economics of Keynes* (Oxford: Oxford University Press, 1968); see also his "Effective Demand Failures," *Swedish Economic Journal*, 75, March 1973; reprinted in *Information and Coordination* (Oxford: Oxford University Press, 1981), pp. 103–129.

9.2.1 The Keynesian Consumption Function

The Keynesian or "current income" consumption function was introduced in Chapter 3 as part of the Keynesian cross and *IS-LM* macromodels. To briefly review the simpler one of these two models, the Keynesian cross is composed of two equations:

$$Y = C + I + G \tag{9.1}$$

$$C = a + B(Y - T) \tag{9.2}$$

where Y is national income, C is consumption, I is net investment, G is government expenditures, and T is net government revenue, i.e., taxes less transfers. Equation (9.1) is the national income identity. It states that national income is equal to consumption plus net investment plus government expenditures. (For simplicity, we assume net exports are zero.) Equation (9.2) is the Keynesian consumption function. It states that consumption spending is a function of disposable income, that is, $Y - T$.

Note that B is referred to as the *marginal propensity to consume*. It indicates how much of an additional dollar of income is consumed. Presumably, this is between zero and 1. The intercept a is referred to as "autonomous consumption." In order for the average propensity to consume to fall as income rises, the intercept a would have to be greater than zero.

The national income identity is, of course, true by definition. What makes the Keynesian cross a useful macromodel is not that the national income identity is true but rather is the set of assumptions — such as there being widespread unemployment — that imply that aggregate demand determines national income. In the context of the Keynesian cross, the insight of the consumption function is that changes in autonomous spending (that is, I, G, and a) can have *multiplied* effects on national income. Solving Equations (9.1) and (9.2) for national income, we get

$$Y = \frac{1}{1 - B}(a + I + G) - \frac{B}{1 - B}T \tag{9.3}$$

where the expression $[1/(1 - B)]$ is known as the *multiplier*. A marginal propensity to consume of, say, 0.8, implies a multiplier of 5. With this marginal propensity to consume, a fall in investment of \$1 billion would result in a fall in national income of \$5 billion.

The Keynesian cross implies that income and employment could be quite volatile and that discretionary monetary and fiscal policies could be used to stabilize the economy. That is, small fluctuations in investment could lead to large fluctuations in national income and employment through the workings of the multiplier. Government expenditures could, for example, be used to achieve a high level of national income and employment in spite of fluctuations in investment.

The reason why small fluctuations in investment lead to large fluctuations in national income and employment is because of the large marginal propensity to consume *out of current income*. When investment spending falls, the incomes of those in the investment sector of the economy fall, and they, in turn, reduce their consumption spending. Their reduced consumption spending, in turn, reduces incomes to others in the economy, which causes them to reduce their consumption spending as well. The multiplier relationship between investment and national income is due to the fact that the spending of some is the income of others and the assumption—as represented in the Keynesian consumption function—that consumption spending is connected to current income.

9.2.2 Problems with the Keynesian Consumption Function

When Keynes presented his theory of consumption, macroeconomic data such as we now have were not available. Nevertheless, as national income accounting was developed and estimates of national income were constructed, Keynes's theory appeared to be verified. Figure 9.1 presents a scatter plot of consumption and personal disposable income for the years 1929 – 1941. These are the data that were available shortly after *The General Theory* was published. As the trend line indicates, consumption during these years does appear to be well described by the Keynesian consumption function. In particular, these data appear to reveal a marginal propensity to consume between zero and 1 and an intercept greater than zero, implying that the average propensity to consume does indeed fall as income rises.

Just as these data appeared to verify the Keynesian consumption function, other data questioned it. Simon Kuznets, as part of a massive historical study, generated estimates of national income, consumption, and saving from 1869 to 1931.[5] A scatter plot of his data is presented in Figure 9.2. The trend line through his data—contrary to the trend line through the 1929 – 1941 data—does not reveal a statistically significant positive intercept. The average propensity to consume does not appear to fall with income but rather appears to be constant (and equal to the marginal propensity to consume). Somehow, economists had to reconcile the behavior of consumption during the 1929 – 1941 period with its behavior during the much longer period studied by Kuznets.

[5]Simon Kuznets, *National Product Since 1869 and National Income, A Summary of Findings* (New York: National Bureau of Economic Research, 1946).

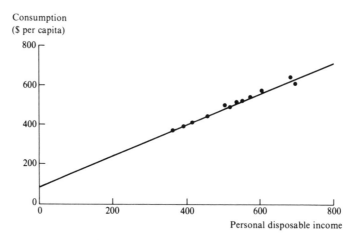

FIGURE 9.1   The Consumption Function, 1929–1941 ($ per Capita).

These are the first data with which macroeconomists could test Keynes's theory of consumption. Notice that the slope of the trend line implies that the marginal propensity to consume is between zero and 1 and that the intercept is positive, implying that the average propensity to consume falls as income rises. These observations appeared to confirm Keynes's theory.

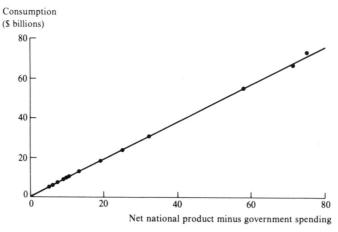

FIGURE 9.2   The "Long-Run" Consumption Function, Kuznets's Data, 1869–1931 ($ Billions).

The dots are Kuznets's estimates of 5-year average income and consumption during the period 1869–1931. Notice that the trend line through these data appears to go through the origin, implying that the average propensity to consume is constant. This observation questioned Keynes's theory of the consumption.

Yet other data questioned the Keynesian consumption function. These are the family budget data obtained periodically in studies of the cost of living. In these studies, families are surveyed as to their incomes and expenditures in order to determine the "market basket" of goods and services to be covered by the consumer price index. Having information on incomes and expenditures, these studies can be used to assess consumption behavior. The data of two such studies are presented in Figure 9.3. Each study, individually, appears to verify Keynes's theory of consumption, having a positive intercept and a slope between zero and 1. However, the consumption functions of these studies appear to shift. Not only do they appear to shift, they appear to shift so as to keep their average propensities to consume more or less constant and approximately equal to the average propensity to consume found in Kuznets's 1869 – 1931 data.

Two of the earlier attempts at reconciling the various observations of consumption behavior were those of James Duesenberry and Franco Modigliani.[6] Duesenberry attempted to explain observed consumption behavior

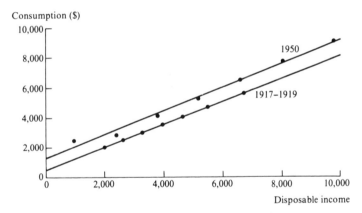

FIGURE 9.3   Cross-Sectional Consumption Studies Based on Budget Studies, 1917 – 1919 and 1950.
The dots are the average income and consumption of families in the income ranges reported by the budget study. Notice that, individually, the trend lines appear to confirm Keynes's theory of consumption. Yet the consumption function appears to shift from one to the other budget study. (Data were converted to 1967 dollars by the authors.)

[6]James S. Duesenberry, *Income, Saving and the Theory of Consumer Behavior* (Cambridge, Mass.: Harvard University Press, 1949); and Franco Modigliani, "Fluctuations in the Saving-Income Ratio: A Problem for Income Forecasting," in *Studies in Income and Wealth No. 11* (New York: National Bureau of Economic Research, 1949).

by arguing that people like to imitate the rich so that—until reality sets in—they tend to consume beyond their means. Modigliani similarly hypothesized that people adjust their consumption downward only with difficulty. Upon a fall in income, rather than reduce consumption, people tend—at least at first—to draw on their past savings.

Duesenberry's and Modigliani's theories, like those of Keynes, were based more on amateur psychology than on rigorous economic theory. None of these theories incorporated the basic paradigm of economics, which is rational decision making or choice given limited means and competing wants. It was for Milton Friedman and Modigliani at a later time to develop seemingly different but fundamentally similar theories of consumption based on rational decision making.

9.2.3 The Permanent Income Consumption Function

In *A Theory of the Consumption Function*, Milton Friedman masterfully reconciled the various observations of consumption behavior. Friedman distinguished between current and "permanent" income and argued that rational consumers would determine their consumption not on what they happen to receive in income in any one year but on what they expect, on average, to receive in income over a longer time period.

To illustrate Friedman's theory of the consumption function, consider a person who is paid once a month. We would not expect this person to concentrate all his or her consumption on that day, but rather to have a relatively smooth flow of consumption through the month. That is, the person's consumption each day would be based on average daily income and not so much on which day happens to be payday. This logic is easily extended to a year, a decade, or a lifetime.

The economic underpinning of Friedman's consumption function is little more than diminishing marginal utility. Because the utility of additional units of consumption goods falls with the total number of units consumed in any particular time period, rational consumers seeking to maximize total lifetime utility will tend to smooth or average out consumption. Ignoring imperfections such as transactions costs and uncertainty, and also ignoring interest, rational consumers would completely smooth consumption. Because of interest, rational consumers will usually seek smoothly growing consumption by, on average, saving part of their income.

Friedman's theory of consumption easily reconciles the observed short- and long-run consumption functions and explains the shifting cross-sectional consumption functions. According to Friedman,

$$C = \beta Y^p \tag{9.4}$$

where C is consumption, β is the marginal propensity to consume out of permanent income, such that $0 < \beta \leqslant 1$, and Y^p is permanent income. Therefore, when economists regress consumption on current income—i.e., estimate the equation

$$C = a + BY \qquad\qquad\qquad (9.5)$$

where Y is current income—they have a bias problem because of mismeasurement of the true independent or right-hand side variable. In econometric jargon, this is called an *errors-in-variables problem*. The expected value of B is not β but is instead $\beta/(1 + \sigma_v^2/\sigma_y^2)$, where σ_v^2 is the variance of the difference between current and permanent income and σ_y^2 is the variance of income. Note that the expected value of B is less than β. Likewise, the expected value of a is not the true intercept, which is zero, but is instead $(\beta - \exp B)\mu_Y$, where $\exp B$ is the expected value of B and μ_Y is the mean of Y.

With Kuznets's "long-run" data, the bias problem is probably small. This is so because his estimates of consumption and income are averages over several years, so that fluctuations in income about its permanent level tend to average out. With the 1929 – 1941 "short-run" data, the bias problem is probably substantial because of the large fluctuations in income about its permanent level during this period.

In any particular cross section, the bias in estimating β may be considered to be a constant. However, as income grows over time, the mean of income μ_Y becomes larger and so the expected value of a, which is $(\beta - \exp B)\mu_Y$, becomes larger. Thus, the cross-sectional consumption function will appear to shift from one budget study to the next.

In *The General Theory*, a major role of the consumption function is to show how fluctuations in investment can lead to multiplied fluctuations in national income and employment. As reformulated by Friedman, the multiplier mechanism is (mostly) destroyed. His consumption function, instead of being an amplifier of fluctuations in investment, maintains consumption and thereby stabilizes aggregate demand in the face of fluctuations in investment.

Actually, with Friedman's consumption function, there are two multiplier-like linkages. The first is the possible effect of current income on permanent income, and the second is spending on durable consumer goods. Current income can sneak into Friedman's consumption function and by doing so partially restore the multiplier process by affecting people's expectations of their permanent income. Let us say that you are a salesperson on commission and that your sales are particularly high this quarter. To some extent you would probably conclude that you were just lucky and that your sales and income will not always be so high. However, you would probably also suspect that your sales potential has at least improved a little bit and that your sales and income will possibly be higher in the future.

This reasoning implies that you would partially adjust your expectation of permanent income upward like so:

$$Y_t^p = \alpha Y_t + (1 - \alpha)Y_{t-1}^p \tag{9.6}$$

where Y_t^p is your new (revised) expectation of permanent income, Y_t is current income, Y_{t-1}^p is your past expectation of permanent income, and α is your adjustment coefficient, where $0 < \alpha < 1$. The size of α, or how fast you adjust your expectation of permanent income to current income, would logically depend on how much randomness, or "noisiness," there is in current income. The more randomness in current income, the slower you would adjust permanent income to current income. The implication of Equation (9.6) is that consumption is partially a function of current income. Substituting Equation (9.6) into Equation (9.4), we get

$$C_t = \alpha \beta Y_t + (1 - \alpha)\beta Y_{t-1}^p \tag{9.7}$$

The second connection between current income and consumption spending in Friedman's consumption function is the distinction between expenditures on durable consumption goods such as automobiles, household appliances, and furniture and the flow of services that these goods provide. Friedman's consumption function implies that consumers will smooth the flow of services from durable consumption goods, not necessarily that they will smooth their purchases of durable consumption goods. Spending on durable consumption goods behaves differently from spending on nondurable consumption goods and services. Instead of being relatively insensitive to fluctuations in income, spending on durable goods is relatively sensitive. See Figures 9.4 and 9.5.

9.2.4 The Life-Cycle Consumption Function

The life-cycle consumption function, developed by Franco Modigliani in a series of articles and recently restated in his 1985 Nobel lecture, is in many ways similar to Friedman's permanent income consumption function. Like Friedman's model, the life-cycle model stresses utility maximization through the smoothing of consumption. And therefore, just as in Friedman's model, current income does not play much of a role in determining consumption. The distinctive contribution of the life-cycle consumption function is its ex-

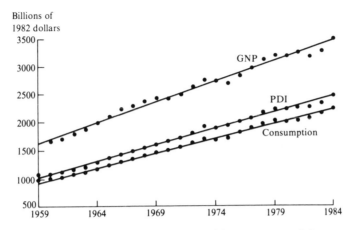

FIGURE 9.4   GNP, Personal Disposable Income, and Consumption Expenditures, 1959–1984.
Compared to the fluctuations of GNP and personal disposable income about their trend lines, consumption expenditures were relatively stable during the period 1959–1984.

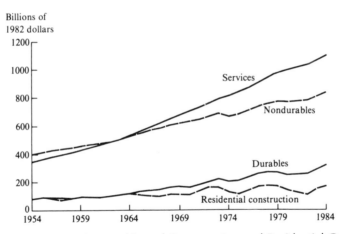

FIGURE 9.5   Composition of Consumption and Residential Construction, 1959–1984.
Consumption expenditures on services was relatively stable during the period 1959–1984. Consumption expenditures on nondurable goods (a principal component of which is fuel) exhibit two marked fluctuations, both in conjunction with increases in the relative price of energy, and both fluctuations more due to microeconomic than macroeconomic behavior. Consumption expenditures on durable goods and residential construction (a component of investment), in contrast, are relatively sensitive to the business cycle.

plicit consideration of people's income, consumption, saving, and wealth over their lifetimes.

A simple yet complete life-cycle model is easy to develop. Assume that people live for N years, working during the first M years and being retired for the remaining $N-M$ years; that they earn Y_t in year t of work, that the interest rate is zero, that consumption in any year features decreasing marginal utility, and that the economic problem is to choose consumption for each year, that is C_t, $t = 1, ..., N$, in order to maximize lifetime utility. In mathematical notation,

$$\text{Max} \sum_{t=1}^{N} U(C_t) \quad \begin{matrix} U' > 0 \\ U'' < 0 \end{matrix} \tag{9.8}$$

subject to

$$\sum_{t=1}^{N} C_t \leq \sum_{t=1}^{M} Y_t \tag{9.9}$$

where $U(C_t)$ is the utility of consumption during time period t. The solution to this problem is

$$C_t = \frac{M}{N}\mu_Y \tag{9.10}$$

for $t = 1, ..., N$, where μ_Y is the mean of income. Notice the similarity between Equations (9.10) and (9.4). Let β equal (M/N) and interpret μ_Y as permanent income; then these two equations are identical. This shows the basic similarity between the permanent income and life-cycle consumption functions.

In order to examine how current income affects consumption in the life-cycle model, assume that a person receives a windfall of Y^w. This windfall changes this person's lifetime budget constraint to

$$\sum_{t=1}^{N} C_t \leq Y^w + \sum_{t=1}^{M} Y_t \tag{9.11}$$

implying that

$$C_t = \frac{1}{M}Y^w + \frac{M}{N}\mu_Y \tag{9.12}$$

for $t = 1, ..., N$. Notice the similarity between Equations (9.12) and (9.7). Let β continue to equal (M/N), let α equal $(1/M)$, continue to interpret μ_y as permanent income and Y^w as current income, and then these two equations are nearly the same. That is, both the permanent income and life-cycle consumption functions imply that the marginal propensity to consume out of current income is relatively small.

This simple life-cycle model is illustrated in Figure 9.6*a*. From age 20 until age 64—during the time the hypothetical person is working—income is higher than consumption. Therefore, the hypothetical person is saving. During these years, he or she is accumulating wealth. From age 65 until age 79—during the time the hypothetical person is retired—income is zero. Nevertheless, he or she maintains consumption by drawing on past savings. At the end of the hypothetical person's seventy-ninth year, on his or her eightieth birthday, exactly as he or she spends his or her last dollar of past savings, he or she steps across the border from this life to the next, where, presumably, balancing income and consumption is no longer a concern!

Figure 9.6*b* presents a more realistic life-cycle model. Income rises during this hypothetical person's young adulthood and then flattens out as this person reaches his or her mature adulthood. In this model, smoothing consumption implies beginning adulthood by going into debt. Notice that until age 29, this hypothetical person is spending more than he or she is receiving in income. The differences are being borrowed. From age 30 until age 38, he or she is paying off the debt accumulated during young adulthood. Then, from age 39 until age 64, he or she is accumulating wealth for retirement. If you ever wondered why young adults have such a difficult time making ends meet, it is because they are typically in the debt-accumulation portion of their life cycle. Given the difficulties involved in borrowing—which are addressed in Section 9.3.5—these are often years of restricted spending relative to permanent income.

While the overall implications of the permanent income and life-cycle consumption functions are quite similar, the life-cycle model adds a great deal of detail to our understanding of income, consumption, saving, and wealth. For one thing, wartime disruptions of the normal process of family formation can lead to uneven age mixes in the population. The World War II ''baby boom'' has had and will continue to have enormous impacts. Some of these impacts have been obvious, such as the boom-and-bust cycle in education as these children made their way through school. Some of these impacts have been subtle, such as the glut of young, unskilled workers when the baby boomers entered their teenage years, followed by a shortage when the baby boomers left. The life-cycle model suggests that another impact of the baby boomers has been to depress the aggregate saving rate

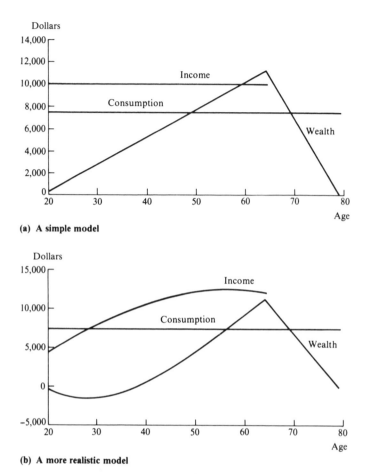

(a) A simple model

(b) A more realistic model

FIGURE 9.6   Life-Cycle Model. (Wealth is divided by 10.)

upon their entry into young adulthood, and the model further suggests that
the aggregate saving rate will recover upon their transition into mature
adulthood.

The life-cycle model also reveals the nature of wealth in a capitalist
economy. While there are people with fortunes ranging from the millions to
the billions, the vast majority of wealth is owned by people in the normal
course of saving over the life cycle. The assets in workers' private pensions,
for example, approximates the total market value of the nation's corporations.
Moreover, borrowing and lending in a capitalist economy is mostly from
people of one age group to people of another age group. Banks and other
financial institutions are only intermediaries in this borrowing and lending.

9.2.5 Consumption with Rational Expectations

The life-cycle and permanent income models are similar in that they argue that consumption is a function not so much of current income but of people's long-term views of income. Friedman, in his particular formulation of the consumption function, operationally defined permanent income as a weighted average of current and past incomes [i.e., Equation (9.6) with recursive substitution]. While this may be an adequate enough approximation for some purposes, it implies that people are mechanistic in forming their expectations to the point of ignoring information other than past income useful in forecasting future income.

Applying rational expectations theory to the consumption function, Robert E. Hall and Thomas Sargent reach some new and even surprising conclusions.[7] Rational expectations would assume that people use all available information in forming their forecasts of future income. This means that only new information—surprises—will cause them to change their forecasts. As a result, expectations of permanent income will behave like a ''random walk.'' Given the permanent income consumption function, this further implies that consumption will behave like a ''random walk.'' Technically, because of population growth, consumption will behave like a ''random walk with drift.''

For a time series to be a random walk, its changes cannot be predictable. Changes *can be* correlated with contemporaneous innovations (surprises) in other time series. In the case of consumption, changes in consumption *can be* caused by innovations in the macro economy that cause people to change their expectations of permanent income.

To say that consumption behaves like a random walk does more than question our ability to forecast future changes in consumption. It also questions the stability of consumption spending, which originally seemed like the most important insight of the permanent income and life-cycle models. When permanent income was seen to change slowly and mechanistically, consumption spending was seen to be a source of stability in the economy. Now that permanent income is seen to be capable of dramatic revision upon major macroeconomic innovations, consumption spending is seen to be a potential source of instability in the economy. To be sure, the nature of this instability is different from the multiplier instability in the Keynesian cross and *IS-LM* macromodels.

[7]Robert E. Hall, ''Stochastic Implications of the Life Cycle Permanent Income Hypothesis: Theory and Evidence,'' *Journal of Political Economy*, 86, December 1978, pp. 971–987; and Thomas S. Sargent, ''Rational Expectations, Econometric Endogeneity and Consumption,'' *Journal of Political Economy*, 86, August 1978, pp. 673–700.

At the beginning of this chapter it was mentioned that Peter Temin has argued that a fall in consumption spending was a major cause of the Great Depression. For Temin, this fall in consumption spending is "an unexplained event" because it does not accord with his econometric estimate of the consumption function. Yet he writes, "In 1929, most people expected good times to continue. By 1933, most people expected bad times to continue. Sometime in the interim, people's vision of what the next few years would bring changed. The question, therefore, is not whether expectations changed in the Depression, but when."

In light of the recent application of rational expectations theory to the consumption function, one could conjecture that during the early 1930s, permanent income fell by more than slow-moving mechanistic estimates of it would indicate. In addition to the 1929 stock market crash, which Temin discusses at length, other macroeconomic innovations of that period included the collapse of the banking system, the Smoot-Hawley tariff, and higher federal income taxes. These events could very well have dampened people's forecasts of their future incomes.

Rational expectations also can be used to explain the sustained and surprisingly strong consumption spending of the mid-1980s. While some fretted over the accumulation of consumer debt, many people borrowed to finance increased consumption, confident of their future earnings. With rational expectations, consumption can be a strong, independent force in the macro economy.

9.3 POLICY IMPLICATIONS AND EXTENSIONS

9.3.1 Temporary Tax Changes

One implication of the permanent income and life-cycle consumption functions is that short-term changes in income do not affect consumption much. This implication questions the effectiveness of discretionary monetary and fiscal policies. In the Keynesian cross and *IS-LM* macromodels, changes in taxes are powerful tools for achieving economic stability and high employment even with fluctuating investment. If investment is high, the inflationary pressure can be offset with a tax increase. If investment is low, the recessionary pressure can be offset with a tax decrease. However, changes in taxes such as these will probably not change aggregate demand much because people probably will not change their expectations of permanent income and their consumption much.

The logic of the permanent income and life-cycle models could potentially be applied to announcements of future tax changes. If the announcement of a future tax reduction is credible, then consumers might immediately adjust their expectations of permanent income and their consumption, treating the delay in the tax reduction as a kind of temporary tax hike. The Tax Reform Act of 1981, in fact, consisted of a series of tax reductions that took effect over the following several years.

Alan S. Blinder and Angus Deaton, in their recent study of consumption, found—as did others before them—that the temporary tax surcharge in 1968 and the temporary tax decrease in 1975 had little, if any, effect on consumption.[8] However, they found no increase in consumption in conjunction with the scheduling of future tax reductions by the Tax Reform Act of 1981. Consumption only increased as the tax cuts took effect. This suggests that people, if they were aware that taxes were scheduled to be reduced, doubted that the cuts would take effect as scheduled.

9.3.2 Deficit Spending

In one of the most controversial papers in macroeconomics of the 1970s, Robert Barro derived what may be called the *deficit neutrality theorem*.[9] In this paper, Barro argued that anticipating that the accumulated debt will have to one day be repaid, people will increase their saving when their governments run deficits. This increase in saving will tend to offset the effects of deficits, such as increased aggregate demand, higher interest rates, and reduced investment. Because the effects of deficits are offset by increased saving, the deficits can be said to be neutral.

This deficit neutrality theorem presumes a level of sophistication in people's expectations that most economists are unwilling to accept. It is one thing to reject adaptive expectations. It is quite another to accept that people accurately derive the implications—years into the future—of deficit spending. The most persuasive argument against adaptive expectations is that it implies that people can be systematically fooled. The effects of deficit spending, however, are generational in nature. With deficit spending, people need only be fooled once each lifetime.[10]

As argued by Modigliani in his Nobel lecture, the permanent income and life-cycle consumption functions offer several suggestions for taxes and deficit spending: Interpersonal equity as well as incentive effects call for

---

[8]Alan S. Blinder and Angus Deaton, ''The Time Series Consumption Function Revisited,'' *Brookings Papers on Economic Activity*, 2:1985, pp. 465–511.

[9]Robert J. Barro, ''Are Government Bonds Net Wealth?'' *Journal of Political Economy*, 82, November-December 1974, pp. 1095–1117.

[10]As George Santayana stated, ''Those who cannot remember the past are condemned to repeat it.''

taxation of consumption rather than current income because that would more nearly tax permanent income. And, abstracting from the financing of government investments, intergenerational equity calls for government budgets to be balanced. Government budgets need not be balanced over calendar years, but rather should be balanced over a more relevant period of time, such as the business cycle. During recessions, when revenues fall, governments should run deficits, maintaining aggregate demand and acting as an automatic stabilizer. During expansions, governments should run surpluses, retiring the debt accumulated during recessions.

9.3.3 Social Security

Another insight of the life-cycle model is the potential impact of social security programs on saving. The life-cycle model argues that the savings of mature adults is what mainly finances capital accumulation and productivity growth. Because social security is an unfunded pension plan, contributions into it do not finance capital accumulation and productivity growth but are disbursed to beneficiaries. Nevertheless, much of the motivation to save is preempted by the provision of retirement income by social security programs. Savings behavior in the United States and internationally, as analyzed by Martin Feldstein, appears to indicate that social security programs have in fact reduced saving.[11]

Actually, the U.S. social security system has two effects on savings. First, by providing income security, it tends to decrease saving. Second, by inducing retirement, it tends to increase saving. Social security induces retirement by taxing the earnings of those over 65 at confiscatory rates. Continuing to work after you reach 65 is not exactly against the law, but if you do — and you earn more than the social security "disallowance" — you forego social security benefits. Add this loss to income taxes, social security taxes, and Medicare and catastrophic health insurance taxes that only the elderly pay, and your effective tax rate can easily approach 100 percent.

Because social security induces retirement, it tends to increase private saving. Many people, realizing that they are effectively forced into retirement at age 65 and not wanting to live only on social security, supplement their public pension with one or more private pensions and additionally accumulate real and financial assets. Feldstein's research suggests that social security's dissaving effect outweighs its saving effect.

[11]See Martin Feldstein, "Social Security, Induced Retirement, and Aggregate Capital Accumulation," *Journal of Political Economy*, 82, September-October 1974, pp. 905–926; and "Social Security and Private Savings: International Evidence in an Extended Life-Cycle Model," in M. Feldstein and R. Inman (Eds.), *The Economics of Public Services* (New York: Macmillan, 1977).

9.3.4 Wealth and Consumption

Contemporary consumption functions distinguish between human and non-human wealth. *Human wealth* is defined as the present value of present and future labor earnings. *Nonhuman wealth* is the market value of real and financial assets, including corporate stocks and bonds. This distinction is important for examining the effect of changes in interest rates and stock prices on consumption. These consumption functions are of the form

$$C_t = \beta Y_t^p + \Gamma W_t \tag{9.13}$$

where C_t is consumption, Y_t^p is permanent income, and W_t is the market value of nonhuman wealth, or simply wealth. Γ is the marginal propensity to consume out of wealth and is generally estimated to be about 4 cents.

Equation (9.13) is useful for examining the possible influence of the stock market crash of 1987 on consumption spending. Following a 39 percent increase from December 31, 1986 to August 25, 1987, the Standard and Poor 500 index of stock prices dropped 16 percent from August 25 to October 16 and then dropped a 1-day record 20 percent on Black Monday, October 19. This fall in stock prices should have, by reason of reducing consumers' nonhuman wealth, reduced consumption.

The Council of Economic Advisors estimates that at the time of the crash, consumers' nonhuman wealth amounted to $15.1 trillion, $2.7 trillion of which was in corporate stocks.[12] During the fourth quarter of 1987, consumer holdings of corporate stocks fell, mainly because of capital losses, by $650 billion. A marginal propensity to consume out of wealth of 4 cents therefore implies a reduction in consumption of $25 billion. Consumption did, in fact, fall during the fourth quarter of 1987 as the saving rate increased by about 2 percentage points. The saving rate remained about 1 point higher through the first three quarters of 1988. Quantitatively, the council concluded that consumption fell by about half of the predicted amount. Apparently, consumers felt that about half of the crash was permanent and the other half transitory.

Surveys by both the Conference Board and the Survey Research Center of the University of Michigan found that consumer confidence fell immediately after the crash. However, later surveys showed recovery of consumer confidence. Importantly, the crash of 1987 was not followed by a major downward revision in consumers' expectations of permanent income. Of course, the crash of 1987 was neither followed by policy blunders such as

---

[12]These figures and most of the following pertaining to the 1987 stock market crash are taken from *Economic Report of the President*, 1989, pp. 271–274.

protectionism and tax increases—although there was political agitation on these issues.

9.3.5 Liquidity and Consumption

Throughout history there has been a general disposition against borrowing, especially borrowing for the purpose of consumption. Adam Smith, in *The Wealth of Nations*, endorsed usury laws because they made it unprofitable to lend to ''prodigals'' and directed savings to others who would ''use it to best advantage.'' The Federal Reserve has used regulations such as mandatory down payments to limit the flow of credit to consumers seeking financing for purchases of automobiles, household appliances, and furniture. In addition, the Tax Reform Act of 1986 removes the tax deductibility of interest on consumer debt. In contrast to this general disposition against borrowing for consumption, the life-cycle model argues that it is natural for young adults to seek to borrow to finance consumption (as well as to finance their acquisition of household and human capital).

Even if there were no usury laws, consumer debt regulations, or adverse tax treatment, there would still be difficulties involved in borrowing for consumption. This is so because of the moral hazard involved in borrowing. A person deeply enough in debt has an incentive to default. A person who borrowed money to buy a house in Houston when the real estate market in that city was booming in the early 1980s might rationally choose to declare bankruptcy and ''walk away'' from his or her debt when the Houston real estate market collapsed in the mid-1980s. However, the moral hazard in borrowing is different from this. The election of bankruptcy because of an adverse turn in *external* conditions is considered nowadays to simply be the exercise of an option built into debt with little moral connotation.

The moral hazard involved in borrowing derives from ''adverse selection'' on the part of the borrower and the costliness of credit evaluation on the part of the lender.[13] Not all borrowers are the same. The thing is, because of the cost involved in credit evaluation, lenders will not perfectly distinguish among their borrowers. Therefore, within the categories into which the lender does classify borrowers, the lender will charge interest rates that reflect the average creditworthiness of borrowers within each category. This rate will be too high for the lender's more creditworthy customers (within each category) and too low for the lender's less creditworthy customers (within each

---

[13]This theory of credit rationing is formally developed by Joseph E. Stiglitz and Andrew Weiss, ''Credit Rationing in Markets with Imperfect Information,'' *American Economic Review*, 71, June 1981, pp. 393–410.

category). Because the interest rate tends to be a bargain for less creditworthy customers, the less creditworthy will tend to increase their borrowing.

An effective solution to the moral hazard problem involved in lending is specification of collateral. With a sufficiently low loan-to-value ratio, the borrower would always have an incentive to repay. Innovations in "securitization," including the home equity line of credit, are enabling consumer finance to be conducted on an increasingly efficient basis.

However, many would-be borrowers do not have assets that can be used as collateral. This is especially true for young adults. In order to manage the risk characteristics of their loan portfolios in the face of "adverse selection," lenders tend to ration or limit credit to their unsecured borrowers. This theory of credit rationing explains why consumer finance companies both charge relatively high interest rates and establish relatively low credit limits. The people whose spending is restricted by reason of credit rationing are said to be *liquidity constrained*.

Returning now to the consumption function, current income—by lifting liquidity constraints—can greatly increase consumption. Indeed, for those who are liquidity constrained, the marginal propensity to consume out of current income is near 1. Studies of consumption often find that it is more sensitive to current income than would be warranted by the permanent income and life-cycle models.[14] One explanation for this excessive sensitivity is the role of liquidity in determining consumption.

9.4 SOME MANAGERIAL IMPLICATIONS

The life-cycle and permanent income consumption functions hold many insights for management. To begin with, consumption spending on durables behaves differently from consumption spending on nondurables and services. The latter two are relatively insensitive to current income, being determined mostly by people's long-term income expectations. Aggregate sales are, therefore, less volatile, and fluctuations in sales are more due to microeconomic factors such as changes in relative prices.

Consumption spending on durable goods, on the other hand, is relatively sensitive to current income. At the same time, this means that firms manufacturing and selling durable consumer goods must carry inventories of finished products and production capacity sufficient to meet unexpected

[14]See, for example, Marjorie Flavin, "The Adjustment of Consumption to Changing Expectations About Future Income," *Journal of Political Economy*, 89, October 1981, pp. 974–1009; and Fumio Hayashi, "The Permanent Income Hypothesis: Estimation and Testing by Instrumental Variables," *Journal of Political Economy*, 90, October 1982, pp. 895–916.

increases in demand and maintain reserves of liquid assets sufficient to survive unexpected decreases in demand. This implies that effective working capital management is a key to success for these firms (see Figure 9.7).

Many durable consumer goods, such as household appliances and furniture, are purchased by young adults in conjunction with family formation. The life-cycle model tells us that such buyers are typically liquidity-constrained consumers. The ability of manufacturers and distributors of these goods to offer financing is, therefore, vitally important. Seller financing is probably efficient because of the seller's unique position to evaluate the "character" of the buyer/borrower and the collateral value of the product.

The movement of the World War II baby boomers through their life

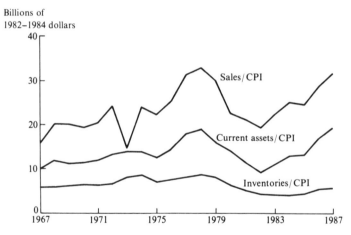

FIGURE 9.7   Ford Motor Corporation, 1967–1987.
Ford Motor Corporation is one of the world's largest manufacturers of automobiles. Notice how volatile has been its sales during the 20-year period 1967–1987. Notice what happened when sales fell sharply during 1974: Ford's inventories increased and its other current assets decreased. Inventories increased because production, pricing, and credit policies were not sufficiently responsive to the sudden fall in demand. The increase in inventories, during a time of reduced net income, absorbed much of Ford's reserve of liquid assets. Notice what happened when sales fell beginning in 1979: Ford's inventories did not increase. New responsiveness in production, pricing, and credit policies enabled Ford to not only survive this fall in demand, but to emerge during the 1980s as a highly competitive and profitable firm. (*Note:* Sales are divided by 2.)
Source: Ford Motor Company, *Annual Reports*, various issues. Used with permission.

cycle will continue to change the composition of consumer demand for years to come. In addition, aggregate saving will probably increase as the baby boomers enter their mature adult years and begin to accumulate wealth in preparation for their retirement years.

9.5 SUMMARY

1. The Keynesian consumption function links consumption to current income. Because of this link, fluctuations in autonomous spending such as investment cause multiplied fluctuations in national income. Also because of this link, discretionary fiscal and monetary policies can be used to stabilize the economy at a high level of employment.

2. The permanent income and life-cycle consumption functions, on the other hand, link consumption to people's long-term expectations of their future income. Because consumption is disconnected from current income, the consumption function is a source of stability instead of an amplifier of instability.

3. The permanent income and life-cycle consumption functions imply that discretionary fiscal and monetary policies such as temporary changes in taxes will not have major effects on aggregate demand. Taxes should be set at levels that balance government budgets over the buiness cycle.

4. Even with the permanent income and life-cycle consumption functions, current income can affect consumption spending in several ways. Current income can affect people's expectations of their future income. Current income can affect spending on durable consumer goods, since this spending is viewed as a form of investment. And, current income can increase the consumption of liquidity-constrained consumers.

5. When people's expectations of future income are formed by rational expectations instead of by slow-moving, mechanistic adaptive expectations, consumption will behave like a random walk with drift. Not only does this mean that future changes in consumption cannot be forecasted, this also means that consumption spending can change dramatically upon major macroeconomic innovations.

6. A key to success for companies that manufacture and sell consumer durables is working capital management. This includes the ability to finance sales when customers are liquidity constrained, having inventories of finished goods and responsiveness in production so as to be able to meet surprise increases in demand, and having reserves of liquid assets such as marketable securities so as to be able to ride through surprise reductions in demand.

9.6 EXERCISES

1. Why is the multiplier relatively low with the permanent income and life-cycle consumption functions?

2. In order to reduce inflationary pressures while a limited war is conducted in Southeast Asia, the President proposes a temporary 10 percent surtax on federal income taxes. How is this likely to affect consumption?

3. Why would ''superrational'' consumers increase their saving when the government runs a deficit? If consumers are not ''superrational'' and do not increase their saving when the government runs a deficit, what will happen to interest rates, investment, and productivity growth?

4. Why do banks not lend to all would-be borrowers at the going interest rate?

5. Why was the stock market crash of 1987 not followed by a large fall in consumption spending and a major recession?

6. How would you modify the life-cycle consumption function to allow for uncertain lifetimes?

9.7 REFERENCES

Ben S. Bernanke, ''Permanent Income, Liquidity and Expenditure on Automobiles: Evidence from Panel Data,'' *Quarterly Journal of Economics,* 99, August 1984, pp. 587–614.

Alan S. Blinder and Angus S. Deaton, ''The Time Series Consumption Function Revisited,'' *Brookings Papers on Economic Activity*, 2:1985, pp. 465–521.

Milton Friedman, *A Theory of the Consumption Function.* Princeton, N.J.: Princeton University Press, 1957.

George Hadjimatheou, *Consumer Economics after Keynes.* Brighton, England: Wheatsheaf Books, 1987.

Robert E. Hall, ''Stochastic Implications of the Life Cycle Permanent Income Hypothesis: Theory and Evidence,'' *Journal of Political Economy*, 86, December 1978, pp. 971–987.

Robert E. Hall and Frederick S. Mishkin, ''The Sensitivity of Consumption to Transitory Income: Estimates from Panel Data on Households,'' *Econometrica*, 50, March 1982, pp. 461–481.

Fumio Hayashi, ''Why is Japan's Savings Rate So Apparently High?'' in Stanley Fischer (Ed.), *NBER Macroeconomics Annual.* Cambridge, Mass.: MIT Press, 1986, pp. 147–210.

George Katona, *The Powerful Consumer.* New York: McGraw-Hill, 1960.

Thomas Mayer, *Permanent Income, Wealth and Consumption.* Berkeley, Calif.: University of California Press, 1972.

Franco Modigliani, "Life Cycle, Individual Thrift, and the Wealth of Nations," *American Economic Review,* 76, June 1986, pp. 297–313.

Thomas S. Sargent, "Rational Expectations, Econometric Endogeneity and Consumption," *Journal of Political Economy*, 86, August 1978, pp. 673–700.

_10_
The International Sector

10.1 INTRODUCTION

The U.S. macro economy is influenced more by international trade nearly every day. While exports and imports together amounted to only 10 percent of GNP in 1960 (approximately 5 percent each), in 1987 both exports and imports together made up nearly 30 percent of GNP (approximately 15 percent each). The United States in recent years has seen a massive infusion of foreign capital, while nearly every major U.S. company is either selling or manufacturing abroad. According to the city of San Francisco, for example, almost as much office space is owned by foreign nationals as by Americans. In most states, the growth of jobs in the international sector has been impressive. The Japanese Honda corporation manufactures cars in Ohio, the Japanese Sharp Electronics Company assembles television sets in Memphis, and the Dutch-owned Shell corporation sells gasoline and oil products nationwide. In Tennessee in 1987, it was estimated by the Department of Economic and Community Development that nearly one out of every five workers works for a foreign-owned firm. Even though we might not have as active a trade sector as some nations, the growth in trade has been phenomenal. The time has long passed from when a domestic business was unaffected by international trade.

Many events in the late 1980s have encouraged growth in international trade. First, the United States has not had any appreciable increase in trade restrictions, while most of our major trading partners in Europe and Asia have. Holding the line on trade restrictions such as tariffs and quotas has encouraged both foreign businesses to invest and export here and American businesses to do more business abroad. Second, the value of the U.S. dollar on international markets fell substantially through 1980 – 1987. As the dollar fell, U.S. product services and investments became cheaper and more attractive to foreign investors and buyers. Foreign buyers and investors encouraged further internationalization of our economy. Third, while wars and political instability appear to be at the forefront of any major news broadcast, the United States has been free of this at home for years. This nationwide confidence in our political and economic stability has encouraged foreigners who see great instability at home to move their wealth and investments to the United States. Once it was more the American investing abroad; today it is foreigners more often bringing investments to the United States. The largest peacetime military force in the United States in the 1980s further encouraged businesses to invest where they saw protection for their assets. Fourth, price instability in the 1970s was a diverting force for international trade. Buyers and investors were uneasy about an economy racked with price instability. In 1978, the price level rose to over 18 percent. The relatively stable prices of the 1980s have encouraged international trade. Price hikes fell from that 18 percent to just under 3 percent in 1986. With U.S. prices rising slower than those of many other countries, international sales became easier. Fifth, the real rate of interest in the United States has been higher than many of its major trading partners in the 1980s. The higher rates in the United States have encouraged foreign investors and savers in the United States. Sixth, resources are becoming more scarce all the time and the United States and its major trading partners have come to rely on each other more than ever for imports of inputs of goods and services for nearly every industrial process. It is no wonder that trade has come to be of such great importance to the United States and the world.

10.2 THE U.S. HERITAGE AND INTERNATIONAL TRADE

Even though there are many reasons for the colonization and eventual independence of the United States from England, it is irrefutable that international trade was a major factor. Our heritage is steeped in a desire for free and unbridled international trade. England originally sought new trading partners in the New World. America was to become not only a new source of raw materials, but a new market for British manufactured goods. It was not until later that tea and stamp taxes and the many restrictions England made on the colonists on how and to whom they could sell their produce finally drew the masses into a long hard fight for U.S. independence. The Boston Tea Party alone was symbolic of the desire of Americans to buy or sell tea from whomever they liked. The restrictions on international trade were no longer tolerated.

When our new government was formed in 1776, it was ironic that the very first tax levied to pay for the continental army was import duties, which in a sense was restricting the very trade we had fought so hard to make free. The first duties, however, were for the most part very low, and even until the late 1980s, U.S. trade restrictions have fallen far below that of our major trading partners in Europe and Asia. It may be this legacy more than any other that has kept the United States from establishing more restrictive trade practices.

10.3 COMPARATIVE ADVANTAGE AND INTERNATIONAL TRADE

David Ricardo is considered to be the father of the concept of comparative advantage. He was born in London into a family of Orthodox Jews who had fled Spain because of persecution. The family traveled first to Holland and then to London, where they settled. At the age of 21, Ricardo renounced his faith and married a young Quaker. He became a stockbroker and dealer in government securities. Within a few years, he was very wealthy, and at the age of 42, he retired to a large country estate in Scotland.

Ricardo soon became a member of the British Parliament. He published his famous *Principles of Political Economy and Taxation* in April of 1817, one of the first economics textbooks. He was famous for his theories on wages, rent, labor, and profits, all of which became extremely controversial. His theory of comparative advantage, however, has long been held as law among most economists. This theory opened the way for world trade. When Ricardo died in 1823, he left an estate that at that time was estimated at £700,000. In today's world, it might approximate $20 million (US). His theories laid the foundation for economic and political thinkers as ideologically different as Karl Marx and John Stuart Mill.

A nation or region is said to have a *comparative advantage* when it can produce a product or service at lower relative economic costs than any other product or service. A nation is said to have an *absolute advantage* when it can produce a good or service using fewer resources than any other nation or region.

10.3.1 Theory of Comparative Advantage

The objective of Ricardo's theory of comparative advantage is to prove that even though a nation might not have an absolute advantage in the production

---

Section 10.3 is based on S. Z. Barr, "A Lesson in International Economics," in R. T. Byrns and G. W. Stone (Eds.), *Great Ideas in Teaching Economics* (Chicago: Scott Foresman, 1984), pp. 198-200.

of any of its goods or services, it still can receive benefits of a higher standard of living by trading that good in which it has a comparative advantage.

Let us examine these concepts, as Ricardo did, using early nineteenth-century Britain and the United States. What would be the advantage of a highly advanced nineteenth-century Britain trading with a growing, but at that time undeveloped America? The following example shows how Ricardo proved trade was a great idea for both Britain and America and, of course, for the United States and the world today.

Consider the case where the United States has only 60 workers and Britain has only 60 workers. Also consider that each produces only wheat and cloth and the only factor of production is labor. Suppose that it takes one man 1 week to produce either 2 yards of cloth or 5 bushels of wheat in the United States. Britain, however, in the nineteenth century could produce more per man-hour per week. Britain could produce 10 yards of cloth and 6 bushels of wheat with that same man per week. Britain had an absolute advantage in the production of both wheat and cloth, since more of each could be produced per unit of input than in the United States.

10.3.2 Comparative Advantage and International Trade

How much wheat and cloth would be produced in Britain and the United States if there were no international trade? If Britain used all 60 workers, 30 to produce wheat and 30 to produce cloth, it could produce 300 yards of cloth and 180 bushels of wheat, or a total of 480 economic units without trade. If the United States used 30 workers to produce wheat and 30 to produce cloth, it would produce 60 yards of cloth and 150 bushels of wheat, or a total of 210 economic units without trade. Together, Britain and the United States would produce 690 economic units without international trade.

Britain realized that even though it had an absolute advantage in the production of both wheat and cloth, it would do better to produce only that good in which it had a comparative advantage. With its 60 workers, Britain could produce 600 yards of cloth per week and could trade with the United States for wheat. The United States enjoyed a comparative advantage in the production of wheat over cloth. It could produce more wheat per man-hour than cloth. The United States could produce 300 bushels of wheat with its 60 workers and trade for cloth with Britain. The United States and Britain could then produce together 900 economic units per week. As a result of free trade, the world production thus increased by 210 economic units: 900 economic units with trade minus 690 economic units without trade equals a 210-unit increase in economic units as a result of trade.

Of course, there are costs of trade not shown in this simple example, such as transportation. However, the underlying idea of trade being efficient, even when a country is less efficient than its trading partner in all outputs, is what makes the Ricardian theory of comparative advantage so timeless. It is no wonder that Ricardo died a very wealthy man!

10.4 INTERNATIONAL TRADE AND THE LEVEL OF MACROECONOMIC EQUILIBRIUM

Aggregate demand AD has been described in Chapter 3 as the sum of planned expenditures in the economy by consumers C, investors I_p, government G, and the foreign sector X_n. This relationship has been defined by Equation (3.1):

$$AD = C + I_p + G + X_n \tag{3.1}$$

Aggregate supply AS has been described in Chapter 3 as the measure of total output of real goods and services in the economy. This relationship has been defined as Equation (3.3):

$$AS = Y$$

At equilibrium in the macroeconomy,

$$AD = AS \tag{3.2}$$

Furthermore, these relationships can be graphed as shown in Figure 10.1. Expanding on Equation (3.1), X_n can be divided into exports X and

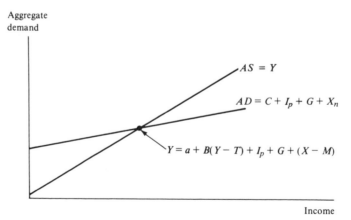

FIGURE 10.1   Basic Aggregate Demand – Aggregate Supply Model.

imports M where

$$X = X - M \tag{10.1}$$

and

$$AD = C + I_p + G + (X - M) \tag{10.2}$$

If there is an increase in the value of exports, all else being equal, aggregate demand will increase or shift upward graphically, and if X decreases, aggregate demand will shift downward. If there is an increase in imports, all else being equal, aggregate demand will decrease or shift downward graphically, and if M decreases, aggregate demand will increase or shift upward (see Fig. 10.2).

This concept can be further understood by looking at the algebraic value for the point of intersection between aggregate supply and aggregate demand. In Chapter 3, Equation (3.7) explained the point of intersection as

$$Y = a + B(Y - T) + I_p + G + X_n$$

which can be expanded to

$$Y = a + B(Y - T) + I_p + G + (X - M) \tag{10.3}$$

by further defining the international sector X_n.

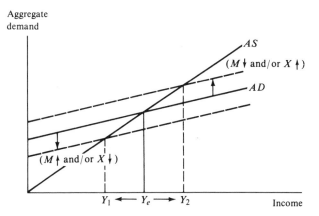

FIGURE 10.2   Exports and Imports on Aggregate Demand.
Increasing X, a decrease in M, or both will raise Y. Decreasing X, an increase in M, or both will lower Y.

It can be seen readily that an increase in X or a decrease in M increases Y, while the reverse also holds true. Therefore, exports tend to increase the level of national income Y, while imports tend to decrease the level of national income Y. The flow of X and M and the impacts of these flows on national income are best understood through measures such as the balance of payments, the balance of payments on the current account, and the balance of trade.

10.5 BALANCE OF PAYMENTS AND THE BALANCE OF TRADE

The most comprehensive measurement of international transactions, the *balance of payments* for a country, is a systematic record of all economic transactions between the residents of that country and the residents of foreign countries during a given reporting period. Whenever and for whatever reason a U.S. resident spends funds abroad, it is considered a debit, and whenever and for whatever reason a foreign resident spends funds here, it is a credit. For example, if a U.S. resident spent the summer in France, all the funds earned here and spent there would be a debit. On the other hand, if a French resident spent the money he or she earned in France here, it would be a credit. The overall balance of all transactions must always, to the accountant, be in balance. The balance of payments must show all debits equal to all credits. In other words, even though transactions in one category, say, goods, might show a deficit—more imports than exports—some accommodating transaction must take place to pay for these excess imports. Either income from investments abroad or official government reserves or some other source of foreign funds must be drawn on to pay for the imbalance. If a nation does not have the funds available, then no international transaction can take place. In other words, if the United States did not receive any income from Japan and therefore received no yen, then the United States would have no yen to purchase goods or services from Japan. Ultimately, the balance of payments is always in balance.

If the balance of payments is always in balance, how is it that the news media has so frequently reported trade deficits? The reason is that the news media reports the international balance of payments on the current account or the international balance of trade. Each leaves some account or accounts out of the total balance. For example, it is like a balance sheet for a corporation being in imbalance because we only counted inventories as an asset and accounts payable as a liability. The *international balance on the current account* is only the sum of merchandise and service exports less merchandise and service imports and unilateral transfers, which are private transfers representing gifts and similar payments and government transfers representing payments associated with foreign assistance programs. The *international balance of trade* is only a measure of the value of merchandise exports minus merchandise imports for one nation for one reporting period. Because the international balance on the current account reports only imports and exports of goods and services and gifts, there can be and usually is an imbalance. The current account balance shows whether or not we are acquiring net claims on foreigners (surplus) or foreigners are gaining net claims on the United States (deficit). This is the balance that relates directly to X_n in Equation (3.1). Surpluses increase the measure of national income, and deficits reduce the measure of national income. The balance of trade also can be in imbalance because it only measures the difference in exports and imports of goods or merchandise. If more merchandise is imported than exported, the trade balance is in deficit. If more merchandise is exported than imported, then the trade balance is in surplus.

The broadest measure, therefore, of international transactions is the international balance of payments. It is always in balance because for every debit there must be an accommodating credit. International balances on the current account, however, show either a deficit or a surplus and hardly ever are in balance. A deficit represents a total of more imports of goods, services, and gifts from foreigners and government transfers to the United States than the total of exports of goods, services, and gifts by Americans and U.S. government transfers to foreigners. A surplus in the international balance on the current account is simply the reverse (see Table 10.1).

The narrowest measure of international transactions is the international balance of trade. It nearly always shows an imbalance because it only measures the flow of merchandise in and out of a country. If the value of merchandise exported exceeds the value of merchandise imported, then it shows a surplus. In the reverse, it shows a deficit.

10.6 INVESTIGATING INTERNATIONAL PAYMENTS

10.6.1 Trends

The international balance of trade since 1961 has been toward greater deficits. In 1961, we exported $20,108 million worth of goods while importing $14,537 million worth of goods. The balance of trade showed a $5571 million surplus. Merchandise exports continued to exceed merchandise imports every year until 1971, when $43,319 million was exported and over $2000 million more was imported. The trade deficit gap has widened, and the United States has imported more than it exported in merchandise every year from 1976 to 1987. In 1986, we imported nearly $148,000 million more

TABLE 10.1 International Balance of Payments on the Current Account, Annual Series, U.S. International Transactions ($ Millions)[a]

	Trade Flows					Capital Flows								
Year	Merchandise Exports	Merchandise Imports	Service Exports	Service Imports	Current Account Balance	Direct Investment Abroad	Direct Investment in U.S.	Security Purchases Abroad	Security Purchases in U.S.	Bank Claims on Foreigners	Bank Liabilities to Foreigners	U.S. Government Assets Abroad	Foreign Official Assets in U.S.	Monetary Base Effect[b]
1961	20,108	14,537	9,829	8,916	3,822	2,653	311	762	475	1,261	928	303	765	-1,061
1962	20,781	16,260	11,022	9,416	3,387	2,851	346	969	68	450	336	-450	1,270	-1,012
1963	22,272	17,048	11,942	9,922	4,414	3,483	231	1,105	138	1,556	898	1,284	1,986	-539
1964	25,501	18,700	13,325	10,402	6,823	3,760	322	677	-231	2,505	1,818	1,509	1,660	-114
1965	26,461	21,510	14,626	11,198	5,432	5,011	415	759	-489	-93	503	380	134	-1,378
1966	29,310	25,493	15,252	12,975	3,031	5,418	425	720	550	-233	2,882	973	-672	-879
1967	30,666	26,866	16,648	14,610	2,583	4,805	698	1,308	881	495	1,765	2,370	3,451	1,748
1968	33,626	32,991	18,737	15,680	611	5,295	807	1,569	4,550	-233	3,871	3,144	-774	-1,540
1969	36,414	35,807	21,108	18,191	339	5,690	1,263	1,459	3,062	570	8,886	3,379	-1,301	-72
1970	42,469	39,866	23,205	20,035	2,331	7,590	1,464	1,076	2,270	967	-6,298	-892	6,908	-355
1971	43,319	45,579	25,519	20,835	-1,433	7,618	367	1,113	2,265	2,980	-6,911	-465	26,879	-922
1972	49,381	55,797	28,114	23,440	-5,795	7,747	949	618	4,468	3,506	4,754	1,572	10,475	-39
1973	71,410	70,499	38,831	28,498	7,140	11,353	2,800	671	3,825	5,980	4,702	2,486	6,026	-328
1974	98,306	103,811	48,360	28,463	1,962	9,052	4,760	1,854	1,075	19,516	16,017	1,101	10,546	-34
1975	107,088	98,185	48,641	34,560	18,116	14,244	2,603	6,247	5,093	13,532	628	4,323	7,027	469
1976	114,745	124,228	56,885	37,881	4,207	11,949	4,347	8,885	4,067	21,368	10,990	6,772	17,693	759
1977	120,816	151,907	63,460	41,857	-14,511	11,890	3,728	5,460	2,971	11,427	6,719	4,068	36,816	-414
1978	142,054	176,001	77,940	53,862	-15,427	16,056	7,897	3,626	4,432	33,667	16,141	3,928	33,678	693
1979	184,473	212,009	102,323	69,650	-991	25,222	11,877	4,726	6,311	26,213	32,607	4,879	-13,665	2,039
1980	224,269	249,749	118,216	83,271	1,873	19,222	16,918	3,568	8,102	46,838	10,743	13,317	15,497	2,947
1981	237,085	263,063	138,674	96,932	6,339	9,624	25,195	5,778	10,122	84,175	42,128	10,272	4,960	1,907
1982r	211,198	247,642	137,467	101,237	-9,131	-2,369	13,792	8,102	13,444	111,070	65,633	11,096	3,593	1,246
1983r	201,820	268,900	131,437	101,480	-46,604	373	11,946	7,007	17,357	29,928	30,342	6,201	5,968	-1,556
1984r	219,900	332,422	140,211	121,988	-106,466	3,858	25,359	5,082	35,818	11,127	33,849	8,654	3,037	-150
1985r	214,424	338,863	144,074	122,328	-117,677	18,752	17,856	7,977	71,359	691	40,387	6,682	-1,324	3,204
1986p	221,753	369,461	148,949	126,665	-140,569	31,922	25,585	4,765	79,992	57,312	77,435	1,666	33,394	3,404

Note: r = revised; p = preliminary. [a]The signs in this table do *not* indicate whether a particular transaction is an inflow or an outflow. In this table a negative sign indicates a reduction in the stock of a particular class of assets during a particular time period.
[b]Begining in 1979, official U.S. holdings of assets denominated in foreign currencies are revalued monthly at market exchange rates. As of July 1980, the monetary base effect includes the addition of official U.S. holdings of Swiss franc–denominated assets. Consequently, this series after July 1980 is not directly comparable to that reported for previous periods.
Source: International Economic Conditions Annual Edition, July 1987. Federal Reserve Bank of St. Louis, St. Louis, Missouri, 1987. Used with permission.

merchandise than we exported, or in current terms, we ran a deficit equal to more than seven times what we had exported back in 1961.

The international balance on the current account also has accumulated deficits since 1961. In 1961, the current account balance was $3822 million in surplus, and we continued to run surpluses every year until 1971. During that year and for 4 of the next 10 years we ran deficits that, nevertheless, did not ever exceed the accumulated surpluses of prior years. The greatest imbalances began in 1983 and continued on throughout 1987, during which deficits on the current account reached nearly $160,000 million.

What has caused these deficits? The deficits are a result of many economic factors. The U.S. economy has undergone a transition from a manufacturing-based economy to a service-based economy. As we changed toward services it was only natural that merchandise imports would rise while our service exports also rose. This helps explain the deficit in our balance of trade, which only measures merchandise flows. However, this does not explain the imbalances in the current account, which also includes services as well as merchandise.

The current account deficits are a strong indication that, first, the United States has continued to import goods and services relatively more freely of government regulation and taxes than our trading partners have accepted our goods and services. For example, while the Japanese can export electronic products freely to the United States with the payment of a minor import tax and easy access to our markets, American firms that hope to sell in Japan must first find a Japanese citizen to buy half or more of their company.

A second reason for the current account deficits has been that foreign nations have tried to encourage their own exports through government assistance programs such as subsidies and credits and our government has not done so to the same degree. For example, it is estimated that the value of the Japanese government subsidy is worth about $800 on each car shipped to the United States; the United States has no such subsidy for American automobile exports.

A third reason for the deficits has been that even though these two balances, the trade and current account balances, are in deficit, accommodating transactions have been the cause as well as the result. In other words, there has been a massive infusion of foreign capital both by foreign governments and by private individuals and businesses into the United States. Many capital transfers are not included in the current account or trade balances. However, they have been the source of billions of dollars worth of foreign funds that have been used to buy foreign products and services. While we have been the beneficiary of a world of new foreign investment, we have lost that capital as a source for sales of our goods and services.

The 1990s may show some change. Many U.S. corporations today look for a relaxation of trade restrictions for their products abroad. Our major trading partners have set up many more trading barriers than we have in recent years. If these trade routes are not opened, then many feel that the source of foreign dollars also will dry up. The U.S. government has in the late 1980s considered hundreds of possible trade restricting regulations to halt the flood of imports. Economists continue to argue, however, that as the theory of comparative advantage shows, free trade might still be best. If we halt imports, then further restrictions on exports might bring our economies down. Economists point out that even though deficits in the current and trade accounts have been mounting, unemployment during that same 1973 – 1987 period has been falling. In 1973 we had 11 percent unemployment, while in 1987 it stands at a mere 6.8 percent. Maybe the sources of new foreign investment capital have been of greater value to the U.S. economy than the loss of exports of goods and services.

10.6.2 Long-Term Effects of Trade Imbalances

Excessive long-term deficits in the current account balance can lead toward dangerously low levels of international financial reserves. If a nation continues to earn less funds abroad than it spends abroad, international settlements may require governments and private financial institutions to use up their reserves of foreign capital. If these reserves are fully depleted, then purchases from abroad will halt because foreign funds for those purchases will not be available. This type of disruption could seriously injure business.

Excessive long-term surpluses in the current account balance can lead toward dangerously high levels of inflation and dangerously low levels of interest. If we have many more funds flowing in than out, then the accumulation of cash assets will increase while our store of goods and services for shipment abroad become depleted. Fewer goods and services for sale at home coupled with massive increases in cash assets might lead toward higher and higher prices. Inflation of this sort can cause great business instability. The accumulation of massive cash assets can cause interest rates to fall. If cash is in abundance, less money is demanded for loans while more is saved. The lower the rate of interest, the more difficult it is for financial institutions to survive. If interest rates, for example, fall below 1 percent, the difference between the savings rates and lending rates falls close to nothing and there is no room for bank profits. A collapse could disrupt all American business.

The best long-term trend certainly is neither a deficit nor a surplus in the international balance on the current account. Japan's massive international trade surplus in 1987 is as much of a destabilizing problem as the U.S. 1987 deficit. Both would benefit in greater economic stability if both ran closer to a current account balance. Ideally, both imports and exports and capital flows should rise in balanced proportions to ensure international financial liquidity and stability in the long run. Amassing either surpluses or deficits should not be any nation's goal, but rather expanded world trade should be the goal. Only in this way can nations fully utilize their comparative advantages.

10.7   EXCHANGE RATE DETERMINATION

There are over 150 separate nation states in the world. Each, for the most part, has chosen its own currency. These currencies each have a different relative value, and each must be measured in terms of another for international trade worldwide to take place. The *Wall Street Journal* reports many of these exchange rates on a daily basis, as shown in Table 10.2.

The exchange rate for each country is reported both as a U.S. dollar equivalent and as currency per U.S. dollar. The *U.S. dollar equivalent* shows you how much in dollars each unit of the foreign currency costs. For example, on Wednesday, January 4, 1989, one British pound cost about $1.81. The *currency per U.S. dollar* is how many units of the foreign currency can be purchased with one U.S. dollar. On the same date, a little over £0.55 is equivalent to one U.S. dollar.

If you were shopping in Britain and found a coat costing £160, you

TABLE 10.2   Exchange Rates: Wednesday, January 4, 1989

Country	U.S. $ Equivalent		Currency per U.S. $	
	Wed.	*Tues.*	*Wed.*	*Tues.*
Argentina (austral)	0.06135	0.06135	16.30	16.30
Britain (pound)	1.8095	1.8230	0.5526	0.5485
30-day forward	1.8038	1.8171	0.5543	0.5503
90-day forward	1.7933	1.8064	0.5576	0.5535
180-day forward	1.7794	1.7918	0.5619	0.5581
Japan (yen)	0.008005	0.008077	124.92	123.80
30-day forward	0.008037	0.008110	124.41	123.29
90-day forward	0.008100	0.008172	123.45	122.36
180-day forward	0.008199	0.008274	121.96	120.85

Source: Selected data from *Wall Street Journal*, January 4, 1989, p. C11, col. 4.

could find the dollar value by either dividing 160 by the currency per dollar or multiplying the amount times the dollar equivalent. In other words, £160 is the same as about $290 (1.81 times 160 or 160 divided by 0.55).

The *Wall Street Journal* also reports, as shown in Table 10.2, the 30-, 90-, and 180-day forward rates. The current rate is called the *spot rate*, such as $1.8095 per British pound, and the *forward rates* are how much pounds cost if they are contracted for today to be delivered and paid for at some future date. If you are willing to wait 30 days for your pounds, the rate is $1.8038 per pound; in 90 days, the rate is $1.7933 per pound; and in 180 days, the rate is $1.7794 per pound. In each case, you can see that the forward price of pounds is less the farther you go in the future, leaving the spot rate the highest exchange rate. In other words, on this date the longer you would be willing to wait for your pounds, the cheaper would be your dollar cost. This shows a market that sees the value of the pound falling in the future and the value of the dollar against pounds rising in the future. Forward rates, however, can either be higher or lower than spot rates. The forward and spot markets alone are an important indicator of the future direction of a currency's value. Speculators watch for discounts or premiums in forward exchange markets because they realize that actual future spot rates may be different from the forward rates quoted today. Such speculators make money on these differences.

When currency is bought or sold by businesses today for transactions done today or when businesses buy or sell currency for future transactions on the forward market, they are hedging against losses due to an unexpected adjustment in exchange rates. Can you imagine the shock of finding out that those goods you ordered today, when delivered in 30 days, now cost twice as much as a result of exchange rate changes. Forward contracts guarantee future currency prices, but there is a chance the future spot rate will actually be cheaper. Speculators take chances and often make fortunes on guessing what others were unable to guess. Forces that cause these changes in exchange rates are discussed later.

10.7.1 The Importance of Exchange Rates

Exchange rates are of primary importance to international business. The prices of goods and services produced here are subject to the rate of exchange when sold abroad. Business selling prices may be competitive or not depending on how expensive the dollar is. If, for example, the dollar doubles in cost, then business products produced here become twice as expensive abroad. Business profits and the returns from foreign sales must ultimately be converted to dollars when reported to investors or stockholders. Sales in England, for example, may rise in pound values for a firm, but if the pound falls enough against the dollar, these same sales as measured in dollars may be less than before. It is no wonder that businesses watch exchange rates carefully. Exchange rates also affect how much must be paid to foreigners in the future. If the rate of exchange for the dollar is rising, you can get more pounds per dollar in the future than you can today. A debt in England, in such a case, would fall in the future. A rising dollar encourages you to borrow more abroad and less at home. This situation would be reversed if the value of the dollar were falling against the pound. In such a case you would be encouraged to borrow less abroad and more at home.

Anyone who has traveled abroad has seen exchange rates for dollars change daily nearly everywhere. Since late in 1971, the value of the dollar has floated. In other words, the value of the dollar reflects the value it has in the open market and *not* what government decrees as its value. Each day, buyers and sellers of currencies through their supplies and demands determine the value of the dollar. If the supply of dollars exceeds demand, the value of the dollar will fall, and if demand exceeds the supply of dollars, then the value of the dollar will rise. As shown earlier in Table 10.2, British pounds in the future are worth more on the reporting day than in the future. This means the supply of pounds is predicted to rise faster than the demand for pounds. The value of the pound is predicted to fall; therefore, the dollar must rise against the pound.

10.7.2 Devaluation and Revaluation

Devaluation is the official term for a reduction in the value of a native currency in terms of a foreign currency. If one U.S. dollar can be traded for 0.6 British pounds today and only 0.5 British pounds tomorrow, then tomorrow the dollar will devalue. *Revaluation* is the official term for an appreciation in the value of a native currency in terms of a foreign currency. If the dollar increases in value from 35 Venezuelan bolivars to 35.5 bolivars, then it has revalued. Currencies can naturally revalue or devalue based on adjustments in their supplies and demands in international markets.

The advantage of a devaluation can be that it makes U.S. exports cheaper to foreign buyers in their currencies and imports more expensive in domestic currency prices. When the price of U.S. goods in foreign currency drops, domestic producers can sell more at the same dollar price. Devaluations can lead to an increase in export earnings, net exports (exports minus imports), and national income. The major disadvantage of a devaluation is that it makes the cost of foreign currency loans greater. As the dollar devalues, the number of dollars needed to pay off a foreign-currency loan increases. Devaluation, therefore, leads to an increase in the dollar value of foreign debts.

The advantage of revaluation is that it makes the cost of foreign loans decrease. If, for example, the dollar doubles in value against the French franc, then only half as many dollars are needed to pay off the same number of francs. The major disadvantage of a revaluation is that it makes domestic products more expensive in foreign currencies and imports cheaper in domestic currency. If, for example, it takes half as many dollars to buy the same amount of French francs, then French products will appear to be half-price to Americans while U.S. products to the French will seem like they have doubled in price. A revaluation can lead to a drop in export earnings, net exports (exports minus imports), and national income.

When business or individuals engage in international trade and either debts or credits are created, currency values become of great importance. A debtor abroad must use more of his or her currency to pay you back when your currency appreciates or revalues. A revaluation, therefore, adds a premium to your return. A devaluation, on the other hand, causes the reverse and can lead to a discount on your foreign-currency return. Currency changes also can affect the level of reportable corporate profits. For example, the 1987 annual report of Black and Decker Manufacturing Company shows that a major proportion of all sales took place in Britain between 1985 and 1987. During this period the pound grew 64 percent against the dollar. This revaluation made Black and Decker profits in England look much brighter when measured in dollars. Currency changes affect tourism, banking, and any commercial dealing involving international exchange.

10.7.3 Trends

On August 15, 1971, President Richard Nixon announced an order that set the dollar floating on world markets. Up to that time, the postwar value of the dollar was fixed by the U.S. government. When the value was first allowed to float, the dollar quickly began to devalue. Our exports began to rise while imports to the United States began to fall. Our trade partners began to complain to the Nixon administration that they needed the United States to move back to a higher priced-controlled dollar. The administration did not change its policy, and the decline continued, giving the United States trade surpluses in 1973 and 1975 and close to trade balances in 1972 and 1974.

This trend changed in early 1980, when the dollar started one of its steepest rises in history. Between the beginning of 1981 and the beginning of 1985, the dollar appreciated upward by 52.4 percent against the currencies of the major U.S. trading partners. This trend led to a reduction in net export earnings and a deficit in the trade and current account balances. Since 1985, the trend again has been reversed. From early 1985 to mid-1988, the dollar

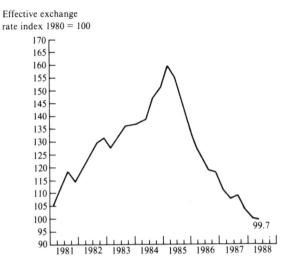

Effective exchange
rate index 1980 = 100

FIGURE 10.3   Movements in U.S. Exchange Rate, 1981 – 1988.
The U.S. dollar exchange rate is an index of the weighted value of
the U.S. dollar against 17 other major currencies. From early 1981
through early 1985, the value of the dollar rose from an index of
105 to an index of 160. This amounts to a 52.38 percent increase in
the value of the dollar. From early 1985 to mid-1988, the U.S. dollar effective exchange rate fell to 99.7. This amounts to a 37.69 percent decrease in the value of the dollar.
Source: Federal Reserve Bank of St. Louis, *International Economic Conditions*, October 1988. Used with permission.

has devalued against the currencies of the major U.S. trading partners by
nearly 40 percent. This devaluation could cause an increase in our net export
earnings and a surplus in our trade and current account balances. This movement in U.S. exchange rates is shown in Figure 10.3.

10.7.4 Macroeconomic Policies that Influence Exchange Rates

Government policies are often directed toward adjustments in the rate of
exchange of a nation's currency. As mentioned earlier, a nation might try to
institute policies that cause a devaluation to discourage imports and encourage exports as well as foreign direct investment at home. On the other
hand, a nation might institute macro policies to revaluate their currency
upward to reduce the size of foreign debts as measured in domestic currency.
The most popular policies to influence exchange rates are discussed in the
following subsections.

10.7.4.1 Exchange Controls

Rationing of foreign currency to maintain favorable exchange rates is one approach. In Venezuela, for example, in 1987 the government controlled all conversions from bolivars to other currencies by instituting a 4- to 6-month waiting period for currency conversions. This type of exchange control is often coupled with a *fixed exchange rate*, or a government-decreed legal rate of exchange, rather than a *floating exchange rate*, in which currency can be exchanged freely and prices are set by market conditions.

10.7.4.2 Currency Intervention

National central banks often try to adjust currency rates in a floating exchange market by either buying or selling currencies. For example, when the Japanese government sells large amounts of yen for dollars in the open international money markets, as it did in the 1980s, it causes the demand for dollars to rise and the supply of yen to rise. The desired effect was to cause the yen value to fall relative to the dollar. One of the reasons for this action was an attempt to make Japanese car prices appear cheaper in the U.S. market. By buying up yen with their accumulated dollars, the Japanese government could create the reverse, or a fall in the dollar and a rise in value of the yen. Japan has been accused in the past by U.S. businesspeople of driving down the yen by selling yen to keep their products more than price competitive.

10.7.4.3 Financing

Governments can take loans from abroad in foreign currency and use them to purchase their own currency. This will drive up the value of the native currency. In reverse, governments can exchange their own currency for the necessary foreign currency to pay off a foreign debt and through this action drive down the value of the native currency.

10.7.4.4 Adjustable Peg

With this policy, the government allows the currency values to fluctuate between a narrow range. The rate of exchange cannot legally fluctuate above a certain ceiling price nor fall below a certain floor price. For example, if the dollar were "pegged" between 1.8 and 2.2 German marks, then between those values the dollar is allowed to fluctuate freely but never above 2.2 or below 1.8 German marks. By pegging currency values, governments attempt to keep favorable rates of trade.

10.7.4.5 Adjusting the Domestic Economy

Through monetary and fiscal policies, governments indirectly intervene in international exchange markets. An expansionary monetary policy, all else being equal, tends to devalue currency, while a contractionary monetary policy tends to revalue currency. This occurs because the supply of the currency is changed with a constant demand and, therefore, so is its price. An expansionary demand-side fiscal policy, all else being equal, drives up domestic demand for imported goods and services and the accompanying demand for foreign currency. The supply of domestic currency demanding foreign currency can devalue the dollar and revalue foreign currencies. A contractionary demand-side fiscal policy could do the reverse and cause the dollar to revalue. Supply-side fiscal policies would have different effects. If a supply-side fiscal policy encouraged more and lower-priced business output, then the quantity of these products being demanded could rise. As foreigners demand more of our products at more competitive prices, they will need to demand more dollars to buy them. The new demand for these dollars could drive up the value of the dollar. An expansionary supply-side policy, therefore, tends to revalue the dollar, while a contractionary supply-side policy tends to devalue the dollar.

10.7.4.6 Forward Operations

A method of raising foreign currency now is to have the government raise the official forward price of domestic currency. Forward operations encourage citizens and foreigners to purchase rights to future domestic currency with foreign currency. With the foreign currency, the government can enter exchange markets to adjust the value of domestic currency. By raising the forward price alone on domestic currency, the spot price should rise. By lowering the forward price of the domestic currency, spot prices should fall. These occurrences are the result of both changing expectations and changes in future currency values.

10.7.4.7 Swaps

Sometimes the central banks of two countries literally swap for each other's currency. By swapping, they not only receive needed foreign exchange, but they also receive funds necessary for currency intervention. As mentioned earlier, greater supplies can drive down prices, while shorter supplies can cause prices to rise for domestic currency.

10.7.4.8 Roosa Bonds

Roosa bonds are bonds distributed by a central government but sold for foreign currency. Both the principal and the future interest on these bonds are paid in another currency. Roosa bonds raise needed foreign currency for governments and can affect the value of domestic currency. The sale of yen bonds in the United States could increase yen prices and consequently devalue the dollar. The buying back of yen bonds by the Japanese government could increase the supply of yen and reduce the value of the yen while revaluing the dollar upward.

10.7.5 The Effects of Interest Rates and Inflation on Exchange Rates

By examining Figure 10.4, you can see that the United States had higher short-term interest rates in August of 1988 (8.66 percent) than either Japan (4.15 percent) or Germany (5.35 percent). When U.S. rates are higher than those of its trading partners, such as was the case in August of 1988, the tendency is for these higher rates, all else being equal, to cause the value of the dollar to rise. Since the Germans and Japanese can earn higher interest rates in the United States, they should be willing to pay more for their dollars to invest here. When the U.S. interest rates fall below those of its trading partners, as it has with Canada (10.15 percent) and the United Kingdom (12.19 percent), all else being equal, then the tendency is for our trading partners to be willing to pay less for the dollar in their currencies. In other words, higher interest rates here tend to cause revaluation; lower interest rates here tend to cause devaluation.

Inflation has the reverse effect that interest rates have on exchange rates. While higher interest rates here tend to give foreigners a premium for saving and investing here, higher inflation here reduces their returns. When the U.S.

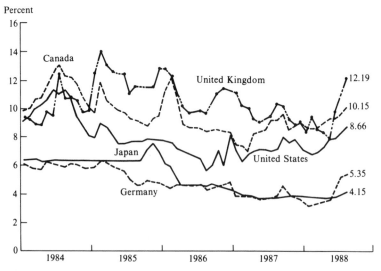

FIGURE 10.4   Short-Term Interest Rates, International, 1984–1988.
Source: Federal Reserve Bank of St. Louis, *International Economic Conditions*, October 1988, with data from Morgan Guaranty Trust. Used with permission.

inflation rate outpaces the rate of inflation of our trading partners, all else being equal, our trading partners are willing to pay less for our currency. The dollar tends to devalue. When the domestic rate of inflation is below that of our trading partners, all else being equal, then our partners are willing to pay more for the dollar and the dollar appreciates.

10.7.6 Purchasing Power Parity

The idea of *purchasing power parity* (PPP) is that there is a predictable relationship between price levels and exchange rates between countries. This appears to make sense because, at least theoretically, goods and services can be bought in one country rather than in another. It also would seem logical that even transportation costs and tariffs should work their way into the balance. In other words, after considering exchange rates, taxes, and transportation costs, one should buy products where the cost is the least. Purchasing power parity, however, is far from perfect. European electrical products use 220 volts and 50 hertz, while the U.S. electrical products use 110 volts and 60 hertz. There can be no price parity when the products are not substitutes. Housing cannot be shipped, and there are vast differences in tastes and preferences from country to country. Not only this, but there may be great differences in monetary and fiscal policies from country to country that can cause excessive pressure on prices unrelated to trade.

For these reasons, purchasing power parity has gotten little attention and limited empirical support, but it does arise from time to time whenever countries move away from fixed exchange rates to a more flexible system. The argument usually is that prices need to adjust to make the exchange rate adjust more favorably. In other words, if prices are lower here, our currency will revalue, and if our prices are higher here, then our currency will devalue. Even though purchasing power parity is not the only determinant of exchange rates, it certainly has some effect on them.

10.8   INTERNATIONAL TRADE POLICY

The political economy of trade barriers is not always based on sound economic logic but rather on the ebb and flow of political pressures. Each of the following is a rallying point from which trade barriers are erected.

10.8.1 Defense

Since all nations want to protect their sovereignty, national defense is nearly always seen as a legitimate role of the central government. Free trade opens the possibility that advanced technological, defense-related outputs could pass to political foes. This possibility is restricted through trade barriers.

The problem with defense as an argument against trade is the extent to which defense should be used as a trade barrier. One could argue that the military uses pencils and soldiers wear boots, and therefore, no pencils or boots should be imported to protect the domestic industry from competition to ensure their existence in time of war. These arguments are often used to extend trade barriers beyond what might be considered a legitimate defense industry. Certainly weapons of all sorts need regulation in trade but not boots!

10.8.2 Retaliation

When foreign nations put trade restrictions on our outputs, we tend to feel that their manufacturers should suffer as well. For example, in early 1985, the United States put a higher import tax on pasta from Italy. In response, Italy put a higher import tax on fresh fruit and nuts from the United States. Retaliation may satisfy the urge to fight back, but it is often misdirected against one industry, such as the U.S. fruit and nut industry, when their business is totally unrelated to the original restriction. The result of retaliation is often further retaliation.

10.8.3 Jealousy

In the 1984 presidential debates between Walter Mondale and Ronald Reagan sponsored by the League of Woman Voters, candidate Mondale was asked what one thing he would like to see as a result of his first 4 years in the White House. He answered that he would like to go to a large department store in the United States and see that all the best products at all the best prices were made in America. Then, he said that he would be proud to be an American and that he had done his best as President. Such a statement evokes pride and nationalism in all of us. We feel we are the best, and therefore, why not hope that the best is American. The problem is that no nation does everything best. We import not to hurt U.S. business, but to get either higher quality or a better price. Foreign products would not adorn our shelves if the same or better was available at home. The thing is that coffee, bananas, scotch, caviar, and many other products are produced better in other places because of climatic or geographic differences. To force such products to all be produced here would destroy our comparative advantages. What works best is to do what we do best, as David Ricardo suggested, and to leave what we do not do so well, such as producing coffee, to others.

10.8.4 National Optimal Tariff

When a foreign manufacturer has a dominating market power, trade restrictions can benefit a nation. A tariff or import tax on the foreign products or services can be more easily passed back onto the foreign manufacturer and not the U.S. consumer if that manufacturer depends heavily on the U.S. market. The more elastic our demand and the more inelastic their supply, the more the foreign manufacturer stands to lose if he or she raises U.S. selling prices. When our demand is elastic, our quantity demand will fall by a greater percentage than any increase in price, thereby discouraging foreign firms from raising prices. When foreign supply to the United States is inelastic, foreign firms must continue to supply nearly the same output to our market even if after tariff they receive a lower selling price. As you can see, the national optimal tariff is most effective in these unique instances. Few markets, however, fit this example, but some do.

10.8.5 Second-Best Arguments

When a nation is faced with a problem in trade of such great significance that an entire industry may disappear, certainly the second-best thing to do is a trade restriction. Most economists oppose trade restrictions; however, restrictions may be necessary in this individual instance. For example, if imported steel was to put the U.S. steel industry out of business, then we would be better off protecting our industry than losing the capacity to ever produce steel again. Steel is a primary industry that is important not only for national defense, but also for economic development.

10.8.6 Lobbying

The control of a decision by the minority over the majority is mostly possible when the cost to the majority is spread thinly and the benefit to the minority is highly concentrated. For example, an import tax or tariff may raise the price of sugar a few cents per pound for all consumers but raise billions of dollars for domestic sugar manufacturers. Industries often discover that it is easier and less expensive to lobby for government action to block foreign competition than it is to spend the necessary capital to mount a massive productivity and quality effort in their businesses.

10.9 BASIC ANALYSIS OF A TARIFF

A *tariff* is either a tax on an imported good or service or a tax on exported goods or services. The most common type of tariff is the import tariff on a good, which is explained in Figure 10.5.

Figure 10.5 is a typical supply-demand graph of the market for televisions in the United States. P_e is the market equilibrium price for televisions in the United States without international trade. P_w is the world price for

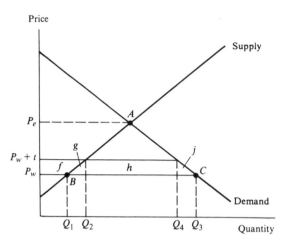

FIGURE 10.5 U.S. Television Industry: Analysis of an Import Tariff.

televisions. If free trade were allowed with no tariffs or trade restrictions and, for the sake of simplicity, no transportation costs, then the price for televisions in the United States would fall to P_w from P_e. This drop in price would drive out the more inefficient U.S. producers along segment AB, who would no longer be able to compete at the lower selling price. This drop in market price also would open the television market to more consumers along segment AC, who now could afford televisions. The new free trade price, therefore, would drive out inefficient U.S. producers and add more U.S. consumers. U.S. manufacturers would now have to either find ways to reduce costs and increase efficiency or be driven permanently from the market.

Assume the U.S. television industry successfully lobbies for an import tariff that raises the market equilibrium price to $P_w + t$, where t is the amount of the tariff. Immediately, domestic sales rise from Q_1 to Q_2, while foreign sales drop from $(Q_3 - Q_1)$ to $(Q_4 - Q_2)$. The effect is an increase in less efficient U.S. business production at a new, higher price to consumers, but certainly jobs are saved in the U.S. television industry. The question then is whether the net increase in the U.S. television industry and jobs is worth the net loss to consumers (who have to pay higher prices) and the net loss resulting from a rise in inefficient business.

The net effect of a tariff for society as a whole can be explained as follows using Figure 10.5. Block f and triangle g represent new revenues for U.S. industries; block h represents new revenues from the tariff for the U.S. government. The gain from the tariff, then, is $f + g + h$. Now consider the losses. First, U.S. consumers lose f, g, and h because they now are paying a higher price. There is a loss of j because higher prices reduced the consumer surplus, since now only wealthier consumers can afford televisions. There is also a loss of g, again because new industries are added that are less efficient. The loss is $f + g + h + j + g$. The net result of the tariff to society as a whole is a dead-weight loss of g and j or $(f + g + h) - (f + g + h + j + g)$. Jobs have been saved, but U.S. industry is less efficient (g) and consumers have been driven from the marketplace through higher prices (j). In conclusion, tariffs cause net losses to societies even though they may greatly satisfy the vested interests of those who stand to gain higher revenues without foreign competition.

10.10 BASIC ANALYSIS OF A TRADE SUBSIDY

The second most popular trade barrier is to subsidize export-based industries or subsidize import-competing industries. The United States has for a long time subsidized its tobacco industry, keeping it relatively free of foreign competition. The Japanese have heavily subsidized their automobile industry to keep it export competitive in the world. The most popular type of governmental protection is the import-competing industry subsidy because, as do tariffs, it theoretically saves U.S. jobs. Figure 10.6 analyzes the net effect of a subsidy on our economy.

Before trade, the U.S. market for televisions is again shown by a basic supply-demand graph where P_e is the equilibrium price and Q_e is the equilibrium quantity produced. The world price is lower at P_w. When the United States enters into free trade, prices fall to P_w, U.S. sales fall from Q_e to Q_1, and $(Q_3 - Q_1)$ is imported. Trade eliminates inefficient, high-priced U.S. industries along segment AC and adds less wealthy U.S. consumers to the market along segment AB. A subsidy then is put in place to try to save jobs

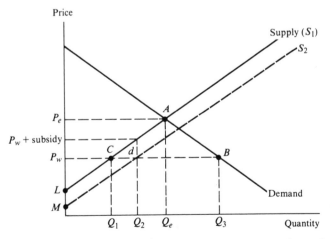

FIGURE 10.6   Analysis of an Import-Competing Industry Subsidy.

in the U.S. television industry. A subsidy of LM is paid to U.S. manufacturers for every television produced and sold. Now assuming, in the best of circumstances, that the entire subsidy is passed on to consumers, S_1 increases to S_2. P_w is maintained as the market selling price, and U.S. sales rise from Q_1 to Q_2 while imports fall from $(Q_3 - Q_1)$ to $(Q_3 - Q_2)$. Now let's look at the overall effect on U.S. society.

The subsidy is a gain of LM times Q_2 for U.S. industry, or the subsidy times output. The government must, however, pay LM times Q_2 to U.S. business, so that again is a loss. This gain and accompanying loss leave society as a whole with the same income, but government revenues have been transferred to business. The net loss to society is represented by triangle d, which illustrates the loss due to inefficiency in the U.S. television industry when less efficient industries returned to the market after the subsidy was added. Subsidies, therefore, leave society with more jobs in the domestic import-competing industries by increasing domestic output, but they result in a net loss to society owing to industrial inefficiencies. The subsidy, though more costly to government, produces less of a net loss to society than a tariff. Since no increase in consumer prices occurs, there is no loss in consumer surplus, as is the case with a tariff.

10.11 OTHER TRADE BARRIERS

Besides trade restrictions such as tariffs and subsidies, there are a whole host of other trade barriers that target restrictions in international trade. These barriers are often set up when an international trade agreement specifically restricts or prevents tariffs or subsidies. As countries of the world have entered into more trading agreements to lower tariffs, they have come to rely more often on the following to continue to restrict trade.

10.11.1 Sanitary Standards

The United States does not allow the importation of raw meats from abroad. This is, according to the Department of Agriculture, to ensure sanitary standards and prevent the spread of disease. This may be the case, but certainly one could argue that Danish or Icelandic raw meat is as healthful as U.S. raw meat and that these restrictions are mainly to prevent foreign competition. Inspections could ensure that the imported meat is healthful.

10.11.2 Quotas

A *quota* is a physical limit on the quantity of a good that may be imported. The idea here is to limit the number of imports and therefore open the remainder of a market to domestic producers. The problem with this idea is that it is difficult to enforce. In addition, limits are often set by giving a restricted number of import licenses, which can create monopolistic powers for sellers. Those who can sell lower-priced imports have an advantage over sellers of higher-priced domestic products. Quotas result in the same losses to society overall as a tariff, but they also create extra externalities.

10.11.3 Mixing Requirements

Governments often require that imports contain a percentage of domestic materials. Often these rules are called *content legislation*. In the early 1980s, while the U.S. automobile industry continued to fight hard against foreign competition, content legislation was considered by the U.S. Congress. The law, if passed, would have required imported cars to have a major portion of U.S. parts. The law was defeated because arguments showed that the law would unduly raise automobile prices to consumers.

10.11.4 Buy-at-Home Rule

This law requires that official state, local, or federal purchases be made of only locally produced goods and services. The idea here is that local governments should support local business. The problem with this idea is that local business may or may not be as price competitive as foreign producers. While the government pays more to local manufacturers and local manufacturers benefit, the taxpaying public must pay more. Gains are felt by a few in a big way, while losses are felt by all in a small way. The summation of losses, even though more widely spread, is greater than the gains by a few.

10.11.5 Differences in Tax Rates

Even though many taxes are paid on both domestic and foreign outputs, they influence trade. For example, a value-added tax or a tax on nonfinal goods raises the cost of goods abroad produced here. A sales tax, however, is only paid on final sales and does not affect our product prices abroad. All taxes that affect prices of goods and services before final sale tend to influence international trade, while taxes on final goods and services have no impact on trade.

10.12 INTERNATIONAL TRADE LEGISLATION

The trend in tariffs since the Smoot-Hawley Tariff (1930) has been downward. According to the U.S. Department of Commerce, the trend in duties as a percentage of dutiable imports has been as follows:

Smoot-Hawley Tariff (1930): 68 percent

Reciprocal Trade Agreement Act (1934): 38 percent

General Agreements on Tariff and Trade (1947): 15 percent

Kennedy Round of GATT (1967): 10 percent

Tokyo Round of GATT (1979): 8 percent

U.S. – Canadian Reciprocal Trade Agreement (1988): 0 percent (applies to limited trade between the United States and Canada only)

Omnibus Trade and Competitiveness Act (1988): (encourages bilateral reductions in trade barriers)*

It is interesting that trade between the United States and its partners has become more free in terms of tariffs when the U.S. Congress has so often threatened more trade restrictions. In fiscal year 1988, for example, over 100 separate pieces of trade-restricting legislation were considered by the U.S. Congress, none of which was passed. Because of the ever-widening trade and current account balance deficits, as explained earlier, Congress and the U.S. people continue to question free trade. Statistics, however, from 1980 to 1989 show ever-increasing employment and a fall in unemployment rates from a high of 10.75 percent in late 1982 to 5.9 percent in early 1989. It appears that trade gaps have not been associated with rising overall unemployment even though there has been a massive shift in the types of jobs most of us now do. Trade has forced us to concentrate more on what we do best and rely more on what others do best for us.

10.13 INTERNATIONAL ORGANIZATIONS

10.13.1 United Nations Affiliates

The world, although greatly diverse, has come to agree on a number of organizations that have either caused greater regional economic cooperation or worldwide cooperation in international economics. The main organizations are listed below and are all linked in some fashion to the United Nations.

The Food and Agricultural Organization (FAO) of the United Nations, headquartered in Rome, is concerned with an improvement in production and distribution worldwide so as to alleviate world hunger. The FAO has

---

*According to the International Trade Commission estimates, this act should actually lower tariffs.

worked for more political and economic power for farmers in governments across the planet. There were 144 member countries in 1980.

The General Agreements on Tariff and Trade (GATT) establish and administer an orderly code for conduct of international trade, assist governments in reducing tariffs, and try to help abolish trade barriers and provide export promotion assistance to developing countries. GATT is headquartered in Geneva, Switzerland, and in 1980 it had 84 participating nations, including the United States.

The International Bank for Reconstruction and Development (IBRD), more commonly called the World Bank, works to further the economic development of its members by loans made to or guaranteed by governments and with technical advice. It is headquartered in Washington, D.C., and in 1980 it had 133 member countries.

The International Development Assistance (IDA) has been formed to further economic development of member nations by providing financing on terms bearing less heavily on the balance of payments than conventional loans. In many instances, IDA issues credit for over 50 years that is interest-free. It is affiliated with the IBRD and shares the same offices and officers in Washington, D.C. In 1980, 120 nations were members.

The International Fund for Agricultural Development (IFAD) grants loans to developing nations to help develop agriculture. It has over a billion dollars in reserves and is one of the newest worldwide agencies. It is located in Rome and has 115 member countries.

The International Monetary Fund (IMF) is probably the most important in terms of international trade. The IMF promotes monetary cooperation among governments to help stabilize the values of their currencies. It assists nations in making foreign currency exchanges and provides advice in meeting international payments. The IMF issues special drawing rights (SDRs), which in exchange for native currencies provide nations with a currency that has international liquidity. SDRs are often called as good as gold because they are highly liquid. They are a world currency, but they can only be held by governments. The IMF keeps reserves of all member currencies to facilitate monetary exchanges. Nations that overvalue or undervalue their currencies beyond negotiated limits are removed from membership and lose the liquidity advantages of their currency. The IMF is located in Washington, D.C., and had 138 member countries in 1980.

The United Nations Industrial Development Organization (UNIDO) was formed to encourage and extend assistance to developing nations for the expansion and modernization of industry. It promotes the full utilization of a nation's natural resources with consultations and advice for developing nations and their trading partners. The UNIDO is located in Vienna and had 120 members in 1980.

10.13.2 Independent World Agencies

Besides those organizations previously listed, there are many organizations not aligned with the United Nations. Some of the more significant ones that have an effect on world trade are listed below.

The European Free Trade Area (EFTA) was organized to eliminate tariffs on industrial goods between members and to negotiate bilateral reductions of trade restrictions on agricultural products. The EFTA has only European members and has not been as successful in reducing trade barriers as the Common Market. The headquarters is in Geneva.

The European Community (EC) is commonly called the Common Market because it was created to make Europe one free common marketplace following World War II. The EC is one of the very few full-fledged customs unions. It has three objectives. First, it attempts to eliminate all internal trade barriers between members. Second, it attempts to align all external trade barriers so that all member nations block imports from outside the union in the same way. Third, it encourages free movement, where possible, of the factors of production: labor, management, capital, and the use of land. It has been very successful, but since the United States is not a member, it has successfully blocked U.S. outputs. It is headquartered in Brussels.

The Organization for Economic Cooperation for Development (OECD) began as an oversight agency over economic development following World War II under the Marshall Plan. Today, its goals are to further economic development and growth in the world. It publishes numerous publications and aids nations in economic planning. It is headquartered in Paris.

The Council for Mutual Economic Assistance (COMECON) attempts to coordinate the economies of members under U.S.S.R. leadership. The membership includes eastern European nations, Cuba, Vietnam, and the U.S.S.R. The headquarters is in Moscow.

10.14 SUMMARY

1. International trade is essential to the world and the U.S. economy. As we have expanded our trading sectors, so have we become dependent on world supplies of goods and services and the sale of our outputs. As David Ricardo pointed out in his theory of comparative advantage, the more free trade becomes, the more everyone benefits from it. For this reason and others, nations have had the foresight from time to time to foster freer trade, as have the many international organizations listed.

2. The macro economy of the United States has felt the pressure of deficits in its trade balances and as a result has seen great restructuring of both the export industries and those which compete with imports. As this transition takes place, many workers have and will be displaced, but with this transition comes a greater and more efficient economy based on comparative not artificial advantages. The problems of the future rest with cooperative efforts between nations to ensure a more balanced growth of trade so as not to upset a fragile international balance of currency and liquidity. Nations that overly restrict imports and/or overly encourage exports strain both the economic and political wills of nations to continue down the more prosperous road of freer trade. Trade barriers can become the barriers to both political and economic cooperation. In the 1990s and beyond, trade will become of greater and greater importance on a planet of dwindling resources.

10.15 EXERCISES

1. Explain and discuss the six events of the 1980s that, according to the text, have most affected international trade.

2. Why does the United States have a history that would, more than many other nations, promote free trade?

3. Use Ricardo's theory of comparative advantage to explain why if Iceland can produce 5 pounds of lamb and 10 pounds of fish per labor hour and the Faroe Islands can produce 15 pounds of lamb and 10 pounds of fish per labor hour that Iceland should produce only fish and the Faroe Islands only lamb. Assume that each nation has only 20,000 workers each. How much more could they produce with free trade than without trading?

4. Graph the aggregate supply and aggregate demand model, and label each curve with its appropriate equation. Label the point of intersection. Show both graphically and algebraically how the point of intersection moves in the northeast direction with an increase in aggregate demand resulting from greater output in the export-based industries.

5. Compare and contrast the balance of payments, the balance of payments on the current account, and the balance of trade. Which measure do you see as most important in understanding the direction of international trade of a nation and why?

6. What have been and will be the prospects for a nation that runs an unending string of deficits in its balance of payments on the current account? Why is it unlikely that a balance of payments on the current account will be maintained without it naturally turning into a surplus?

7. If the dollar is worth 42 Icelandic krona today, 45 Icelandic krona in 30 days, and 50 Icelandic krona in 60 days, is the U.S. dollar projected to devalue or revalue? How much does an Icelandic wool coat costing 5000 krona cost in dollars today? How much does the same 5000 krona coat cost with dollars

purchased in 30 days and in 60 days? Is the Icelandic krona worth more on the spot or forward exchange market against the dollar?

8. Devaluation of U.S. currency against the British pound will cause what to happen to the dollar value of U.S. profits in England as reported on a U.S. company's annual report? Should a U.S. company with major overseas profits hope for a devaluation or revaluation of the U.S. dollar and why?

9. What are the major differences between a floating and a fixed exchange rate, and how might a nation use currency intervention to cause a nation's currency to devalue?

10. If the U.S. interest and inflation rates were higher than those of its trading partners, then what, all else being equal, should happen to its exchange rate?

11. Name an international agency that affects U.S. trade with Europe or the developing world. Use the library to report on current events related to that agency.

12. Compare and contrast various types of trade barriers. Be specific about the advantages and disadvantages of each.

13. Why or why not might it be better or worse for the United States to join the European Community (EC)? Use your own opinion based on the information learned about trade agreements in this chapter.

10.16 REFERENCES

1. John Adams, *The Contemporary International Economy: A Reader*. New York: St. Martins Press, 1984.

2. Federal Reserve Bank of St. Louis, *National Economic Trends* (monthly).

3. Federal Reserve Bank of St. Louis, *Annual U.S. Economic Data* (annually).

4. Federal Reserve Bank of St. Louis, *International Economic Conditions* (monthly).

5. International Monetary Fund, *International Financial Statistics* (monthly).

6. Peter H. Lindert, *International Economics*. Homewood, Ill.: Irwin, 1986.

7. Organization for Economic Cooperation for Development, *Main Economic Indicators* (monthly).

8. U.S. Department of Commerce, *Survey of U.S. Business* (monthly).

PART FOUR

Macroeconomic Problems

11
Inflation

11.1 INTRODUCTION

> *in • fla • tion* (*n*): an increase in the volume of money and credit relative to available goods resulting in a substantial and continuing rise in the general price level.[1]

For a long time it was thought that the dollar was ''as good as gold'' — meaning that its purchasing power was certain. When the authors were youngsters, the idea that the dollar had a constant value was firmly entrenched. We all ''knew,'' for example, that a candy bar cost 5 cents. We so believed in the value of a nickel that as post-World War II inflation began, manufacturers began making smaller candy bars so that they could continue to sell them at their ''known'' price of 5 cents. Today, after a generation of inflation, the American public has learned to live with an unstable dollar. Today, children are not surprised and do not resist increases in the prices of candy bars. Accordingly, candy bars are once again their full ''5 cent'' size, although they now cost thirty-five cents or more.

This chapter surveys several important issues concerning inflation, including the quantity theory of inflation, hyperinflation, inflation and debt, taxes, and accounting. The first part of the chapter deals mainly with the phenomenon of inflation itself: what it is and where it comes from. The second part of the chapter mainly concerns doing business in an inflationary environment. Although inflation has recently moderated in the United States, continuing inflation over a period of time, even at moderate rates, can have significant effects. Moreover, as long as the dollar is a fiat currency, there is

---

[1]*Webster's Seventh New International Dictionary.*

always the possibility of a return of galloping inflation. Most important, however, in many places around the world inflation continues at high rates. Without adjusting for the effects of inflation, multinational corporations could easily find themselves unable to profitably conduct business.

11.2 DEFINITION AND MEASUREMENT

Inflation can be defined as the annualized percentage change in a general price index such as the GNP deflator or the consumer price index (CPI). Another useful price index for measuring inflation is the producer price index (PPI), formerly known as the wholesale price index (WPI). Inflation, then, refers not to the rise in any single price but to a general rise in prices. To be precise, inflation refers to the extra money cost of the specific set of goods and services incorporated into the general price index. The consumer price index represents the current money cost of a market basket of consumer goods and services relative to the market basket's money cost in the base year. The GNP deflator represents the current money cost of all final goods and services relative to the money cost of these final goods and services in the base year. The producer price index (formerly the wholesale price index) represents the current money cost of commodities, including raw materials and manufactured goods at various stages of production, relative to their money cost in the base year. Alternately, *inflation* can be defined as the fall in the purchasing power of the dollar, i.e., how much less $1 can buy in one year compared to the previous year.

These simple definitions mask the difficulty in actually measuring inflation. In practice, measuring inflation involves collecting a great many prices and then, somehow, averaging them. The U.S. Bureau of Labor Statistics, in estimating the CPI, collects thousands of prices from dozens of metropolitan areas every month. These include the prices of food in supermarkets and restaurants; of new and used automobiles; of clothing, furniture, and appliances; of gasoline, heating, and electricity; and of medical care, education, and a great many other services; and they include rental costs of homes and apartments. A weighted average of these is then calculated using weights derived from the actual amounts of these goods and services purchased by American families in the bureau's periodic survey of consumer expenditures. The CPI, then, is a fixed-weight price index until new weights are phased in every 10 years or so.

Probably the most difficult problem in calculating the CPI is the constantly changing quality of retail goods and services in a contemporary capitalist economy. In former times, the great bulk of consumer purchases were of relatively homogeneous commodities such as wheat flour, whole milk, meats, and vegetables. Today, Americans spend as much money on food at restaurants as they do on food at supermarkets, and even the food bought at supermarkets is in various stages of preparation from ready-to-eat cereals to complete microwave dinners. The basically conservative approaches taken by the Bureau of Labor Statistics in adjusting prices for quality differences is widely thought to overstate the rate of inflation. This bias may amount to 1 percent or so per year.

Another problem with measuring inflation is the "representativeness" of prices. With producers' prices, this problem manifests itself in list prices, which are readily available, being different from actual transactions prices, which are typically only known to professional purchasers. This is similar to the problem of bargaining over the price of a new car or bargaining over prices at a flea market or a Mideast bazaar. List prices, in these cases, are usually just starting points for negotiation. Today, the Bureau of Labor Statistics attempts to use actual transactions prices, when available, as opposed to list prices in constructing the producer price index. With consumer prices, this problem manifests itself in "home-ownership costs" based largely on vintage mortgages that are no longer representative and in rents in rent-controlled cities such as New York where rent-controlled apartments are not readily available. Today, the bureau uses rental costs and not home-ownership costs in constructing the consumer price index. The problem of unrepresentative, controlled prices is relatively minor in the United States, but it is a major problem in certain other countries.

Figure 11.1 displays the history of prices in the United States. Several episodes of inflation are noteworthy:

1. The paper money issued by the Continental Congress during the Revolutionary War (1776 – 1783) resulted in inflation. The expression "not worth a continental"—meaning not worth a Continental dollar—was coined during this period.

2. From 1796 to 1821, and initially because of the French Revolution and the Napoleonic Wars, Britain suspended convertibility of the pound. Of course, the result was inflation in Britain. In addition, the gold that left Britain increased the money supply throughout the rest of the world. Thus, inflation also affected the United States.

3. During the Civil War (1861 – 1865), the Federal government issued paper money referred to as "Greenbacks." After a long period of gradual deflation, the gold standard was resumed at its prewar parity in 1879.

4. During World War I (1917 – 1918), convertibility was first suspended in Europe and was then suspended in the United States. After the war, Britain and the United States attempted to maintain prices above their prewar levels, and only *partially deflate*, by instituting a gold exchange standard. Only Britain and the United States tied their currencies directly to gold, allowing concentration of the world's supply of gold and an expanded

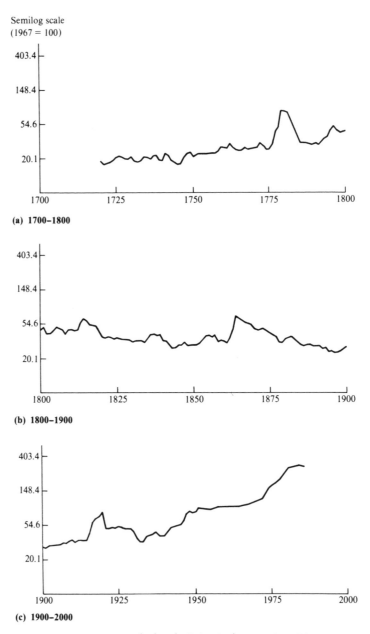

FIGURE 11.1   U.S. Wholesale Price Index, 1720–1986.

world money supply. This system broke down; the result was severe deflation and the Great Depression.

5. During World War II (1940 – 1947), as during prior wars, governments resorted to inflationary finance. After the war, Britain and the United States attempted to stabilize prices through fixed exchange rates of all major currencies into the U.S. dollar combined with convertibility of the dollar into gold for balance of payments.

6. In 1971 the last tie between the dollar and gold was severed. No longer was the dollar convertible into gold for balance of payments. Instead, monetary restraint and wage and price controls were supposed to keep inflation in check.

11.3 THEORIES OF INFLATION

11.3.1 The Early Quantity Theory

The *quantity theory* was formulated during the European inflation of the fifteenth to seventeenth centuries. This inflation, known as the *price revolution*, was caused by the influx of silver and gold into Europe from Spanish conquests in the New World. At first, this inflation was attributed to debasement, i.e., to the recasting of coins with base metal, such as copper substituted for precious metal. Debasement was formerly a common cause of inflation and is found in the ancient histories of Mesopotamia, Egypt, and Rome.

In 1568, Jean Bodin of France correctly identified the reason for the price revolution as the increase *in the quantity of money*, i.e., of silver and gold, that resulted from the Spanish conquests. The quantity theory was further developed during the late seventeenth and eighteenth centuries. John Locke, in 1691, made the clear but wrong statement that prices were *always* proportional to the quantity of money. Richard Cantillon, in 1755, and David Hume, in 1752, made the more correct argument that variations in the quantity of money *will cause* proportional variations in prices.

According to Cantillon and Hume, an increase in silver and gold production will first increase the purchasing power of miners, enabling them to increase their purchases of food, clothes, and so on. In a second round, merchants selling to the miners will enjoy increased profits, and these profits, as well as optimistic expectations of additional profits, will lead the merchants to increase their production, employment, and purchases of supplies. In third and subsequent rounds, other merchants as well as farmers, manufacturers, and workers enjoying increased business will increase their own spending.

At each round of spending, as the new money moves through the economy, upward pressure is put on the prices of the particular goods being bought. Eventually, when the new money is completely diffused throughout the economy, all prices will be raised in proportion to the increase in the money supply. However, *here's the important point*: the increase in the money supply has important short-run business-cycle effects.

11.3.2. The Modern Quantity Theory

During the early twentieth century, the quantity theory came to be associated with Irving Fisher's *equation of exchange*. Fisher's equation emphasized the medium of exchange role of money, or its use in transactions. The equation of exchange can be written as

$$MV = PY \tag{11.1}$$

where M is the money supply, V is the velocity of money, or how many times, on average, money is spent and respent in the course of a year, P is the price level, and Y is real GNP. As written, the equation of exchange can be viewed as merely a definition of the velocity of money; that is $V = PY/M$. What makes the equation of exchange into the quantity *theory* is the argument that in the long run Y and V are exogenous with respect to M, so that variations in M *cause* proportional variations in P.

Fisher argued that the quantity of money could not affect the productivity of farms or factories and so could not affect real GNP. He also argued that the quantity of money could not affect the speed of banks in clearing checks and so could not affect the velocity of money. With Y and V fixed, it is obvious from the equation of exchange that doubling, for example, M, would cause P to double.

The long-run relationship between prices and money envisioned by Fisher can be tested by plotting the inflation rates of different countries against their money supply growth rates. To abstract from short-run influences, averages over several years should be used. Such a test is presented in Figure 11.2 using 10-year averages of 93 countries over the period 1974–1983. Notice that the regression line through the scatterplot appears to have an intercept of about −4 percent and a slope of +1. This confirms the tendency of inflation in the long run to equal the growth of the money supply less the growth of real GNP.

Regarding the short-run effects of an increase in the money supply, Fisher did not offer the kind of detailed analysis found in the early quantity theory. Fisher described the equation of exchange, that is, $MV = PY$, as a kind of train. Once it got going, the engine—M—would pull the rest of the cars—V, P, and Y—along nice and smoothly. However, when first getting started, movements of the cars would be rough. In the short run, prices would

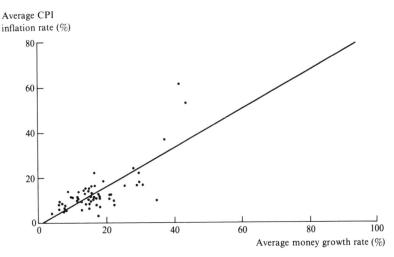

FIGURE 11.2   Money and Inflation, 93 Countries, 1974–1983.
The regression line confirms that over the long run, the tendency is
for inflation to equal the growth in the money supply less trend
growth in real GNP.
Source: *International Financial Statistics*, various issues. Used with permission.

not move proportionally to the money supply, so that velocity and real GNP
would have to be somewhat affected.

Fisher's main analysis of business cycles derived not from the effects
of changes in the quantity of money as such, but from the effects of (unexpected) changes in prices. When prices increased unexpectedly, borrowers
—including farmers and corporations—found that the real burden of their
debt was decreased. On the other hand, lenders found that their wealth was
decreased. When prices decreased unexpectedly, borrowers found that the
real burden of their debt was increased. In fact, after a severe deflation,
borrowers were often bankrupted. Accordingly, an unexpected fall in prices
did not necessarily benefit lenders. Because of this concern, Fisher advocated
stabilization of the value of money and, as a private-sector substitute, indexation of debts.

11.3.3 Monetarism

The worldwide surge of inflation during the 1970s sparked a renewed interest
in the quantity theory—now known as *monetarism*—and in Milton Friedman, who had become its leading proponent. Friedman, like Fisher, emphasizes the long-run effects of changes in the money supply. Illustrative of
his abstraction of the short-run effects, Friedman assumes that the way new
money enters an economy is that it is simply dropped from a helicopter!

Friedman is particularly well known for his development of the demand for money. Friedman argues that while the velocity of money—V—may not be a constant, it is a stable function. Friedman's formulation of the demand for money may be stated as

$$\frac{M}{P} = f(X_1, X_2, \ldots, Y) \tag{11.2}$$

where the X's and Y are the determinants of the demand for money. Notice that the demand for money is a demand for real money balances, the money supply *divided by* the price level. This preserves the essence of the quantity theory. The demand for real money balances is given by the function f and is largely determined by nonmonetary or real factors such as the real GNP. Since the monetary authority, i.e., the Federal Reserve, determines the money supply M, equilibrium is obtained by adjustment of prices P.

Monetarists admit that the demand for real money balances is not completely exogenous with respect to monetary policy. Increasing the rate of money growth, and therefore increasing the rate of inflation and the level of nominal interest rates, decreases the demand for real money balances. Monetariests view a fall in real money balances to be harmful because of the use of real resources to economize on cash balances and the reduced efficiency of an economy operating with less liquidity and unstable prices. Furthermore, as a result of the fall of real money balances, the rate of inflation in hyperinflations is *faster* than the rate of money growth, or changes in prices are more than proportional to changes in the growth of the money supply.

Like others who have examined the demand for money, Friedman includes "the" interest rate among the determinants of the demand for real cash balances. However, unlike others who include only "the" interest rate, Friedman argues that the entire term structure of interest rates, the expected rate of return on equity, the expected rate of inflation, and other variables may potentially be included among the X's. In practice, however, Friedman and his followers usually identify a small number of variables to include in their list of determinants. For example, Philip Cagan, in his study of hyperinflation, only included the rate of inflation among his X's.

11.4 HYPERINFLATION

Hyperinflation can be defined as inflation that reaches a specific high rate. Cagan specifies this rate to be 50 percent per month. More descriptively, *hyperinflation* can be defined as rapidly accelerating rates of inflation, such as when inflation passes from ''creeping'' inflation—single-digit rates of 1 to 9 percent per year—to ''galloping'' inflation—double-digit rates of 10 to 99 percent per year to triple-digit rates and beyond.

Until the twentieth century, hyperinflations were very rare. A prominent example of pre-twentieth century hyperinflation occurred during the French Revolution, during which time the most common reason for execution by the guillotine was violation of the price controls imposed by the radical government attempting to hold inflation in check while rapidly printing paper money. A reason for the rarity of hyperinflation was that prior to the twentieth century, gold and silver coins and paper currency redeemable in gold and silver were widely believed to *be* money. With the twentieth century, nonredeemable paper money, or *fiat money*, came into widespread use, allowing continuing inflations and hyperinflations.

Cagan studied hyperinflations in Austria, Germany, Greece, Hungary (twice), Poland, and Russia that occurred following World Wars I and II. These hyperinflations were short periods—typically 10 to 16 months long—during which prices exploded. They include the famous German hyperinflation of $1922 - 1923$ that bankrupted that country's middle class and paved the way for Adolph Hitler. They also include the world's ''greatest'' hyperinflation, the Hungarian hyperinflation of $1945 - 1946$, during which prices rose by a factor of 3.81×10^{27}, or 3.81 billion billion billion times. During this hyperinflation, the world's largest denomination of money was printed, the *Egymilliard B.- Pengo*, worth 1,000,000,000,000,000,000,000,000,000 pengos, and not worth the paper it was printed on! This hyperinflation was used by the occupying Soviets to destroy Hungary's middle class and pave the way for communism.

A recent example of hyperinflation occurred in Bolivia, where the rate of inflation reached over 10,000 percent per year. Inflations reaching 100 percent per year are rather common nowadays, triple-digit inflation being the norm for certain countries—Argentina and Brazil, for example.

Hyperinflations are generally thought to result from grave fiscal imbalance, from the government attempting to spend a much larger fraction of GNP than it raises in taxes. In the case of the German hyperinflation of $1922 - 1923$, this grave fiscal imbalance resulted from the attempt of the victorious governments of World War I to impose severe reparation payments on the defeated governments. In other situations, this imbalance results from the inability to collect (explicit) taxes because of civil disorder (war, revolution, etc.) or a large underground or even criminal economy. Finally, this imbalance results from governments attempting to raise more than they can on a sustained basis from printing money.

Figure 11.3 tracks the dynamics of hyperinflation in Bolivia. During

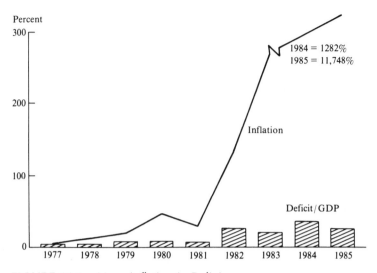

FIGURE 11.3   Hyperinflation in Bolivia.
When deficit spending increased from an average of 8 percent of
gross domestic product during 1979 – 1981 to an average of 27 percent during 1982 – 1985, a hyperinflation was set off. Inflation was
1,282 percent in 1984 and 11,748 percent in 1985.
Source: *International Financial Statistics*, various issues. Used with permission.

1977 – 1978, deficit spending averaged about 4 percent of the gross domestic
product (GDP) (a measure similar to gross national product), increasing to
8 percent during 1979 – 1981. During these years, inflation (merely) ran in
the double digits. However, during 1982 – 1985, deficit spending increased
to an average of 27 percent of GDP, and prices started exploding. Inflation
jumped from double digits to triple digits and from there to quadruple and
quintuple digits.

In the short run, government can raise enormous amounts of money
simply by printing it. This additional money results in inflation. With increasing inflation, expectations of inflation are adjusted upward. With greater
expected inflation, government has to print even more new paper money in
order to obtain the same purchasing power. In a sense, government has to
leap-frog inflation expectations in order to continue to raise more than the
maximum sustainable revenue from inflationary finance. One or two rounds
of leap-frogging results in expectations of further leap-frogging. At this point,
inflation and expectations of inflation are exploding. People in the economy
are thinking, ''Inflation was 100 percent last week. This means inflation will
be 200 percent this week.''

Once inflation and expectations of inflation reach this point of leap-frogging, the economy can be said to be experiencing a hyperinflation. The money issued by the government soon becomes replaced, even if illegally, by foreign money, gold and silver, and barter. During the German hyperinflation of 1923, wives would go to the factories where their husbands worked in order to receive their husbands' pay — workers were then being paid twice a day — in order to spend the money as fast as possible. On weekends, people would take whatever they had bought during the week to the country in order to barter for food with farmers.

Hyperinflation is indeed a calamity. The only controversy regarding hyperinflation is if it is itself the fundamental problem or only a manifestation of other, deeper problems in the political economy.

11.5 INFLATION AND REDISTRIBUTION

Until recently it was commonly believed that inflation—by eroding the value of the dollar—transferred wealth from creditors to debtors. Let's say that in 1967 one person (the debtor) borrowed $10,000 from another (the creditor), with provision for repayment of the principal in 20 years, i.e., in 1987. And let's say that from 1967 to 1987, because of continuing, gradual inflation, the general price level increased from an index number of 100 to 300. Then, the argument is, inflation transfers two-thirds of the value of the original principal from the creditor to the debtor, or the debtor only repays one-third of the value of the original principal. That is, the value (or inflation-adjusted value or the purchasing power) of the repayment of principal is equal to $(P_{1967}/P_{1987}) \times \text{principal} = 1/3 \times \text{principal}$.

This argument was essentially correct prior to the days of continuing inflation and interest rates that reflected expectations of inflation. Low, fixed-rate, long-term interest rates ranging from 4 to 6 percent were the norm for U.S. Treasury bonds, high-grade corporate and municipal bonds, and residential mortgages prior to the inflationary 1970s. These interest rates incorporated little if any "premium" for expected inflation. Consequently, the inflation of the 1970s really did transfer value from creditor to debtor. Investors in long-term debt, either directly or through their pensions and whole-life insurance policies, found that they received back less value than they had invested. Borrowers of long-term debt found that they paid back less value than they borrowed.

The 1970s were a period when older Americans, living on "fixed" incomes, i.e., their life savings, pensions, and so on, were impoverished. It is no wonder that the political system reacted by increasing the generosity of social security benefits and by indexing these benefits. The 1970s also were a period when younger Americans, paying off home mortgages, farm mortgages, and business and corporate debt, found that financial leverage worked to their advantage. Financial leverage "worked" because it involved the purchase of real estate, farm land and equipment, and business plant and equipment, and inventories—which generally rose in money value with the rate of inflation—with debt that was fixed in money terms. Borrowers bought real goods of roughly constant value and paid for them in future dollars of greatly decreased value.

With continuing inflation, a "premium" for expected inflation came to be incorporated into interest rates by the 1970s. This inflation premium in interest rates changed the nature of the wealth transfer from creditors to debtors affected by inflation. No longer did inflation *as such* transfer wealth. Instead, the extent to which inflation *differed* from what was expected caused a transfer of wealth. Let's say a borrower and lender contract for a 1-year loan of $100 at an interest rate of 16 percent equal to a "real interest rate" of 6 percent and an inflation premium of 10 percent (*note*: tax complications arising from the taxability of interest income and tax deductibility of interest expenses are being ignored). Furthermore, let's say that the actual rate of inflation during the year of the loan winds up being, exactly as expected, 10 percent. Then, in spite of the inflation, *no* transfer of wealth takes place.

Table 11.1 presents calculations of gain or loss to the creditor upon different assumptions regarding expected inflation and actual inflation. Column A can be considered the baseline case. Here no inflation is expected or built into interest rates, and no inflation occurs. The creditor is repaid at the end of 1 year, with $106 having the purchasing power of $106 in terms of the value of the dollars that were originally lent. Column B can be considered the historical effect of inflation on transfers of wealth from creditor to debtor. Again, no inflation is expected or built into interest rates, *but* the actual rate of inflation turns out to be 10 percent. The creditor is repaid with $106, but this money has the purchasing power of only $96 in terms of the value of the dollars that were originally lent. Inflation has transferred $10 in value from creditor to debtor.

The next three columns represent the contemporary situation regarding the transfer of wealth by inflation. In column C, 10 percent inflation is expected, is built into interest rates, and actually occurs. The creditor is repaid with $116, having the purchasing power of $106 in terms of the dollars that were originally lent. Notice that this is the same value that is found in column A. In column D, *more* inflation occurs than is expected. This has a result similar to that found in column B; i.e., inflation at a faster rate than expected and built into interest rates transfers wealth from creditor to debtor. In column E, *less* inflation occurs than is expected. This has the opposite result; i.e., inflation at a rate slower than expected transfers wealth in the opposite di-

TABLE 11.1   Inflation and Redistribution

	A	B	C	D	E
Expected inflation	0%	0%	10%	10%	10%
Real interest rate	6%	6%	6%	6%	6%
Nominal interest rate	6%	6%	16%	16%	16%
Total dollars	106	106	116	116	116
Actual inflation rate	0%	10%	10%	20%	0%
Value of $1	1.00	0.91	0.91	0.82	1.00
Value total dollars	106	96	106	96	116
Loss/gain	0	− 10	0	− 10	+ 10

rection, from debtor to creditor (this is assuming the debtor does not default on the loan).

The scenario illustrated in column E is representative of the 1980s. During the disinflationary years of the 1980s, the inflation that was expected and built into interest rates did not materialize. The result was a transfer of wealth from debtors to creditors, where loans were repaid, as well as numerous bankruptcies. Borrowers, including working-age families, farmers, businesses, local and national governments, and the third world, found paying their debts very burdensome. In many instances, banks and other financial intermediaries were forced to foreclose on mortgages, renegotiate "stretched out" loan payments, and write off bad debts. The burdens of debt inhibited family formation and investment in productive capacity and so slowed economic growth.

The other side of the coin is that lenders generally made out like bandits. While standards of living fell and poverty rose among working-age families and their children, the opposite was happening among older Americans with substantial savings and pension accumulations. Not all that was lost by borrowers, however, was gained by lenders. The disruption of normal economic activity associated with bankruptcy involves losses to all, losses of borrowers that are not gains to lenders. A similar loss to all occurs when excessive debt burdens resulting from disinflation curtail the normal flow of borrowing needed to finance new projects.

11.5.1 Inflation and Banks

Sometimes there is confusion as to how inflation affects banks and other financial intermediaries. Because most people borrow from banks, they believe that inflation transfers wealth from banks to themselves. Contributing to this belief was the fall in the burden of mortgage payments, originally contracted at low interest rates during the 1960s, when inflation accelerated during the 1970s.

Actually, inflation does not directly have much of an effect on banks and other financial intermediaries. While it is true that banks are major *lenders*, they are also major *borrowers!* At the same time that inflation erodes the value of the loans that banks make, inflation also erodes the value of the deposits that banks take in. To a large extent, then, the wealth-transfer effect of inflation nets to zero as far as banks are concerned. The real transfer of inflation is not from banks to mortgage holders, but from depositors to mortgage holders.

There is a second, somewhat subtle way in which inflation *can* affect banks and other financial intermediaries. This subtle way involves banks that "borrow short" and "lend long," that is, that borrow—mainly by taking in deposits—at fluctuating, short-term interest rates and then lend this money out at fixed, long-term interest rates. Banks that engage in this practice are said to be "maturity transforming," and they are gambling that the normally positive spread between long-term and short-term interest rates will prove profitable. However, if inflation accelerates, then future short-term interest rates will be higher than the banks' locked-in, fixed, long-term interest rates. Many savings and loan institutions, which specialize in mortgage lending, suffered significant losses during the 1970s because of the acceleration of inflation and the resulting rise in interest rates.

11.5.2 Indexation

Almost 100 years ago, economists began to argue that bonds, mortgages, loans, pensions, and other long-term financial agreements should be indexed because of the potential of inflation or, rather, unexpected inflation to transfer wealth from creditor to debtor. Irving Fisher, who is noted for advocating indexation, even succeeded in getting a corporation, the Rand Kardex Corporation, to issue indexed bonds in the 1920s. However, the concept of indexed bonds was then and may still today be ahead of its time.

While economists were concerned about the potential variations in the value of money back in the days when gold was money, the real world of finance in the late nineteenth century and early twentieth century was more concerned with variations in the value of money due to devaluation, suspension of the gold standard, and to "silver agitation," i.e., adoption of a devalued silver standard. Adequate protection against the possibility of transfer of wealth from creditor to debtor was thought to be obtained by the "gold clause" that was then standard in long-term bonds. The gold clause provided for payment of interest and principal in gold coins of specified weight and fineness. Therefore, if the U.S. Congress changed the definition of the dollar so as to allow inflation, creditors would be able to demand payment in gold.

In 1933, during the Great Depression and amidst falling prices and widespread bankruptcies, the U.S. Congress passed a resolution making ownership of gold illegal, voiding the gold clause, and banning all forms of indexation. In 1978, when the Congress decriminalized gold and indexation, economists again started to advocate indexing bonds and other financial agreements.

While the case for indexation was much stronger after a decade of accelerating inflation than with a gold standard, the real world of finance did not appear enthusiastic. An alternative to indexing had been developed, almost by accident, during the time that indexation itself was illegal. This alternative was *floating-rate debt*, also referred to as *adjustable-rate* and *variable-rate debt*. Floating interest rates originated with the bank lending practice of quoting interest rates to business as prime plus an amount appropriate to a borrower's creditworthiness. A bank's best customers would be able to borrow at the prime interest rate. Customers with lower creditworthiness would pay higher interest rates, such as the prime rate plus 1 percentage point. Before inflation gathered steam, the prime interest rate remained constant over relatively long periods of time, and this policy of tying interest rates to the prime rate was not recognized to constitute floating-rate lending. However, when inflation began to accelerate and the prime rate began to be reset on a regular basis, the practice of tying interest rates to the prime rate automatically resulted in floating-rate lending.

A number of financial innovations have occurred in recent years. Among these are

1. *Indexed bonds* and *price-level adjusted mortgages*. These pay interest in constant dollars. Let C be the constant dollar annual coupon. Then, the coupon in year t will be $(P_t/P_0) \times C$, where P_t is the general price level in the year t and P_0 is the general price level in the year of issue.

2. *Price-linked bonds*. These pay interest according to functions of *specific* prices, for example, gold, silver, and oil prices. Thus, interest in year t is $(p_t/p_0) \times C$, where p is the price of gold.

3. *Floating rate, adjustable rate*, and *variable rate loans, bonds, mortgages*, and *preferred stock*. These pay interest and dividends that *vary* according to a formula linked to market interest rates. For example, the interest rate may be equal to the 3-month Treasury bill rate plus 0.50 percent subject to a minimum of 4 percent and a maximum of 15 percent. Most Eurodollar bonds carry interest rates that vary according to the London Inter-Bank Offering Rate, LIBOR, which is the short-term interest rate London banks offer for deposits.

4. *Extendable bonds, Dutch auction stock,* and *remarketable preferred stock.* These pay interest and dividends that are periodically re-set to make the demand for these securities equal the supply at market value equal to par. That is, the returns on these securities are totally adjustable according to market conditions as opposed to being fixed as in conventional bonds or adjustable rate bonds that vary according to a specified formula.

5. *Income bonds* and *participating preferred stock.* These pay interest and dividends that are tied to a company's income or common stock dividends. In a sense, interest and dividends are tied directly to the fortunes of the company. However, because of managerial discretion over income and common stock dividends, utilization of these securities is not widespread.

6. *Convertible bonds* and *preferred stock.* These pay interest and dividends that may or may not be fixed. Nevertheless, these securities offer a kind of inflation hedge because, if rising prices diminish the value of the bonds or preferred stock, the holder has the option of conversion into common stock.

11.5.3 Floating-Rate vs. Indexed vs. Price-Linked Debt

Floating-rate debt approximates indexed debt because a series of short-term forecasts of inflation will, on average, tend to be correct. In any particular year, the expected rate of inflation can differ significantly from the actual rate of inflation. However, over a long period of time it is reasonable to believe that overforecasts of inflation will offset underforecasts of inflation. For example, during the 1970s, inflation tended to race ahead of expectations. Interest rates therefore tended to undercompensate for the falling value of the dollar. During the 1980s, the opposite was the case. Inflation fell faster than expectations, and interest rates tended to overcompensate for the falling value of the dollar. A long-term floating-rate bond or mortgage covering both the 1970s *and* 1980s, therefore, would have more or less correctly compensated for the effects of inflation.

An important question is whether floating-rate securities are an *adequate enough* approximation of indexed securities. For example, during the 1970s, creditors were undercompensated for the effects of inflation with floating-rate instruments because inflation ran ahead of expectations. Then, during the 1980s, creditors were overcompensated, when debtors did not default, for the effects of inflation with floating-rate instruments because disinflation ran ahead of expectations. While floating-rate instruments may not be exact approximations of indexed instruments, they do offer countervailing advantages of having well-known legal and tax consequences and enjoying active secondary markets. Until and unless indexed debt features these advantages, an individual borrower may correctly feel that issuing indexed debt would be more costly than issuing floating-rate debt.

Individual borrowers may find their needs better served by *price-linked debt* rather than floating-rate or indexed debt. A company producing a product such as gold, silver, or oil with a highly volatile price can find that its income is not highly correlated with the overall rate of inflation. In such a case, the company may prefer to issue price-linked debt, where interest is linked to specific prices. In years where the price of gold, for example, is up, the company would be obligated to *and would be able to pay* a high interest rate. In years where the price of gold is down, the company would not be obligated to pay *and would not be able to pay* a high interest rate. Therefore, the interest rate the company would have to pay would be correlated with its own income. This would *hedge* the company's interest expense against its income. Furthermore, this correlation of interest expense and income would nearly eliminate the incentive to default when the fortunes of the company are low. A financial intermediary, such as a bank, insurance company, or pension trust fund, can invest in a number of *different* price-linked securities and create a portfolio that as a whole correlates well with the overall rate of inflation.

11.6 INFLATION AND TAXES

Inflation itself can be considered a tax, a tax on cash balances. In a sense, the revenue obtained by government from the printing of new money is derived from the erosion of value of the already existing money in an economy. In this section, the induced or indirect taxes of inflation—as opposed to the tax on cash balances—are examined. These induced taxes include "bracket creep," historical cost accounting, and capital gains taxation.

11.6.1 "Bracket Creep"

"Bracket creep" refers to the combined effect of inflation and a nonindexed progressive income tax. A progressive income tax provides for higher tax *rates* on higher levels of income, e.g., a tax rate of 15 percent on income up to a certain level and a tax rate of 28 percent on income above that level. The levels of income on which higher tax rates are applied are called *brackets*. And unless the income tax is indexed, inflation has the effect of pushing taxpayers into higher and higher tax brackets, from which comes the expression "bracket creep." During the period from 1965 to 1980, Robert J. Barro and Chaipat Sahasakul estimate that the average marginal income tax rate rose from 21 to 30 percent mostly due to the continuing effects of inflation.[2]

In order to offset "bracket creep," the income tax has been both indexed and flattened. Indexation of the income tax involves recomputation of the brackets and personal exemption according to the value of the dollar. Flattening of the income tax involves reducing the number of brackets so that remaining imperfections in the indexation of the tax structure cannot push many taxpayers into increasingly higher brackets.

11.6.2 Historical Cost Accounting

Inflation combined with historical cost accounting affects taxes on business in two important ways: inventory valuation and depreciation. In both instances, accounting income is an overstatement of economic income, and taxes calculated on the basis of accounting income are higher. The biases of historical cost accounting during a period of inflation can be said to cause "inflationary profits." These inflationary profits are not completely an illusion, however, because the taxes to be paid on them are real.

Let's say that a manufacturer sells 100 units of a product per month and makes these products out of an equal number of raw materials over a 2-month cycle. Ignoring any precautionary or speculative inventories, the manufacturer will require 200 units in inventory in order to maintain a steady flow of raw materials coming in and finished products going out.

If the manufacturer uses first-in, first-out (FIFO) inventory valuation, then the cost of materials is determined by the oldest inventory in stock—in the present case by the money cost of the supplies purchased 2 months previously. If there is 1 percent inflation per month, then the cost of materials on a FIFO basis is about 2 percent less than the "replacement cost" of the inventory used in production. This understatement of cost of materials corresponds to an overstatement of profits and results in a higher tax.

Because of the bias of FIFO inventory valuation during a period of rising prices, many large corporations switched to last-in, first-out (LIFO) inventory valuation during the 1970s. With LIFO, cost of materials is determined by the money cost of the newest inventory in stock. This method approximates replacement cost accounting in the calculation of profits and, therefore, in determining taxes.

A related problem concerns the understatement of replacement cost depreciation by historical cost accounting during a period of rising prices.

[2]Robert J. Barro and Chaipat Sahasakul, "Measuring the Average Marginal Tax Rate from the Individual Income Tax," *Journal of Business*, 56, 1983, pp. 419–452.

Depreciation apportions the costs of plant and equipment over their useful lives. The basic idea of depreciation is to *match* the costs of production, including fixed or overhead costs, to sales. Since buildings, vehicles, tools, and so on contribute to production over long periods of time, their costs are to be matched against the sales generated over these periods of time. What historical cost depreciation does is spread the original money cost of depreciable assets over their useful lives using a formula such as the straight-line method.

This method would be appropriate if the dollar enjoyed a constant value. However, because of the effect of continuing inflation, depreciation charges relating to past investments can substantially understate the current money cost of replacing plant and equipment. With depreciation understated, income is overstated and a larger tax results.

The 1981 accelerated capital recovery system mitigated this problem by allowing accelerated depreciation schedules. Instead of being depreciated over their useful lives, plant and equipment were to be depreciated over very short periods of time. With accelerated depreciation, there would not be enough time for the effect of continuing inflation to become significant. Acceleration of depreciation, however, was a hodge-podge solution to the bias of historical cost depreciation. Therefore, after inflation moderated during the 1980s and acceleration was no longer appropriate, the Tax Reform Act of 1986 returned depreciation schedules to something like their pre-1981 time schedules.

11.6.3 Capital Gains

Capital gains refers to the increase in money value from the time of purchase until the time of sale of an asset, usually a durable asset such as real estate, gold, collectibles, and common stocks. (Depreciation usually offsets any increase in the value of a unit of a nondurable asset such as vehicles and equipment.) During an inflationary era, capital gains can accrue to ownership of durable assets simply because of the falling value of the dollar. A house can go from $50,000 to $150,000 in money value over a period of time just because inflation raises the general price level from an index number of 100 to 300.

Taxation of capital gains amounts to another induced tax during a period of inflation. The house just described, if sold, could expose the owner to a tax on a capital gain of $100,000. Fortunately, a number of provisions of the tax code mitigate the effects of capital gains taxation. First, capital gains taxes can often be postponed if the proceeds from the sale of an asset are used to purchase a like asset. Specifically, if the family selling the house just described bought another house of the same or higher value, the tax on the capital gain would not be payable at that time. The capital gain would, instead, be rolled into the next house, and the tax on it and any additional capital gain would become payable upon final liquidation of the family's investment in housing.

Second, the capital gain in one's residence is subject to a once-in-a-lifetime exclusion. Accordingly, as long as you keep buying new houses of equal or higher value than the ones you sell, then you may never have to pay a capital gains tax. Simply maintain your investment in housing until you are over the required age for the exclusion before liquidating any part of your investment in housing. At that time, you can decide to invest in a less valuable house, such as a Florida condo, or no house at all, i.e., become a renter, and pocket the accumulated capital gain. Unfortunately, this exclusion, combined with the already high transactions costs in real estate, makes investments in housing quite illiquid.

Third, capital gains taxes can be avoided through estate planning. This is the big tax loophole that the government does not know how to close, commonly referred to as death. While you cannot take it with you, you *can* keep the IRS from taking it with them![3] Often in these situations the recipient of appreciated property such as common stock picks up the property for tax purposes at the current market value. This means that the capital gains during the lifetime of the giver are tax-free. Fourth, until the Tax Reform Act of 1986, long-term capital gains were taxed at a low rate relative to taxes on ordinary income. With the Tax Reform Act of 1986, capital gains, whether long-term or not, became taxable at ordinary income tax rates. Even so, taxation of capital gains still receives favorable treatment in many jurisdictions, e.g., in Japan, where there is no tax at all on capital gains. In addition, some form of capital gains tax advantage may be returned to the U.S. tax code.

Fifth, and finally, capital gains taxes are often evaded through the nonreporting of gains in sales — often cash sales — of gold and collectibles such as coins, stamps, gems, art, antiques, rare books, baseball cards, and so forth. Altogether, it is very difficult to determine the net effect of inflation combined with capital gains taxation because of the variety of legal and illegal methods used to avoid capital gains taxation. It seems fair to say, however, that to the extent inflation increases capital gains, it induces utilization of these tax avoidance measures and so distorts the normal incentives involved in saving and investment.

---

[3] Yes, people *are* dying to avoid taxes. Benjamin Franklin was wrong, it is not death *and* taxes, it is death *or* taxes.

11.6.4 Inflation and the Stock Market

The taxes induced by inflation partially explain why common stocks did not prove to be an inflation hedge during the 1970s. As inflation heated up during the 1970s, common stocks performed poorly. In fact, the market value of corporations fell substantially below the replacement cost value of their assets. Perhaps the stock market was irrationally valuing corporations; or else something was being left out of the equation. Perhaps it was the taxation of inflationary profits. Alternatively, it may have been the overall riskiness of conducting business in a highly inflationary economy.[4] In any case, what is now obvious is that the stock market enjoyed one of its strongest rallies in history after inflation moderated during the 1980s.

11.7 SUMMARY

1. According to the quantity theory it is the quantity of money, not its precious-metal content, that in the long run determines the price level.

2. In the long run, prices will tend to rise by the rate of money supply growth less about 4 percent (i.e., the long-run growth rate of real GNP).

3. Hyperinflation is characterized by rapidly accelerating rates of inflation, is usually indicative of other, more fundamental fiscal and monetary problems in the political economy, and is characterized by inflation running at much faster rates than the rate of money supply growth.

4. Actual inflation greater than the expected inflation rate built into interest rates transfers wealth from creditor to debtor. Actual inflation less than the expected inflation built into interest rates transfers wealth from debtor to creditor, when the debtor does not default, as well as induces defaults.

5. Variable-rate debt mitigates the effects of unstable money by replacing one long-term forecast of inflation with a series of short-term forecasts. Theoretically, indexed and price-linked debt would be superior.

6. Inflation induces a variety of taxes including "bracket creep," taxation of inflationary profits, and capital gains taxes.

---

[4]The issue of rational valuation of common stocks during the inflationary 1970s is discussed by Martin Feldstein, "Inflation and the Stock Market," *American Economic Review*, 70, December 1980, pp. 839 – 847; Franco Modigliani and Richard A. Cohn, "Inflation, Rational Valuation and the Market," *Financial Analyst Journal*, March-April 1979, pp. 24 – 44; and Patrick H. Hendershott, "The Decline in Aggregate Share Values: Taxation, Valuation Errors, Risk and Profitability," *American Economic Review*, 71, December 1981, pp. 909 – 922.

11.8 EXERCISES

1. Use the quantity theory to determine the implications of the following:
   a. Debasement in which the king "calls in" all the gold and silver coins and melts them down, recasting twice as many coins containing only 50 percent of the precious metal content of the original coins, returning one of the new coins to the owners of the original coins for each of the original coins turned in, and using the extra new coins to finance his government's spending.
   b. Debasement in which the king "calls in" all the gold and silver coins and melts them down, recasting the same number of coins containing only 50 percent of the precious metal content of the original coins, returning one of the new coins to the owners of the original coins for each of the original coins turned in, and keeping the extra gold and silver coins safe and sound—and idle—in his government's treasury.
   c. The issue of paper currency and subsidiary coins by the monetary authority in a multiple amount such as four-to-one of its gold and silver reserves, with convertibility of its paper currency and subsidiary coins into gold and silver.
   d. Repudiation of convertibility into gold and silver of paper currency and subsidiary coins, which repudiation itself does not increase the money supply.

2. In light of Figure 11.1, discuss the major cause(s) of inflation under the classic (nineteenth century) gold standard.

3. Identify the winners and losers upon an unanticipated acceleration in inflation.

4. Why is it that indexed bonds would in theory be preferred to fixed-rate bonds during a period of unstable prices? Why is it that, with the legalization of indexation in 1978, indexed bonds have not become commonplace in the United States?

5. Why is it that wage-and-price controls would in theory be useful as complements to fiscal and monetary policies to disinflate an economy? Why is it that, in practice, wage-and-price controls are hardly ever actually used as complements to fiscal and monetary policies for the purpose of disinflating an economy?

11.9 REFERENCES

Philip Cagan, "The Monetary Dynamics of Hyperinflation," in M. Friedman (Ed.), *Studies in the Quantity Theory of Money.* Chicago: University of Chicago Press, 1956.

Richard Cantillon, *Essai sur la nature du Commerce en general.* Translated by Henry Higgs. London: Royal Economic Society, 1931 (orig. 1755).

Stanley Fischer, *Indexing, Inflation and Economic Policy.* Cambridge, Mass: MIT Press, 1986.

Irving Fisher, *The Purchasing Power of Money.* New York: Macmillan, 1911.

J. Huston McCulloch, *Money and Inflation*, 2d Ed. New York: Academic Press, 1982.

David Tweedie and Geoffrey Whittington, *The Debate on Inflation Accounting*. Cambridge: Cambridge University Press, 1984.

Leland B. Yeager, *Experiences with Stopping Inflation*. Washington, D.C.: American Enterprise Institute, 1981.

Managerial Case 1

INFLATION OUT OF CONTROL: THE MARXIST EXPERIMENT IN CHILE

On September 11, 1973, the world's first, and thus far only, freely elected Marxist government was overthrown. Comrade Salvadire Allende Gossens, who was elected President of Chile in November of 1970, was found in his palace riddled with bullets. The official police autopsy determined the cause of his death to be suicide. Allende, supposedly, killed himself with machine-gun fire, stopping once, while shooting himself, to reload.

Some may dismiss this overthrow of a Latin American government as a not unusual event. Others blame it on the CIA or AT&T. Yet even the casual observer must be impressed with the almost total collapse of the Chilean economy during the months immediately preceding the coup.

During these months, in spite of — or perhaps because of — government attempts to control wages, prices, credit, and foreign exchange; to ration consumption and to direct production; to nationalize industry; and to "reform" agriculture, the economy was in chaos. Flour, sugar, meat, dairy products, fuel, and other necessities were extremely scarce. Copper miners, factory workers, dock workers, and truck drivers were on strike. Hoarding of goods was rampant. Prices were rising faster and faster, rising in the last month of Allende's regime at an annual rate of 750 percent.

Exhibit 11.1 shows that money supply growth accelerated to about 100 percent per year during 1971–1972 following the election of Allende in 1970. At first, and because of price controls, the rate of inflation actually fell; but soon, inflation too started accelerating. By 1973, a hyperinflationary spiral was underway.

How did this economic anarchy come about? What brought Chile to such ruin?

Allende's first budget featured massive new government spending, financed by added taxes and paper money. Agrarian reform was accelerated, and selected industries — including banking — were nationalized. In order to contain the inflationary pressure of increasing the money supply, price controls were extended throughout the economy.

At first, the controls seemed to work. But soon, signs of trouble appeared. The government reacted by tightening price and foreign exchange controls.

By mid-1972, in spite of controls, inflation was exploding, rising to over 100 percent per year. Food shortages began to appear. Strikes were becoming numerous as workers resisted wage controls during the rapid inflation. By late 1972, Allende declared a state of "war economy."

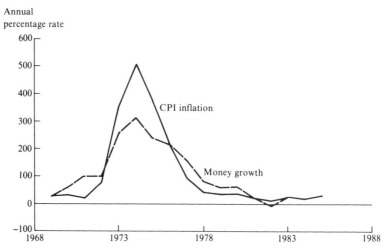

Exhibit 11.1 Money and Inflation in Chile, 1969 – 1985.
An increase in money supply growth is obvious immediately after
the election of Allende in 1970. Inflation, however, actually slows
down because of the imposition of price controls. As the money
supply continues to grow rapidly and as the price controls fall apart,
inflation explodes, and a devastated economy ushers in a military
coup.
Source: *International Financial Statistics*, various issues. Used with permission.

Early in 1973, states of emergency were declared in the provinces of Santiago and O'Higgin. A wheat reserve was created to supervise the distribution of
wheat from farm regions to urban areas. However, there was little wheat to supervise. Agrarian reform had turned into a nightmare. Reform was supposed to redistribute land from the wealthy to the poor. Instead, reform replaced the estates
of the wealthy with government communes. The poor remained landless. In addition, armed bands of leftist revolutionaries and right-wing reactionaries roamed
the countryside terrorizing farmers.

In the midst of this upheaval, in the May 1973 congressional elections, the
Popular Unity Party of Allende increased its share of the votes and seats in Congress. Even though still a minority government, the Unity Party was returned to
power for 4 more years.

In September, the military moved. General Augusto Pinochet Ugarte of the
army, joined by officers of the other branches of the military, acted to overthrow
the government.

In the coup, some 2000 to 3000 people were killed in short, but bloody
conflicts. Dozens of Unity Party officials were imprisoned, and thousands more
were detained at the Santiago football stadium. Leftist parties were banned, and
other parties were given a ''recess.'' Military tribunals replaced courts. Only two

center-right papers were allowed to publish. Several thousand refugees fled to U.N. centers. Strikes were banned. University autonomy was ended. A draconian ''state of siege'' was upon the land.

Fifteen years later, while there had been some progress, freedom still seemed far from Chile. The wholesale adoption of radical socialist economic policies simply did not work. Government controls did not control, but replaced the ''invisible hand'' of the market with anarchy. Deficit spending and rapid expansion of the money supply resulted first in higher prices and eventually in a ruined economy. And then the collapse of the economy ushered in an even more authoritarian regime.

Managerial Case 2

PRICE STABILIZATION THROUGH "INCOMES POLICY": ARGENTINA, BRAZIL, AND ISRAEL

After years of triple-digit inflation, Argentina, Brazil, and Israel, in June of 1985, February of 1986, and July of 1985, respectively, sought to end inflation while avoiding recession by combining fiscal and monetary restraint with ''incomes policies.'' Wage-and-price controls were to quickly and painlessly break the inflationary spiral.

The Cruzado Plan of Brazil, for example, involved the issue of a new monetary unit, the cruzado, at the rate of 1 cruzado for 1000 cruzeiros (the former monetary unit). In addition, prices were frozen, wages were deindexed, and the exchange rate of the cruzado was fixed at 13.80 for one U.S. dollar. In addition, the purchasing power values of rents and mortgage payments were stabilized, and interest rates on nonindexed debt were reduced.

At first, all three stabilization efforts appeared enormously successful. Not only were rates of inflation dramatically reduced, major recessions were not experienced.[1] However, success may have been too easy. As Exhibit 11.2 shows, triple-digit inflation soon returned to Argentina and Brazil. Israel, on the other hand, appears to have achieved more lasting success.

In Argentina and Brazil, the return of triple-digit inflation clearly indicates that wage-and-price controls were used—as they usually are—as substitutes for real fiscal and monetary reform. In spite of talk of reform, little was actually done. In fact, the apparent success of the wage-and-price controls may have undermined any intent to reform. Why adopt policies of monetary and fiscal restraint when all that is necessary is wage-and-price controls?

In Israel, the difference may well have been $1.5 billion in supplementary aid—equal to 7.5 percent of that country's annual gross national product—from

---

[1]For detailed descriptions of these plans and their early successes, see Rudiger Dornbusch and Mario Henrique Simonsen, ''Inflation Stabilization with Incomes Policy Support: A Review of the Experience in Argentina, Brazil and Israel'' (New York: The Group of Thirty, 1987).

CPI annual
inflation rate

Exhibit 11.2   Stabilization with "Incomes Policy": Argentina, Brazil, and Israel.
Inflation is significantly reduced immediately after adoption of "incomes policies" (wage-and-price controls) in Argentina (in June 1985), Brazil (in February 1986), and Israel (July 1985). However, because of failures to implement real fiscal and monetary reforms, rapid inflation soon returns to Argentina and Brazil.
Source: International Financial Statistics, various issues. Used with permission.

the United States, enabling Israel to significantly reduce its budget deficit. In addition, the incomes policy was temporary: a freeze of wages and prices, followed by a 1-year phaseout of wage-and-price controls.

_____ *Managerial Case 3* _____

ACCOUNTING FOR INFLATION

From 1980 to 1986, large corporations were required to include certain inflation-adjusted estimates in footnotes to their standard historical cost financial statements in their annual reports. These supplementary disclosures confirmed what had been generally understood, that historical cost accounting during a period of rising prices overstates income and so increases taxes. Moreover, detailed analysis of these inflation-adjusted figures indicates that the biases induced by historical cost accounting differed across firms and so distorted trend analysis and financial analysis.[2] In 1986, by reason of a controversial four to three vote by the Financial Accountants Standards Board, the ''experiment'' with inflation-adjusted accounting was terminated. Large corporations were no longer required to disclose inflation-adjusted estimates in their annual reports.

Even though large corporations are no longer required to report inflation-adjusted figures, the concept of restating a firm's financial position remains valid. Indeed, multinational corporations restate income and assets of overseas subsidiaries in terms of U.S. dollar values in order to state all figures on a comparable basis and in terms of a relatively stable currency. This restatement is called *translation* and is governed by detailed instructions from the Financial Accountants Standards Board. Firms operating in highly inflationary economies such as Brazil routinely restate their own books using general price level accounting. Sometimes this even involves restatement between publication of the official general price level using the exchange rate of the local currency into the U.S. dollar.

Basically, inflation-adjusted accounting takes two forms: constant-dollar (or general price level) accounting, and replacement-cost (or current cost or specific price) accounting. In *constant-dollar accounting*, all accounting entries from prior years are adjusted to account for the accumulated effect of inflation. Let's say a depreciable asset was purchased for $10,000 ten years ago and was being straight-line depreciated over a useful life of 20 years. Then, constant-dollar accounting would record this year's depreciation relating to this particular asset as $(P_t/P_{t-10}) \times \$500$, where P_t is the general price level in the current year. And, constant-dollar accounting would record this year's undepreciated balance, or book value, as $(P_t/P_{t-10}) \times \$5000$. Notice that historical cost accounting involves biases on both the income statement and the balance sheet.

Replacement-cost accounting adjusts accounting entries from prior years using changes in the money prices of the specific goods in which the company does business. In practice, this can either be done via direct pricing or by application of detailed price indexes. Sometimes this requires engineering studies in order to take technological obsolescence into account. Using detailed price indexes, the methodology is similar to constant-dollar accounting. Relating to the preceding example, replacement-cost depreciation would be $(p_t/p_{t-10}) \times \$500$, where p_t is the relevant price index, and replacement-cost book value would be $(p_t/p_{t-10}) \times \$5000$.

Exhibit 11.3 presents historical-cost and replacement-cost income statements for Georgia-Pacific for the year 1982. First, notice that cost of sales as restated is only slightly higher than the historical-cost entry. This is because Georgia-Pacific was using LIFO inventory evaluation. Next, notice that depreciation and depletion as restated is substantially higher than the historical-cost entry. This illustrates the effect of moderate but continuing inflation over a period of time. Because of this bias, the company is actually suffering economic losses as opposed

[2]Clifford F. Thies and Thomas Sturrock, ''What Did Inflation-Adjusted Accounting Tell Us?'' *Journal of Accounting, Auditing and Finance*, 2, Fall 1987, pp. 375–391.

EXHIBIT 11.3   Income Statement, Georgia-Pacific, 1982 ($ Millions).

	Historical Cost	*Replacement Cost*
Net sales	5402	5402
Costs of sales	4475	4477
Selling, general and administrative	394	394
Depreciation and depletion	356	518
Interest	186	186
Other income, net	(76)	(76)
Income (loss) before taxes	67	(97)
Taxes	15	15
Income (loss)	52	(112)

Source: From 1982 *Annual Report* of Georgia-Pacific. Used with permission.

to earning economic profits, as may be inferred from the historical-cost figures. Finally, notice that Georgia-Pacific is paying $15 million in taxes because of the profits it supposedly is making even though the company is actually suffering a loss. Taxes on inflationary profits are no illusion!

12
Unemployment

12.1 INTRODUCTION

> A "recession" is when your neighbor is out of work. A "depression" is when you're out of work.

The modern economy consists of a wide range of work and job opportunities. In addition to the traditional jobs on farms and in factories, there is an ever-expanding list of jobs in the emerging service sector. Long ago, the task of finding a productive place in society was relatively easy. You did what your father did if you were male or what your mother — and almost all women — did if you were female. The clergy and the New World provided a kind of safety valve, allowing the talented and ambitious some opportunities, but by and large, economies were static and traditional, and the challenge of finding work did not fall heavily on the individual person.

Today the task of finding a job is itself a job. Matching your own skills and preferences to an available position — or creating such a position for yourself — is a sometimes frustrating exercise in comparison shopping. This is so because most people consider more than just the wage in choosing jobs. Among other considerations are fringe benefits, working conditions, opportunities for advancement, job security, and geographic location. For most people, the eventual decision involves some degree of compromise and some element of luck. The efficiency of the market process, during normal times, in matching people to jobs may be considered amazing. Nevertheless, it is understandable how costly can be the loss of a job and how costly can be the inability of many to find jobs during periods of recession.

This chapter examines unemployment, how it is measured, and how it behaves over time. In this chapter, the concept of the "natural rate" of unemployment is carefully developed. Deviations from this natural rate resulting from the vagaries of the business cycle and structural shifts in the economy are also examined. The role of expectations in contributing to unemployment is pursued, and some public policies that affect the unemployment rate, including unemployment insurance, are analyzed.

12.2 MEASURES OF UNEMPLOYMENT

Being unemployed is defined as (1) not being employed and (2) looking for work. The U.S. Bureau of Labor Statistics, in fact, places all persons at least 16 years of age in one of the following three categories: employed, unemployed, or not in the labor force.

Every month the Bureau of Labor Statistics conducts a survey of some 70,000 households in order to estimate the number of persons in each of the preceding three categories for the U.S. population as a whole as well as for a number of subgroups. The interviewer for the Bureau of Labor Statistics first asks if members of the household were working for pay during the previous week, whether part time, full time, or at a temporary job. These people are counted as employed. For persons not employed, the interviewer asks if they were on temporary layoff waiting recall or had looked for work during the past 4 weeks. "Looking for work" includes applying for work with an employer, registering with an employment agency, checking with friends, and other job-search activities. These people are counted as unemployed. Remaining people, such as housekeeping spouses, students, retirees, and institutionalized persons, who are not employed or looking for employment are counted as not in the labor force.

Given the number of people classified as employed, unemployed, and not in the labor force, the unemployment rate is then calculated at $U/(E+U)$, where U is the number of persons unemployed and E is the number of persons employed. Table 12.1 displays the composition of the U.S. labor force during 1979 and 1983, the first a year of relatively low unemployment and the second a year of relatively high unemployment. Table 12.2 displays the composition of the group of persons not in the labor force. Notice that some people who are not in the labor force say they are not looking for a job because they do not feel they could find one and that the number of people in this category is higher during a period of high unemployment. These people are referred to as the "discouraged unemployed."

12.2.1 Advantages and Disadvantages of the Official Unemployment Rate

The ideal labor market index would indicate the deviation of the actual matching of people to jobs from what would be a perfect matching given the job

TABLE 12.1   Composition of the U.S. Labor Force

	1979	1983
Population		
16 years and older	166,460	175,891
Labor force	106,559	113,226
Employed	100,421	102,510
Unemployed	6,137	10,717
Unemployment rate		
$U/(E+U)$	5.8%	9.5%

Source: Handbook of Labor Statistics, Bulletin no. 2217, U.S. Bureau of Labor Statistics, June 1985, p. 6.
Note: Annual averages of monthly figures, in millions, except for unemployment rate, which is in percent.

TABLE 12.2   Composition of Group of Persons Not in the Labor Force

	1979	1983
Total	59,900	62,665
Do not want a job now	54,472	56,161
Going to school	6,144	6,583
Ill, disabled	4,610	3,915
Housekeeping	29,581	28,356
Retired	10,143	13,019
Other	3,944	4,288
Want a job now	5,427	6,503
Going to school	1,470	1,608
Ill, disabled	757	765
Housekeeping	1,268	1,413
Think cannot get a job	771	1,641
Job market reason	515	1,248
Personal reason	257	394
Other	1,161	1,076

Source: Handbook of Labor Statistics, Bulletin no. 2217, U.S. Bureau of Labor Statistics, June 1985, p. 38.
Note: Annual average of monthly figures, in millions.

skills and preferences involved. Persons completely without work and looking for a full-time job would be counted as unemployed. Persons with part-time jobs and looking for full-time jobs would be counted as partially employed and partially unemployed. Persons with jobs not fully utilizing their skills and looking for jobs that would would likewise be counted as partially employed and partially unemployed.

Such an ideal measure of unemployment would involve considerable subjectivity. In addition, it would be difficult to compare this ideal measure to unemployment figures from the past. Nevertheless, in its monthly household survey, the Bureau of Labor Statistics does ask some supplemental questions that allow construction of expanded measures of unemployment. For example, an unemployment concept that accounts for those who are working part time for economic reasons in addition to (fully) unemployed registered 12.4 percent in December of 1982, the bottom of the recession then underway, compared to the conventionally measured unemployment rate of 10.7 percent.

Despite its limitations, the official unemployment rate has two important advantages: objectivity and comparability. The most important judgment in classifying people concerns whether a person has actually looked for work in the past 4 weeks. This judgment is aided by enumeration of several methods of job search and is ultimately made by the interviewed members of households. In addition, from time to time, controversies are raised in classifying people. Recently, it was argued that with an all-volunteer military, those in the armed forces should be simply included among the employed without a distinction being made between the civilian labor force and the military. In the past, categorization of persons in federal manpower programs—such as job-training programs—varied among all three categories of employed, unemployed, and not in the labor force.[1]

Comparability is provided by use of the same definition for a long period of time. Whatever biases are in the measurement of unemployment, they presumably affected comparable past data as they do the present. Therefore, the unemployment rate is a useful index of changes in labor market conditions.

12.2.2 Other Measures of Labor Market Efficiency

At least four other measures of labor market efficiency are available: the insured unemployment rate (based on unemployment insurance data), the

---

[1]Michael Darby argues that counting persons employed in state and federal job programs during the 1930s as ''unemployed'' understates the strength of the recovery from the Great Depression. ''Three-and-a-Half Million U.S. Employees Have Been Mislaid: Or an Explanation of Unemployment, 1934–1941.'' *Journal of Political Economy*, 84, February 1976, pp. 1–16.

registered unemployment rate (based on employment agency figures), the employment rate (based on establishment data), and job vacancies (based on help-wanted advertising). These other measures of labor market efficiency have, from time to time and country to country, served as the main labor market indicator. Table 12.3 presents unemployment rates of seven countries as originally stated and as re-stated on a consistent basis by the Organization for Economic Cooperation and Development. Today, for the United States, they help to verify trends observed with the unemployment rate constructed from the Bureau of Labor Statistics' household survey. In addition, the set of measures gives a more complete picture of labor market conditions. Notice the broad similarities among all ten measures of labor market conditions presented in Figure 11.1. (Also notice which of these measures are graphed upside-down.)

1. Insured unemployment. *Insured unemployment* is the number of persons receiving unemployment compensation. Both the total number of insured unemployed and the number of *new* insured unemployed are key business condition indicators. These measures focus on workers on layoff and job losers who are covered by unemployment insurance.

2. Registered unemployment. The *registered unemployment* rate is the number of persons registered at employment agencies, usually at the "official" or government-run agencies, relative to the total of registered unem-

TABLE 12.3   International Unemployment Rates, 1985

	As Originally Stated	OECD Standardized Unemployment Rates
United States	7.2%	7.1%
Japan	2.6	2.6
Germany	8.3	7.2
France	10.2	10.1
United Kingdom	11.7	11.3
Italy	10.1	10.5
Canada	10.5	10.4

Source: OECD Economic Outlook, No. 41, June 1987, pp. 30–31. Used with permission.

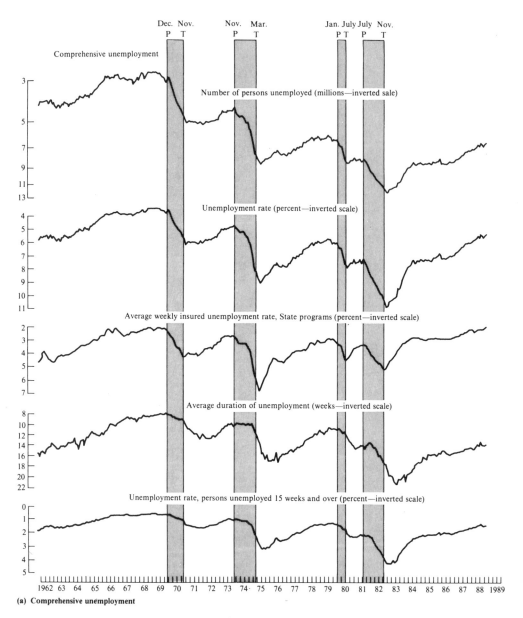

FIGURE 12.1 Unemployment Indicators.
Parts (a) and (b) demonstrate the relations among the major unemployment indicators. The uppermost indicator in Figure 12.1a is the number of persons unemployed (notice that this and several other series are inverted). The number of persons unemployed rises dramatically during recessions (the shaded areas in the figures). However, the number of persons unemployed drifts upward over time

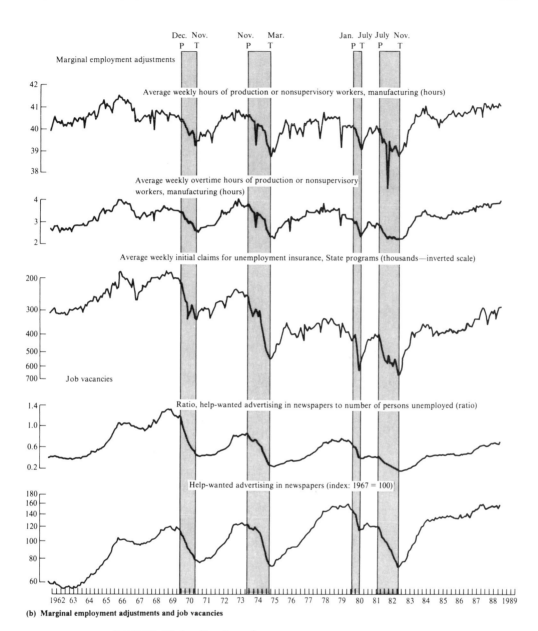

FIGURE 12.1   Continued

owing to increases in the population and labor force participation and to changes in labor force composition. The next two indicators are the (official) unemployment rate and the insured unemployment rate.

Source: *Business Conditions Digest*, November 1988, pp. 16 and 18. Redrawn with permission of *Business Conditions Digest* and The Conference Board.

ployed and employment. Today, in a number of other countries, the registered unemployment rate is the main unemployment indictor.

A disadvantage of both insured and registered unemployment as overall measures of labor market conditions is their limited coverage. With unemployment insurance, most important is that labor force entrants and reentrants, such as young adults leaving school and women returning to the labor force, are not covered and that unemployment insurance expires after so many weeks of coverage. Because of limited coverage, the insured unemployed rate is an undercount of the total unemployed. Furthermore, since they are receiving unemployment compensation, the insured unemployed are arguably not as badly off as the uninsured unemployed. Registered unemployment only counts those without work seeking jobs through specified employment agencies. Job seeking in the modern economy includes many modes of search in addition to registering at employment agencies. Thus registered unemployment is also an undercount of unemployment.

3. Employment. Separately from its household survey, the Bureau of Labor Statistics conducts a monthly survey of establishments, or workplaces, in order to estimate the total number of people at work. Prior to World War II, figures similar to these were the main labor market indicator in this country. Aside from some technical differences, the estimate of employment from this survey should equal that in the household survey, verifying trends in employment. Continuing changes in the labor market, however, require continuing adjustment of the estimates derived from the establishment surveys to maintain comparability with the estimates derived from the household survey.

4. Vacancies. An index of help-wanted advertising is constructed by the Conference Board, a privately funded research organization, by measuring the inches of job listings in major newspapers across the country. This index is considered a measure of vacancies. This index looks at the labor market from the opposite standpoint of the other indexes considered. Instead of measuring unemployed workers, this index measures the unfilled jobs.

12.3 TYPES AND CAUSES OF UNEMPLOYMENT

Logically, there are five ways a person can become unemployed: (1) A person not in the labor force, who never before was employed, starts to look for a job. This person is called a *new entrant*. Young adults dominate this category. (2) A person not in the labor force, who was formerly employed, starts to look for a job. This person is called a *reentrant*. Young people, who switch back and forth from school to work, and women, who switch from childbearing and raising to work, dominate this category. (3) A person voluntarily

TABLE 12.4   Reasons for Unemployment

	1979	1983
Unemployment rate	5.8%	9.6%
Job losers	2.5	5.6
Job leavers	0.8	0.7
New entrants	1.7	2.2
Reentrants	0.8	1.1

Source: Handbook of Labor Statistics, Bulletin no. 2217, U.S. Bureau of Labor Statistics, June 1985, p. 64.

quits a job and starts to look for another. (4) A person is put on temporary layoff and waits for recall. (5) A person permanently loses a job and starts to look for another.

While there always are some people unemployed for each of these five reasons, a major difference between a smoothly operating economy and a recession is a large increase in layoffs and (involuntary) job losers, i.e., reasons number 4 and 5. In Table 12.4, contrast the portion of total unemployment due to "Job losers" in 1983, a year of high unemployment, to that in 1979. Another major difference is the average length of time it takes people, once unemployed, to find an acceptable job. This length of time is referred to as a *spell of unemployment*. During recessions, the average duration of spells of unemployment increases.

12.3.1 Frictional Unemployment

The unemployment that seems, inevitably, to accompany searching for a job is sometimes referred to as *frictional unemployment*. The analogy is to the operation of a real-world machine, its moving parts rubbing against each other and causing some waste heat in the process.

Sometimes this same unemployment is referred to as the *natural rate of unemployment*. This analogy invokes not wasted effort, but *optimal* job search. The argument is that finding the right job takes time, effort, and some degree of luck. Job searchers do not often accept the first job they find, but rather conduct a search to find the best job available given their job skills and preferences. The search is conducted in part to gain information on the jobs that are "out there," i.e., to form expectations about the available jobs. This is similar to "price shopping" when planning a major, but infrequent purchase such as buying a car. Once these expectations are formed, the search is conducted until the best match that can be reasonably hoped for is found.

The natural rate of unemployment varies considerably from one demographic group to another. As Table 12.5 shows, teenagers have higher unemployment rates than older workers. Their high unemployment rate results from the frequency with which teenagers enter and leave the labor force. Adult women tend to have higher unemployment rates than adult men. (However, this was not the case during 1983.) Because of the continued entry of women into the labor force, and because of the maturing of the post-World War II baby-boom generation, the composition of the labor force has changed considerably during the last few years. Through the mid-1980s, demographic groups with high natural rates of unemployment were growing components of the labor force, and this increased the overall natural rate. Therefore, it is generally felt that an unemployment rate today of about 6 percent corresponds, economically, to an unemployment rate of about 4 percent during the early 1960s.[2]

One reason why frictional unemployment is so high is because many who are unemployed are waiting for a job not currently open to come open. Consider an unemployed librarian in a metropolitan area with 100 jobs appropriate for this person's skills. In any given year, several of these positions

TABLE 12.5   Unemployment Rates of Demographic Groups

	1979	*1983*
All	5.8%	9.6%
Men 20 years and older	4.2	8.9
Women 20 years and older	5.7	8.1
Men and Women 16 to 19 years old	16.1	22.4
Whites	5.1	8.4
Blacks	12.3	19.5
Hispanics	8.3	13.7
Unemployed 15 weeks or more	1.2	3.8
Average (mean) duration	10.8 weeks	20.0 weeks

Source: Handbook of Labor Statistics, Bulletin no. 2217, U.S. Bureau of Labor Statistics, June 1985, pp. 64 and 78.

[2]Keynesian economists tend to argue that 4 percent during the early 1960s and 6 percent during the early 1980s were the natural rates of unemployment. Monetarist economists tend to argue that the natural rates were higher. For more on this topic, see Stuart E. Weiner, "The Natural Rate of Unemployment: Concepts and Issues," *Economic Review of the Federal Reserve Bank of Kansas City,* January 1987, pp. 11–24.

will come open because of factors such as death, retirement, relocation, promotion, and so on. If all 100 positions are currently filled, the unemployed librarian does not have to give up hope of ever finding a librarian position in that metropolitan area. The librarian can consider ''waiting'' for a position to come open. Of course, other unemployed librarians may be waiting for positions to come open. When positions do come open, this particular librarian may find that someone else always gets the job. After a while, this would indicate a more fundamental problem than frictional unemployment.

As the market economy develops, specialists in job placement come into demand. These include both (part of) personnel departments in large organizations and job agencies. These specialists act as clearing houses for job searchers and vacancies. Depending on the number of job searchers and vacancies involving a particular skill, these specialists in job placement may operate over a metropolitan, regional, or national area. Some universities, professional associations, and other organizations, as a service to their students and members, sponsor ''job fairs,'' at which prospective hirers come to meet prospective new hirees in a round-robin of interviews. Recently, temporary job agencies have come into demand. These organizations match people—who may or may not be looking for permanent work—with temporary positions. At first, these temporary job agencies made markets only in clerical skills. Today they are expanding into a wide range of skills, including chief executive officers.

The problem of frictional unemployment is altogether different from the problems of cyclical unemployment and structural unemployment covered below. Frictional unemployment can be viewed as part of the cost of finding a job in a highly specialized, constantly changing market economy. Cyclical and structural unemployment, on the other hand, are not costs borne in anticipation of benefits. Rather, these are the aftermath of mistakes, in some cases, avoidable mistakes, and therefore truly represent waste.

12.3.2 Structural Unemployment

Structural unemployment is defined as unemployment resulting from an underlying mismatch of jobs and job seekers. Structural unemployment can result from many causes: a person may have an obsolete job skill, suffer discrimination, or be legally barred from working. The distinction between structural and search unemployment may sometimes be subtle. However, with structural unemployment, more than continued search is necessary to eventually find employment. To clarify the concept of structural unemployment, three causes of structural unemployment are discussed below: inflexibility of wages, inflexibility of human capital, and discrimination.

12.3.2.1 Inflexibility of Wages

Sometimes wages are insufficiently flexible to clear labor markets. For example, legal minimum wage laws can prohibit wages from falling to levels that would encourage employers to hire all persons seeking work. Teenagers and other workers with limited job skills find that the number of job seekers exceeds the number of jobs, and unemployment is permanently high.

Union wage scales, "equal pay" and "comparable pay" laws, and mandatory benefits laws can have the same effect. Union wage scales typically "flatten" wage schedules, eliminating much, if not all, wage differentials among coworkers. For example, beginning workers are paid not much differently from senior workers. This flattening of wage schedules results in low-productivity workers being unemployable.

Equal pay laws require that members of identified minority groups be paid the same as others for the same work, and comparable pay laws require that they be paid the same for work that, according to some authority, is of equal value to the employer. While these laws may be directed to achieving fairness, they inhibit the market from creating jobs to fit each person's individual circumstance.

Mandatory benefits laws, such as employer social security contributions and health insurance in certain states, including Massachusetts, raise the total cost of hiring workers and should be considered part of a worker's wage. These laws effectively raise the minimum wage for low-skilled workers.[3] Certain mandatory benefits laws pertaining to job tenure make hiring "permanent" full-time workers especially risky. This is so because job tenure rights make terminating workers costly. This risk makes employers reluctant to hire workers, especially workers they consider to be marginal.

In addition to laws and union agreements, expectations create "social" minimum wages. A person may be "overqualified" and therefore be denied a relatively low-paying job. Perhaps it is thought that the person will leave when another, better position comes open. A company may itself feel that

[3]Many states require that firms *that provide* health insurance *include* coverage for certain benefits, including chiropractic services in 40 states, alcohol and drug treatment in 38 states, and acupuncture in Nevada. Maryland, for example, mandates coverage for 32 benefits, raising the cost of providing health insurance to workers by 12 percent. One way for (large) firms to avoid the cost of these required benefits is to self-insure, because, under federal law, self-insurers are exempt from these state regulations. More than 70 percent of employers of more than 500 workers self-insure. Another way firms can avoid the cost of these required coverages is by not providing health insurance at all. Perhaps one out of five small companies not providing health insurance to their workers in 1985 would have provided health insurance if their states' required coverages were dropped. David Stipp, "Laws on Health Benefits Raise Firms' Ire," *Wall Street Journal*, December 28, 1988, p. B1.

fairness requires that it pay all professionals a certain minimum even though there may be many fully qualified unemployed persons in certain professions.

Whether because of laws or expectations, inflexibility of wages curtails the ability of the market to absorb oversupplies of workers. The result is unemployment. This is not to say that wages should be totally flexible. For example, perceptions of fairness within a company probably have some impact on productivity and therefore have to be considered in the formulation of wage policies. However, the cost of wage inflexibility—which is unemployment—has to be weighed against whatever is the benefit.

12.3.2.2 Inflexible Human Capital

Many job skills are expensive in time and money to acquire. ''Investment'' in these job skills is justified by people, typically when they are young, by the anticipation of a lifetime of higher wages. However, job skills acquired long ago can become obsolete. Moreover, decisions regarding the acquisition of job skills can be incorrect. In these cases, imbalances can exist between the supply and demand of particular job skills that wage adjustments cannot, at least not immediately, compensate for.

Consider obsolescence of job skills. Often this occurs in conjunction with technological progress. Sometimes this occurs in conjunction with changes in government policies regarding trade, regulation, and taxation. Typically, older workers, unable to justify the costs of retraining, hang on as best they can in their occupation. Younger workers, better able to justify retraining costs, leave their occupation and find a new one.

It is the fall in wages in the occupation that encourages younger workers to depart and leaves room for the older workers to remain. If wages did not fall, younger workers would not leave, and new workers might even enter. The oversupply of the obsolete job skill would persist and might even worsen.

A similar thing occurs when employment falls in a particular community. Workers who are best able to leave are encouraged to do so by the depressed wages and unemployment in the community. This leaves the remaining jobs for those for whom the costs of relocating are the highest.

All this is not to diminish the real losses suffered by those in occupations or communities in which employment is falling. Adjustments are not made easily or quickly. Part of the reason is that workers must realize that the situation has changed permanently. Rather than retrain or relocate immediately, most workers will wait for a period of time to pass to confirm that the changed situation is permanent. During this period of time, they will be unemployed.

Since this type of unemployment stems from changes in the economy, its cost must be weighed against the benefit of a dynamic, changing economy. Imagine resisting a miracle cure for cancer on the basis that the cure would obsolete the skills of health professionals who treat cancer victims!

Nevertheless, to the extent a dynamic, changing economy enriches us, we can protect against the "hazard" of unemployment through insurance. Unemployment insurance is the obvious example. Additional examples include plant closing insurance, retraining insurance, early retirement, and "golden parachutes" for managers. Political resistance to change often reflects that insurance, as it has so far developed, is insufficient.

12.3.2.3 Discrimination

It seems that all through history people have suffered discrimination—racism, sexism, antisemitism—whether codified into law or enforced by vigilantism and genteel social pressure. It should be obvious that when arbitrary considerations such as a person's color are included, the efficiency of the market in matching jobs to job seekers is curtailed.

With completely flexible wages, those suffering discrimination would be able to find employment by working for lower wages. The lower wages give employers a profit incentive to hire those discriminated against. It is the combination of discrimination and inflexible wages that results in persistent unemployment among those discriminated against.

A special form of discrimination is *statistical discrimination*. This refers to the use of statistical correlations of one's appearance (race, sex, and so on) with job-related behavior. For example, not all women leave jobs in order to have children, but many do. Thus firms that provide workers with specific job training would be understandably reluctant to hire women. It is just as understandable for particular women who have no intention to leave shortly after receiving the specific training to feel discriminated against when they are denied these jobs simply on the basis of their sex.

12.3.3 Cyclical Unemployment

Cyclical unemployment occurs when there is a shortfall in the total number of jobs relative to the labor force. Periods of relatively high unemployment are, by definition, periods of cyclical unemployment. Cyclical unemployment is conceptually different from unemployment due to job searches or underlying mismatches between jobs and job seekers. In reality, however, it is difficult to identify which specific unemployed persons are in this category versus one of the two other categories of unemployment. Figure 12.2 presents the relationship between changes in the unemployment rate and percentage changes in real GNP. Notice that unemployment goes up when GNP goes down.

During recessions, persons with obsolete job skills or persons who are discriminated against suffer particularly high rates of unemployment. New entrants and reentrants find it unusually difficult to locate satisfactory employment. In fact, the normal fluidity in the labor market associated with the creation and disappearance of jobs, and the turnover of persons in jobs, is reduced. Companies are reluctant to hire new or replacement workers, and current job holders are reluctant to (voluntarily) quit in order to look for better positions.

For a long time, economists have debated whether unemployment during recessions is ''voluntary'' or ''involuntary.'' By definition, an unem-

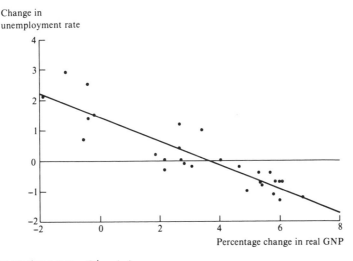

FIGURE 12.2 Okun's Law.
Arthur M. Okun, chairman of the Council of Economic Advisors during the Johnson Administration, estimated that for every 1 percentage point fall in the unemployment rate, the real GNP increases by 3 percent. This relationship has, ever since, been referred to as *Okun's law*. Actually, there are two parts to Okun's law. The first is that because of an increasing labor force, 2.5 to 3 percent growth in real GNP is required to keep the unemployment rate from increasing. The second concerns the relationship between percentage changes in real GNP and changes in the unemployment rate. Contemporary estimates of the latter range from 2 to 2.5:1 rather than the ratio of 3:1 that Okun estimated. Notice that the relationship between changes in the unemployment rate and real GNP is 2 to 3:1, instead of 1:1. Among the reasons why are that a vibrant economy more fully employs already employed persons and draws more persons into the labor force.

ployed person is looking for work. However, an unemployed person does not have to accept any job offered. A job may be rejected if the pay or other conditions associated with the job are unacceptable. It is possible, then, for a person to be voluntarily unemployed in the sense that he or she is rejecting unacceptable jobs and will continue searching for one that is acceptable.

As was discussed earlier, sometimes a company will not offer a job to a person considered to be overqualified because it fears the person will be dissatisfied and will soon leave. A person who is refused employment in such a situation may be said to be involuntarily unemployed. More precisely, *involuntary unemployment* refers to when job seekers cannot obtain employment by offering to work for lower wages. Involuntary unemployment, as it is commonly understood, goes beyond the problem of individual job seekers being overqualified. Involuntary unemployment occurs when job seekers are *generally* unable to obtain employment by offering to work for lower wages. The problem is that there is relatively high unemployment at the prevailing structure of wages *and* there is no process of wages being lowered so as to absorb the unemployed into new jobs.

Involuntary unemployment may be caused by legal or social restrictions on wages or by expectations on the part of workers and firms about future wages. Legal minimum wage laws obviously prevent wages from falling to the level that would correspond with full employment. Similarly, union-bargained wage scales may make wages inflexible, and political exhortation may maintain wages in the face of unemployment.

More frequently, expectations that recessionary conditions are temporary and that permanent changes in wages are not necessary are what maintain wages in the face of recessionary conditions. Rather than lower wages and maintain employment, firms adjust to recessionary conditions by maintaining wages and reducing employment. Employment is reduced through reduced average hours of work per week, layoffs, and nonhiring.

12.4 POLICIES TO DEAL WITH UNEMPLOYMENT

The problem of unemployment is, for most people and for most of the time, a manageable one. During their infrequent and brief spells of unemployment, most people rely on a combination of unemployment insurance, earnings of other family members, and past savings in order to maintain their standard of living. Many people use the ''free'' time provided by such spells of unemployment to advantage, e.g., doing home repairs while waiting recall from temporary layoff.

On the other hand, for some people, unemployment is endemic. For these people, work life consists of a series of jobs often broken by spells of unemployment. The *labor force attachment* of these people—meaning their commitment to work or willingness and ability to devote themselves to work —may simply be low. A lifestyle of casual work, spells of unemployment, and participation in government income-maintenance programs may be their preference. This possibility is difficult for people with traditional values to accept. Job training and counseling may be recommended.

For people who want a good-paying, steady job—and are willing to make the necessary commitment—job training and counseling may very well be cost-beneficial. However, the record of government job-training and counseling programs, such as those provided by the Comprehensive Training and Employment Act (CETA), which was phased out during 1981 – 1982, has been disappointing.

Another group of people finds that, from time to time, the normal provisions for unemployment prove insufficient. Unemployment insurance runs out. Savings run out. Medical bills or other large expenses occur while income is low because of unemployment. This distressful unemployment usually happens during recessions, when it is difficult to find satisfactory work. When people who normally are able to take care of themselves suffered this type of unemployment during the early 1980s, they were termed the ''new poor.''

Table 12.6 gives a detailed picture of unemployment. This table demonstrates that even during a normal year such as 1979 a large number of people, nearly 16 percent, experience unemployment. However, during a normal year, most people who experience unemployment are unemployed for only a relatively short period of time. During a year of high unemployment such as 1983, an even larger number of people, nearly 20 percent, are unemployed. In addition, more people suffer long periods of unemployment. Almost all the increase in unemployment from 1979 to 1983 occurs in the categories of ''did not work at all'' and ''worked less than 50 weeks and unemployed 15 weeks or longer.'' These categories are important not only because of the long period of unemployment, but because many of these people either did not qualify for unemployment insurance or saw their unemployment insurance run out.

12.4.1 Unemployment Insurance

The obvious answer to the problems of unemployment is unemployment insurance. And yet there is a problem that the insurance industry would refer to as ''moral hazard'' associated with *full* unemployment insurance: Even if unemployment insurance were determined by the free market, it would not completely replace the income lost from unemployment.

Moral hazard refers to insurance that, by reason of its poor design,

TABLE 12.6   Extent of Unemployment

	1979	*1983*
Labor force	116,983	121,634
Unemployment	18,468	23,794
Percent of labor forces	15.8%	19.6%
Did not work at all	1,990	3,916
Worked part of the year	16,478	19,883
Worked 50 weeks or more and unemployed 1 or 2 weeks	856	920
Worked less than 50 weeks and unemployed		
1 to 4 weeks	4,264	3,367
5 to 10 weeks	3,542	3,608
11 to 14 weeks	2,335	2,549
15 to 26 weeks	3,378	4,980
27 weeks or more	2,102	4,460

Source: Handbook of Labor Statistics, Bulletin no. 2217, U.S. Bureau of Labor Statistics, June 1985, p. 86.

encourages the insured to act against what would be his or her interest without the insurance. The classic example is fire insurance on a building for more than the building's value, giving the insured an incentive to "torch" the building. With unemployment insurance, the problem of moral hazard derives from near complete replacement of income lost to unemployment, which replacement reduces the incentive of the unemployed person to search for and accept a new job.

Martin Feldstein, a chairman of the Council of Economic Advisors during the Reagan administration, has examined the issue of moral hazard in unemployment insurance. Feldstein demonstrates that unemployment insurance replaces a large fraction of many workers' after-tax wages. He argues that as a result, many workers on layoff do not search for new jobs but simply wait to be recalled to their old job. Furthermore, because firms realize that laid-off workers will not search for new jobs, they feel free to lay off workers when demand for their products is low, not fearing the loss of their laid-off workers to other employers. The existence of unemployment insurance, therefore, increases unemployment and decreases wage flexibility.[4]

[4]Martin S. Feldstein, "The Importance of Temporary Layoffs: An Empirical Analysis," *Brookings Papers on Economic Activity*, 1975, pp. 725–744.

The *replacement rate* is the ratio of unemployment benefit to earnings. The higher the replacement rate, the greater is the income security provided by unemployment insurance, but the less is the incentive to find a job while receiving unemployment benefits. While estimates vary, a 10 percentage point increase in the before-tax replacement rate may lead to a 1-week increase in the average duration of unemployment.[5] Additional evidence of the disincentive effect of unemployment insurance is provided by surveys of persons who have exhausted their unemployment benefits. These studies find high rates of reemployment during the first and second months following exhaustion of unemployment benefits.[6]

While there undoubtedly are disincentives with unemployment insurance, this does not necessarily imply that unemployment insurance should be abolished. The cost of these ''side effects'' of unemployment insurance have to be compared to the benefits of unemployment insurance. These benefits include — at the micro level — mitigating the loss of income suffered by the unemployed and enabling unemployed persons to conduct more extensive searches for new jobs and — at the macro level — an automatic stabilizer for aggregate demand. Without unemployment insurance, political support of a dynamic, capitalistic economy would certainly be much less, meaning that the benefits of technological progress, deregulation, and worldwide economic integration would be threatened.

Although run by the government for over 50 years now, unemployment insurance originated in the private sector, by workers in occupations where the availability of work was sensitive to the business cycle and to other hazards such as weather. Some supplementary private-sector forms of unemployment insurance are taking shape. Certain unions today bargain for guarantees of work for their members. Home mortgages and other consumer debts are beginning to incorporate provisions for forgiveness of monthly payments while the borrower is unemployed. Top managers demand ''golden parachute'' provisions in their contracts, providing (generous) compensation should they be fired from their jobs. These supplementary forms of unemployment insurance reflect that for many people the level of coverage provided by the government-run program is not sufficient. For at least these people, the benefits of unemployment insurance outweigh the cost.

---

[5]Daniel S. Hamermesh, *Jobless Pay and the Economy* (Baltimore: Johns Hopkins University Press, 1977), pp. 32–39.

[6]Raymond Mintz and Irwin Garfinkel, *The Work Disincentive Effects of Unemployment Insurance* (Baltimore: Johns Hopkins University Press, 1974), pp. 41–45.

12.4.2 Wage Indexation

During the early 1970s, an increasing number of labor union contracts began to feature *cost-of-living allowances* (COLAs), providing for automatic increases in wages upon specified increases in the consumer price index. Many of the formulas providing for cost-of-living allowances only partially adjusted wages for the effects of inflation. Nevertheless, the idea of hedging against inflation uncertainty through indexation became firmly established. As inflation accelerated through the 1970s, COLA adjustment periods were reduced and caps on COLA adjustments were lifted in many contracts (see Fig. 12.3). In addition, indexation spread to social security, federal government wages, and income tax schedules.

In the absence of indexation, accelerations of inflation erode the value of labor union–bargained wages. This, in turn, often results in strikes and other collective-bargaining activity costly to both labor and management. Indexation of union contracts, then, is supposed to keep wages in line with changes in the cost of living and preclude strikes. In fact, an analysis of strike activity during the 1970s found that unanticipated inflation led to fewer strikes where labor union contracts featured uncapped COLAs.[7]

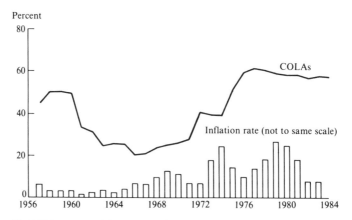

FIGURE 12.3 COLAs in Labor Contracts.
Notice the decreased use of COLAs with the stable prices of the 1950s through early 1960s and the increased use of COLAs in labor union contracts with the accelerations of inflation from the mid-1960s through the 1970s.
Source: Data from Wallace E. Hendricks and Lawrence M. Kahn, *Wage Indexation in the United States* (Cambridge, Mass.: Ballinger, 1985), pp. 36–37.

[7]Wallace E. Hendricks and Lawrence M. Kahn, *Wage Indexation in the United States* (Cambridge, Mass.: Ballinger, 1985), pp. 221–238.

In theory, indexation of wages could make them flexible so that upon changes in aggregate demand, wages could adjust and employment remain stable. However, indexation of private-sector wages did not work this way during the disinflation and recession of the early 1980s. The problem with indexation of wages is identifying an index and a formula that both (1) protect the worker from erosion of the purchasing power of wages through the effects of continued inflation and (2) match the wage bill of the company to its revenue. For the federal government, indexation to the CPI ''works'' because the revenues of the federal government are highly correlated with the CPI inflation rate. However, for the private sector, indexing wages to the CPI does not adequately accomplish the second objective, since the prices of the goods and services sold by individual companies seldom change exactly with changes in the CPI.

Let's say that, overall, consumer prices are rising, but prices of the goods and services of a particular company are not rising. At a constant rate of employment and production, this company will find its costs rising faster than its revenues. It will be under pressure to cut back on employment. Indexation, during a period of disinflation such as the early 1980s, will contribute to the recession. No wonder companies sought to remove COLAs from their labor contracts.

12.4.3 Profit Sharing and Worker Ownership

Alternatives to CPI indexation that nevertheless make wages flexible include programs that tie workers' wages to the economic fortune of the company. In 1982, the New York Stock Exchange surveyed 49,000 companies regarding innovations in human resource management. Fully 25 and 21 percent, respectively, were found either to already have or to be planning to have profit-sharing and stock-purchase plans.[8]

In Japan, a major portion of workers' wages is comprised of bonuses.[9] *Profit sharing* allows firms to maintain employment through periods of falling demand because their costs automatically fall along with the fall in revenue. On the other hand, if inflation results in an increase in revenue, workers' wages are automatically increased. The interests of both the workers and the company are protected.

An even more direct link of labor costs to the revenue of a firm occurs when there is *worker ownership*. An increasing number of companies are

---

[8]''People and Productivity: A Challenge to Corporate America,'' New York Stock Exchange, 1982, p. 44.

[9]See Martin L. Weitzman, ''Macroeconomic Implications of Profit Sharing,'' in Stanley Fischer (Ed.), *NBER Macroeconomics Annual 1986* (Cambridge, Mass.: MIT Press, 1986), pp. 147–210.

coming to be owned by their workers, including Publix Supermarkets of Florida (100 percent employee-owned) and U.S. Sugar (43 percent employee-owned). Many of the firms in the recently deregulated airline and trucking industries feature significant employee ownership, as do many firms in hi-tech industries. Worker ownership has been found successful in the reorganization of "smokestack" companies such as Weirton Steel.[10]

A correct form of indexation protects the interests of workers while enabling firms to maintain employment through the course of the business cycle. The alternative is to lay off workers when demand falls. The fact is that the act of hiring workers for permanent positions is an implicit contract or informal agreement between the employer and employee. Both usually spend time and money in hiring/accepting the job and in training/learning the job. This effort constitutes an investment by both parties that is justified by the profits/wages that are expected to accrue in the future. The wages and other conditions of the bargain are not easily renegotiated. That is, wages are inflexible. However, if wages are indexed, then they will be automatically adjusted upon changing conditions. The key question is how to index wages. Simply indexing wages to the CPI may not be sufficient.

12.5 SUMMARY

1. The unemployment rate is defined as the ratio of the unemployed to the labor force, where by *unemployed* is meant not working and actively seeking employment and by *labor force* is meant the total of employed and unemployed.

2. Other measures of labor market efficiency include the insured unemployed, registered unemployed, employment, and job vacancies.

3. Conceptually, unemployment can be divided into three categories: frictional unemployment, or the unemployment associated with normal job search; structural unemployment, or unemployment associated with underlying mismatches between jobs and job seekers; and cyclical unemployment, or the increase in unemployment associated with recessionary phases of the business cycle.

4. Frictional unemployment is due to the multitude of different jobs in a modern economy and the difficulty involved in finding a good match between a job and a job seeker. Sometimes referred to as the natural rate of unemployment, the level of frictional unemployment changes over time with changes in the composition of the labor force. The more young workers and

[10]Corey M. Rosen, Katherine J. Klein, and Karen M. Young, *Employee Ownership in America* (Lexington, Mass.: Lexington Books, 1986), pp. 3–4.

more female workers there are—groups of workers that tend to have high natural rates—then the higher is the overall natural rate.

5. Structural unemployment is usually identified with problems such as inflexible wages, inflexible human capital, and discrimination. For example, legal minimum wages may prevent the market from creating jobs for all low-skilled workers looking for work. The available jobs for low-skilled workers may be rationed to applicants on the basis of race or some other arbitrary criterion. While job-training programs have been recommended to deal with structural unemployment, the record of such programs has been disappointing.

6. Cyclical unemployment may make people normally able to provide for themselves into "new poor." During recessions, companies cut back hours of employment, reduce hiring, and lay off workers. Workers with jobs become reluctant to voluntarily quit in order to seek new and better jobs. As a result, the normal fluidity of the labor market is reduced, and satisfactory jobs become difficult to find. Depending on the state of expectations, wages may be inflexible and workers may be "involuntarily" unemployed.

7. Unemployment insurance provides partial coverage for the loss of income while unemployed. The extent of its replacement of lost income reflects a tradeoff: the benefit of income security versus the cost of reduced incentive to seek and accept a new job.

8. In order to maintain employment through the business cycle, index-ation of wages should both (1) protect workers against inflation's erosion of the value of wages and (2) match the wage bill of the company against its revenues. In Japan, this combination is achieved through bonuses. In America, this combination is increasingly achieved through profit sharing and worker ownership.

12.6 EXERCISES

1. Why does the (official) unemployment rate *understate* the extent of unemployment?

2. How would you restate an unemployment rate based on registered unemployment in order to make it consistent with the U.S. definition of unemployment?

3. Why is an unemployment rate greater than zero consistent with "full" employment?

4. In what way can unemployment be viewed as a risky investment?

5. What is the moral hazard associated with unemployment insurance?

6. Why is unemployment insurance an automatic stabilizer?

7. Why is unemployment much lower in Japan than it is in the United States and in western Europe?

8. Distinguish between "voluntary" and "involuntary" unemployment.

12.7 REFERENCES

Clair Brown and Joseph A. Pechman (Eds.), *Gender in the Workplace*. Washington, D.C.: Brookings Institute, 1987.

Council of Economic Advisors, "The Dual Problems of Structural and Cyclical Unemployment." In *Economic Report of the President*. Washington, D.C., 1983. Pp. 29 – 50.

Council of Economic Advisors, "Women in the Labor Force." In *Economic Report of the President*. Washington, D.C., 1987. Pp. 209 – 226.

Richard B. Freeman and Harry J. Holzer (Eds.), *The Black Youth Employment Crisis*. Chicago: University of Chicago Press, 1986.

Stephen M. Hill (Ed.), *The Changing Labor Market*. Lexington, Mass.: Lexington Books, 1986.

S. A. Lippman and J. J. McCall, "The Economics of Job Search: A Survey," *Economic Inquiry*, 14, June 1976, pp. 347 – 368.

Ray Marshall and Richard Perlman (Eds.), *An Anthology of Labor Economics*. New York: Wiley, 1972.

A. C. Pigou, *The Theory of Unemployment*. New York: Macmillan, 1933.

Lloyd G. Reynolds, *Labor Economics and Labor Relations*. Englewood Cliffs, N.J.: Prentice-Hall, 1982.

—————— *Managerial Case* ————————————————————————————

MINIMUM WAGES AND UNEMPLOYMENT

Minimum wages are not set so high in the United States as to cause widespread unemployment. Usually, only low-skilled workers, such as teenagers, are affected.[1] Moreover, the main effect appears to be reduction in the nonwage terms of employment, including on-the-job training, fringe benefits, and working conditions that offset the higher wages mandated by minimum wages.[2] However, it was not always

---

[1]C. Brown, C. Gilroy, and A. Kohen, in their survey of the literature, find that a 10 percent increase in the minimum may reduce teenage employment by 1 to 3 percent. "The Effect of the Minimum Wage on Employment and Unemployment," *Journal of Economic Literature*, 20, June 1982, pp. 487 – 528.

[2]See Walter J. Wessels, *Minimum Wages, Fringe Benefits, and Working Conditions* (Washington, D.C.: American Enterprise Institute, 1980); and Masanori Hashimoto, *Minimum Wages and On-the-Job Training* (Washington, D.C.: American Enterprise Institute, 1981).

this way in the United States and it is not this way in many of the developing countries today.

In 1933, as part of President Franklin Roosevelt's "100 days" legislative agenda, Congress passed the National Recovery Act, establishing the National Industrial Recovery Administration (NIRA). From then until 1935, when it was declared to be unconstitutional by the Supreme Court, the NIRA set minimum wages as well as formed cartels, enabling monopoly price setting, in many industries. As a result, wages and prices were stabilized or actually raised. Thus, the deflationary pressures in the economy contributed to unprecedented unemployment instead of lowering wages and prices. As Michael Weinstein in a recent history of the NIRA states, "It was the codes and not, as previously suggested, dysfunctional labor markets which explain the inflation amidst massive unemployment during the NIRA period."[3]

Today, many developing nations use minimum wage laws as instruments of income redistribution and development policy.[4] Compared to the United States, minimum wages in these nations are set higher relative to average manufacturing wages. For example, while the minimum wage is usually about 40 percent of the average manufacturing wage in the United States, it is usually about 50 percent of the average manufacturing wage in Mexico. The result is that minimum wages in these nations have significant macroeconomic effects. Relatively high minimum wages lead to widespread unemployment among low-skilled workers, and inflation — mainly by eroding the value of these minimum wages — leads to increased employment.

[3]*Recovery and Redistribution under the NIRA* (New York: North-Holland, 1980).
[4]G. Starr, *Minimum Wage Fixing* (Washington, D.C.: International Labor Office, 1981).

_13_
Interest Rates

13.1 INTRODUCTION

> Then you should have invested my money with the bankers, and on my return
> I would have gotten my capital with interest.[1]

Interest rates are sometimes referred to as "the price of money." This is
potentially misleading terminology. First, there are *many* interest rates.
Among these are short- and long-term interest rates, fixed and variable interest rates, risk-free and risky interest rates, tax-free and taxable interest
rates.

Second, instead of being "the price of money," interest rates are the
rental cost of money. Interest rates are what it costs to borrow money, not
what it costs to buy money. The *price* of money is its value in terms of goods
and services or its purchasing power. Interest rates reflect the price of money
today in terms of money *tomorrow*. The difference in value between money
today and money tomorrow includes a pure return—sometimes called the
time value of money—and a number of premiums, including premiums for
inflation, uncertainty, and taxation. Actual, real-world interest rates almost
always contain several of these premiums in addition to the pure time-value
component of interest rates.

Depending on the context, when economists talk of "the" interest rate,
they may be referring to the interest rate on short-term, highly liquid, default
risk-free money-market securities such as Treasury Bills. Alternately, "the"
interest rate may refer to a (possibly hypothetical) risk-free, after-tax, real
interest rate. In this chapter, both definitions of "the" interest rate will be
studied.

[1]Matthew 25:27

316

13.2 "THE" INTEREST RATE

For centuries, philosophers have debated the morality of interest. The early Christian church taught that interest—referred to as *usury*—was immoral, and lending at interest was prohibited. Even today, Islam teaches that (pure) interest is immoral and that investors must participate in risk in order to justifiably participate in profit. Marxism treats interest as exploitation. (Nevertheless, modern communist economies use interest.) Certain early Keynesians argued that interest rates could and should be lowered through monetary and fiscal policies in order to achieve a more egalitarian distribution of wealth and income.

The idea of interest as usury was exploded by Eugen von Bohm-Bawerk in his classic, *Capital and Interest*. (For a contemporary work, see Jack Hirshleifer's *Investment, Interest and Capital*.) In the late nineteenth century, economics discovered *marginal utility*. Simply put, this is the idea that value is subjective, dependent on the prospective use of the marginal or next unit of a good or service. This idea contrasts with the prior classical—and Marxist—idea that value is objective and dependent on the cost of production.

Bohm-Bawerk applied the newly discovered concept of subjective marginal utility to interest rates. The value of "money today"—or, to be precise, the goods and services that money could buy today—*could be* different from the value of the same amount of money (in terms of purchasing power) tomorrow. That the two sets of goods and services were physically identical did not necessarily mean that their value had to be the same.

Furthermore, the value of "money today" necessarily had to be greater than "money tomorrow" because one of the potential uses of "money today" is to simply hold onto it until tomorrow. Therefore, whatever a given amount of "money tomorrow" could buy could be bought with the same amount of "money today." For example, a student anticipating graduation in a year could hold onto any money held in excess of current needs. Through the act of holding onto this money, it would become "money tomorrow." *However*, in addition to being able to buy everything "money tomorrow" could buy, "money today" also can buy things "right now" and at any time between "right now" and "tomorrow."

Having "money today," available from "right now" until "tomorrow," is itself valuable. This money is available for unplanned expenditures—bargains or unforeseen needs—between "right now" and "tomorrow." This is the *liquidity service* offered by cash balances. Money is a reserve of spending power. It is available not only for planned expenditures, but for unplanned expenditures as well.

There is a story of a little girl who asked her father why good horses were so expensive. "Good horses are expensive," explained her father, "because they are rare." "But," interjected the little girl, "aren't good horses which are cheap *even more rare*?'' Money today is valuable because it enables you to buy the ''good horse'' that is ''cheap'' when you have the good fortune to find such a horse. Cash balances are not ''idle.'' They are reserves of spending power available for unplanned expenditures and are valuable just like ''excess'' water in municipal reservoirs and ''excess'' capacity in electrical generators are valuable.

13.2.1 Interest and Investment

It is important to clarify the relation between interest and investment. For some, investment *justifies* interest because (1) the saving that finances the investment constitutes a sacrifice of current consumption for which increased future consumption is a reward, and (2) the investment increases future productivity, enabling producers to repay investors without diminution of their own income.

While these arguments are basically correct, they miss an important point. The sacrifice of current consumption implicit in investment does not *guarantee* an increase in future productivity. In a free-market economy, there is a connection because of the choices made by savers. In a socialist economy, where choices are made by bureaucrats with possibly different values, this connection may be broken.

Imagine that there are three soda machines on campus. One soda machine, located right where students are, dispenses 8 ounces of soda for 50 cents. The two other soda machines are located some distance away. One of these two other machines dispenses 8 ounces of soda for 50 cents, and the other dispenses 8 ounces of soda for 25 cents. Given these assumptions, what will be the observed pattern between distance and the price of soda?

Some students, for convenience, will buy soda from the immediately available machine at 50 cents. Others, to economize on money, will buy soda from the cheaper of the two distant machines at 25 cents. Notice that there is no technologically necessary reason for distant soda machines to feature soda at a lower price. It is technologically possible for students to buy soda from a distant machine at the same price as from the nearby machine. However, students doing so would not be acting in a thinking, economic way. Because of choice, the relationship that would actually be observed involves a tradeoff between price and distance: convenient but high-priced soda versus inconvenient but low-priced soda.

In a similar way, investments do not necessarily increase productivity. The two are connected because people who are free to choose will only save if investment is anticipated to lead to increased productivity. It is because of choice, Bohm-Bawerk argued, that ''round-about'' means of production had to feature higher productivity than more direct means of production. If a particular technique featuring no investment would lead immediately to 10 units of output, then a freely chosen alternative technique that featured some investment, and some delay in consumption, *must* lead in the future to more than 10 units of output.

Notice that the connection between investment and productivity can break down in a socialistic economy. If bureaucrats in a centrally planned economy decide to build a steel mill, the designation of this expenditure as an "investment" does not necessarily mean that this will increase productivity. The construction of this steel mill may very well divert resources from other, more promising investments. The fact that the government has to intervene in order to get the steel mill built suggests that it would not be built otherwise and is in fact such a diversion.

Building steel mills because this is what, in past times, increased productivity is like concluding that it is always less expensive to buy soda in distant machines. But, the cheaper of the distant machines may have run out of soda. Of course, those saying you should buy soda from distant machines also will tell you the exercise is good for you!

13.2.2 Geometric Analysis

The determination of interest rates in a free-market economy can be represented geometrically. At any given time, an economy features an "intertemporal production possibilities curve." This production possibilities curve might look like Figure 13.1.

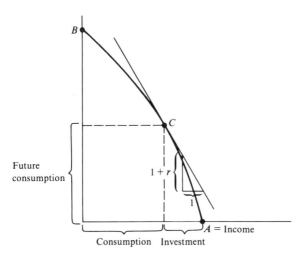

FIGURE 13.1   The Geometry of Interest Rates.

Point *A* represents the maximum possible "present consumption." Point *A* would involve consuming everything today and saving and investing nothing for the future. Point *B* represents the maximum possible "future consumption." Point *B* results from saving and investing everything.

The slope from point *A* to point *B* would be curved in the manner indicated, first being steeply sloped and then less steeply sloped, because of choice. That is, the first units of present consumption sacrificed for future consumption—i.e., saved and invested—would be those which most increase future consumption. Subsequent units of present consumption sacrificed will increase future consumption by lesser and lesser amounts. Therefore, the slope of the curve falls as one moves along the production possibilities curve from point *A* to point *B*.

Although the slope of the production possibilities curve falls from point *A* to point *B*, it never falls below a slope of -1. This is so because of the productivity of (freely chosen) investments. Investments always increase future consumption by at least the present consumption sacrificed. As a result, the future consumption available at point *B* is necessarily greater than the present consumption available at point *A*.

In a free-market economy, interest rates are determined by the supply and demand for credit. The supply and demand for credit cannot be easily incorporated into Figure 13.1, but their effect can be illustrated in this figure. At the point where the supply equals the demand for credit, which is point *C*, the tradeoff between present and future consumption—which is the slope of the line tangent to the intertemporal production possibilities curve—just equals the ratio $1:1 + r$, where *r* is the interest rate.

This interest rate *r* reflects the ability of the economy, at the margin, to transform present consumption into future consumption, i.e., to direct resources through saving and investment away from producing "consumer goods" and into producing "capital goods" that will enable increased production of consumer goods in the future. This interest rate is determined, fundamentally, by the productivity of investment, as represented by the intertemporal production possibilities curve, and "impatience" to consume, or the general disposition of people to prefer goods and services today rather than in the future.

13.3 INFLATION AND INTEREST RATES

Irving Fisher is generally credited with distinguishing "real" from "nominal" interest rates. *Nominal interest* rates are interest rates as stated. *Real interest* rates are nominal interest rates less the expected inflation rate. Distinguishing real from nominal interest rates is important because during a period of inflation, an apparently high interest rate may represent little or no return in terms of purchasing power.

Suppose that the interest rate on a 1-year loan is 10 percent and that the rate of inflation during the next year is 20 percent. At the end of the year, the borrower repays the lender $110 for every $100 borrowed. The purchasing power of these dollars relative to the dollars borrowed is $110/1.20 = $92. The borrower repays less value than was originally borrowed. The interest rate, while apparently high, is "really" negative.

Fisher did more than distinguish real from nominal interest rates. He argued that interest rates incorporate a premium for expected inflation. When prices in general are expected to rise, interest rates will tend to be high, and when prices are expected to remain stable or to fall, interest rates will tend to be low. Nominal interest rates vary with expected inflation, and real interest rates are not affected by expected inflation.

Let i represent the nominal interest rate, r the real interest rate, and x the expected inflation rate. The *Fisher equation* states that

$$i = r + x \qquad\qquad\qquad\qquad\qquad (13.1)$$

If the real interest rate r is relatively constant, changes in nominal interest rates i reflect changes in the expected rate of inflation x.

Fisher made his argument in a series of books and articles, beginning with *Appreciation and Interest* in 1896 and continuing through *The Theory of Interest* in 1930. He explained that during periods of rising prices, business executives find that they enjoy rising money profits. These profits result from selling inventories at higher money prices than the prices at which they were purchased. These rising money profits encourage business executives to increase their borrowing in order to expand their businesses. This increase in the willingness of business executives to borrow is what directly causes interest rates to rise so as to reflect expected inflation.

Figure 13.2 illustrates Fisher's argument. This figure presents a supply and demand analysis of interest rate determination. The horizontal axis measures the quantity of credit—or loanable funds—and the vertical axis measures its price—or the interest rate. The demand for loanable funds is negatively sloped because business executives are willing to borrow more at lower interest rates. In Figure 13.2a, the supply of loanable funds is considered—for simplicity—to be fixed. From an initial condition of no expected inflation, where the nominal interest rate equals the real interest rate, expectations of inflation increase the willingness of business executives to borrow and "push" the demand curve out. The result is a nominal interest rate that is higher by the amount of expected inflation.

Figure 13.2b takes this analysis one step further. In this figure, the

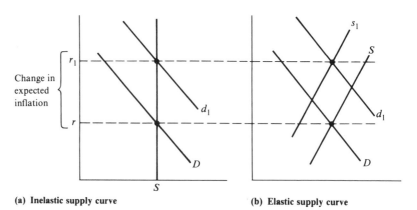

(a) Inelastic supply curve   **(b) Elastic supply curve**

FIGURE 13.2   Interest Rates and Expected Inflation.
(a) With inflation, business executives find that their money profits
increase. Expectations of continuing inflation-driven profits cause
them to increase their demand for credit. With an inelastic supply
curve, the only result is higher interest rates by the amount of inflation expectations. (b) With an elastic supply curve, the result of
higher business demand for credit is, at first, interest rates that are
higher (but not as much higher as the amount of inflation expectations) and an increased quantity of credit. However, as savers come
to recognize the inflation that is taking place, the supply of credit
shifts up and the only result is higher interest rates by the amount of
inflation expectations.

supply curve is positively sloped, indicating that at higher interest rates more
credit is supplied. Expectations of inflation, as before, push the demand curve
out. Expectations of inflation also push the supply curve in, reflecting that
savers are less willing to provide credit because inflation means that the
interest and return of principal they will receive in the future will have less
purchasing power. The result of the shifts in both the demand and supply
curves is an interest rate that is higher by the amount of expected inflation.

This analysis can be conducted using algebra. Let the supply and demand of credit be given as follows:

$$S = s_0 + s_1(i - x) \tag{13.2a}$$
$$D = d_0 - d_1(i - x) \tag{13.2b}$$
$$S = D \tag{13.2c}$$

The first equation is the supply curve, the second is the demand curve, and
the third is the equilibrium condition (i.e., quantity supplied equals quantity
demanded). Notice that both the supply and demand curves depend only on

the real interest rate. Neither borrowers nor lenders have "money illusion"; they are not fooled by the nominal interest rate. Solving for the nominal interest rate, we get

$$i = r + x \qquad\qquad\qquad\qquad\qquad (13.3)$$

where r equals $(s_1 + d_1)/(d_0 - s_0)$. That is, we get the Fisher equation.

13.3.1 The Historical Record

Today, the evidence that interest rates adjust for changes in expected inflation is overwhelming. For example, Table 13.1 presents inflation and interest rates from 1984 to 1986 in seven major OECD countries. Notice the high correlation between inflation and interest rates across these countries.

The relationship between interest rates and expected inflation was not so obvious when Fisher made his argument. At that time, inflations and deflations were episodic, associated with wars and their aftermaths, and difficult to project into the future. Fisher's theory was, at the time he presented it, dismissed as irrelevant. It has only been with the emergence of persistent inflation since the late 1960s that Fisher's theory has come to be widely accepted.

Prior to recent times, interest rates had a high correlation with *the level* of prices as opposed to *the rate of change* of prices (i.e., inflation). As Figure 13.3b shows, it used to be that when prices were high, interest rates were high, and when prices were low, interest rates were low. John Maynard

TABLE 13.1   Interest Rates and Inflation (Percent), Major OECD Countries, 1984–86

	1984		1985		1986	
	Inflation Rate	Interest Rate	Inflation Rate	Interest Rate	Inflation Rate	Interest Rate
United States	4.3	9.5	3.5	7.5	2.0	6.0
Japan	2.2	6.1	2.1	6.5	0.4	6.5
Germany	2.4	6.0	2.2	5.4	−0.2	5.4
France	7.4	11.7	5.8	9.9	2.7	7.7
United Kingdom	5.0	9.3	6.1	11.6	3.4	10.3
Italy	10.6	17.3	8.6	15.3	6.1	13.4
Canada	4.3	11.2	4.0	9.6	4.2	9.2

Source: OECD Economic Outlook, 41, June 1987, pp. 30–31. Used with permission.

Keynes described this relationship as the "Gibson paradox" after the British statistician who (Keynes thought) discovered it. Keynes described the relationship as a paradox because it contradicted his theory of interest rates.

Keynes saw interest rates as the "price of money" and thought that more money in the economy would simultaneously raise prices and lower interest rates. He therefore expected to see a negative correlation between prices and interest rates. However, for centuries, the relationship was positive.

For Irving Fisher, the Gibson paradox is explained by *the lag* between

WPI: 1867–1877 = 100

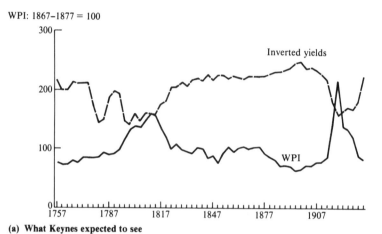

(a) What Keynes expected to see

WPI: 1867–1877 = 100

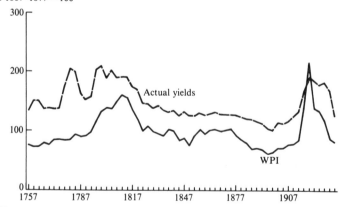

(b) What Keynes saw

FIGURE 13.3   The Gibson Paradox.
Definitions: WPI–British commodity prices, 1867–1877 = 100, from various sources, concluding with the Sauerback *Statist Index*; British Consol rate.

actual and expected inflation. As prices rise from low to high, inflation is positive. *After* people experience this inflation, people expect it to continue. Expected inflation will be at its peak—and interest rates that contain a premium for expected inflation will be at their peak—when prices are at their peak. Therefore, prices and interest rates should have, as they did, a positive correlation.

13.3.2 Money, Inflation, and Interest Rates

It is relatively easy to incorporate Keynes's theory of interest rates—his liquidity preference theory—into an overall analysis of interest rates. When the Federal Reserve increases the rate of money growth, the supply of loanable funds is increased. Interest rates are (temporarily) lowered, lending is increased, and additional investment spending is financed. This is illustrated in Figure 13.4a.

As this new money works its way into the economy, prices are increased, and borrowers and lenders come to expect inflation. These inflationary expectations "push up" both the supply and demand for loanable funds. Eventually, all the new money accomplishes is an increase in the rate of inflation and the nominal interest rate. This is illustrated in Figure 13.4b.

The mechanisms by which and the speed with which interest rates move

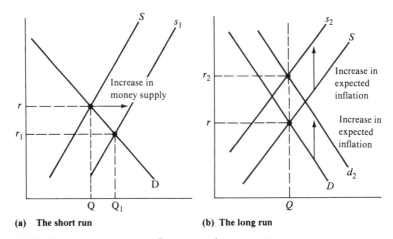

(a) **The short run**   (b) **The long run**

FIGURE 13.4   *Money, Inflation, and Interest Rates.*
In the short run, panel (a), an increase in the rate of growth of the money supply pushes out the supply of loanable funds, lowering interest rates and increasing the quantity of credit. In the long run, panel (b), however, the new money raises prices and inflationary expectations. This shifts both the supply and demand for loanable funds up, with the result only of higher interest rates.

from the short run to the long run are vitally important questions. In a "rational expectations economy," interest rates jump to their long-run levels, and the short run is simply bypassed. This roughly describes economies that have adapted to high and varying rates of inflation. Starting from an economy with stable-valued money, it may take some time before expectations are affected. In the meantime, the increase in the rate of money growth can fuel an inflationary boom. This expansion may be followed by a recessionary bust, i.e., the new money may engender a business cycle.

13.3.3 Measuring Inflation Expectations

Macroeconomics places a heavy emphasis on expectations, especially on inflationary expectations. The Fisher hypothesis, covered in this chapter, states that interest rates contain a premium for expected inflation. Yet expectations are subjective. One way to incorporate expectations into empirical macroeconomic analysis is to use survey data. Several surveys have tracked inflation expectations during the postwar period.

Soon after World War II, the financial columnist for the *Philadelphia Enquirer*, Joseph A. Livingston, began a semiannual survey of economists in which he asked their forecasts of the GNP, CPI, and other macroeconomic variables. The responses to these surveys have been used to construct a time series known as the *Livingston expectations data.*

Also soon after World War II, the Survey Research Center of the University of Michigan began a survey of households that has been used to construct a time series of consumer inflation expectations. One of the authors has used about a dozen surveys of the expectations of business executives to construct a time series of business inflation expectations.

Figure 13.5*a* presents the actual rate of inflation and the inflationary expectations of economists during the post-World War II period. Notice that immediately after World War II, economists expected deflation (and collapse back into the Great Depression). Instead, prices jumped upon the lifting of World War II price controls. During the 1960s and 1970s, expected inflation tended to lag actual inflation instead of forecasting the future path of inflation. The lag, however, appears to be relatively short, economists predicting that inflation will be next year what it was last year.

Figure 13.5*b* presents the inflationary expectations of business executives. Notice that business executives were not persuaded by economists' forecasts of deflation (and collapse back into the Great Depression) immediately after World War II. Since then, however, business expectations have been similar to those of economists. This similarity should not be surprising, since business executives obtain forecasts from the economists on their staffs, as well as from the economists employed by their professional associations and who write for their business magazines.

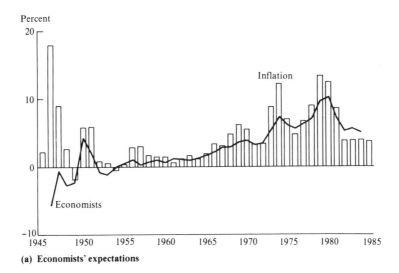

(a) Economists' expectations

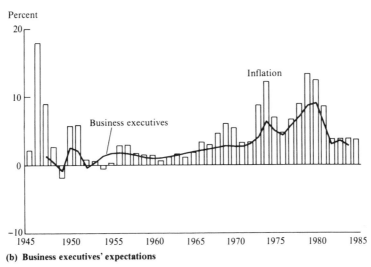

(b) Business executives' expectations

FIGURE 13.5   Inflation Expectations, 1945 – 1985.

13.3.4 Inflation Uncertainty

Whether expectations are rational or not, it is clear that inflation expectations have been poor predictors of actual inflation. With respect to the historical experience, Irving Fisher stated, "When the cost of living is not stable, the rate of interest takes the appreciation and depreciation into account to some extent, but only slightly and in general indirectly." Fisher was not saying that interest rates do not reflect expected inflation. Rather, he was saying that the expectations of inflation that are incorporated into interest rates are poor predictors of future inflation. With respect to recent experience, as inflation has become persistent, expectations have become only moderately more accurate.

Table 13.2 presents information on interest rates, expected inflation, and actual inflation over the 20-year period from 1965 to 1984. In 1965, inflation was and was expected to continue to be low. Interest rates were, accordingly, low. The annual average 3-month Treasury Bill rate, given in the table, was only 4.0 percent, and the annual average Treasury Bond rate was only 4.2 percent. Inflation then embarked on a roller-coaster ride of increases and decreases. Expected inflation and interest rates roughly followed the same pattern but with a lag.

TABLE 13.2   Actual and Expected Inflation, 1965–1984

	Expected Inflation Rate (1)	Actual Inflation Rate (2)	Nominal Interest Rate (3)
1965	1.1	1.7	4.0
1966	2.1	2.9	4.9
1967	2.4	2.9	4.3
1968	3.1	4.2	5.3
1969	3.4	5.4	6.7
1970	3.7	5.9	6.5
1971	4.1	4.3	4.4
1972	3.8	3.3	4.1
1973	4.2	6.2	7.0
1974	6.8	11.0	7.9
1975	5.7	9.1	5.8
1976	5.9	5.8	5.0
1977	6.0	6.5	5.3
1978	6.6	7.7	7.2
1979	8.5	11.3	10.0
1980	10.1	13.5	11.5
1981	8.6	10.4	14.1
1982	5.7	6.1	10.7
1983	4.9	3.2	8.6
1984	5.5	4.3	9.6
Average	5.1	6.3	7.1

Forecasts for inflation were, in any particular year, not very accurate. However, over the entire 20-year period, the average expectation for inflation, 5.1 percent, was only slightly below the average actual rate, 6.3 percent. Similarly, realized real interest rates, calculated as the nominal interest rate less the actual inflation rate, varied considerably and were negative from 1974 to 1980. However, over the 20-year period, the average nominal interest rate, 7.1 percent, *was* higher than the average actual inflation rate.

Inflation uncertainty had a major impact on the long-term bond market. A person who had, in 1965, lent money for 20 years at the Treasury Bond rate of 4.2 percent would have lost purchasing power at the rate of 2.1 percent per year. Today, long-term, fixed-rate bonds, instead of being "safe" investments, make or lose purchasing power depending on the actual rate of inflation versus the expected rate. Because of this new form of risk in long-term bonds, much of corporate finance has switched to short-term and variable-rate instruments.

With a variable-rate loan, the interest rate is periodically restated, usually according to a formula based on short-term interest rates. Instead of having one 20-year forecast of inflation, which is bound to be inaccurate, the loan will have a series of twenty 1-year forecasts. While each of the twenty 1-year inflation forecasts may be inaccurate, the 20 forecasts will probably average something like the actual average rate of inflation.

Variable-rate loans originated in commercial bank lending to business during the late 1960s and early 1970s. From there it spread, during the middle to late 1970s, to corporate bonds, mortgages, and consumer finance. During the 1980s, new forms of hedges against inflation uncertainty appeared, such as corporate bonds linked to the prices of silver, gold, oil, and other specific commodities; corporate bonds linked to relatively stable-valued currencies such as the Japanese yen, German mark, and Swiss franc; and corporate bonds linked to equities.

Therefore, it has been inflation uncertainty — and not inflation itself — that has led to the proliferation of new debt instruments, including variable-rate loans, adjustable-rate mortgages, and price-linked and indexed bonds. These new forms of debt *hedge* against inflation uncertainty. By allowing the nominal interest rate to be variable, they attempt to stabilize the real interest rate.

13.4 THE STRUCTURE OF INTEREST RATES

There are many interest rates: short-term interest rates and long-term interest rates, taxable and tax-free interest rates, deposit rates, and loan rates. The "structure" of interest rates is quite intricate. This section examines the structure of interest rates, identifying the major compensating differentials, and discusses their macroeconomic behavior.

13.4.1 Taxes and Interest Rates

The interest on securities issued by *municipal* authorities are exempt from federal income taxes. (Municipal authorities include states, local governments, school districts, and water, bridge, tunnel, and toll road utilities. Certain industrial development and pollution control bonds also enjoy exemption from federal income taxes. This interest may have to be included in the computation of the "alternative minimum tax." As always with taxes, consult your tax specialist.) Because of this exemption, municipal securities are attractive to high marginal tax rate taxpayers. They are usually issued at interest rates lower than those on corporate bonds of similar default risk.

Until the mid-1970s, economists did not believe that municipal interest rates had much effect on Treasury or corporate rates. Instead of being an integral part of the overall financial market, markets in municipal securities were thought to be "segmented." *After* Treasury and corporate interest rates were determined, *then* municipal rates were determined. These municipal rates were determined by the rates in taxable money and bond markets and by the income tax structure.

During the mid-1970s, four important papers incorporated taxes into the theory of interest rates. Papers by Michael Darby and Martin Feldstein considered interest rates in an economy where interest is tax-deductible to the borrower and taxable to the lender, both borrower and lender paying taxes at the marginal tax rate t. They demonstrate that, in such an economy, the taxable interest rate would equal $1/(1-t)$ times the interest rate that would exist in a tax-free economy, or that interest rates adjust for the effect of taxation. This adjustment leaves after-tax incentives for saving and investment unaffected by taxation, *even at high marginal tax rates*. This adjustment of interest rates for the effects of taxation has come to be known as the *Darby-Feldstein effect*.

Let m be the interest rate in a tax-free economy. Then a taxable rate $i = [1/(1-t)]m$ would change neither the after-tax cost of borrowing nor the after-tax return from lending. The borrower would pay i in interest and would save taxes in the amount of $t \cdot i$ for a net-of-taxes cost of borrowing of $(1-t)i$. This equals m if $i = [1/(1-t)]m$. The lender receives i in interest and would pay taxes in the amount of $t \cdot i$ for a net-of-taxes return of $(1-t)i$. Again, this equals m if $i = [1/(1-t)]m$. Therefore, even though the tax rate may be high, it does not affect the after-tax cost of borrowing or reward for lending.

Combining the Darby-Feldstein effect with the Fisher effect, the following equation determines taxable nominal interest rates:

$$ i = \frac{1}{1-t}r + \frac{1}{1-t}x \tag{13.4} $$

where r is the after-tax real interest rate and x is expected inflation. This implies that taxable nominal interest rates should adjust by more than the expected rate of inflation. If the tax rate equals 33.3 percent, then the coefficient of expected inflation equals 1.5. The Darby-Feldstein effect, when presented, was quite controversial because a coefficient such as 1.5 was much larger than what researchers were obtaining in econometric analysis of interest rates.

A paper by Arthur Gandolfi considered a tax structure with two tax rates: income taxes at the rate t and capital gains taxes at the rate t_g. He demonstrates that with such a tax structure, the taxable nominal interest rate i equals $(1 - t_g)/(1 - t)$ times m. This implies a coefficient of expected inflation in a Fisher equation *between* the Darby-Feldstein effect of $1/(1 - t)$ and the Fisher effect of 1. If the income tax rate is 33.3 percent, and if the capital gains tax rate is one-half that, then the coefficient of expected inflation should equal 1.2. This is roughly in line with the findings of econometric researchers. However, the actual average rate of capital gains taxation prior to the Tax Reform Act of 1986 has been estimated to have been about 6 percent. This estimate of t_g implies a coefficient of about 1.4. This is still large relative to the findings of econometric researchers.

A paper by Merton Miller considered a tax structure with corporations paying income taxes at a rate of t_c and individuals paying income taxes at graduated rates, with many having higher marginal tax rates than the corporate tax rate and paying taxes on capital gains at the capital gains tax rate of t_g. (For convenience, Miller assumed that t_g equals zero. Here we will assume that t_g equals 6 percent.) Miller demonstrates that with such a tax structure, the tax rate incorporated into taxable interest rates would equal $(1 - t_g)/(1 - t_c)$ times m. With a corporate income tax rate of 48 percent, this implies a coefficient of expected inflation of 1.8, which is even larger than the Darby-Feldstein coefficient. This implied coefficient is very far out of alignment with the estimates that were being obtained by econometric researchers.

One reaction to these theories concerning the effect of taxes on interest rates was to conclude that financial markets suffer "fiscal illusion," that the determination of interest rates did not incorporate the effect of taxation. Another reaction was to conclude that the after-tax real interest rate has not been constant but was strangely negative during the 1970s. These negative after-tax real interest rates are illustrated in Figure 13.6.

The concern of economists for the effect of taxes—or inflation combined with taxes—on interest rates makes the interest rates on municipal securities potentially useful for analysis. If municipal securities are an integral part of the overall financial market, then they can be used as estimates

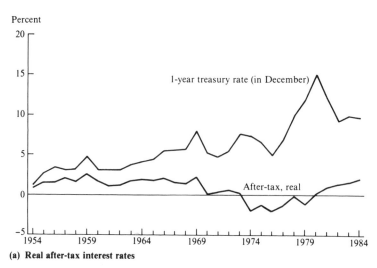

(a) Real after-tax interest rates

FIGURE 13.6   Real Interest Rates, 1954 – 1984.
Definitions and sources: Real after-tax interest rate $= (1 - t)i - x$, and
real municipal interest rate $= m - x$, where t is the average marginal
personal tax rate (from Robert J. Barro and Chaipat Sahasakul,
"Measuring the Average Marginal Tax Rate from the Individual Income Tax," *Journal of Business*, 56, October 1986, pp. 419 – 452), i
is the 1-year Treasury rate, m is the 1-year prime municipal rate
(these two being the rates in December, from Salomon Brothers,
Inc.), and x is the end-year CPI inflation rate forecast of the Livingston survey of economists.

of the hypothetical tax-free rate in Treasury and corporate securities of comparable default risk. In this case, the implied tax rate in taxable securities
would be $1 - m/i$. Such calculations for Treasury and "prime" (or default
risk-free) municipal securities deliver large implied tax rates from short-
term interest rates and smaller implied tax rates from long-term interest rates.

The large implied tax rates in short-term interest rates are generally
consistent with Miller's model, indicating that the corporate income tax is
embedded in taxable interest rates. In contrast, the smaller implied tax rates
in long-term interest rates are more consistent with the Darby-Feldstein and
Gandolfi models, indicating that the marginal personal income tax rate is
embedded into taxable interest rates. The difference in implied tax rates
between short- and long-term interest rates also may reflect some degree of
segmentation in long-term municipal securities.

Corporations, primarily banks, are attracted to short-term municipal

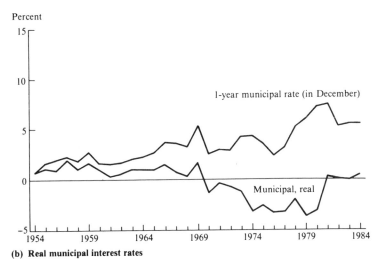

(b) Real municipal interest rates

FIGURE 13.6 Continued

securities, thus embedding the corporate tax rate into short-term municipal rates. However, because of the interest rate sensitivity of the market value of long-term municipals, banks shy away from long-term municipals, leaving individual investors to embed the marginal personal income tax rate into long-term municipal rates.

Recent tax legislation has significantly altered the way taxes affect interest rates. First, both the 1981 and 1986 Tax Reform Acts flattened the personal income tax structure and lowered personal income tax rates relative to the corporate tax rate. Second, the 1986 act eliminated the capital gains exclusion and the tax deductibility of interest payments on some forms of consumer debt. These changes in the tax structure should reduce taxable interest rates relative to tax-free interest rates. Moreover, presuming that elimination of the capital gains exclusion is either temporary or ineffective, the effect of changes in expected inflation on taxable interest rates would fall, but not all the way to the Fisher effect of 1.

If the elimination of the capital gains exclusion is effective and permanent, then both the Gandolfi and Miller models would imply that the effect of changes in expected inflation on taxable interest rates would fall all the way to the Fisher effect of 1. This is a potential time bomb. Whether by design or accident, the prereform tax structure allowed taxable nominal interest rates to adjust for the combined effect of taxation and inflation. As a result, taxes—even at high rates—did not greatly affect the after-tax, after-inflation cost of borrowing or return to lending. It would be ironic if tax reform—and lower tax rates—winds up distorting saving and investment.

13.4.2 The Term Structure of Interest Rates

The *term structure of interest rates* refers to the relationship of short- to long-term interest rates on securities of similar default risk. Usually, Treasury securities are used to construct term structures. Treasury Bills of 1 to 52 weeks to maturity provide most of the data for the short end, Treasury Notes of up to 5 years to maturity provide most of the data for the middle, and Treasury Bonds of up to 30 years to maturity provide the data for the long end of the term structure. "Yield curves," constructed from these data, can be found in the *Treasury Bulletin*, and "constant maturity yields," also constructed from these data, can be found in the *Federal Reserve Bulletin*. To be sure, yield curves can be constructed from the data of other sets of securities, provided sufficient variation in term to maturity is available.

13.4.2.1 Yield Curves

Construction of a yield curve is, essentially, a two-step procedure. First, yields to maturity are calculated for a set of securities. These yields are obtained from the following formula:

$$P = \sum_{i=1}^{M}\left(\frac{1}{1+y}\right)^{i}C + \left(\frac{1}{1+y}\right)^{M}100 \tag{13.5}$$

where P is the market price of the bond, expressed in percent of par value, M is the term to maturity, C is the annual coupon, expressed in percent of par value, and y is the yield to maturity. This formula is an *implicit function* in yield, meaning that the formula cannot be rearranged so that yield y is isolated on the left-hand side as an explicit function of the other variables. Yield to maturity is, therefore, solved through a process of iterative approximation. Programs to do this are nowadays common in financial calculators and are available for computers. In former days, yields were read out of books with page after page of yield tables.[2]

Note that when the security is issued, term to maturity is the stated term of the bond. However, term to maturity falls as time transpires. Ten years after issue, a bond with an original term of 20 years has 10 (remaining) years to maturity. Nineteen years after issue, this originally 20-year bond has a term to maturity of 1 year.

Furthermore, if the bond is issued at par, yield to maturity is the stated

---

[2]It should be pointed out that contemporary yield curves are constructed by econometric techniques beyond the scope of this book.

coupon rate. However, as market interest rates change, the market price of the bond changes so as to bring the yield of the bond into alignment with market rates. If the bond is issued at 10 percent and the market rate falls to 8 percent, then the price of the bond will rise so as to bring yield down to 8 percent. This bond will trade at a premium. If the market rate rises to 12 percent, then the price of the bond will fall and the bond will trade at a discount. In practice, market price of the bond is what is determined in buying and selling, whether at a premium, a discount, or exactly at par, and yield is calculated using the preceding formula.

The second step in constructing a yield curve is to plot the yields to maturity of a set of securities on a graph with term to maturity on the horizontal axis and yield to maturity on the vertical and then to draw a curved line through the scatter of points. Historically, yield curves have taken four shapes: rising, falling, flat, and humped. These are pictured in Figure 13.7. Flat yield curves may be considered the limiting case of rising curves and falling yield curves the limiting case of humped curves.

Rising yield curves are the historical norm. From the earliest times that interest rates are available, long-term interest rates have normally been higher than short-term rates on securities of similar default risk. Because rising yield curves are the norm, falling or humped curves are said to be *inverted*. The shape of the yield curve is strongly correlated with the business cycle. Rising yield curves are generally observed prior to the trough of recessions and into the following expansion. Humped yield curves are generally observed at the peak of expansions and prior to the following recession.

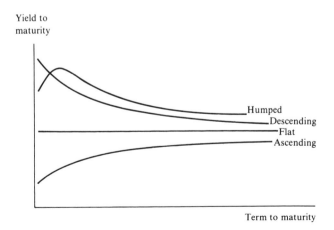

FIGURE 13.7   The Term Structure of Interest Rates.

13.4.2.2 Theories of the Term Structure

The regularities in yield curves have motivated economists to develop theories of the term structure. Why are long-term interest rates normally higher than short-term rates? Why are yield curves inverted at business-cycle peaks? Why are "dished" curves—yield curves with a reverse hump—rarely observed? Three theories have been advanced: the expectations, modified expectations, and preferred habitat theories.

The *expectations theory* of the term structure posits that long-term interest rates are averages of the current and *expected future* short-term rates. The argument is that if long-term interest rates are not such averages, then speculators would have an incentive to borrow short term and lend long term, or to borrow long term and lend short term, depending on the discrepancy, and their borrowing and lending would bring long-term interest rates into alignment with current and expected future short-term interest rates.

Imagine that the 1- and 2-year interest rates were both 10 percent, but speculators expected that in 1 year the 1-year rate would be 13 percent. These speculators could profit by borrowing long term and lending short term. A speculator could borrow $1 million for 2 years at 10 percent and invest the proceeds for 1 year at 10 percent with the intention of reinvesting this money at the end of the year at the expected future 1-year rate of 13 percent. Over the 2-year period, the speculator will earn $230,000 in interest and pay $200,000 in interest, for a profit of $30,000.

The very act of this speculator will tend to bring the long-term rate into alignment with the current and expected future short-term rates. By borrowing long term, the speculator will raise the long-term rate, let's say to 11 percent, and by lending short term, the speculator will lower the short-term rate, let's say to 9 percent. Now the long-term rate (11 percent) equals the average of the current short-term rate (9 percent) and expected future short-term rate (13 percent). The long-term rate is brought into alignment with the current and expected future short-term rates, and there is no longer any incentive for other speculators to borrow in one market and lend in the other.[3]

The expectations theory of the term structure explains the rise in yield curves observed at the business-cycle troughs by saying that at these times, interest rates are expected to rise (which is what generally happens), and it explains the fall in yield curves observed at business-cycle peaks by saying that at these times, interest rates are expected to fall (which, again, is what generally happens).

The expectations theory does not offer a satisfying explanation for the

---

[3]To be precise, the long-term rate would have to equal the geometric average of the current and expected future short-term rates; also, the above calculations of interest ignore compounding.

normal rise in yield curves. The theory would imply that speculators have biased expectations for future short-term interest rates, expecting them always to be rising. Nor does the expectations theory offer a satisfying explanation for the observation of humped yield curves but not dished yield curves. The theory would imply that when the yield curve is humped, speculators expect interest rates to first rise and then fall. If speculators can entertain this type of forecast, why do they not expect—with equal frequency—interest rates to first fall and then rise, whereupon dished yield curves would be exhibited?

The *modified expectations theory* of the term structure explains both the normal rise in yield curves and the periodic observation of humped but not dished yield curves. The modified expectations theory accepts that speculators do play a role in bringing long-term interest rates into alignment with current and expected future interest rates. The modified expectations theory then *adds* a second, independent determinant of the shape of the yield curve, namely, the liquidity premium.

The *liquidity premium* can be thought of as the service offered by the "moneyness" of short-term securities. Short-term securities are automatically turned into cash upon their maturity. Transactions costs, which would be involved in the selling of long-term securities in the secondary market, are avoided. Short-term securities can be used as a "secondary reserve," since they offer a mix of interest and liquidity.

The liquidity premium also can be thought of as the value of the price stability offered by short-term securities. The prices of long-term securities, in contrast, are subject to fluctuations depending on changes in market interest rates. Long-term securities are of limited usefulness as a secondary reserve because their prices are less predictable.

According to the modified expectation theory, long-term interest rates equal a biased average of current and expected future long-term interest rates; that is, $(1 + y_2)^2 = (1 + y_1 + \Theta)(1 + y \, Y_1^e)$, where Θ is the liquidity premium. This liquidity premium can be estimated as the average of $2(y_2 - y_1)$.[4]

The liquidity premium explains why long-term interest rates are nor-

---

[4]Let Θ equal the liquidity premium. The modified expectations hypothesis states that

$$(1 + y_2)^2 = (1 + y_1 + \Theta)(1 + y_1^e)$$

Taking logs,

$$2 \log (1 + y_2) = \log (1 + y_1 + \Theta) + \log (1 + y_1^e)$$

which for moderate interest rates, is approximately

$$2y_2 = y_1 + \Theta + y_1^e$$

Given rational expectations, y_1^e will equal, on average, y_1. Making this substitution,

$$2y_2 = 2y_1 + \Theta$$

Therefore,

$$\Theta = 2(y_2 - y_1)$$

mally higher than short-term rates. Furthermore, it explains why yield curves are humped at business-cycle peaks; i.e., the yield curve first rises because of the liquidity premium. Indeed, the liquidity premium would be rather large at peaks because of tightness in the money market. Then, because interest rates can be expected to fall during a recession, the yield curve would be falling. The modified expectations theory also effectively preempts dished yield curves.

The *preferred habitat theory* of the term structure is not so much a theory but an explanation of why the term structure may differ from its regular pattern. Sometimes referred to as the *segmented markets theory*, this theory says that interest rates are determined in each market by the forces of supply and demand in that market and without the influence of speculators who can borrow in one market and lend in another to bring interest rates into alignment with expectations.

According to this theory, institutional investors such as banks and insurance companies dominate each segment of the market. These institutional investors are wedded, by the nature of their business or by regulation, to certain segments, which are called their *preferred habitats*. Banks, for example, are wedded to the short-term segment, and insurance companies are wedded to the long-term segment. Short-term interest rates are normally lower than long-term interest rates because—by chance—demand for short-term securities is relatively stronger than the demand for long-term securities. Presumably, it could be different.

The evidence for the preferred habitat theory is very weak. During the early 1960s, the Kennedy administration decided to rearrange the maturity structure of the federal debt in order, they thought, to simultaneously raise short-term interest rates while keeping long-term rates low. The high short-term rates were supposed to strengthen the balance of payments, and the low long-term rates were supposed to encourage investment spending. This was called "Operation Twist" because the Kennedy administration was going to "twist" the normal pattern of the term structure by changing the relative supplies of short- versus long-term securities.

Econometric analysis of the results of Operation Twist revealed only a small, transitory effect on the term structure. While it may be possible to change around the term structure with a large enough shift in the relative supplies of securities, financial markets appear capable enough of rationally aligning interest rates for the variations in relative supplies that do occur.

13.4.3 Default Risk

U.S. Treasury securities are thought to be free of default risk. This is so because these securities are denominated in U.S. dollars, which the government—through the Federal Reserve—could print if necessary. The risk in Treasury securities, realistically speaking, is not that the government will fail to make good on them, but that the value of the dollars with which the government repays its debt could be lower than expected. That is, the risk in Treasury securities is that of inflation, not that of default.

On the other hand, the debts of private corporations and nonincorporated businesses, families and households, and even local governments *do* embed default risk. These borrowers cannot print the money needed to repay their debts. These borrowers have to generate the money they need to repay their debts through sales, wages, other earnings, or taxes. If income should fall below expectations, these borrowers may not be able to repay their debts. In such an instance, they would default, and the lender would lose some or all of the promised return.

Even the debt of *national* governments can embed default risk. This would be the case if the national government borrows in a currency that it itself does not issue. For example, a foreign government that issues bonds denominated in U.S. dollars, Japanese yen, or another "hard currency" may not "earn" the foreign exchange needed to repay its debts. The Third World debt crisis of the 1980s was due, in a sense, to the fact that the "external" debt of nondeveloping countries was denominated in "hard currencies." Default by national governments on their debts is referred to as *sovereign risk*. This is a special kind of default risk because of the difficulties in enforcing contracts with national governments.

13.4.3.1 Bond Ratings

Rating agencies such as Moody's and Standard & Poor's publish ratings of bonds, a list of which is presented in Table 13.3. These ratings are published for a fee, which is paid by the issuer of the bonds. Issuers are willing to pay this fee because rated bonds are more marketable. Rated bonds are more marketable because their "investment quality" is immediately obvious to potential buyers. Potential buyers do not each have to conduct the financial analysis necessary to evaluate the investment quality of the bond but can rely on the rating agency's evaluation.

Note that it is efficient for the cost of determining investment quality to be borne once, by the issuer, instead of being borne many times by the many buyers of "public" bond issues. In contrast, ratings are usually not obtained for "private" issues, i.e., bond issues that are purchased in their entirety by a single buyer, since it is immaterial who—the issuer or (one) buyer—pays for the cost of the financial analysis necessary to evaluate the bonds.

By convention, bonds rated Baa/BBB or higher are said to be of *in-*

TABLE 13.3   Rating Agency Classifications

Moody's	Standard & Poor's	Description
Aaa	AAA	Highest quality
Aa	AA	High quality
A	A	Upper-medium grade
Baa	BBB	Medium grade
Ba	BB	Lower-medium grade
B	B	Speculative
Caa	CCC, CC	Poor (may be in default)
Ca	C (income bonds)	Often in default
C	DDD, D	Lowest grade (in default)

Note: Moody's and Standard & Poor qualify bonds *within* their rankings Aa/AA through
Ba/BB as follows: Aa-1 or AA + (using Aa/AA bonds as an example), highest within
grade; Aa-2 or AA, middle within grade; and Aa-3 or AA − , lowest within grade.

vestment quality. Bonds rated Ba/BB or lower, especially at issue, are said
to be *junk bonds*. Since evaluation of investment quality involves judgment,
there may not be much difference between a Baa/BBB bond—which is an
investment quality bond—and a Ba/BB bond—which is a junk bond. Nevertheless, there *is* considerable difference in investment quality between Aaa/
AAA and Aa/AA bonds compared to Ba/BB and B/B bonds.

Rating agencies grade bonds using many sources of information, including company financial statements, economic analyses, and management
interviews. Factors such as the size of the firm, the level and consistency of
profits, use of financial leverage, and industry analyses weigh heavily in the
process. Ratings are reviewed periodically to ensure that published ratings
reflect new developments. Typically, a highly rated bond will not all of a
sudden fall into default but will first go through a series of downgradings.
It should be noted that rating agencies are slow relative to financial markets.
Almost always the market prices of bonds fall prior to their downgradings
by rating agencies.

13.4.3.2 Risk Structure of Interest Rates

Interest rates on low-quality bonds are, of course, higher than the interest
rates on high-quality bonds. However, this does not necessarily mean that
investors in low-quality bonds expect to make more money. The *expected*
return on low-quality bonds depends not only on the "promised" return, but
also on the probability of and loss upon default. For a simple illustration, a
1-year bond with an interest rate or promised rate of return of 10 percent, a
probability of default of 2 percent, and a loss upon default of 50 percent,

has an expected rate of return of 9 percent; i.e., promised return less the probability of default times the loss upon default. The loss upon default does not have to be 100 percent, but depends on loan collateral and priority of claim.

If capital markets were perfect, then the higher interest rate on low-quality bonds would merely compensate investors for default risk. The expected return on risky bonds would equal the return on risk-free bonds. However, because capital markets are not perfect, the realized returns on portfolios of risky bonds—adjusted for losses on defaults—has been somewhat higher than the return on risk-free bonds.

The structure of interest rates on risky bonds is illustrated in Figure 13.8. The risk premium for short-term high-grade bonds—i.e., the high-grade rate minus the default-free rate—is quite small. This risk premium is somewhat higher for long-term high-grade bonds. The reason why the risk premium is so small for short-term high-grade bonds is that there is little time for the issuer's strong financial condition to deteriorate and throw the bond into default. However, for the long-term high-grade bond, there is time enough for this possibility. Therefore, its risk premium is higher.

On the other hand, the short-term low-grade bond features a large risk premium. This is so because the issuer is already in weak financial condition and will have difficulty paying the principal on maturing debt. The issuer has a high probability of being ''financially embarrassed'' when the bonds come due. This is referred to as the *crisis at maturity*. For long-term low-grade bonds, there is sufficient time for the weak financial condition of the company to improve. Therefore, the risk premium is lower. [As illustrated, the long-term low-grade risk premium is still greater than the long-term high-grade risk premium.]

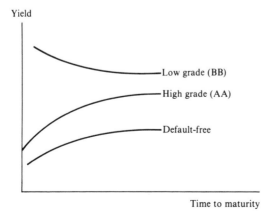

FIGURE 13.8   The Risk Structure of Interest Rates.

13.5 SUMMARY

1. Interest rates incorporate the time value of money and a number of premiums, including premiums for inflation, taxation, and default risk. In a free-market economy, the hypothetical ''pure'' interest rate reflects the liquidity service of cash balances, the economy's ''impatience to consume,'' and the productivity of investment.

2. The Fisher equation refers to the relation between nominal and real interest rates. The real interest rate is, by definition, equal to the nominal interest rate less the expected inflation rate. The Fisher hypothesis is that the real interest rate is not affected by expected inflation, so that the nominal interest rate fully adjusts for changes in expected inflation. Contemporary interest rates, in this and other countries, appear to support the Fisher hypothesis.

3. Inflation and interest-rate uncertainty has led to indexation of much long-term debt.

4. Interest rates appear to adjust for tax treatment of interest income and expense. Before-tax interest rates of taxable securities are higher, leaving after-tax interest rates to lender and borrower more or less equal to what interest rates would be in the absence of taxes. Recent changes in the U.S. tax codes may, however, alter this relation.

5. The term structure of interest rates refers to the relation between interest rates of short- and long-term bonds of similar default risk and marketability. Normally, short-term interest rates are lower than long-term rates. However, at business-cycle peaks, inverted or humped term structures are observed.

6. Risky bonds offer higher promised return than risk-free bonds. However, the risk premiums in these bonds do little more than compensate lenders for expected losses on defaults.

13.6 EXERCISES

1. What is the short- and the long-term effect of increasing the rate of growth of the money supply on nominal interest rates?

2. Let the average marginal personal income tax rate be 33 percent, the corporate income tax rate 46 percent, and the average effective capital gains tax rate 6 percent. What would be the effect of a one-point increase in expected inflation on short-term taxable interest rates according to the (a) Darby-Feldstein model, (b) Gandolfi model, and (c) Miller model?

3. How does the Tax Reform Act of 1986 affect the relationship between taxable interest rates and expected inflation?

4. Distinguish among the expectations theory, the modified expectations theory, and the preferred habitat theory of the term structure of interest rates.

5. According to the modified expectations theory, why are inverted or humped term structures usually observed at cyclic peaks?

6. Why is it that the fact that bonds rated BBB/Baa offer a higher interest rate than bonds rated AAA/Aaa does not necessarily mean that the BBB/Baa-rated bonds will realize a higher return or even that the BBB/Baa-rated bonds are expected to realize a higher return?

7. Why is it that short-term AA/Aa-rated bonds offer a lower risk premium than do long-term AA/Aa-rated bonds?

8. Using the data in Table 13.1, regress the average of the three years of nominal interest rates on the average of the three years of inflation rates.

13.7 REFERENCES

Eugen von Bohm-Bawerk, *Capital and Interest*. South Holland, IL: Libertarian Press, 1959.

John A. Carlson, "Expected Inflation and Interest Rates," *Economic Inquiry*, 17, October 1979, pp. 597 – 608.

Michael R. Darby, "The Financial and Tax Effects of Monetary Policy on Interest Rates," *Economic Inquiry*, 13, June 1975, pp. 266 – 276.

David Durand, *Basic Yields of Corporate Bonds, 1900 – 1942* (Technical Paper No.3). New York: National Bureau of Economic Research, 1942.

Eugene Fama, "Short-Term Interest Rates as Predictors of Inflation," *American Economic Review*, 65, June 1975, pp. 269 – 282.

Martin S. Feldstein, "Inflation, Income Taxes, and the Rate of Interest: A Theoretical Analysis," *American Economic Review*, 66, December 1976, pp. 809 – 820.

Irving Fisher, *The Rate of Interest*. New York: Macmillan, 1907.

Irving Fisher, *The Theory of Interest*. New York: Macmillan, 1930.

Jack Hirshleifer, *Investment, Interest and Capital*. Englewood Cliffs, N.J.: Prentice-Hall, 1970.

Sidney Homer, *A History of Interest Rates*. New Brunswick, N.J.: Rutgers University Press, 1963.

Burton G. Malkiel, *The Term Structure of Interest Rates*. Princeton, N.J.: Princeton University Press, 1966.

J. Huston McCulloch, "Measuring the Term Structure of Interest Rates," *Journal of Business*, 44, January 1971, pp. 19 – 31.

J. Huston McCulloch, "An Estimate of the Liquidity Premium," *Journal of Political Economy*, 83, February 1975, pp. 96 – 119.

David Meiselman, *The Term Structure of Interest Rates*. Englewood Cliffs, N.J.: Prentice-Hall, 1962.

Robert C. Merton, "On the Pricing of Corporate Debt: The Risk Structure of Interest Rates," *Journal of Finance*, 29, May 1974, pp. 449 – 470.

Clifford F. Thies, "New Estimates of the Term Structure of Interest Rates: 1920 – 1939," *Journal of Financial Research*, 8, Winter 1985, pp. 297 – 306.

Clifford F. Thies, "Business Price Expectations, 1947 – 1983, "*Journal of Money, Credit and Banking*, 18, August 1986, pp. 336 – 354.

——— *Managerial Case* ———

CAN REAL AFTER-TAX INTEREST RATES BE NEGATIVE?

While interest rates generally appear to adjust for the effects of taxes and expected inflation, during the middle to late 1970s real after-tax interest rates were negative. This is illustrated in Figure 13.6. Negative real after-tax interest rates should be considered unusual. Who would save if saving meant *less* purchasing power in the future?

First, note that—without inflation—negative real after-tax interest rates would be (nearly) impossible. This is so because zero is a kind of natural floor under nominal interest rates. People can simply hold onto money rather than invest at negative nominal interest rates.[1] Second, without taxation of nominal capital gains, negative real after-tax interest rates also would be (nearly) impossible. This is so because investments in gold, real estate, and collectibles almost certainly will rise in money value with inflation. Therefore, two necessary conditions for negative real after-tax interest rates are inflation and taxation of nominal capital gains.

Even with these two necessary conditions, the normal productivity of investment would be sufficient to ensure a positive real after-tax interest rate. A third factor, cited by some economists in their analysis of interest rates during the 1970s, that contributed to negative real after-tax rates was the sudden rise in energy prices. Because energy is a complement to physical capital, the sudden rise in energy prices reduced the "optimal capital stock," i.e., the quantity of physical capital demanded, below the existing stock of physical capital. Because physical capital is durable, the existing stock could not quickly adjust downward but could only adjust downward over time, through the slow workings of economic depreciation. During the time there was an excess supply of physical capital, the normal productivity of investment did not factor into interest rates.

Three factors, therefore, conspired to drive real after-tax interest rates negative during the middle to late 1970s: inflation, taxation of nominal capital gains, and the sudden rise in energy prices.

---

[1]To be precise, interest rates can be slightly negative because there are some costs, such as storage and insurance, to physically holding money. Also, certain state and federal taxes apply to bank deposits. During the Great Depression, there was a time that the interest rate on Treasury Bills was slightly negative. See Stephen Cecchetti, "The Case of Negative Nominal Interest Rates," *Journal of Political Economy*, 96, December 1988, pp. 1111 – 1141, for a discussion of anomalous negative yields on Treasury securities during the 1930s.

Business Conditions Analysis

You have now developed a solid understanding of various models that are useful in explaining how macroeconomic variables interrelate to determine the overall level of economic activity in the United States. These models provide a framework that is useful in making predictions about the future course of the economy and its major sectors. Without an understanding of the past and without a paradigm of the system to be forecast, it would be extraordinarily difficult to make predictions about what might be expected to occur in some future time period.

Every business decision depends on some type of forecast. Sometimes these forecasts are developed in a very judgmental way, based on the intuition of managers who have a wealth of accumulated knowledge about the economy and the industry in which they operate. However, in recent years, there has been an increase in the use of a variety of quantitative techniques that have been demonstrated to improve forecast accuracy in many situations. There is no one method that always works the best, and it often takes considerable experience and experimentation to identify the methods that work the best.

In this section of the text we provide an overview of economic forecasting, a discussion of some of the most popular quantitative methods used in forecasting today, an introduction to business cycles and economic indicators, and examples of applications that include GNP and two major components of the consumption sector of the economy, housing starts and domestic automotive sales. The three chapters that comprise this section of the text, as well as the appendix on input/output analysis, have been written in such a way that each can be used as a stand-alone chapter. Some instructors may wish to cover only a subset of this material.

14

Economic Forecasting: An Overview

14.1 INTRODUCTION

Forecasts about the future level of various economic variables are the basis for many decisions in both the private and public sectors of the economy. Virtually every functional area of a business relies on forecasts. Examples include the following:

Functional Area	Typical Need for Forecasting
Personnel	Employment requirements
Finance	Interest rates
Production	Raw material inventory needs
Marketing	Promotional budgets
Accounting	Tax planning

In the public sector, forecasts are equally important. The federal government relies on forecasts of aggregate economic activity in determining each year's budget, estimating staffing needs, and for other planning purposes. State and local governments forecast the demand for various public services, such as the number of students who will be in each grade level, the demand for fire and police protection, and social services demand, as well as expected levels of revenues.

14.2 LEVELS OF ECONOMIC FORECASTS

There are four major levels of forecasts that are useful for particular purposes. The broadest level of forecasting involves making projections about various

347

macroeconomic variables such as personal consumption expenditures, the unemployment rate, the consumer price index (CPI), disposable personal income, and gross national product (GNP). Macroeconomic variables are often viewed as ''prime movers'' in the sense that they provide the basis for changes in other variables that may be of more direct concern.

As you have seen in your study of macroeconomics, there are a number of conceptual models that help to explain how various macroeconomic variables are interrelated. An understanding of the relationships that exist between macroeconomic variables can be useful in making predictions about those variables. For example, knowing that interest rates are expected to rise may be helpful in judging what may happen to the level of investment and employment. Consider also the basic consumption function

$$C = f(DPI)$$

$$C = a + b(DPI)$$

where C is personal consumption expenditures (in billions of dollars), DPI is disposable personal income (in billions of dollars), a is autonomous consumption, and b is the marginal propensity to consume. Suppose that this relationship has been empirically estimated and that $a = -32$ and $b = 0.93$.[1] The consumption function then becomes

$$C = -32 + 0.93DPI$$

If DPI is $3000, then personal consumption expenditures would be $2758 (remember that this would be in billions of dollars):

$$C = -32 + 0.93(3000)$$
$$= \$2758$$

Now suppose that you wanted to make an estimate of personal consumption expenditures if disposable personal income were to rise to $3062. You would estimate personal consumption expenditures to be

$$C = -32 + 0.93(3062)$$
$$= \$2816$$

This was the actual value of DPI for the first quarter of 1987 (87.1), and the equation was based on data for the first quarter of 1976 through the last

---

[1]We will discuss the regression techniques that form the basis of such estimates in the next chapter.

quarter of 1985. The actual level of personal consumption expenditures for 87.1 was 2854, so our forecast would have been low by about 1 percent.

Personal consumption expenditures is itself a broad macroeconomic series that may be broken down into segments. The three segments of particular interest are usually durable goods, nondurable goods, and services. Recently, durable goods have been about 14 percent of personal consumption expenditures, nondurable goods have been about 36 percent, and services have been about 50 percent. Other macroeconomic series often can be broken down similarly. For example, the unemployment rate may be broken down by sex, race, and age groupings. The consumer price index can be disaggregated into indices related to durable goods, nondurable goods, and services, as well as to finer divisions within these segments, such as the CPI for housing, automobiles, medical care, or energy.

The second level of forecasting is the industry level. Examples of this level would include making a forecast for particular durable goods, such as cars, new homes, refrigerators, televisions, or home computers. Each of these involves an industry composed of some number of individual producers of the products. The nondurable goods and service sectors also can be broken into specific industries, such as the clothing industry, food processing, hospitality services (motels, hotels, restaurants, and so on), nursing care, and so forth. A forecast of the future level of activity for an industry is often based, in part, on a prediction about what will happen to one or more of the macroeconomic ''prime movers.''

The next level of forecasting is for an individual firm. In addition to looking at and/or preparing macroeconomic and industry-level forecasts, each firm ultimately needs to generate a forecast of its own sales. General Motors is concerned about the direction of the entire economy because overall economic trends influence the automotive industry, which, in turn, affects the sales of General Motors cars. Procter and Gamble is likewise concerned about macroeconomic variables as well as forecasts for the industries in which its products are sold, but in the end, the most concern is with making projections of the future sales of Procter and Gamble products. Forecasts at the firm level are important in financial planning and in the determination of labor needs, for example.

Finally, forecasts must be made at the product-line level. The number of each model of General Motors cars must be forecast. Someone has the responsibility to predict the sales of Corvettes each year. At Procter and Gamble, a forecast of the sale of Ivory products such as Ivory bath soap, Ivory shampoo, and Ivory hair conditioner must be made. These forecasts are critical for production management decisions, including procurement of raw materials, and for marketing decisions, such as inventory control.

At the firm and product-line levels, the forecasts also may be broken down by region, by channel, and/or by customer. For example, a publisher of popular trade books may want to make forecasts of sales by region to help in decisions about how many copies of particular books to keep in inventory in various parts of the country or even in decisions concerning where to have books printed and/or bound. The publisher also may want to forecast the number of copies that are likely to be sold through department stores, book stores, and mail-order outlets (i.e., by channel of distribution) as well as by ultimate customer (e.g., by sex of buyer, age, and so on).

14.3 METHODS USED IN ECONOMIC FORECASTING

Quite a wide array of methods have been and are being used in developing economic forecasts. These can usually be put into one of three main categories: judgmental methods, time-series methods, and econometric methods.[2] Let us start by considering some of what would be classified as judgmental approaches to forecasting. These methods are probably most frequently used at the firm and industry levels. One such approach is often called the *sales force composite method*. This involves having each member of the sales force make an estimate of the level of sales he or she expects to have during the forecast period. These individual estimates are then combined to form a total forecast for the period. This has an advantage in that sales personnel often have a very good "professional feel" or "intuition" about what will happen in the industry and are thus able to incorporate many diverse and often subjective factors into their forecasts. A major concern about using this method is that a bias may develop when the firm's reward structure is related in some way to the individual's forecast. Specifically, consider what might happen if the forecast is used as a benchmark against which performance is evaluated and that personal promotions and/or bonuses are based on those evaluations. Forecasts may be artificially low so that meeting or exceeding them will result in easily obtained favorable evaluations.

A second judgmental forecasting method is the *jury of executive opinion approach*. In this approach, the individual who is responsible for making the forecast consults with other experts in the field and discusses likely outcomes with them. These opinions are subjectively weighed, and the forecaster arrives at a prediction based on his or her own personal knowledge and experience as well as the shared wisdom of others who are knowledgeable about the series to be forecast. This method, therefore, takes advantage of

[2]For a different and more comprehensive discussion of these three approaches to forecasting, see Robert Fildes, "Forecasting: The Issues," in Spyros Makridakis and Steven C. Wheelwright (Eds.), *The Handbook of Forecasting: A Managers Guide* (New York: Wiley, 1982), pp. 92–100.

a wealth of accumulated expertise. However, as with other subjective approaches to forecasting, the final forecast that results is very highly dependent on the particular individual who makes the forecast and his or her subjective weightings of the information received from others. This means that it is often difficult to replicate forecasts or to transfer forecasting responsibility to another individual. As an example, when the person in charge of forecasting sales of a line of coatings for a division of a major oil company retired in the late 1970s, the company found that the quality of forecasts fell off sharply. The main reason was that this type of approach to forecasting had been used by the individual who retired. He was not able to pass along his intuitive ability to sort through the mass of qualitative and quantitative data that he had typically incorporated into his judgmental forecasts. Whatever he did worked well. However, the process was not sufficiently well defined and documented to be picked up and adopted by others despite the person's sincere effort to imbue his talents into his successor's standard operating procedures.

The *Delphi method*[3] is a judgmental approach to forecasting that is in some ways an adaptation of the jury of executive opinion method. The Delphi method begins with the selection of a panel of people who are knowledgeable about the area to be forecast. There are no firm rules about the size of the panel, but five to seven people may be appropriate. These people are then sent a set of questions regarding the area involved in the forecast. They respond independently and anonymously to the panel coordinator. The results are summarized and reported back, again anonymously, to the panel members, who are asked to review the summary and to once again submit their individual judgments. This process is repeated until the group response appears to stabilize. When strongly divergent views are forthcoming, panel members may be asked to provide justifications for their positions, which are shared, with anonymity, with other members of the panel. Complete agreement may not result. This ability of the Delphi method to incorporate extreme opinions is often seen as a strength. Often a person with an extreme view will move his or her response toward the median when shown the response of others, and yet there is no pressure to do so. Because of the anonymity of the Delphi method, dominant personalities are not likely to affect the group outcome as much as if the process were accomplished in a committee setting. This method is particularly useful in long-term and technological

---

[3]The Delphi method was developed at the Rand Corporation in the early 1960s. An excellent discussion by one of its developers can be found in Olaf Helmer, *The Use of the Delphi Technique — Problems of Educational Innovations* (Santa Monica, Calif.: Rand Corporation, 1966). An overall evaluation of this approach is available in H. Sackman, *Delphi Critique* (Lexington, Mass.: Lexington Books, 1975).

forecasting. For example, we might use the Delphi method in developing a forecast of what the home entertainment market might be like 20 years from now. Computer networking can be used to facilitate the Delphi method and to speed up the process.

Time-series methods involve the knowledge of a variable's past history as the only basis for making a forecast of what that variable may be in the future. There is an almost endless array of possible time-series models. The simplest may be to assume that the variable of interest will take on the same value in the next time period as it had in the immediately preceding period. Thus, if UR_t represents the unemployment rate at time period t, the forecast of the unemployment rate for the following period $(t + 1)$ would be

$$UR_{t+1} = UR_t$$

Starting from this simplistic approach, various time-series techniques add differing layers of sophistication. For example, the forecast used above could be modified by a growth rate as follows:

$$UR_{t+1} = UR_t\left(\frac{UR_t}{UR_{t-1}}\right)$$

Here we see that if UR_t was arrived at from below (that is, UR_{t-1} was less than UR_t), the forecast of the unemployment rate for the time period $t + 1$ will be greater than UR_t. However, if UR_t was arrived at from above (that is, UR_{t-1} was greater than UR_t), the forecast of the unemployment rate for the time period $t + 1$ will be lower than UR_t.

There are four particular time-series models that get the bulk of the attention in forecasting. These are *trend projection*, *exponential smoothing*, *time-series decomposition*, and *ARIMA models* (ARIMA is an acronym for *autoregressive integrated moving average*). The ARIMA models, also frequently referred to as *Box-Jenkins models* after the primary developers of this method, are by far the most complex, and a discussion of them is beyond the scope of this text.[4] Trend projection, exponential smoothing, and time-series decomposition will be discussed and applied to specific forecasts in the next chapter.

Econometric approaches to forecasting involve the use of causal relationships in predicting the value that the variable of interest will have under some set of circumstances at a future date. Simple bivariate regression

---

[4]See the original work in G. F. P. Box and G. M. Jenkins, *Time Series Analysis: Forecasting and Control* (San Francisco: Holden-Day, 1970). An introduction to this method can be found in J. Holton Wilson and Barry Keating, *Business Forecasting* (Homewood, Ill.: Irwin, 1990).

models, such as the consumption function discussed earlier in this chapter, are the simplest of the econometric approaches to forecasting. In the consumption function, the dependent variable is the level of personal consumption expenditures. It is hypothesized that the primary causal factor that influences this variable is disposable personal income. Regression methods are used to test this hypothesis and to estimate the equation that best represents the manner by which personal consumption expenditures are determined by the level of personal disposable income.

Simple bivariate regression methods can easily be extended to multiple regression models in which more than one causal variable may be incorporated into the regression equation. For example, suppose we wanted to model automotive sales. Variables we might hypothesize as having a causal relationship to new car sales (*NCS*) might include some measure of income (*INC*) and interest rates (*R*), a measure of the number of people in age brackets for which an automotive purchase is likely (*POP*), and the price of new cars (*P*). The model would then be

$$NCS = f(INC, R, POP, P)$$
$$= b_0 + b_1 INC + b_2 R + b_3 POP + b_4 P$$

where b_0 is the intercept and b_1, b_2, b_3, and b_4 are the slope terms related to income, interest rate, population, and price, respectively. The use of bivariate and multiple regression models will be discussed in more detail, and specific examples will be presented, in the following chapter.

Other econometric approaches to forecasting include simultaneous equation models and input/output models. In reading other sections of this text, you have seen the use of simultaneous equation models to explain structural relationships in the macro economy. Consider, for example, the following simple model of the economy:

$$Y = C + I + G + X_n$$
$$C = f(Y)$$
$$I = f(i)$$
$$G = G_0$$
$$X_n = f(Y, E)$$

where Y is income, C is personal consumption expenditures, I is gross private domestic investment, G is government spending, and X_n is net exports (exports minus imports). Consumption is a function of the level of income, investment is a function of the interest rate i, government spending is exogenously determined (i.e., is at some amount, G_0, specified by government policies), and net exports are a function of the level of income and perhaps some exchange rate variable E. In such a simultaneous equation model there are several dependent, or endogenous, variables (Y, C, I, and X_n in this model) that are determined simultaneously. The causal, or exogenous, variables in this case are the interest rate i, the level of government spending G_0, and the exchange rate variable E. Once the model has been specified (i.e., the equations have been estimated), future values of the dependent variables may be estimated based on assumptions (or predictions) about the values of the exogenous variables.

14.4 ACCURACY AND COST ISSUES

The bottom line in forecasting is accuracy.[5] That is, we are often a bit less concerned with evaluating how the forecast is developed than we are with how accurate the results are. There are a number of measures of accuracy that can be used. Three commonly used measures are the *mean absolute deviation* (MAD), the *mean absolute percentage error* (MAPE), and the *root mean squared error* (RMSE). The formulas for calculating each of these are as follows:

$$\text{MAD} = \frac{\Sigma |A - F|}{n}$$

$$\text{MAPE} = \frac{\Sigma |(A - F)/A|}{n}$$

$$\text{RMSE} = \sqrt{\frac{\Sigma (A - F)^2}{n}}$$

where A represents the actual value for each period, *F* represents the forecast value for each period, and *n* is the number of periods used in the calculation. For each of these measures, a lower value is preferable to a higher value.

Let us consider an example based on the U.S. unemployment rate (*UR*) for the period $1970 - 1985$, with a forecast for 1986. The data represent the annual unemployment rate in percent, as shown in the second column of Table 14.1. A forecast of the unemployment rate (*URF*) is shown in the third

---

[5]For example, Mentzer and Cox have found that "accuracy is normally the overwhelming criterion used to evaluate forecasting techniques." See John T. Mentzer and James E. Cox, Jr., "Familiarity, Application, and Performance of Sales Forecasting Techniques," *Journal of Forecasting*, 3(1), 1984, p. 33.

column of the table starting with 1971. The forecasting model used is the following simple naive model:

$$URF_{t+1} = UR_t$$

That is, the prediction of what the unemployment rate will be for any year is equal to what the actual unemployment rate was in the previous year.

In addition to the unemployment rate (UR) and the forecast (URF), Table 14.1 shows the forecast error (E) for each period. The values for the mean absolute deviation (MAD), the mean absolute percentage error (MAPE), and the root mean squared error (RMSE) are also shown on a year-by-year basis.

The unemployment data given in Table 14.1 are plotted in Figure 14.1. You will find that looking at time-series plots of data that are to be forecasted

TABLE 14.1   U.S. Unemployment Rate and Naive Forecast with Determination of MAD, MAPE, and RMSE

Year	UR	URF	E	AE	SAE	MAD	APE	SAPE	MAPE	SSE	RMSE
1970	4.90	NA	NA	NA	NA	NA	NA	NA	NA	NA	NA
1971	5.90	4.90	1.00	1.00	1.00	1.00	0.17	0.17	0.17	1.00	1.00
1972	5.60	5.90	−0.30	0.30	1.30	0.65	0.05	0.22	0.11	1.09	0.74
1973	4.90	5.60	−0.70	0.70	2.00	0.67	0.14	0.37	0.12	1.58	0.73
1974	5.60	4.90	0.70	0.70	2.70	0.68	0.13	0.49	0.12	2.07	0.72
1975	8.50	5.60	2.90	2.90	5.60	1.12	0.34	0.83	0.17	10.48	1.45
1976	7.70	8.50	−0.80	0.80	6.40	1.07	0.10	0.94	0.16	11.12	1.36
1977	7.10	7.70	−0.60	0.60	7.00	1.00	0.08	1.02	0.15	11.48	1.28
1978	6.10	7.10	−1.00	1.00	8.00	1.00	0.16	1.18	0.15	12.48	1.25
1979	5.80	6.10	−0.30	0.30	8.30	0.92	0.05	1.24	0.14	12.57	1.18
1980	7.10	5.80	1.30	1.30	9.60	0.96	0.18	1.42	0.14	14.26	1.19
1981	7.60	7.10	0.50	0.50	10.10	0.92	0.07	1.49	0.14	14.51	1.15
1982	9.70	7.60	2.10	2.10	12.20	1.02	0.22	1.70	0.14	18.92	1.26
1983	9.60	9.70	−0.10	0.10	12.30	0.95	0.01	1.71	0.13	18.93	1.21
1984	7.50	9.60	−2.10	2.10	14.40	1.03	0.28	1.99	0.14	23.34	1.29
1985	7.20	7.50	−0.30	0.30	14.70	0.98	0.04	2.03	0.14	23.43	1.25
1986	NA	7.20	NA	NA	NA	NA	NA	NA	NA	NA	NA

Note: UR = unemployment rate in percent; URF = naive forecast of unemployment rate; E = forecast error ($E = UR - URF$); AE = absolute value of E; SAE = cumulative sum of AE; MAD = mean absolute deviation ($MAD = SAE/n$, where n is number of years); APE = absolute percentage error; $SAPE$ = cumulative sum of APE; $MAPE$ = mean absolute percentage error ($MAPE = SAPE/n$); SSE = cumulative sum of squared errors; $RMSE$ = root mean squared error ($RMSE = \sqrt{SSE/n}$).

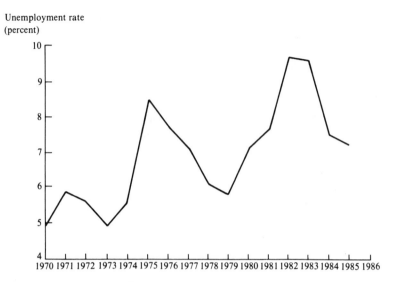

FIGURE 14.1   Unemployment Rate by Year, 1970 – 1985.
This figure shows the unemployment rate data given in Table 14.1 in
graphic form. Movements in a data series are usually easier to see
and understand in a graphic presentation than in tabular form.

is very helpful. Most people are able to recognize trends, cycles, and outliers
in data much more readily in such a plot than when they look at tabular
representations of the same data. We will look at more specific series in this
way in the next chapter.

There is no convincing evidence that any one forecasting method is
consistently more accurate than others across different series or different time
frames. A good deal of the work that confronts anyone who has forecasting
responsibilities is to sort through the available methods to find those which
work well for the series to be forecast. Stekler has suggested that when using
the results of professional forecasters of macroeconomic variables we should
look not for one that is "best" but for those which are generally "better"
than the others. He also suggests a methodology for making that selection.[6]

The cost of using an explicit forecasting system is difficult to pin down,
as is the cost of not forecasting with a nonjudgmental method. There are a
number of types of costs that are associated with implementing an explicit
forecasting system. There are costs involved in gathering data and in maintaining the data base. There are personnel costs, including training expenses

---

[6]H. O. Stekler, "Who Forecasts Better?" *Journal of Business and Economic Statistics*, 5(1),
January 1987, pp. 155 – 158.

and salaries and fringe benefits for people who develop, maintain, and implement the forecasting system. There are also computer costs, since in today's environment virtually all forecasting is done with the aid of computer technology. As long ago as 1966, ''Reichard found in a survey of business use of forecasting that 68 percent of the companies surveyed were at that time using the computer in this manner.''[7] Recently, it was found in a survey of economists that over 93 percent of respondents used either a mainframe or a microcomputer (or both) in developing their forecasts.[8]

Some estimates of cost have been developed by Makridakis, Wheelwright, and McGee. Figure 14.2 has been prepared based on results of their findings as they relate to methods described in this chapter and those which

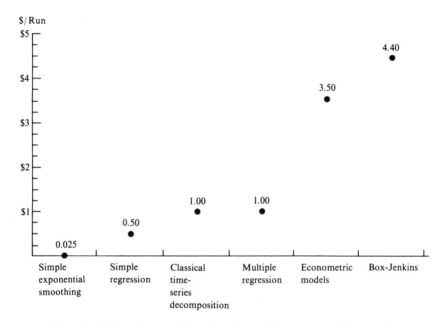

FIGURE 14.2   Cost per Run for Selected Quantitative Forecasting Techniques.

As the forecasting methods increase in complexity, the cost per run increases.

Source: Spyros Makridakis, Steven C. Wheelwright, and Victor E. McGee, *Forecasting Methods and Applications*, 2d Ed, (New York: Wiley, 1983), pp. 784-785. The authors use the term *econometric models* to refer to what we have called *simultaneous equation models*.

[7]Spyros Makridakis, Steven C. Wheelwright, and Victor E. McGee, *Forecasting: Methods and Applications*, 2d Ed. (New York: Wiley, 1983). p. 782.

[8]Barry Keating and J. Holton Wilson, ''Forecasting: Practices and Teachings,'' *Journal of Business Forecasting*, 6(4), Winter 1987–1988, pp. 10–13.

follow. In the figure we see that along the horizontal axis six quantitative forecasting techniques have been arrayed from the least to the most sophisticated or complex. The vertical axis measures the cost estimates on a per-computer-run basis using 1980 data. The absolute values are not as important as the relative values. We see that as we move from the simpler quantitative methods to those which are more complex, the cost per run increases.

As implied earlier, it is not clear whether those added costs are worthwhile in terms of a gain in accuracy. J. Scott Armstrong, a noted authority in the field of forecasting, has said that "highly complex models may reduce accuracy. While these complex models provide better fits to historical data, this superiority does not hold for forecasting." Further, he observes that "for the practitioner, the implications are clear: Relatively simple extrapolation methods . . . are adequate. . . . These methods provide accuracy equivalent to more complex methods at a lower cost, and they are easier to understand."[9]

14.5 SELF-GENERATED VERSUS PURCHASED ECONOMIC FORECASTS

There are many macroeconomic forecasting services available that will, for a fee, provide forecasts of a variety of economic series. Some of the most widely known of these vendors are Citibank, the Conference Board, Data Resources Incorporated, the Kent Economic & Development Institute, and the WEFA Group. The size of the economic models and the number of variables included vary among these, but they are all large and can provide forecasts of a wide array of series. The Kent model is probably the largest, forecasting over 40,000 variables.

These vendors and others have devoted years to the development of their models and their forecasts. As a result, one can be confident that their forecasts are well constructed and as accurate as possible. Because different models are used, with different underlying assumptions about the interaction of various parts of the economy, the forecasts of one vendor are likely to differ from those of other vendors.

Firms can, and sometimes do, develop similar models inhouse to forecast macroeconomic series. Doing so is a costly proposition, and it may be well to use the principle of comparative advantage and to subscribe to one of the forecasting services. Their expertise can be of benefit to the inhouse personnel who are more specifically involved with forecasting at the industry, firm, and product-line levels.

---

[9]J. Scott Armstrong, "Forecasting by Extrapolation: Conclusions from 25 Years of Research," *Interfaces*, 14(6), November-December 1984, pp. 55 and 58.

There is also considerable evidence that using a consensus forecast may be preferable to relying on any single forecast. For example, Zarnowitz has found that "combining corresponding predictions from different sources can result in significant gains; thus the group mean forecasts are on the average over time more accurate than most of the corresponding sets of individual forecasts."[10]

14.6 THE ROLE OF JUDGMENT IN FORECASTING

At every level of forecasting it is important not to become too enamored with computerized quantitative forecasting techniques. There may be a temptation to take the results of a computer-generated forecast as more precise than is warranted. Computer models are of a tremendous aid in forecasting and can be of significant help in improving our ability to forecast accurately. But these models are either void of expert judgment or only allow for judgments as they reflect on the selection of particular models and/or model parameters.

There is no substitute for the qualitative, often intuitive, judgments of individuals who have an expert knowledge of the phenomena being forecast. The years of experience that provide a "feel" for how some recently passed legislation may affect an economic series have not at this time been factored into forecasting software packages. A business professional's sense of how likely a strike may be and how that may influence sales or how much impact the potential entry of a new competitor will have on the firm's market share is likewise outside the realm of computerized methods. Human judgments are a necessary complement to quantitative methods in developing usable forecasts.

Frequently, management requests a single-point-estimate forecast. This is unfortunate, since such a forecast is almost certain to be incorrect. It may be close, but it is unlikely to be exactly on target. It is better to use some type of forecast range. If statistically based models, such as regression models, are used, it may be possible to provide a confidence interval estimate centered on the best point estimate. When nonstatistically based methods are used, such confidence intervals are unavailable. In such cases, it is useful to look at several alternative forecasts. Once more, professional judgments become important.

---

[10]Victor Zarnowitz, "The Accuracy of Individual and Group Forecasts from Business Outlook Surveys," *Journal of Forecasting*, 3(1), 1984, p. 11. See also Spyros Makridakis and Robert L. Winkler, "Averages of Forecasts: Some Empirical Results," *Management Science*, 29(9), September 1983, pp. 987–996; David Ahlers and Josef Lakonishok, "A Study of Economists' Consensus Forecasts," *Management Science*, 29(10), October 1983, pp. 1113–1125; and Peter L. Bernstein and Theodore H. Silbert, "Are Economic Forecasters Worth Listening To?" *Harvard Business Review*, September-October 1984, pp. 32–40, in which the authors conclude, "We should bet with the consensus" (p.40).

In developing a forecast range, a forecaster should consider several different models, preferably including different fundamental approaches. Three to five models may be appropriate. From the results of these different approaches, a three-tiered range consisting of an optimistic, a most likely, and a pessimistic forecast can be developed. Note that these levels are not necessarily the high, middle, and low values from the models used. The models simply provide important input to the expert, who then combines that information with his or her "feel" for the activity being forecast.

14.7 SOURCES OF DATA

There is no shortage of readily available data for most macroeconomic and industry-level forecasting. Some of the data are published privately and can be expensive to obtain, but a great deal are published by federal and state governments and are available for free or for a nominal cost. It would not be practical to provide an exhaustive listing of data sources in this text. However, we will identify some of the most fruitful sources in this section.

There are two publications of the U.S. Department of Commerce Bureau of Economic Analysis (BEA) that are of particular importance to economic forecasters. These are the *Survey of Current Business* and *Business Conditions Digest*. Each month the *Survey of Current Business* publishes data related to the national income and product accounts (NIPA) for the U.S. economy. (These accounts were discussed in Chapter 2 of this text.) In addition, each issue has 32 pages (blue pages in the middle of each issue) of data covering a wide range of economic series in monthly or quarterly form. The following major headings will give you some idea of the breadth of the data included. Following each broad heading are just two examples, from many, of specific series found within that heading:

General business indicators (starts on page S-1)
  Personal consumption expenditures
  Business inventories
Commodity prices (starts on page S-5)
  Consumer price index—housing
  Producer price index—capital equipment
Construction and real estate (starts on page S-7)
  New housing units started
  Construction cost indexes
Domestic trade (starts on page S-8)
  Sales at food stores
  Automotive dealer sales

Labor force, employment, and earnings (starts on page S-9)
    Civilian labor force
    Total employees in durable goods manufacturing
Finance (starts on page S-13)
    Consumer installment credit
    Money stock measures
Foreign trade of the United States (starts on page S-16)
    Exports to Japan
    Value of imported petroleum and products
Transportation and communication (starts on page S-18)
    Air passenger-miles (revenue)
    Restaurant sales index
Chemicals and allied products (starts on page S-19)
    Production of chlorine gas
    Imports of potassium chloride
Electric power and gas (starts on page S-20)
    Electric utilities production
    Revenue from gas sales to residential customers
Food and kindred products; tobacco (starts on page S-20)
    Beer production
    Rice production
Leather and products (starts on page S-23)
    Producer price index for leather
    Exports of footwear
Lumber and products (starts on page S-23)
    Production of hardwoods
    Shipments of Western pine
Metals and manufacturers (starts on page S-24)
    Imports of steel mill products
    Factory shipments of room air conditioners
Petroleum, coal, and products (starts on page S-27)
    Bituminous coal exports
    Domestic gasoline demand
Pulp, paper, and paper products (starts on page S-28)
    Woodpulp exports
    U.S. production of newsprint
Rubber and rubber products (starts on page S-29)
    Synthetic rubber production
    Production of automotive pneumatic casings
Stone, clay, and glass products (starts on page S-30)
    Production of glass containers

Crude gypsum imports
Textile products (starts on page S-30)
    Cotton production
    Men's apparel cuttings: suits
Transportation equipment (starts on page S-32)
    Retail sales of imported passenger cars
    Total new passenger car registrations

You can see from this representative listing that the *Survey of Current Business* is a valuable source of data for use in developing economic forecasts. Historical data can be found in *Business Statistics*, which is also published by the BEA.

Business Conditions Digest contains approximately 300 economic time series and is also published monthly by the BEA. Each series has a reference number ranging from 1 to 978 (numbering is not consecutive). Some of the series that are of particular interest to economic forecasters would include the following (series number followed by series title):

12. Index of net business formation
28. New private housing units started
37. Number of persons unemployed
43. Unemployment rate
47. Index of industrial production
50. Gross national product in 1982 dollars
58. Index of consumer sentiment
59. Sales of retail stores in 1982 dollars
67. Bank rates on short-term business loans
85. Change in money supply *M1*
225. Disposable personal income in 1982 dollars
231. Personal consumption expenditures in 1982 dollars
241. Gross private domestic investment in 1982 dollars
255. Net exports of goods and services in 1982 dollars
263. Federal government purchases of goods and services in 1982 dollars
267. State and local government purchases of goods and services in 1982 dollars
292. Personal saving
441. Civilian labor force

500. Federal government surplus or deficit

910. Composite index of eleven leading indicators

These and the other series are defined and discussed in detail in the *Handbook of Cyclical Indicators*, which is a supplement to *Business Conditions Digest* and is also published by the BEA. The most recent issue of the *Handbook* is the 1984 edition. This extraordinarily valuable publication also contains historical data for the series, usually as far back as the late 1940s.

Many other data sources are available.[11] *International Financial Statistics*, published by the International Monetary Fund, has a wealth of international data. The *Federal Reserve Bulletin*, published monthly by the Federal Reserve Board, is a useful source of monetary data. The censuses of population, manufacturers, and trade are also sources that are readily available. The Council of Economic Advisors publishes *Economic Indicators* and the *Economic Report of the President*, each of which contains useful data series. State governments and trade organizations also can be fruitful sources of data. Other sources include the Conference Board publications *Business Outlook* and *Guide to Consumer Markets*; Sales and Marketing Management's *Survey of Buying Power*; the first issue of *Business Week* each year includes an "Industrial Outlook"; the Department of Commerce's annual *U.S. Industrial Outlook*; and syndicated data from market research firms such as A. C. Nielsen and Selling Areas-Marketing, Inc. (SAMI). Forecasters working within a firm should not overlook data available in accounting records, established management information systems, and other internal data bases as well as annual reports.

14.8 SUMMARY

1. Macroeconomic theory provides a basis upon which forecasts can be developed. Business economists normally look at forecasts at four levels:

Macroeconomic forecasts
Industry forecasts
Forecasts for the firm
Product-line forecasts

2. Macroeconomic variables such as GNP, disposable personal income, gross private domestic investment, the unemployment rate, and personal

---

[11]A more comprehensive list of data sources can be found in Barry Keating and J. Holton Wilson, *Managerial Economics* (New York: Academic Press, 1986), Appendix C, pp. 661–673.

consumption expenditures are often useful as determinants of sales at lower levels. These important macroeconomic variables are often referred to as "prime movers" because they have such an important role throughout the economy.

3. There was a time when all forecasts were made in a purely judgmental manner. However, the use of quantitative forecasting models has been shown to improve forecast accuracy. The quantitative forecasting techniques can be classified as either time-series or econometric methods. A subset of these will be described in more detail in the following chapter and applied to particular data series taken from the U.S. economy.

4. In preparing and using forecasts, one always strives toward increased accuracy. Some people have assumed that greater accuracy would be obtained by using ever more sophisticated and complex computer-based forecasting models, such as the Box-Jenkins type of time-series analysis and simultaneous equation econometric models. Empirical evidence does not appear to support this proposition, however. It would seem that the conventional wisdom today is to try to get by with relatively simple methods that are less costly to use and which are more easily explained to end users.

5. While more and more quantitative techniques are being used in the preparation of forecasts at all levels, it is important not to neglect the role of personal judgments. There is no substitution for the accumulated expertise of experts who have had years of experience in the area that is the focal point of the forecasting effort. It is recommended that thoughtful judgments be used in determining a likely range for any forecast rather than to rely on any single point estimate as *the forecast*.

14.9 EXERCISES

1. Suppose that you are a financial manager for a large toy manufacturer. What macroeconomic and demographic variables would you be most interested in tracking and forecasting? Explain why.

2. In this chapter and earlier in the text you read about a model of personal consumption expenditures. Explain that model in your own words, and discuss how it might be useful in preparing an economic forecast of personal consumption expenditures. Go to the library and look up annual data on the three components of personal consumption expenditures starting with 1965 data (remember that the three components are durable goods, nondurable goods, and services). Prepare a time-series plot of these data. What does this plot imply for the U.S. business community?

3. If you were a mortgage lending officer at a large financial institution, you might be interested in forecasting housing starts. Suggest five independent variables that might be useful in forecasting housing starts, and explain how you expect each to influence the dependent variable.

4. Write an essay in which you discuss the issues involved in evaluating the cost versus accuracy tradeoff that some people have suggested.

5. Explain how the demand for new cars may be influenced by the following variables:
   a. Price
   b. Population growth and distribution
   c. Income
   d. Unemployment rate
   e. Prices of other things
   f. Tastes and preferences

6. Look up annual data on the percent of women in the labor force from 1960 to the most recent year available. Pick some industry and explain what implications this trend may have for that industry. Is the trend likely to continue at its present rate?

7. Pick the industry in which you hope to find employment after completing school or use the industry in which you are currently employed, and suggest ways in which macroeconomic variables influence that industry.

8. How do you think macroeconomic factors influence the demand for mainframe and microcomputers? Would you expect government policy to have any impact on this industry? If so, how?

9. What factors do you think might be important in forecasting the exchange rate between the U.S. dollar and the Japanese yen? Explain.

14.10 REFERENCES

Richard Ashley, "On the Usefulness of Macroeconomic Forecasts as Inputs to Forecasting Models," *Journal of Forecasting*, 2(3), 1983, pp. 211 – 223.

Dale G. Bails and Larry C. Peppers, *Business Fluctuations: Forecasting Techniques and Applications*. Englewood Cliffs, NJ: Prentice-Hall, 1982, especially Chapter 1 "Business Forecasting: Economy, Region, Industry, and Company," pp. 3 – 30.

Robert Fildes, "Quantitative Forecasting: The State of the Art: Econometric Models," *Journal of the Operational Research Society*, 36(7), 1985, pp. 549 – 580.

Howard Keen, Jr., "Economists and Their Forecasts: Have the Projections Been that Bad?," *Business Economics,* January 1987, pp. 37–40.

William M. Lupoletti and Roy H. Webb, "Defining and Improving the Accuracy of Macroeconomic Forecasts: Contributions from a VAR Model," *Journal of Business*, 59(2), 1986, pp. 263 – 285.

Spyros Makridakis, "The Art and Science of Forecasting: An Assessment and Future Directions," *International Journal of Forecasting*, 2, 1986, pp. 15 – 39.

Spyros Makridakis and Steven C. Wheelwright (Eds.), *The Handbook of Forecasting: A Manager's Guide*. New York: Wiley, 1982.

John J. McAuley, *Economic Forecasting for Business: Concepts and Applications*. Englewood Cliffs, N.J.: Prentice-Hall, 1986.

Lloyd M. Valentine, *Business Cycles and Forecasting*, 7th Ed. Cincinnati, Ohio: South-Western Publishing, 1987.

MANAGERIAL CASE

THE COUNCIL OF ECONOMIC ADVISORS' 1987 LONG-TERM FORECAST

On January 23, 1987, Chairman Beryl W. Sprinkle and other members of the Council of Economic Advisors submitted to President Reagan their economic forecast for 1988 – 1992. The following is a slightly abridged version of their predictions:[1]

> The administration's long-term economic projections represent expected trends and should not be interpreted as year-to-year forecasts. They reflect long-run economic goals of the Administration and the long-run trends in the economy. Specifically, it is assumed that the incentives for economic activity embodied in the reduced marginal tax rates contained in the Tax Reform Act of 1986 are preserved and that further gains are made in reducing government spending and the burden of government regulation. Also, the Federal Reserve is assumed to continue a policy that is both consistent with gradual achievement of the long-term goal of price stability and not so restrictive as to impair economic growth.
>
> The Full Employment and Balanced Growth Act of 1978 requires the *Economic Report of the President*, together with the *Annual Report of the Council of Economic Advisors*, to . . . review progress in achieving goals specified in the Act. The projections for 1987 through 1992 summarized in Exhibit A constitute the ". . . annual numerical goals for employment and unemployment, production, real income, productivity and prices, . . . " prescribed by this Act. The projections go far in achieving the goals specified in the Act for unemployment and inflation, while achieving many other aims of the legislation such as balanced growth, reduced federal spending, adequate productivity growth, an improved trade balance, and increased competitiveness in agriculture, business, and industry. Although the goal of 4 percent unemployment, specified in the legislation, is not attained by 1992, this does not indicate a lack of commitment to achieving full employment. . . . There are no quick fixes to reach the legislation's stated goals; government best serves these goals by allowing private enterprise to flourish. . . .
>
> Specifically, the Administration's economic projections detailed in Exhibit [14.1]

[1]Based on the *Economic Report of the President, 1987* (Washington, D.C.: U.S. Government Printing Office, 1987, pp. 11 and 60 – 61.

EXHIBIT 14.1   Administration Economic Assumptions, 1987–1992

Item	Percent Change, Year to Year					
	1987	*1988*	*1989*	*1990*	*1991*	*1992*
Real GNP	2.7	3.5	3.6	3.6	3.5	3.4
Real compensation per hour[a]	.8	2.0	1.8	1.7	1.8	1.9
Output per hour[a]	.9	2.2	2.0	1.9	1.9	1.9
Consumer price index[b]	3.0	3.6	3.6	3.2	2.8	2.2
	Annual Level					
Employment (millions)[c]	113.5	115.8	118.0	120.2	122.0	123.9
Unemployment rate (percent)[d]	6.7	6.3	6.0	5.8	5.6	5.5

[a]Nonfarm business, all persons.
[b]For urban wage earners and clerical workers.
[c]Includes resident armed forces.
[d]Unemployed as percent of labor force, including armed forces.

show real GNP growth rising to 3.6 percent in 1989 and declining slowly to 3.4 percent in 1992. Stronger real growth reflects the long-term benefits of tax reform, as well as factors that will improve growth in the current year and carry forward in later years. Further improvements in real net exports are expected, especially 1988. Higher production will lift incomes and consumption, and business investment should strengthen further in 1988 and beyond. Production is projected to grow sufficiently rapidly to lower the unemployment rate to 5.5 percent by 1992 . . . the inflation rate is projected to decline to 2.2 percent by 1991. Productivity growth is projected to improve. . . . Coincident with this improvement in productivity growth, increases are expected in real compensation per hour.

These projections reflect the Administration's policies to promote long-term, noninflationary growth by encouraging investment in physical and human capital and improvements in productive technology. The Administration believes that creating an economic environment that provides strong incentives for work and production is the best policy for promoting investment and productivity growth. Reduced disparities in the rate of taxation on different economic activities contributes to this result by encouraging resources to be allocated to activities where they can be used most productively.

15
Some Forecasting Methods

15.1 INTRODUCTION

There is a very wide array of forecasting methods used by economic fore-casters. The purposes of this chapter are to introduce some of the methods that are commonly used to establish a basis upon which further study of forecasting can be built and to provide examples of how some economic series might be forecast. In the following chapter we will look at additional examples as we develop forecasts for some important economic sectors.

15.2 TIME-SERIES FORECASTING

The data used in forecasting can be either cross-sectional or time-series. The latter are the most common in economic forecasting and are all that will be used in this text. Therefore, in some sense, all of what we will discuss will be time-series forecasting. However, that phrase, *time-series forecasting*, is also used to describe a subset of forecasting methods in which forecasts are based only on the history of the particular series in question. There are no other variables included, and so there is no attempt to establish causal rela-tionships. We simply try to find a pattern to the data that allows us to make a reasonable projection of that series into the future. In this section on time-series forecasting models, we will look at three of the simplest time-series techniques:

Note: Some instructors may wish to skip this chapter if time constraints prohibit coverage of forecasting methods or if their students have studied these concepts in other courses. However, students may want to use this chapter as a reference on the basic methodology for the common forecasting methods discussed herein.

Trend projections

A simple autoregressive model

Exponential smoothing

15.2.1 Forecasting with a Time Trend

We will begin with *trend projections*. Each of the two panels in Figure 15.1 shows a time series of data for the period 1981 − 1989. The nine data points (shown as dots) in the left-hand panel have a generally positive trend. That is, the overall movement of the sales series for product *A* is upward over time. The opposite is true of the data shown in the right-hand panel. There we see a data series that falls over time. That is, sales of product *B* have been falling.

In each panel of Figure 15.1, a line is drawn that shows the general trend in each of the series. The line has a positive slope in the left-hand panel and a negative slope in the right-hand panel. These lines are called *trend lines* because they show the general overall movement in the series over time. By extending the trend lines into future time periods, we can make forecasts of the sales of each of the two products. Forecasts for 1990 and 1991 are shown by the circles in each panel of Figure 15.1. The actual forecast value

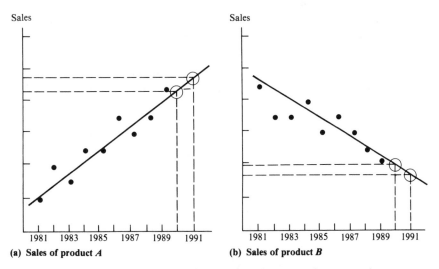

(a) **Sales of product** *A*   (b) **Sales of product** *B*

FIGURE 15.1   Time-Series Plot of Sales of Two Products *A* and *B*. The left-hand plot shows sales of a product *A*, which are generally increasing over the time period 1981–1989. The right-hand plot shows sales of another product *B*, which are decreasing over the 1981–1989 time period. In both cases, the trend lines can be used to forecast sales for 1990 and 1991.

for the sales of product *A* and product *B* could then be read from the vertical axes of panel (a) and panel (b), respectively.

In this example, the trend lines have been fit (i.e., placed in the graphs) by a freehand or visual method. We have simply drawn in the line that appears to best capture the trend in each of the series. While this simple method is sometimes satisfactory, different analysts are likely to draw somewhat different lines. To avoid this problem of possible inconsistency, a more formal regression-based technique is recommended. We hypothesize that sales are a linear function in time. That is,

$$\text{Sales} = f(T)$$

$$\text{Sales} = a + bT$$

where *T* represents time (for example, 1981 would equal 1, 1982 would equal 2, etc.) *a* represents the algebraic intercept of the line, and *b* represents the slope of the line. The slope term tells us the average rate at which sales increase (or decrease) per time period.[1] Once the values of the intercept and slope have been estimated, the equation can be used to forecast sales for future time periods by substituting appropriate values for the time variable *T*.

Let us apply this method to an actual macroeconomic series for the U.S. economy. For illustrative purposes, we will forecast the consumer price index using data from the first quarter of 1970 (1970.1) through the fourth quarter of 1986 (1986.4) to make a forecast for the four quarters of 1987. These data are shown in Table 15.1. In this table, the first column of numbers for the CPI shows first-quarter values, the second column has values for second quarters, and so on.

The time-trend model for this example is

$$\text{CPI} = f(T)$$

$$\text{CPI} = a + bT$$

where *T* represents time ($T = 1$ for 1970.1 and 68 for 1986.4). The values of the intercept *a* and the slope *b* were estimated with the following result:[2]

---

[1]The simple bivariate regression model is discussed in more detail in Section 15.2.

[2]The R^2 value for this model is 0.97, which means that 97 percent of the variation in CPI is explained by this regression. The *t* ratio for the slope term is 28.4. While these statistics are good, they must be interpreted with caution, because this model has severe positive autocorrelation. *Autocorrelation* exists when there is a significant time pattern in the error terms from the regression. Such a pattern violates one of the underlying assumptions of regression analysis. There are econometric procedures to deal with autocorrelation that are beyond the scope of our discussion. Using those methods in this case, however, does not substantially alter the slope and intercept terms found in the simple model reported. The *t* ratio for time is cut about in half but is still at an acceptable level.

TABLE 15.1   Consumer Price Index: All Urban Consumers
(1967 = 100)

Observation	First Quarter	Second Quarter	Third Quarter	Fourth Quarter
1970	113.90	115.73	117.03	118.57
1971	119.47	120.83	122.03	122.70
1972	123.67	124.67	125.80	126.93
1973	128.70	131.53	134.43	137.57
1974	141.43	145.43	149.87	154.23
1975	157.03	159.50	162.90	165.50
1976	167.10	169.17	171.87	173.80
1977	176.87	180.67	183.30	185.33
1978	188.47	193.37	197.93	201.93
1979	206.97	214.07	221.13	227.60
1980	236.47	245.00	249.63	256.17
1981	262.93	269.03	276.73	280.70
1982	283.00	287.33	292.77	293.37
1983	293.23	296.90	300.47	303.07
1984	306.37	309.73	313.07	315.37
1985	317.43	321.23	323.60	326.50
1986	327.30	326.50	328.93	330.80

Source: Citibase: Citibank economic database (New York: Citibank, N.A., 1986).

$$CPI = 84.41 + 3.76T$$

Substituting the appropriate values for T, the forecasts for 1987 are obtained as follows:

1987.1 CPI $= 84.41 + 3.76(69) = 343.85$

1987.2 CPI $= 84.41 + 3.76(70) = 347.61$

1987.3 CPI $= 84.41 + 3.76(71) = 351.37$

1987.4 CPI $= 84.41 + 3.76(72) = 355.13$

The values that would be obtained by using this trend equation for the entire period from 1970.1 through 1987.4 are plotted in Figure 15.2 along with the actual data for the CPI from 1970.1 through 1986.4. The series predicted from the equation is labeled TFCPI, for trend forecast of consumer price index, and is shown by the dotted line in Figure 15.2.

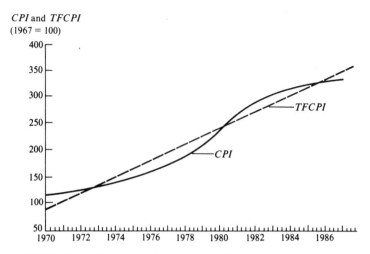

FIGURE 15.2   Consumer Price Index with Trend Forecast.
The consumer price index (CPI) for 1970.1 through 1986.4 is seen to
fluctuate above and below the long-term trend line (TFCPI) used to
forecast the consumer price index into 1987. The forecast values for
1987 are 343.85, 347.61, 351.37, and 355.13 for the first through
fourth quarters, respectively.

15.2.2 A Simple Autoregressive Model

Autoregressive models are models that include a lagged value of the variable
to be estimated in the prediction equation. The most simple general form of
such a model is

$$Y_{t+1} = Y_t$$

where Y_{t+1} is the forecast value of the series one time period into the future
$(t+1)$, and Y_t is the current value of that same series. An example of such
a model is shown in Table 15.2, where a sales series is forecast. If S is used
to represent sales, the model is

$$S_{t+1} = S_t$$

The arrows indicate how each forecast value is derived from the previous
period's actual sales.

These sales data are also graphed in Figure 15.3. Note how the forecast
series shown by the dashed line and circles follows the same pattern as the
original data series. Arrows in Figure 15.3 are used again to illustrate how
the forecast values are related to the original sales data. In both Table 15.2
and Figure 15.3 you see that the 1991 forecast equals the 1990 forecast. That

TABLE 15.2   A Simple Autoregressive Sales Forecast

Year	Actual Sales (S_t)	Forecast Sales (S_{t+1})
1985	40	—
1986	60	40
1987	100	60
1988	120	100
1989	100	120
1990	—	100
1991	—	100

is so because we do not have a 1990 actual value on which to base the 1991 forecast. Thus we assume that the forecast for 1990 will be correct (i.e., will prove to be the actual value for 1990), and thus the 1991 forecast should equal that value (100 in Table 15.2 or Figure 15.3). If we wanted to forecast several more years, this same assumption would be made, and thus forecasts of sales for 1992, 1993, and 1994 also would be 100.

This simple autoregressive model is used more often than one might

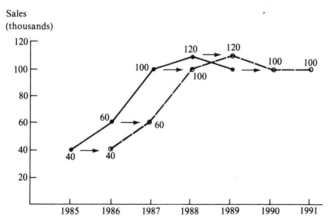

FIGURE 15.3   A Simple Autoregressive Forecast of Sales.
The actual sales data are shown by the black dots. Forecast values are shown by the circles. For each period, you can see that the forecast is the actual value from the previous period. When no actual value is available (e.g., 1990), the forecast value for the next period is assumed to equal the previous forecast value (e.g., the 1991 forecast equals the 1990 forecast).

think. It is the equivalent of being asked what you think the weather will be like tomorrow and, in the absence of any information about weather changes, you answer that tomorrow's weather will be essentially today's weather. For this reason, the simple autoregressive method is sometimes called a *naive forecasting model.*

To further illustrate the simple autoregressive model, let us apply it to the consumer price index data given originally in Table 15.1. The last year's data, along with the simple autoregressive forecast for 1987, are shown in the following table:

Period	Actual CPI	Autoregressive Forecast of CPI
1986.1	327.30	—
1986.2	326.50	327.30
1986.3	328.93	326.50
1986.4	330.80	328.93
1987.1	—	330.80
1987.2	—	330.80
1987.3	—	330.80
1987.4	—	330.80

Note that as the arrows indicate, the forecast for each quarter is the actual value from the previous quarter. For 1987.2, 1987.3., and 1987.4, there are no actual values for the previous quarter. For these periods, the previous forecast is assumed to be correct (i.e., actual = forecast) and so is used to forecast the next period as well.

Figure 15.4 shows the actual values of the consumer price index (CPI) from 1985.1 through 1986.4 along with the forecast values (SARF-CPI) for 1985.1 through 1987.4 based on the simple autoregressive forecasting model. (SARF is an acronym for simple autoregressive forecast.) You can see in this figure that the forecast series parallels the actual series with a one-quarter lag and that the forecast levels off at the 1987.1 level based on the assumption stated earlier.

Since we have used two different models to forecast the consumer price index, it would be useful to illustrate one method for evaluating which method works the best.[3] We will use the root mean squared error (RMSE), which is calculated using the following equation:

$$RMSE = \sqrt{\Sigma(A - F)^2/n}$$

[3]Several methods for evaluating forecasting models were presented in Chapter 14. These were mean absolute deviation (MAD), mean absolute percentage error (MAPE), and root mean squared error (RMSE). A formula for use in calculating each of these can be found on page 354.

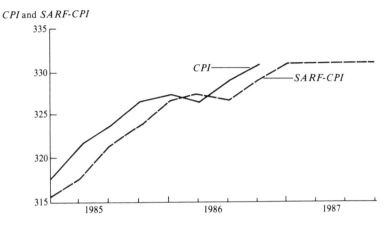

FIGURE 15.4   Consumer Price Index with Simple Autoregressive Forecast.
The simple autoregressive forecast of sales follows the original series in
a parallel manner showing the one quarter lag between the forecast
value (SARF-CPI) and the actual value (CPI).

where A represents the actual value, F represents the forecast value, and n represents the number of periods used in the calculation. For our purposes, the RMSEs are calculated using the 67 periods from 1970.2 through 1986.4 (1970.1 could not be used because there was no forecast using the simple autoregressive model for that period). The results are as follows:

Forecast Method for CPI	Root Mean Squared Error
Trend	11.60
Autoregressive	3.83

Thus we can conclude that for this time period (i.e., 1970.2 through 1986.4) and for this series (CPI), the simple autoregressive model worked better than the time-trend model. The actual data for the consumer price index and both forecasts are given for 1970.1 through 1987.4 in Table 15.3.

15.2.3 An Exponential Smoothing Model

There is a good deal of evidence that exponential smoothing models can be used very effectively in forecasting many time series.[4] There are many var-

---

[4] See, for example, Everette S. Gardner, Jr., and David G. Dannenbring, "Forecasting with Exponential Smoothing: Some Guidelines for Model Selection," *Decision Sciences*, 11, 1980, pp. 370–383; and John T. Mentzer and James E. Cox, Jr., "Familiarity, Application, and Performance of Sales Forecasting Techniques," *Journal of Forecasting*, 3(1), 1984, pp. 27–36.

TABLE 15.3 Consumer Price Index and Two Forecasts of the CPI

Observation	Time	Consumer Price Index	Trend Forecast	Simple Autoregressive Forecast
1970.1	1.00	113.90	88.17	NA
1970.2	2.00	115.73	91.93	113.90
1970.3	3.00	117.03	95.68	115.73
1970.4	4.00	118.57	99.44	117.03
1971.1	5.00	119.47	103.20	118.57
1971.2	6.00	120.83	106.95	119.47
1971.3	7.00	122.03	110.71	120.83
1971.4	8.00	122.70	114.47	122.03
1972.1	9.00	123.67	118.22	122.70
1972.2	10.00	124.67	121.98	123.67
1972.3	11.00	125.80	125.74	124.67
1972.4	12.00	126.93	129.49	125.80
1973.1	13.00	128.70	133.25	126.93
1973.2	14.00	131.53	137.00	128.70
1973.3	15.00	134.43	140.76	131.53
1973.4	16.00	137.57	144.52	134.43
1974.1	17.00	141.43	148.27	137.57
1974.2	18.00	145.43	152.03	141.43
1974.3	19.00	149.87	155.79	145.43
1974.4	20.00	154.23	159.54	149.87
1975.1	21.00	157.03	163.30	154.23
1975.2	22.00	159.50	167.06	157.03
1975.3	23.00	162.90	170.81	159.50
1975.4	24.00	165.50	174.57	162.90
1976.1	25.00	167.10	178.32	165.50
1976.2	26.00	169.17	182.08	167.10
1976.3	27.00	171.87	185.81	169.17
1976.4	28.00	173.80	189.59	171.87
1977.1	29.00	176.87	193.35	173.80
1977.2	30.00	180.67	197.11	176.87
1977.3	31.00	183.30	200.86	180.67
1977.4	32.00	185.33	204.62	183.30
1978.1	33.00	188.47	208.38	185.33
1978.2	34.00	193.37	212.13	188.47
1978.3	35.00	197.93	215.89	193.37
1978.4	36.00	201.93	219.64	197.93
1979.1	37.00	206.97	223.40	201.93

TABLE 15.3   Continued

Observation	Time	Consumer Price Index	Trend Forecast	Simple Autoregressive Forecast
1979.2	38.00	214.07	227.16	206.97
1979.3	39.00	221.13	230.91	214.07
1979.4	40.00	227.60	234.67	221.13
1980.1	41.00	236.47	238.43	227.60
1980.2	42.00	245.00	242.18	236.47
1980.3	43.00	249.63	245.94	245.00
1980.4	44.00	256.17	249.70	249.63
1981.1	45.00	262.93	253.45	256.17
1981.2	46.00	269.03	257.21	262.93
1981.3	47.00	276.73	260.96	269.03
1981.4	48.00	280.70	264.72	276.73
1982.1	49.00	283.00	268.48	280.70
1982.2	50.00	287.33	272.23	283.00
1982.3	51.00	292.77	275.99	287.33
1982.4	52.00	293.37	279.75	292.77
1983.1	53.00	293.23	283.50	293.37
1983.2	54.00	296.90	287.26	293.23
1983.3	55.00	300.47	291.02	296.90
1983.4	56.00	303.07	294.77	300.47
1984.1	57.00	306.37	298.53	303.07
1984.2	58.00	309.73	302.28	306.37
1984.3	59.00	313.07	306.04	309.73
1984.4	60.00	315.37	309.80	313.07
1985.1	61.00	317.43	313.55	315.37
1985.2	62.00	321.23	317.31	317.43
1985.3	63.00	323.60	321.07	321.23
1985.4	64.00	326.50	324.82	323.60
1986.1	65.00	327.30	328.58	326.50
1986.2	66.00	326.50	332.34	327.30
1986.3	67.00	328.93	336.09	326.50
1986.4	68.00	330.80	339.85	328.93
1987.1	69.00	NA	343.60	330.80
1987.2	70.00	NA	347.36	330.80
1987.3	71.00	NA	351.12	330.80
1987.4	72.00	NA	354.87	330.80

Source: Consumer Price Index is from Citibase: Citibank economic database (New York: Citibank, N.A., 1986).

iations of the basic simple exponential smoothing model that we will not present here. The model has been extended to include both trend and seasonality components, as well as other enhancements.[5] The most basic exponential smoothing model may be written as

$$F_{t+1} = wA_t + (1 - w)F_t$$

where F_{t+1} is the forecast value for time period $t+1$ (i.e., one time period ahead), A_t is the actual value of the series at the time period t, F_t is the value that was forecast for period t, and w is a weighting factor that is between 0 and 1. A weight of 0 (that is, $w=0$) would give no consideration to the most recently observed actual value and full weight to the last forecast. At the other extreme, a weight of 1 (that is, $w=1$) gives full weight to the value we most recently observed and ignores the last forecast. Note that if $w=1$, this model is the same as the simple autoregressive model presented in the preceding section.

The exponential smoothing model has the desirable feature of "learning" from past errors. This can be shown if we use some algebraic manipulations to allow us to write the model in an alternative form. We start with the original model:

$$F_{t+1} = wA_t + (1 - w)F_t$$

Multiplying through the parentheses by F_t yields

$$F_{t+1} = wA_t + F_t - wF_t$$

Rearranging the order of terms, we have

$$F_{t+1} = F_t + wA_t - wF_t$$

Now, factoring out w from the last two terms leaves

$$F_{t+1} = F_t + w(A_t - F_t)$$

In this form we see that the forecast for the next time period is equal to the last forecast plus some fraction of the error that resulted from the last forecast (the error is $A_t - F_t$).

---

[5]More complete discussions of exponential smoothing and related models can be found in Robert S. Pindyck and Daniel L. Rubinfeld, *Econometric Models and Economic Forecasts*, 2d Ed. (New York: McGraw-Hill, 1981); and Spyros Makridakis, Steven C. Wheelwright, and Victor E. McGee, *Forecasting: Methods and Applications*, 2d Ed. (New York: Wiley, 1983).

While at first glance it appears that this model only uses information from one period past, in truth, all the data available are used. Every actual observation and all previous forecasts are included. However, the earliest actual and forecast values are given progressively smaller weights as we work backward in time. This can be demonstrated as follows starting with the original form of the model once more:

$$F_{t+1} = wA_t + (1 - w)F_t$$

It follows that

$$F_t = wA_{t-1} + (1 - w)F_{t-1}$$

Substituting this into the original model for F_t, we have

$$F_{t+1} = wA_t + (1 - w)[wA_{t-1} + (1 - w)F_{t-1}]$$
$$= wA_t + (1 - w)wA_{t-1} + (1 - w)^2F_{t-1}$$

But

$$F_{t-1} = wA_{t-2} + (1 - w)F_{t-2}$$

Substituting this into the equation immediately above the word *but*, we get

$$F_{t+1} = wA_t + (1 - w)wA_{t-1} + (1 - w)^2[wA_{t-2} + (1 - w)F_{t-2}]$$
$$= wA_t + (1 - w)wA_{t-1} + (1 - w)^2wA_{t-2} + (1 - w)^3F_{t-2}$$

We could keep doing this for as far back as we have data, but the issue should now be clear. The weights that are assigned to previous values become successively smaller and smaller as we go further back. For example, suppose $w = 0.8$, then in forecasting to time period $t+1$, the weights given to the actual value at times t, $t-1$, and $t-2$ are as follows:

Time Period	Weight for Actual Value
t	$w = 0.8$
$t - 1$	$(1 - w)w = (0.2)(0.8) = 0.16$
$t - 2$	$(1 - w)^2w = (0.2)^2(0.8) = 0.032$

The weight for the forecast value at $t-2$ would be $(1-w)^3 = (1-0.8)^3 = (0.2)^3 = 0.008$. So, while all previous values of the series have some impact on the forecast, their importance diminishes "exponentially." Thus the method is called *exponential smoothing*. Note that if w is small, less weight is given to the actual values and more weight is given to forecast values. If w were equal to 0.1, the three weights shown above would be for t, 0.1; for $t-1$, 0.09; and for $t-2$, 0.009. The weight for F_{t-2} would be $(1-0.1)^3$ or $(0.9)^3$, which is 0.729 (i.e., a larger weight than the 0.008 when $w=0.8$).

To use the exponential smoothing model, we have to assign some value for the forecast at the first observation, since at the start we have no forecast. One approach is to assign the actual observation at time period 1 as the forecast for that period. Other approaches include finding the average of all the actual values or the first two actual values and use either of these for the first period forecast. Since the importance of this early value diminishes rapidly, this decision is usually not critical, especially when a long series is available.

To illustrate the calculation of a simple exponential smoothing forecast, we will use the sales data first shown in Table 15.2. We will use a weighting factor of $w=0.8$, and for the initial forecast value, we will use the average of the first two observations. The calculations are illustrated in Table 15.4.

The sales data and the exponential smoothing forecast of sales are shown in a time-series plot in Figure 15.5. The forecast values were calculated using a 0.8 weighting factor, as described earlier, and are shown by the dotted line.

The simple exponential smoothing model can be used to forecast a series *if* the series is relatively stationary (i.e., has no long-term positive or negative

TABLE 15.4   Sales Forecast Using Simple Exponential Smoothing ($w = 0.8$)

Period	Actual Sales (A)	Forecast Sales (F)	Determination of F^a
1985	40	50[b]	$(40+60)/2 = 50$
1986	60	42	$0.8(40)+0.2(50)=42.0$
1987	100	56.4	$0.8(60)+0.2(42)=56.4$
1988	120	91.28	$0.8(100)+0.2(56.4)=91.28$
1989	100	114.26	$0.8(120)+0.2(91.28)=114.26$
1990	—	102.85	$0.8(100)+0.2(114.26)=102.85$
1991	—	102.85[c]	$0.8(102.85)+0.2(102.85)=102.85$

[a] For all but the first or "seed" forecast value, the following equation is used to determine the forecast for each period:

$$F_{t+1} = wA_t + (1 - w)F_t$$

[b] We have used the average of the first two actual values as the "seed" value.

[c] For the calculation of a forecast value for 1991, we need an actual value for 1990, but since such a value is unavailable, we assume that the 1990 forecast will be correct and thus have used 102.85 as the actual 1990 value.

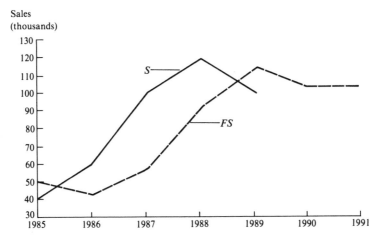

FIGURE 15.5 Simple Exponential Smoothing Forecast of Sales. The actual sales data are shown by the line marked with an *S*. The forecast values are shown by the dotted line. Note how the forecast value reacts to the actual value with a lag.

trend). The weighted-average exchange value of the U.S. dollar is such a series. (While the short period used may appear to have a trend, a longer-term series has been reasonably stable.) Table 15.5 shows the actual value of this index for 1975.1 through 1986.4, along with the exponential smoothing

TABLE 15.5 Weighted-Average Exchange Value of U.S. Dollar With a Simple Exponential Smoothing Forecast ($w = 0.7$)

Observation	Exchange Rate	Forecast Exchange Rate
1975.1	95.02	95.89
1975.2	95.00	95.28
1975.3	101.12	95.08
1975.4	102.87	99.31
1976.1	103.99	101.80
1976.2	106.55	103.34
1976.3	106.31	105.59
1976.4	105.66	106.09
1977.1	105.29	105.79
1977.2	104.51	105.44
1977.3	103.18	104.79

(continued)

TABLE 15.5 Continued

Observation	Exchange Rate	Forecast Exchange Rate
1977.4	100.41	103.67
1978.1	95.91	101.39
1978.2	95.20	97.55
1978.3	90.65	95.91
1978.4	87.81	92.22
1979.1	88.14	89.13
1979.2	89.79	88.44
1979.3	86.97	89.38
1979.4	87.37	87.69
1980.1	87.38	87.47
1980.2	87.78	87.41
1980.3	85.41	87.67
1980.4	88.96	86.09
1981.1	94.54	88.10
1981.2	103.08	92.61
1981.3	110.05	99.94
1981.4	105.36	107.01
1982.1	109.92	105.86
1982.2	114.02	108.70
1982.3	119.82	112.43
1982.4	122.22	117.60
1983.1	119.38	120.83
1983.2	123.01	119.82
1983.3	128.71	122.05
1983.4	130.20	126.71
1984.1	131.62	129.15
1984.2	132.77	130.88
1984.3	141.74	132.20
1984.4	147.24	138.88
1985.1	156.47	144.73
1985.2	149.06	152.95
1985.3	139.21	150.23
1985.4	128.20	142.52
1986.1	119.49	132.49
1986.2	114.24	123.39
1986.3	108.34	116.98
1986.4	107.01	110.94
1987.1	NA	108.19
1987.2	NA	108.19
1987.3	NA	108.19
1987.4	NA	108.19

Source: Exchange rate data are from Citibase: Citibank economic database (New York: Citibank, N.A., 1986).

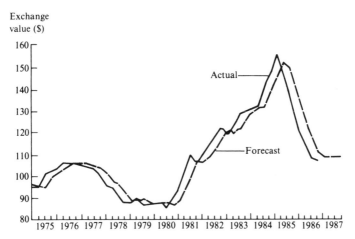

FIGURE 15.6   Simple Exponential Smoothing Forecast of the Weighted-Average Exchange Value of the U. S. Dollar.
The forecast of the weighted-average exchange value of the U.S. dollar is shown by the dotted line and was developed using the model $F_{t+1} = WA_t + (1 - w)F_t$, with $w = 0.7$.

forecast values for 1975.1 through 1987.4. The weighting constant w used for this forecast was 0.7.

The simple exponential smoothing forecast of the weighted-average exchange value of the U.S. dollar is shown along with the actual series in Figure 15.6. The forecast values are shown by the dotted line, which you see follows the same general pattern as the original series. There is a lag as the forecast adjusts to the actual observations and "learns" from previous forecast errors.

15.3   THE BIVARIATE LINEAR REGRESSION MODEL

Bivariate regression analysis is a statistical procedure that enables us to estimate the functional relationship between a dependent variable Y and an independent, or causal, variable X. The basic population bivariate (meaning two variables) regression model can be expressed as follows:

$$Y = f(X)$$
$$Y = \beta_0 + \beta_1 X + e$$

where Y is the dependent variable, X is the independent variable, β_0 is the true population regression intercept, β_1 is the true population slope term associated with X, and e is the error term. In practice, we do not know this true population regression function, so we estimate it based on sample data.

The estimated bivariate regression equation is expressed as

$$\hat{Y} = b_0 + b_1 X$$

where $\hat{Y}$ is the value of Y estimated by the regression equation, b_0 is the estimate of β_0, and b_1 is the estimate of β_1. The estimators b_0 and b_1 are determined using an ordinary least-squares procedure that finds the values of b_0 and b_1 that minimize the square of the difference between actual observations of the dependent variable Y and the values that are estimated by the regression equation ($\hat{Y}$). That is, we want values of b_0 and b_1 that minimize

$$\Sigma(Y - \hat{Y})^2 = \Sigma(Y - b_0 - b_1 X)^2$$

Taking the partial derivatives of this function with respect to b_0 and b_1, setting them equal to zero, and then solving for b_0 and b_1 yields

$$b_1 = \frac{n\Sigma XY - \Sigma X \Sigma Y}{n\Sigma X^2 - (\Sigma X)^2}$$

$$b_0 = \frac{\Sigma Y}{n} - b_1 \frac{\Sigma X}{n}$$

where n equals the number of observations on X and Y. These are called the *normal equations*.

As a simple example, let us apply this method to the hypothetical sales data first shown in Table 15.2. We will hypothesize that sales Y are a function of time X, where $X = 1$ for 1985. The data are then

Year	Sales Y	Time X	XY	X²
1985	40	1	40	1
1986	60	2	120	4
1987	100	3	300	9
1988	120	4	480	16
1989	100	5	500	25
	$\Sigma Y = 420$	$\Sigma X = 15$	$\Sigma XY = 1440$	$\Sigma X^2 = 55$

From the preceding normal equations, we calculate b_0 and b_1 as follows:

$$b_1 = \frac{5(1440) - 15(420)}{5(55) - 15^2}$$

$$= \frac{7200 - 6300}{275 - 225}$$

$$= \frac{900}{50}$$

$$= 18.0$$

$$b_0 = \frac{420}{5} - 18.0\frac{15}{5}$$

$$= 84 - 54$$

$$= 30$$

The estimated regression equation for sales Y as a function of time X is then

$$\hat{Y} = 30 + 18X$$

This model can then be used to forecast sales for 1990 and 1991 by letting X equal 6 and 7, respectively. The forecasts are

For 1990:

$$\text{Sales} = 30 + 18(6) = 138$$

For 1991:

$$\text{Sales} = 30 + 18(7) = 156$$

These results are shown in Figure 15.7

Such regression models are normally not calculated by hand but are done using a computer. When large data sets are used, it is far more efficient to use a computer, and in addition, the output one obtains almost always includes various statistics that are useful in evaluating the results. A complete discussion of these statistical evaluations is beyond the scope of this text.[6]

---

[6]For a complete discussion of bivariate regression models, including the underlying assumptions, see Robert S. Pindyck and Daniel L. Rubinfeld, *Econometric Models and Economic Forecasts*, 2d Ed. (New York: McGraw-Hill, 1981), Chaps. 1 to 3.

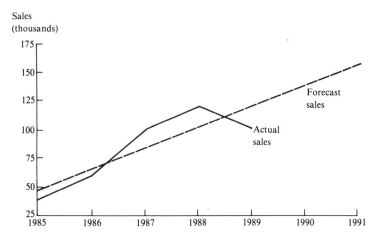

FIGURE 15.7   Actual Sales and Forecast Sales.
The original sales series is shown along with the simple linear trend
through sales as determined using a bivariate regression model. The
model of sales (Y) as a function of time (X) is $\hat{Y} = 30 + 18X$.

However, we will consider three questions you should always ask when using
a regression model:

1. Does the sign of the coefficient for the independent variable (i.e.,
   for b_1) make sense?

2. Is the coefficient for the independent variable sufficiently different
   from zero that rejection of the following null hypothesis is
   warranted?

$$H_0:\beta_1 = 0 \qquad \text{vs.} \qquad H_1:\beta_1 \neq 0$$

3. How much of the variation in the dependent variable is explained
   by the regression equation?

Let us consider how we can answer each of these questions.

First, does the sign on the slope term make sense? This answer must
come from your own knowledge of the activity that is being modeled. For
example, if you were working with the sales data used earlier and were to
look at a plot of sales over time, you would certainly expect the slope term
to be positive. That is, in Figure 15.7, sales appear to increase over time.
Thus the slope term of $+18$ makes sense.

Second, we want to test $H_0:\beta_1 = 0$, because if the true slope is zero, this means that there is no relationship between X and Y (i.e., X does not affect Y). However, if the slope is significantly different from zero, we conclude that X does affect Y (or in this simple example we would conclude that there is a significant positive trend to sales). The hypothesis is tested using a t test in which the calculated t ratio (t_c) is found as follows:

$$t_c = \frac{b_1}{\text{standard error of } b_1}$$

The standard error of b_1 is a normal part of regression output, as is t_c. For our sales problem, the standard error of b_1 is 6.0, and thus $t_c = 18/6 = 3.0$. We compare this value against the table t value (t_T) at $n - 2$ degrees of freedom and whatever significance level we desire (typically 5 percent). In this small example we have $5 - 2$, or 3, degrees of freedom, and at a 5 percent significance level, the table value of t is 3.182. The rule is that we reject H_0 if the absolute value of $t_c > t_T$. In this case, $3.0 < 3.182$, so we fail to reject H_0 and conclude that we do not have enough evidence to say that the slope is significantly different than zero.[7] When there are a large number of observations ($n > 30$), a rule of thumb is that H_0 can be rejected if the absolute value of t is greater than 2 (that is, if $|t_c| > 2$, we can say that there is a significant relationship between X and Y).

Third, we want to be able to make a statement about how much of the variation in the dependent variable is explained by this regression model. The value of the coefficient of determination provides this information. The coefficient of determination is

$$R^2 = \frac{\text{variation in } Y \text{ explained}}{\text{total variation in } Y}$$

In computer output, this will appear as "R-SQUARED." For our sales example, $R^2 = 0.75$. Thus 75 percent of the variation in sales is explained by this model.[8]

---

[7]As developed here, this implies a two-tailed hypothesis test because we are testing only to see if the slope term is *different* from zero. If we wanted to test to see if it is greater or less than zero, a one-tailed test would be appropriate and the alternative hypothesis would be either $H_1:\beta_1 > 0$ or $H_1:\beta_1 < 0$. For a two-tailed test, the table value of t is found under the column that is headed with a number that represents the desired significance level divided by 2. Thus, for our example with a significance level of 5 percent (0.05), we used the 0.025 column of the t table. For a one-tailed test, we would use the column with the heading value that corresponds to our significance level. Thus, in this example for a one-tailed test, the table t value would be 2.353 and we would reject H_0 because $t_c > t_T$.

[8]Actually, in this case, we are not supposing that time is really a causal factor. In our next example a more clearly causal relationship will be examined.

Now that we have the basic bivariate linear regression model in hand, let us apply it to a model for predicting existing home sales (*EHS*) in the United States. We will hypothesize that sales of existing homes are a function of the level of employment (*EMP*). That is, our regression model will be

$$EHS = b_0 + b_1 EMP$$

The data for this estimating model are shown in Table 15.6 for the time frame covering July 1982 (1982.07) to March 1987 (1987.03) and are plotted in Figure 15.8. It is always a good idea to look at the data graphically as well as in tabular form to get a better feel for the relationship between the variables.

TABLE 15.6 Existing Single-Family Home Sales in Thousands *(EHS)* and Total U.S. Civilian Employment in Thousands *(EMP)*

Observation	EHS	EMP
1982.07	1890.00	99493.00
1982.08	1900.00	99633.00
1982.09	1960.00	99504.00
1982.10	2090.00	99215.00
1982.11	2230.00	99112.00
1982.12	2290.00	99032.00
1983.01	2600.00	99168.00
1983.02	2440.00	99112.00
1983.03	2620.00	99189.00
1983.04	2630.00	99573.00
1983.05	2760.00	99671.00
1983.06	2770.00	100573.00
1983.07	2800.00	101216.00
1983.08	2800.00	101597.00
1983.09	2820.00	102024.00
1983.10	2780.00	102049.00
1983.11	2720.00	102720.00
1983.12	2860.00	102980.00
1984.01	2890.00	103199.00
1984.02	2900.00	103856.00
1984.03	2960.00	103964.00
1984.04	3030.00	104374.00
1984.05	2970.00	105219.00
1984.06	2920.00	105545.00

TABLE 15.6   Continued

Observation	EHS	EMP
1984.07	2790.00	105446.00
1984.08	2770.00	105164.00
1984.09	2730.00	105468.00
1984.10	2740.00	105646.00
1984.11	2830.00	105967.00
1984.12	2870.00	106200.00
1985.01	2980.00	106291.00
1985.02	2890.00	106605.00
1985.03	3000.00	106965.00
1985.04	3020.00	106949.00
1985.05	3040.00	106995.00
1985.06	3070.00	106541.00
1985.07	3170.00	106842.00
1985.08	3430.00	107136.00
1985.09	3480.00	107602.00
1985.10	3530.00	107792.00
1985.11	3450.00	107978.00
1985.12	3520.00	108149.00
1986.01	3300.00	108892.00
1986.02	3270.00	108557.00
1986.03	3200.00	108807.00
1986.04	3570.00	108969.00
1986.05	3450.00	109165.00
1986.06	3390.00	109613.00
1986.07	3470.00	109887.00
1986.08	3610.00	110067.00
1986.09	3770.00	109987.00
1986.10	3810.00	110192.00
1986.11	3910.00	110432.00
1986.12	4060.00	110637.00
1987.01	3480.00	111011.00
1987.02	3690.00	111382.00
1987.03	3710.00	111368.00

Source: Citibase: Citibank economic database (New York: Citibank, N. A., 1987).

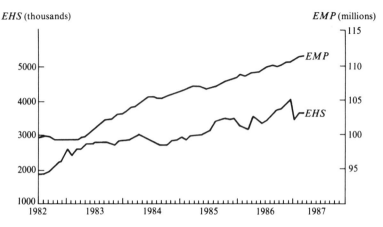

FIGURE 15.8   Existing Single-Family Home Sales (*EHS*) and total U.S.
Civilian Employment (*EMP*).
Existing home sales (*EHS*) and civilian employment (*EMP*) both
increase over the time period from July 1982 to March 1987. Home
sales are in thousands of units measured on the left scale, and
employment is in millions of people measured on the right scale.

Statistical results for the bivariate regression model $EHS = b_0 + b_1 EMP$
are as follows:[9]

Coefficients	Standard Error	t Ratio
$b_0 = -8977.69$	798.1	-11.2
$b_1 = 0.114$	0.0076	15.0
$R^2 = 0.804$		
Standard error of regression $= 223.1$		

[9]This model also has positive first-order autocorrelation, which results when the error terms for
one period are correlated with the error from the immediately preceding period. The Durbin-Watson
statistic is one test for the autocorrelation that often occurs in doing regression analyses with time-series
data. When autocorrelation exists, the *t* tests may suggest statistical significance when it is not warranted.
A Durbin-Watson statistic close to 2.0 is desired. The value of 0.804 found for this model is indicative
of positive autocorrelation. One possible cure for an autocorrelation problem is to use first differences of
the variables. The problem also may be corrected by including additional independent variables. Another
approach is to use a regression technique known as the *Cochrane-Orcutt procedure*. Applying that method
in this example gives a Durbin-Watson statistic of 2.3 and generally improves the model. A more complete
discussion of autocorrelation is beyond the scope of this text. Readers are encouraged to pursue the topic
in Robert S. Pindyck and Daniel L. Rubinfeld, *Econometric Models and Economic Forecasts*, 2d Ed.
(New York: McGraw-Hill, 1981).

Thus the regression equation may be written as follows:

$$\widehat{EHS} = -8977.69 + 0.114EMP$$

There were 57 observations used to estimate the equation, so we have 55 degrees of freedom ($55 = 57 - 2$) in performing a t test for the null hypothesis: $H_0:\beta_1 = 0$ versus $H_1:\beta_1 \neq 0$. At a 5 percent significance level and 55 degrees of freedom, the table value of t is 1.96. Thus, since $t_c > t_T(15.0 > 1.96)$, we can reject H_0 and conclude that there is a statistically significant relationship between existing single-family home sales and the level of employment. The coefficient of determination R^2 is 0.804. This tells us that 80.4 percent of the variation in existing single-family home sales is explained by this regression model (i.e., by changes in employment).

In the statistical results given above you also see something called the *standard error of the regression*. (It is sometimes also called the *standard error of the estimate*.) This measure can be used to provide an approximate 95 percent confidence interval around the point estimate derived from the regression model. Let us assume that employment is 100 million (i.e., $EMP = 100,000$, since the employment data are in thousands). Our best point estimate for existing single-family home sales *(EHS)* would be

$$\widehat{EHS} = 8977.69 + 0.114(100,000)$$
$$= 2422.31$$

However, point estimates are almost sure to be wrong, so we often want to give some interval estimate. In economic work it is common to use a 95 percent confidence interval. Such an interval can be *approximated* using the standard error of the regression as follows:

Approximate 95% confidence interval = point estimate ± 2 (standard error of the regression)

In our current problem, this would be

Approximate 95% confidence interval $= 2422.31 \pm 2(223.1)$
$$= 2422.31 \pm 446.2$$
$$= 1976.11 \text{ to } 2868.51$$

Our objective is to use the regression model as the basis for a forecast of *EHS*. To do so, we must first forecast employment (*EMP*) through the forecast period, which for this example will be the remaining 9 months of 1987. A simple exponential smoothing forecast of *EMP* was made, and those

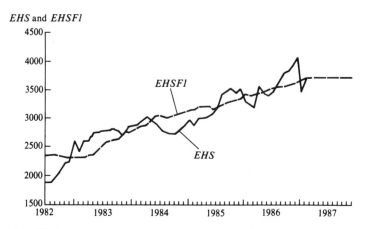

FIGURE 15.9   Existing Home Sales (*EHS*) and a Bivariate Regression Model
Forecast (*EHSF1*).
This graph helps us see how well the regression model fits the
historical time period (1982.07 to 1987.03) as well as what the
forecast for 1987.04 to 1987.12 looks like in comparison with what
has actually been observed.

values were substituted into the regression model for 1987.04 through
1987.12 (i.e., April through December 1987). The results are shown in
Figure 15.9. The dotted line represents the values of *EHS* predicted using
the regression equation (for 1982.07 through 1987.03, the actual values of
EMP were used, and for 1987.04 through 1987.12, forecast values of *EMP*
were used). The predicted, or forecast, values of existing single-family housing sales are labeled *EHSF1* in Figure 15.9. (*EHSF1* stands for "existing
home sales forecast 1." We will shortly develop a second forecast called
EHSF2.) The root mean squared error for this model was 219.15. Note that
the forecast is level for the period 1987.04 to 1987.12. This is so because
the simple exponential smoothing method of forecasting *EMP* provides the
same value throughout the forecast period. That value was *EMP* = 111,368,
and the corresponding value for existing housing sales was *EHSF1* = 3704.83.

15.4 MULTIPLE LINEAR REGRESSION MODELS[10]

Multiple linear regression is an extension of the bivariate linear regression
model in which more than one independent, or causal, variable is used. If *Y*

---

[10]We will discuss only the basics of the multiple regression model. For more detail, see Robert
S. Pindyck and Daniel L. Rubinfeld, *Econometric Models and Economic Forecasts*, 2d Ed. (New York:
McGraw-Hill, 1981), especially Chaps. 4 to 6 and 8.

is the dependent variable and X_1 and X_2 are two independent variables that are believed to have a causal affect on Y, the true population regression model can be expressed as follows:

$$Y = \beta_0 + \beta_1 X_1 + \beta_2 X_2 + e$$

where β_0 is the intercept, and β_1 and β_2 are the true population slope parameters that reflect how X_1 and X_2, respectively, are related to Y. The error term is given by e.

The population parameters are estimated in a manner parallel to the estimation of the bivariate regression parameters. The model, as estimated, is

$$\hat{Y} = b_0 + b_1 X_1 + b_2 X_2$$

Conceptually, many more independent variables could be included, but practically, there are advantages to keeping forecasting models relatively simple.

A number of excellent mainframe and microcomputer packages are available to estimate multiple regression equations. These programs provide values for the estimates of the population parameters (i.e., for b_0, b_1, and b_2) as well as other summary statistics, including standard errors for the b values, t ratios, the Durbin-Watson statistic, the standard error of the regression, and the coefficient of determination (R^2). In addition, an adjusted coefficient of determination is normally provided. This is usually called the "ADJUSTED R-SQUARED" or the "CORRECTED R-SQUARED" on computer output. In writing, we usually denote it as $\overline{R}^2$ ("R-bar squared"). The simple R^2 is adjusted in multiple regression analysis to take into account the loss of degrees of freedom as additional independent variables are added to a model. As new variables are added, the R^2 will always increase, even if the new variables are nonsense variables. By adjusting R^2, such artificial increases are prevented. The adjustment process is as follows:

$$\overline{R}^2 = 1 - (1 - R^2)\left(\frac{N-1}{N-K}\right)$$

where N is the number of observations, and K is the number of independent variables in the regression model.

In evaluating a multiple linear regression model, we should ask the same basic questions as with the bivariate linear regression model:

1. Do the signs of the coefficients make sense?
2. Are the coefficients statistically different from zero?

3. What percent of the variation in the dependent variable is explained by the model?

The answer to the first question must be based on our understanding of the theoretical basis for including each variable in the model. For example, if we have a model with sales as a function of price and income, we would expect the coefficient for price to have a negative sign and the coefficient for income to have a positive sign. These expectations have nothing to do with the mathematics of the regression model. They are determined by the analyst's knowledge of an underlying theoretical or logical connection between the independent variables and the dependent variable.

To determine whether the coefficients are statistically different from zero, we test a hypothesis for each independent variable's coefficient. The null hypothesis is

$$H_0: B_i = 0$$

And the alternative hypothesis[11] is

$$H_1: B_i \neq 0$$

For multiple regression, the number of degrees of freedom for the t test is equal to $N - (K + 1)$, where N is the number of observations, and K is the number of independent variables. Otherwise, the t test is the same as for bivariate regression. If the absolute value of t_c is greater than t_T, the null hypothesis can be rejected.

To answer the third question, we should consider the adjusted R^2. For example, if the adjusted R^2 is 0.625, we would say that 62.5 percent of the variation in the dependent variable is explained by the regression model.

Let us now return to the model of existing single-family home sales *(EHS)*. Our original model was a bivariate regression model with *EHS* a function of the level of employment *(EMP)*. Suppose we also hypothesize that *EHS* also may be a function of the mortgage rate *(MR)*; we will use the fixed-rate, conventional mortgage rate as *MR*. Our multiple linear regression model is then

$$\widehat{EHS} = b_0 + b_1 EMP + b_2 MR$$

We would conjecture a positive sign for b_1 and a negative sign for b_2. That is, home sales would be expected to rise as employment increases and home

[11]This form of the alternative hypothesis implies a two-tailed statistical test. For a comparison to a one-tailed test, refer to footnote 7.

sales would be expected to fall as mortgage rates rise (and vice versa). We have already looked at a graph of *EHS* and *EMP* over time (see Figure 15.8). Figure 15.10 shows a similar plot of existing home sales and the mortgage rate. You see in this figure that there is some support for the notion that there is an inverse relationship between *EHS* and *MR*.

The data for the three variables used in this regression are shown in Table 15.7. Summary statistics for this regression are as follows:

	Standard Error	*t Ratio*
$b_0 = 188.99$	1320.83	0.14
$b_1 = 0.0506$	0.0098	5.16
$b_2 = -201.13$	26.27	-7.66

$R^2 = 0.906$; adjusted $R^2 = 0.903$

Standard error of the regression = 155.91

The algebraic equation for the model is

$$\widehat{EHS} = 188.99 \text{ to } 0.0506EMP - 201.13MR$$

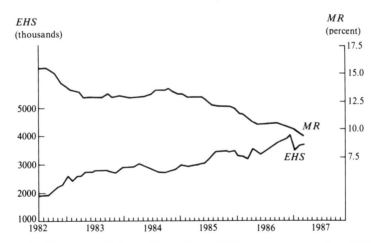

FIGURE 15.10   Existing Home Sales (*EHS*) and Mortgage Rate (*MR*), July 1982 through March 1987.
The conventional fixed-rate mortgage rate (*MR*) is measured in percent terms, as shown on the right-hand scale. Existing home sales (*EHS*) are in thousands of units, as measured on the left-hand scale. It appears that increasing home sales are associated with decreases in the mortgage rate.

TABLE 15.7 Existing Single-Family Homes Sales in Thousands (*EHS*), Total U.S. Civilian Employment in Thousands (*EMP*), and Fixed-Rate Conventional Mortgage Rate (*MR*)

Observation	EHS	EMP	MR
1982.07	1890.00	99493.00	15.53
1982.08	1900.00	99633.00	15.55
1982.09	1960.00	99504.00	15.19
1982.10	2090.00	99215.00	14.97
1982.11	2230.00	99112.00	14.20
1982.12	2290.00	99032.00	13.98
1983.01	2600.00	99168.00	13.54
1983.02	2440.00	99112.00	13.47
1983.03	2620.00	99189.00	13.29
1983.04	2630.00	99573.00	12.82
1983.05	2760.00	99671.00	12.92
1983.06	2770.00	100573.00	12.79
1983.07	2800.00	101216.00	12.80
1983.08	2800.00	101597.00	12.89
1983.09	2820.00	102024.00	13.13
1983.10	2780.00	102049.00	12.94
1983.11	2720.00	102720.00	12.97
1983.12	2860.00	102980.00	13.00
1984.01	2890.00	103199.00	12.82
1984.02	2900.00	103856.00	12.85
1984.03	2960.00	103964.00	12.82
1984.04	3030.00	104374.00	12.91
1984.05	2970.00	105219.00	12.96
1984.06	2920.00	105345.00	13.09
1984.07	2790.00	105446.00	13.46
1984.08	2770.00	105164.00	13.47
1984.09	2730.00	105468.00	13.47
1984.10	2740.00	105646.00	13.67
1984.11	2830.00	105967.00	13.41
1984.12	2870.00	106200.00	13.16
1985.01	2980.00	106291.00	13.10
1985.02	2890.00	106605.00	12.93
1985.03	3000.00	106965.00	12.87
1985.04	3020.00	106949.00	12.90
1985.05	3040.00	106995.00	12.94
1985.06	3070.00	106541.00	12.63
1985.07	3170.00	106842.00	12.23
1985.08	3430.00	107136.00	12.14
1985.09	3480.00	107602.00	12.02

TABLE 15.7   Continued

Observation	EHS	EMP	MR
1985.10	3530.00	107792.00	12.12
1985.11	3450.00	107978.00	11.99
1985.12	3520.00	108149.00	11.88
1986.01	3300.00	108892.00	11.41
1986.02	3270.00	108557.00	11.24
1986.03	3200.00	108807.00	10.87
1986.04	3570.00	108969.00	10.56
1986.05	3450.00	109165.00	10.33
1986.06	3390.00	109613.00	10.38
1986.07	3470.00	109887.00	10.51
1986.08	3610.00	110067.00	10.58
1986.09	3770.00	109987.00	10.47
1986.10	3810.00	110192.00	10.39
1986.11	3910.00	110432.00	10.28
1986.12	4060.00	110637.00	10.13
1987.01	3480.00	111011.00	9.81
1987.02	3690.00	111382.00	9.50
1987.03	3710.00	111368.00	9.36

Source: Citibase: Citibank economic database (New York: Citibank, N. A., 1987).

Do the signs of the coefficients make sense? Yes. We expected a positive coefficient for employment and a negative coefficient for the mortgage rate based on economic reasoning. Are the coefficients significantly different from zero? Using a 5 percent significance level and 54 degrees of freedom for a two-tailed test, the table t value is $t_T = 2.00$. Since the absolute values of both calculated t ratios are greater than 2.00, we can reject the two null hypotheses ($H_0:\beta_1 = 0$ and $H_0:\beta_2 = 0$) and conclude that both independent variables have a statistically significant influence on *EHS*.[12]

The adjusted $R^2 = 0.903$ tells us that this regression model accounts for 90.3 percent of the variation in existing home sales (*EHS*). Compare this to the R^2 of 0.804 for our bivariate regression model.

[12]As is often the case with applications of regression in economics, this model has positive auto-correlation. Using corrective procedures, the Durbin-Watson statistic can be improved from the 0.84 for the model given here to about 1.9. The slope term for *MR* in the corrected model is not significant at a 5 percent level but is significant at a 10 percent level. *EMP* is significant at a 5 percent level in the corrected model as well as in the basic model used here.

We can use this model to make a point estimate of *EHS* for $EMP = 100,000$ and $MR = 12.0$ as follows:

$$EHS = 188.99 + 0.0506(100,000) - 201.13(12.0)$$
$$= 2835.43$$

An *approximate* 95 percent confidence interval can be constructed as follows:

$$95\% \text{ Confidence interval} = EHS + 2(\text{standard error of the regression})$$
$$= 2835.43 \pm 2(155.91)$$
$$= 2835.43 \pm (311.82$$
$$= 2523.61 \text{ to } 3147.25$$

Note that the standard error of the regression is smaller for this multiple regression model than it was for the bivariate regression model (155.91 vs. 223.1).

Once more, our objective is to use this model to forecast existing home sales (*EHS*). To do this, we must now forecast both employment (*EMP*) and the mortgage rate (*MR*) through the forecast period (April 1987 through December 1987). An exponential smoothing model was used for both forecasts with the following results:

For 1987.04 to 1987.12,

$$MRF = 9.36$$

For 1987.04 to 1987.12,

$$EMPF = 111,368$$

where *MRF* and *EMPF* refer to forecast values of the mortgage rate and employment, respectively. These forecast values are the same throughout the period because simple exponential smoothing was used to develop the forecasts. Substituting these values into the regression model yields the following forecast for *EHS*:

For 1987.04 to 1987.12,

$$EHS = 3940.7$$

The values for existing home sales predicted by the regression model for the historical period as well as the forecast period are labeled *EHSF2* in Figure 15.11, where that series is plotted along with the original data (*EHS*).

If you compare this figure with Figure 15.9, you will see that *EHSF2* follows the historical data more closely than *EHSF1* did. The root mean squared error for *EHSF2* is 151.76 (recall that it was 219.15 for *EHSF1*). The forecast of existing home sales is constant throughout the forecast period because the values forecast for employment and the mortgage rate are constant as well.

15.5   TIME-SERIES DECOMPOSITION

The last forecasting technique we will describe is known as *classical time-series decomposition*. This approach provides a methodology for breaking a time series into several components (i.e., for decomposing the series). It is a strictly time-series method like those discussed in Section 15.1 in that the only variable involved is the one for which the forecast is sought. Historical data for the series are analyzed for certain patterns that are then projected into the future to provide the economic forecast.

The time-series decomposition approach to forecasting assumes that the time series is composed of four components:

A long-term trend

Seasonal variations

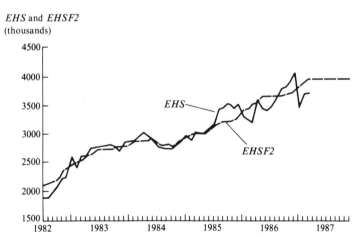

FIGURE 15.11   Existing Home Sales (*EHS*) and a Multiple Regression Model Forecast (*EHSF2*).
This graph shows how well the multiple regression model of existing home sales (*EHS*) as a function of employment (*EMP*) and the mortgage rate (*MR*) fits the actual data through the historical period (1982.07 to 1987.03). We also see what the predicted level of existing home sales is for the forecast period (1987.04 to 1987.12).

Cyclical fluctuations

Irregular movements

The model we will develop postulates a multiplicative relationship between these components. If we let Y represent the data series we want to forecast, the model can be written as

$$Y = T \times S \times C \times I$$

where T is the trend component, S is the seasonal component, C is the cyclical component, and I is the irregular component. Each of these will be described below, and then the use of this method will be explained in the context of developing a forecast for manufacturers' shipments of mobile homes.

The trend represents the long-term movement of the data over a period of many years. If the series is stationary (i.e., flat), then only seasonal, cyclical, and irregular movements will exist. The method can still be used in this case, although it may be that some other technique, perhaps exponential smoothing, would be called for. The trend component is usually estimated using linear regression analysis with the deseasonalized data series as a function of time. When the deseasonalized series appears to be nonlinear, it is a simple matter to fit a nonlinear trend to the data. The seasonal component reflects regular movements in the data that are repeated at the same time of the year, year after year. Most often the seasonal pattern is measured on a monthly or quarterly basis, but it could be measured for longer (e.g., semiannually) or shorter (e.g., weekly) periods. Many economic series have a strong seasonal pattern that may be related to weather conditions, national or religious holidays, the school year, sports seasons, and so forth.

The cyclical component represents long wavelike movements around the long-term trend in the series. These cycles may be more correctly called *long-term business fluctuations* because they rarely have a consistent amplitude (height and depth) and periocity (distance from trough to trough or peak to peak). The fact that these fluctuations are not very regular makes them particularly difficult to project. Thus determination of the cycle factor is the most difficult and limiting factor in using the time-series decomposition method.

The irregular component of the model represents random shocks to the series that occur in an unpredictable manner. These shocks might include such things as wars, strikes, floods, fire, unexpected and transitory political events, and so forth. These events cannot be modeled in a formal way owing to their random nature and thus are, in effect, omitted from applications of the model. Since the model is multiplicative the seasonal (S), cyclical (C), and irregular (I) components are modeled as percentage adjustments to the long-term trend (T). As such, since we have no basis on which to estimate the irregular component, I is assumed to equal 1.

15.5.1 Deseasonalizing Data

We mentioned earlier that the long-term trend is estimated by using a regression model with the deseasonalized data as a function of time. Deseasonalizing the data removes much of the "noise" from the series and provides a cleaner set of data on which to base the trend. Moving averages are used to take out the effect of seasonality. If our data are quarterly, a four-period moving average is used, and if the data are monthly, a twelve-period moving average is appropriate. Since the manufacturers' mobile home shipments data we will use to illustrate this forecasting technique are quarterly, we will develop the model using four-period moving averages.

For our purpose, a four-quarter moving average may be defined as follows:

$$MA_t = \frac{Y_{t-2}+Y_{t-1}+Y_t+Y_{t+1}}{4}$$

Thus the moving average for period 3 would be

$$MA_3 = \frac{Y_1+Y_2+Y_3+Y_4}{4}$$

Note that a moving average cannot be calculated for periods 1 and 2 because we do not have observations prior to time period 1. The next moving average (MA_4) is found in a similar manner except that the four quarters are moved forward by one quarter. The first quarter is dropped and the fifth quarter is included. Thus

$$MA_4 = \frac{Y_2+Y_3+Y_4+Y_5}{4}$$

Subsequent moving averages are found in a like manner. Notice that in calculating four-quarter moving averages, three observations will be lost. A moving average cannot be calculated for the first two or the very last observations because we must have data for two prior quarters and one future quarter for each quarterly moving average. Each moving average contains some first quarter, some second quarter, some third quarter, and some fourth quarter data. When the mean of the four quarters is found, it has representation from every part of the year. Therefore, the mean, or moving average, does not reflect any one season more than any other.

The data for our analysis are found in Table 15.8. There are 11 columns of data in that table, each of which will be explained as we move through the discussion of the time-series decomposition model. The first column, headed "Observation," lists the observation quarters starting with the first quarter of 1959 (1959.1) and extending through the fourth quarter of 1987 (1987.4). The second column, headed "Time," contains a simple time index equal to 1 for 1959.1 and increasing by one each quarter such that at 1987.4, Time = 116. The third column is headed "*MHS*," which stands for "mobile home shipments." This is the raw data to be used in our analysis and is in thousands of units. The raw data are also plotted in Figure 15.12. Thus, in the first quarter of 1959, 26,230 units were shipped, and in the fourth quarter of 1986, 56,100 units were shipped. Note that the *MHS* data do not extend into 1987. That is the period for which we will be making a forecast.

Let us now illustrate how to find moving averages based on the mobile home shipments data. We denote the moving averages in this example as *MAMHS*, which stands for "moving average mobile home shipments." As indicated in the fourth column of Table 15.8 (headed *MAHMS*), we cannot calculate a moving average for the first two observations (NA appears, meaning "not applicable"). The moving averages for the third and fourth quarters are found as follows:

$$MAMHS_3 = \frac{26.23 + 34.09 + 31.92 + 28.26}{4} = 30.125$$

$$MAMHS_4 = \frac{34.09 + 31.92 + 28.26 + 25.08}{4} = 29.838$$

The other moving averages are found in a similar manner.

Technically, each of these moving averages should be placed at the midpoint of the set of four quarters used for the calculation. For example, the first moving average we calculated should be right between the second and third quarters. However, then it would not correspond to any one time period. To get around this problem and to get a moving average that corresponds correctly to each quarter, we calculate a centered moving average (*CMA*). The general form for the centered moving averages is as follows:

$$CMA_t = \frac{MA_t + MA_{t+1}}{2}$$

TABLE 15.8 Mobile Home Shipments Data for Time-Series Decomposition (Data in Thousands of Units)

Observation	Time	MHS	MAMHS	CMAMHS	SF	CMAT	CF	SI	MHSF	PCER
1959.1	1.000	26.230	NA	NA	NA	52.883	NA	0.879	NA	NA
1959.2	2.000	34.090	NA	NA	NA	53.178	NA	1.117	NA	NA
1959.3	3.000	31.920	30.125	29.981	1.065	53.472	0.561	1.084	32.500	−1.816
1959.4	4.000	28.260	29.837	29.331	0.963	53.767	0.546	0.920	26.985	4.513
1960.1	5.000	25.080	28.825	28.311	0.886	54.062	0.524	0.879	24.886	0.775
1960.2	6.000	30.040	27.798	26.861	1.118	54.357	0.494	1.117	30.004	0.120
1960.3	7.000	27.810	25.925	25.298	1.099	54.652	0.463	1.084	27.422	1.393
1960.4	8.000	20.770	24.670	24.060	0.863	54.947	0.438	0.920	22.135	−6.573
1961.1	9.000	20.060	23.450	22.836	0.878	55.242	0.413	0.879	20.073	−0.065
1961.2	10.000	25.160	22.222	22.386	1.124	55.537	0.403	1.117	25.005	0.614
1961.3	11.000	22.900	22.550	23.132	0.990	55.832	0.414	1.084	25.076	−9.501
1961.4	12.000	22.080	23.715	24.774	0.891	56.127	0.441	0.920	22.792	−3.224
1962.1	13.000	24.720	25.833	26.834	0.921	56.422	0.476	0.879	23.587	4.584
1962.2	14.000	33.630	27.835	28.667	1.173	56.717	0.505	1.117	32.022	4.783
1962.3	15.000	30.910	29.500	30.218	1.023	57.012	0.530	1.084	32.756	−5.971
1962.4	16.000	28.740	30.935	31.981	0.899	57.307	0.558	0.920	29.423	−2.376
1963.1	17.000	30.460	33.028	34.281	0.889	57.602	0.595	0.879	30.133	1.073
1963.2	18.000	42.000	35.535	36.623	1.147	57.897	0.633	1.117	40.907	2.602
1963.3	19.000	40.940	37.710	38.891	1.053	58.192	0.668	1.084	42.158	−2.975
1963.4	20.000	37.440	40.072	41.504	0.902	58.487	0.710	0.920	38.183	−1.986
1964.1	21.000	39.910	42.935	44.550	0.896	58.782	0.758	0.879	39.159	1.881
1964.2	22.000	53.450	46.165	46.998	1.137	59.077	0.796	1.117	52.496	1.785
1964.3	23.000	53.860	47.830	48.576	1.109	59.372	0.818	1.084	52.657	2.234
1964.4	24.000	44.100	49.322	49.885	0.884	59.667	0.836	0.920	45.894	−4.068
1965.1	25.000	45.880	50.447	51.246	0.895	59.962	0.855	0.879	45.045	1.819
1965.2	26.000	57.950	52.045	53.081	1.092	60.257	0.881	1.117	59.292	−2.315
1965.3	27.000	60.250	54.117	54.121	1.113	60.552	0.894	1.084	58.667	2.627
1965.4	28.000	52.390	54.125	54.565	0.960	60.847	0.897	0.920	50.200	4.181

(continued)

TABLE 15.8 Continued

Observation	Time	MHS	MAMHS	CMAMHS	SF	CMAT	CF	SI	MHSF	PCER
1966.1	29.000	45.910	55.005	55.024	0.834	61.142	0.900	0.879	48.366	−5.349
1966.2	30.000	61.470	55.042	54.684	1.124	61.436	0.890	1.117	61.082	0.632
1966.3	31.000	60.400	54.325	54.214	1.114	61.731	0.878	1.084	58.768	2.702
1966.4	32.000	49.520	54.103	54.413	0.910	62.026	0.877	0.920	50.060	−1.089
1967.1	33.000	45.020	54.722	55.716	0.808	62.321	0.894	0.879	48.975	−8.784
1967.2	34.000	63.950	56.710	58.400	1.095	62.616	0.933	1.117	65.233	−2.006
1967.3	35.000	68.350	60.090	62.484	1.094	62.911	0.993	1.084	67.732	0.904
1967.4	36.000	63.040	64.878	67.021	0.941	63.206	1.060	0.920	61.660	2.190
1968.1	37.000	64.170	69.165	71.582	0.896	63.501	1.127	0.879	62.921	1.946
1968.2	38.000	81.100	74.000	76.754	1.057	63.796	1.203	1.117	85.734	−5.714
1968.3	39.000	87.690	79.507	82.609	1.062	64.091	1.289	1.084	89.548	−2.119
1968.4	40.000	85.070	85.710	88.951	0.956	64.386	1.382	0.920	81.835	3.803
1969.1	41.000	88.980	92.193	95.403	0.933	64.681	1.475	0.879	83.859	5.755
1969.2	42.000	107.030	98.613	100.893	1.061	64.976	1.553	1.117	112.697	−5.295
1969.3	43.000	113.370	103.173	101.738	1.114	65.271	1.559	1.084	110.284	2.723
1969.4	44.000	103.310	100.302	100.486	1.028	65.566	1.533	0.920	92.447	10.515
1970.1	45.000	77.500	100.670	101.111	0.766	65.861	1.535	0.879	88.877	−14.680
1970.2	46.000	108.500	101.552	100.926	1.075	66.156	1.526	1.117	112.735	−3.903
1970.3	47.000	116.900	100.300	101.787	1.148	66.451	1.532	1.084	110.338	5.614
1970.4	48.000	98.300	103.275	106.262	0.925	66.746	1.592	0.920	97.761	0.548
1971.1	49.000	89.400	109.250	113.338	0.789	67.041	1.691	0.879	99.624	−11.436
1971.2	50.000	132.400	117.425	120.775	1.096	67.336	1.794	1.117	134.906	−1.893
1971.3	51.000	149.600	124.125	128.275	1.166	67.631	1.897	1.084	139.050	7.052
1971.4	52.000	125.100	132.425	135.938	0.920	67.926	2.001	0.920	125.063	0.030
1972.1	53.000	122.600	139.450	139.462	0.879	68.221	2.044	0.879	122.588	0.010
1972.2	54.000	160.500	139.475	141.725	1.132	68.516	2.069	1.117	158.307	1.366
1972.3	55.000	149.700	143.975	145.837	1.026	68.811	2.119	1.084	158.088	−5.603
1972.4	56.000	143.100	147.700	149.163	0.959	69.106	2.158	0.920	137.230	4.102
1973.1	57.000	137.500	150.625	150.100	0.916	69.400	2.163	0.879	131.938	4.045

TABLE 15.8 Continued

Observation	Time	MHS	MAMHS	CMAMHS	SF	CMAT	CF	SI	MHSF	PCER
1973.2	58.000	172.200	149.575	145.675	1.182	69.695	2.090	1.117	162.719	5.506
1973.3	59.000	145.500	141.775	135.387	1.075	69.990	1.934	1.084	146.760	-0.866
1973.4	60.000	111.900	129.000	121.313	0.922	70.285	1.726	0.920	111.607	0.261
1974.1	61.000	86.400	113.625	105.975	0.815	70.580	1.501	0.879	93.152	-7.815
1974.2	62.000	110.700	98.325	90.313	1.226	70.875	1.274	1.117	100.879	8.872
1974.3	63.000	84.300	82.300	76.738	1.099	71.170	1.078	1.084	83.183	1.325
1974.4	64.000	47.800	71.175	64.700	0.739	71.465	0.905	0.920	59.524	-24.527
1975.1	65.000	41.900	58.225	55.263	0.758	71.760	0.770	0.879	48.576	-15.932
1975.2	66.000	58.900	52.300	52.713	1.117	72.055	0.732	1.117	58.880	0.034
1975.3	67.000	60.600	53.125	54.750	1.107	72.350	0.757	1.084	59.349	2.064
1975.4	68.000	51.100	56.375	57.862	0.883	72.645	0.797	0.920	53.233	-4.175
1976.1	69.000	54.900	59.350	60.000	0.915	72.940	0.823	0.879	52.740	3.934
1976.2	70.000	70.800	60.650	61.100	1.159	73.235	0.834	1.117	68.249	3.604
1976.3	71.000	65.800	61.550	61.700	1.066	73.530	0.839	1.084	66.883	-1.646
1976.4	72.000	54.700	61.850	62.487	0.875	73.825	0.846	0.920	57.488	-5.098
1977.1	73.000	56.100	63.125	64.450	0.870	74.120	0.870	0.879	56.652	-0.983
1977.2	74.000	75.900	65.775	67.512	1.124	74.415	0.907	1.117	75.411	0.644
1977.3	75.000	76.400	69.250	70.000	1.091	74.710	0.937	1.084	75.880	0.681
1977.4	76.000	68.600	70.750	70.788	0.969	75.005	0.944	0.920	65.125	5.066
1978.1	77.000	62.100	70.825	70.325	0.883	75.300	0.934	0.879	61.816	0.458
1978.2	78.000	76.200	69.825	69.375	1.098	75.595	0.918	1.117	77.492	-1.695
1978.3	79.000	72.400	68.925	68.850	1.052	75.890	0.907	1.084	74.633	-3.085
1978.4	80.000	65.000	68.775	69.100	0.941	76.185	0.907	0.920	63.572	2.197
1979.1	81.000	61.500	69.425	69.800	0.881	76.480	0.913	0.879	61.354	0.237
1979.2	82.000	78.800	70.175	69.762	1.130	76.775	0.909	1.117	77.925	1.111
1979.3	83.000	75.400	69.350	68.738	1.097	77.070	0.892	1.084	74.511	1.178
1979.4	84.000	61.700	68.125	64.413	0.958	77.364	0.833	0.920	59.260	3.955
1980.1	85.000	56.600	60.700	58.588	0.966	77.659	0.754	0.879	51.498	9.013

(continued)

TABLE 15.8 Continued

Observation	Time	MHS	MAMHS	CMAMHS	SF	CMAT	CF	SI	MHSF	PCER
1980.2	86.000	49.100	56.475	55.950	0.878	77.951	0.718	1.117	62.496	−27.283
1980.3	87.000	58.500	55.425	55.213	1.060	78.249	0.706	1.084	59.850	−2.308
1980.4	88.000	57.500	55.000	57.625	0.998	78.544	0.734	0.920	53.015	7.800
1981.1	89.000	54.900	60.250	61.163	0.898	78.839	0.776	0.879	53.762	2.073
1981.2	90.000	70.100	62.075	61.163	1.146	79.134	0.773	1.117	68.319	2.541
1981.3	91.000	65.800	60.250	60.050	1.096	79.429	0.756	1.084	65.094	1.073
1981.4	92.000	50.200	59.850	59.575	0.843	79.724	0.747	0.920	54.809	−9.181
1982.1	93.000	53.300	59.300	58.962	0.904	80.019	0.737	0.879	51.828	2.762
1982.2	94.000	67.900	58.625	59.262	1.146	80.314	0.738	1.117	66.196	2.509
1982.3	95.000	63.100	59.900	61.150	1.032	80.609	0.759	1.084	66.287	−5.050
1982.4	96.000	55.300	62.400	64.100	0.863	80.904	0.792	0.920	58.972	−6.640
1983.1	97.000	63.300	65.800	68.125	0.929	81.199	0.839	0.879	59.882	5.400
1983.2	98.000	81.500	70.450	72.188	1.129	81.494	0.886	1.117	80.633	1.063
1983.3	99.000	81.700	73.925	74.488	1.097	81.789	0.911	1.084	80.744	1.170
1983.4	100.000	69.200	75.050	75.200	0.920	82.084	0.916	0.920	69.184	0.023
1984.1	101.000	67.800	75.350	75.013	0.904	82.379	0.911	0.879	65.936	2.749
1984.2	102.000	82.700	74.675	74.300	1.113	82.674	0.899	1.117	82.993	−0.354
1984.3	103.000	79.000	73.925	73.238	1.079	82.969	0.883	1.084	79.389	−0.493
1984.4	104.000	66.200	72.550	72.125	0.918	83.264	0.866	0.920	66.355	−0.234
1985.1	105.000	62.300	71.700	71.413	0.872	83.559	0.855	0.879	62.772	−0.757
1985.2	106.000	79.300	71.125	71.050	1.116	83.854	0.847	1.117	79.363	−0.079
1985.3	107.000	76.700	70.975	70.450	1.089	84.149	0.837	1.084	76.368	0.433
1985.4	108.000	65.600	69.925	68.363	0.960	84.444	0.810	0.920	62.894	4.126
1986.1	109.000	58.100	66.800	65.138	0.892	84.739	0.769	0.879	57.256	1.453
1986.2	110.000	66.800	63.475	62.288	1.072	85.034	0.733	1.117	69.575	−4.154
1986.3	111.000	63.400	61.100	NA	NA	85.328	0.730e	1.084	67.522	−6.502
1986.4	112.000	56.100	NA	NA	NA	85.623	0.730e	0.920	57.505	−2.504
1987.1	113.000	NA	NA	NA	NA	85.918	0.730e	0.879	55.131	NA
1987.2	114.000	NA	NA	NA	NA	86.213	0.760e	1.117	73.189	NA

TABLE 15.8 Continued

Observation	Time	MHS	MAMHS	CMAMHS	SF	CMAT	CF	SI	MHSF	PCER
1987.3	115.000	NA	NA	NA	NA	86.508	0.790e	1.084	74.082	NA
1987.4	116.000	NA	NA	NA	NA	86.803	0.850e	0.920	67.880	NA

Source: Manufacturers' Mobile Home Shipments (*MHS*) are from Citibase: Citibank economic database (New York: Citibank, NA., 1987). All other columns have been calculated from *MHS*.

Note: *MHS* = manufacturers' mobile home shipments; *MAMHS* = the four-period moving average of mobile home shipments; *CMAMHS* = the centered moving average of mobile home shipments; *SF* = seasonal factors (*SF* = *MHS*/*CMAMHS*); *CMAT* = long-term trend based on linear regression of *CMAMHS* = *f*(time); *CF* = cycle factors (*CF* = *CMAMHS*/*CMAT*) (those followed by an *e* were estimated based on the graph of the cycle factor in Figure 15.15); *SI* = seasonal indices (normalized mean of seasonal factors); *MHSF* = mobile home shipments forecast (*MHSF* = *CMAT* × *IS* × *CF*); and *PCER* = percent error in forecast {*PCER* = [(*MHS* − *MHSF*)/*MHS*]100}.

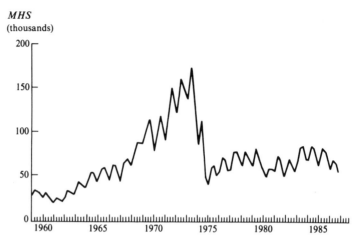

FIGURE 15.12   Manufacturers' Shipments of Mobile Homes.
This series (*MHS*) show a slight upward trend, strong seasonality, and
a considerable cyclical movement.

For our example, we denote the centered moving averages as *CMAMHS*,
which stands for "centered moving average mobile home shipments." The
first of these we can calculate is for period 3:

$$CMAMHS_3 = \frac{MAMHS_3 + MAMHS_4}{2}$$

$$= \frac{30.125 + 29.837}{2} = 29.981$$

Since the third quarter moving average ($MAMHS_3$) should really be between
quarters 2 and 3 and the fourth quarter moving average ($MAMHS_4$) should
be between quarters 3 and 4, it makes sense to use the average of $MAMHS_3$
and $MAMHS_4$ for quarter 3.

It is the series of centered moving averages that is used to represent the
deseasonalized data. If you compare the numbers in the column of Table
15.8 headed "*CMAMHS*" with the original data in the column headed
"*MHS*," you will see that the former has much less erratic movement than
the latter. This also can be seen by comparing the smoother *CMAMHS* line
with the original, more jagged series in Figure 15.13.

15.5.2 Determining Seasonal Factors and Indices

The deseasonalized data, as given by the centered moving averages, is used
to calculate seasonal factors (*SF*). A *seasonal factor* measures how much

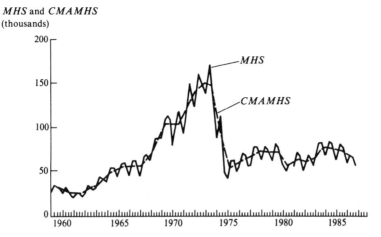

FIGURE 15.13   Mobile Home Shipments and the Centered Moving
Average of Mobile Home Shipments.
The original data for mobile home shipments (*MHS*) has very regular
sharp up and down movements representing seasonal fluctuations.
The smoother series representing the centered moving average of
mobile home shipments (*CMAMHS*) runs through the series in a less
jagged manner.

any quarter's observation is above or below the yearly average on which it
is centered (i.e., the centered moving average). In general, for the series Y,
the seasonal factors are calculated as follows:

$$SF_t = \frac{Y_t}{CMA_t}$$

If the seasonal factor is greater than 1, that quarter is a strong quarter in
comparison to the yearly average. If the seasonal factor is less than 1, it is
a weak quarter.

For our example data on mobile home shipments, the first two seasonal
factors are calculated as follows:

$$SF_3 = \frac{MHS_3}{CMAMHS_3} = \frac{31.920}{29.981} = 1.065$$

$$SF_4 = \frac{MHS_4}{CMAMHS_4} = \frac{28.260}{29.331} = 0.963$$

Thus it appears that the third quarter is a relatively strong quarter, while the
fourth quarter is relatively weak. The remaining seasonal factors are calcu-

lated in a similar manner and are shown in the column headed "*SF*" in Table 15.8. While there is some similarity between the first quarter seasonal factors, they are not all identical. The same can be said for the other quarters. This can be seen better by arraying the seasonal factors in columns by quarter. This is done in Table 15.9. Since there is variation in the seasonal factors within each quarter, we normalize them to determine seasonal indices for use in forecasting.

Since we are using quarterly data, the means for the seasonal factors should sum to 4. If they do not, we normalize them by multiplying each seasonal factor by a standardization factor that is found by dividing 4 by the sum of the mean quarterly seasonal factors. This process is shown at the bottom of Table 15.9. The standardized seasonal factors are called *seasonal indices*, and these are used to prepare forecasts. For our mobile home shipments data, the seasonal indices are

Quarter 1: 0.879

Quarter 2: 1.117

Quarter 3: 1.084

Quarter 4: 0.920

Note that these do add to 4. These seasonal indices are also shown in the column headed "*SI*" in Table 15.8.

15.5.3 Determination of the Long-Term Trend

The long-term trend of the data series is based on the deseasonalized data as given by the centered moving averages. Unless there are compelling reasons to do otherwise, a linear trend is used. The equation for the trend is found by regressing the centered moving average as a function of time. The values calculated on the basis of this equation are called the *centered moving average trend (CMAT) values*. For the mobile home shipments data, the *CMAT* equation is

$$CMAT = 52.588 + 0.295(\text{time})$$

where time = 1 for the first quarter of 1959.

The trend (*CMAT*) is plotted in Figure 15.14. You see that there is a modest positive long-term trend in the mobile home shipments data. The data underlying the trend line in Figure 15.14 are shown in the column headed *CMAT* in Table 15.8.

TABLE 15.9 Seasonal Factors for Mobile Home Shipments Data

Observation	First Quarter	Second Quarter	Third Quarter	Fourth Quarter
1959	NA	NA	1.065	0.963
1960	0.886	1.118	1.099	0.863
1961	0.878	1.124	0.990	0.891
1962	0.921	1.173	1.023	0.899
1963	0.889	1.147	1.053	0.902
1964	0.896	1.137	1.109	0.884
1965	0.895	1.092	1.113	0.960
1966	0.834	1.124	1.114	0.910
1967	0.808	1.095	1.094	0.941
1968	0.896	1.057	1.062	0.956
1969	0.933	1.061	1.114	1.028
1970	0.766	1.075	1.148	0.925
1971	0.789	1.096	1.166	0.920
1972	0.879	1.132	1.026	0.959
1973	0.916	1.182	1.075	0.922
1974	0.815	1.226	1.099	0.739
1975	0.758	1.117	1.107	0.883
1976	0.915	1.159	1.066	0.875
1977	0.870	1.124	1.091	0.969
1978	0.883	1.098	1.052	0.941
1979	0.881	1.130	1.097	0.958
1980	0.966	0.878	1.060	0.998
1981	0.898	1.146	1.096	0.843
1982	0.904	1.146	1.032	0.863
1983	0.929	1.129	1.097	0.920
1984	0.904	1.113	1.079	0.918
1985	0.872	1.116	1.089	0.960
1986	0.892	1.072	NA	NA
1987	NA	NA	NA	NA
Raw means	0.877	1.114	1.082	0.918
Standardized means	0.879	1.117	1.084	0.920

Note: Sum of means = 3.991; standardization factor = (4.000/3.991) = 1.00226; standardized mean = 1.00226(raw mean). The standardized means are used as seasonal indices.

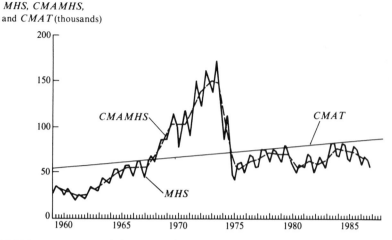

FIGURE 15.14   Mobile Home Shipments, Centered Moving Average of Mobile Home Shipments, and the Long-Term Trend.
In this diagram, the long-term trend (*CMAT*) is plotted along with the original data and the centered moving average. The linear trend is seen to slope slightly upward over time.

15.5.4 Finding and Projecting the Cycle Factor

The *cycle factor* measures the long wavelike movements of the deseasonalized data around the long-term trend. The deseasonalized data are the centered moving averages (*CMA*), and the long-term trend is given by the centered moving average trend (*CMAT*). It should make sense, then, that the cycle factor (*CF*) is calculated as the ratio of *CMA* to *CMAT*. That is,

$$CF_t = \frac{CMA_t}{CMAT_t}$$

For our example, the first two cycle factors are calculated as follows:

$$CF_t = \frac{CMAMHS_t}{CMAT_t}$$

$$CF_3 = \frac{29.981}{53.472} = 0.561$$

$$CF_4 = \frac{29.331}{53.767} = 0.546$$

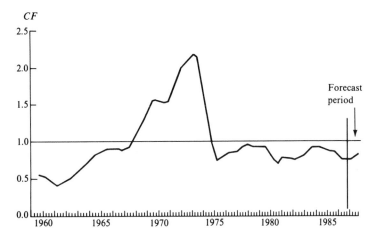

FIGURE 15.15   Cycle Factor for Mobile Home Shipments.
The cycle factor (*CF*) moves slowly around the line at 1.0 over time.

The remaining cycle factors are calculated in a similar manner. These are shown in column eight of Table 15.8, which is headed "*CF*." Notice that these values change relatively slowly and move around 1 (at $CF=1$, $CMA=CMAT$, so the wavelike cycle crosses the long-term trend).

The cycle factors are plotted in Figure 15.15. The cycle factors for the forecast period, 1987, have been estimated, along with the cycle factors for the last two quarters of 1986. In Table 15.8, these values are followed by an *e* to indicate that they were estimated rather than calculated. The estimation of cycle factors can be very difficult. To do so, we look carefully at the pattern of the historical *CF* series and attempt to make an educated projection of it through the forecast period. Other techniques such as exponential smoothing and regression analysis are sometimes helpful in projecting the cycle factor.

In the opening part of Section 15.4 we noted that the irregular component cannot be predicted. For this reason, there is no column for this part of the time-series decomposition model in Table 15.8. The irregular component is for practical applications assumed equal to unity.

15.5.5. Using Time-Series Decomposition to Forecast

Recall that the basic time-series decomposition model for the series *Y* is

$$Y = T \times S \times C \times I$$

where T represents the long-term trend, S represents the seasonal component, C represents the cyclical component, and I is the irregular component. For our mobile home shipments example, the forecast values of mobile home shipments are denoted *MHSF* (for "mobile home shipments forecast"). These are calculated as follows:

$$MHSF = CMAT \times SI \times CF$$

These are shown in column ten (headed "*MHSF*") of Table 15.8. (You may note slight differences in the values reported in Table 15.8 and those you might calculate by hand because values for *CMAT*, *SI*, and *CF* have been rounded to three decimal places in the table.)

The forecast or estimated values (*MHSF*) are also plotted in Figure 15.16 along with the original series (*MHS*). You see that through the historical period the values estimated by the model (dotted line) follow very closely the actual raw data (solid line). The forecast of mobile home shipments for 1987 is shown by the dotted line in the far right section of Figure 15.16 marked "Forecast Period." The forecast values are

1987.1:

$$MHSF = 55.131$$

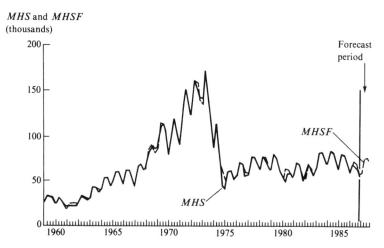

FIGURE 15.16   Mobile Home Shipments and Forecast Mobile Home Shipments.
The actual raw mobile home shipments data (*MHS*) are shown by a solid line. The values estimated by the time-series decomposition model (*MHSF*) are shown by a dotted line. The forecast for 1987 is shown at the right side of the figure.

1987.2:

  $MHSF = 73.189$

1987.3:

  $MHSF = 74.082$

1987.4:

  $MHSF = 67.880$

The accuracy of the forecasts for 1987 is unknown, since that period represents the forecast horizon. For the historical period, the accuracy of the model can be seen by looking at the percent error (*PCER*) for each period, as shown in the last column of Table 15.8.

15.6 SUMMARY

1. In this chapter you have learned about some of the quantitative forecasting methods that are widely used by business economists as they try to forecast such economic series as GNP, personal income, unemployment, inflation, exchange values of the dollar, and so on. These techniques have all been found to be extremely helpful to business economists, although no one method is universally the best. One method may work well for a particular series but not work well at all for another series. Part of the job of the business economist is to find the methods that are most consistently on target for each economic series to be forecast.

2. It is generally wise to use more than one forecasting technique when preparing a forecast, and it may be wise to use at least two substantially different techniques. That is, use one time-series analysis method, such as exponential smoothing, and one regression-based causal model. These quantitative methods should then be combined with judgments drawn from experience with the activity being forecast before a conclusion is reached. It is desirable to prepare a scenario that includes a "most likely" forecast as well as a "most optimistic" and a "most pessimistic" forecast.

3. Time-series forecasting models include the simplest of models, such as the model that predicts the next period to be the same as the current period (that is, $Y_{t+1} = Y_t$), and very simple linear trends of the form $Y = a + bT$. However, time-series models also can include more complex methods such as exponential smoothing. You have read about the simple exponential smoothing model, but there are more sophisticated models in this general class that include trend and/or seasonal components. Time-series models also include some very sophisticated methods, the most widely known of which are the Box-Jenkins models.[13] Empirical evidence is mixed concerning how much better these sophisticated models are in practical applications.

4. Regression analysis has become an important part of the business forecaster's tool kit. Both bivariate linear regression and multiple linear regression can be very helpful in developing an understanding of the structural linkage between variables. This in turn becomes useful as we try to forecast the future path of economic series. The linear regression models discussed in this chapter represent a starting place in the application of regression methods. Nonlinear and simultaneous equation models can add further insight into the behavior of economic variables. Students who are serious about learning more about forecasting should consider taking some course work in econometrics or business/economic forecasting.

5. An approach to forecasting called time-series decomposition allows the forecaster to isolate important components within a time series and to measure the impact of each component. These are the trend, seasonal, cyclical, and irregular components. The time-series decomposition model is useful not only because it is relatively simple to use, but also because it works well in many applications.

6. In using the forecasting methods discussed in this chapter and/or other quantitative methods, it is wise to use the simplest models that work well for the purpose at hand. Some people fall into the trap of becoming enamored with complex, sophisticated models and use those even when a simpler model would have worked as well. There are at least two important reasons to follow the "keep it simple" philosophy in business and economic forecasting. First, and perhaps most important, at some point the forecast must be communicated to managerial personnel who will use it in their decision-making process. Thus it is important that the results, and how they were obtained, be communicated clearly and convincingly. Second, the simpler the model, the fewer are the data and computer resources that will be necessary to support the forecasting effort. This means savings in both time and money.

7. As a final note, we should mention that there are many good forecasting software packages available that allow many methods to be done on personal computers as well as on mainframes. All the methods discussed in this chapter can be done easily in a spreadsheet format that makes them

---

[13]G. F. P. Box and G. M. Jenkins, *Time Series Analysis: Forecasting and Control* (San Francisco: Holden-Day, 1970).

accessible for use by almost anyone in today's business and/or academic setting.

15.7 EXERCISES

1. Write a brief essay in which you compare time-series forecasting methods with regression-based techniques. Include in your essay the strengths and weaknesses you see in each.

2. Suppose that you work in the consumer credit division of a large national bank and that you have been asked to prepare a forecast of consumer installment credit outstanding (*CICO*) for 1986 based on annual data starting with 1960 and ending with 1985. The data are as follows:

Year	CICO ($Millions)	Year	CICO ($Millions)
1960	44,335	1973	152,910
1961	45,438	1974	162,203
1962	50,375	1975	167,043
1963	57,056	1976	187,782
1964	64,674	1977	221,475
1965	72,814	1978	261,976
1966	78,162	1979	296,483
1967	81,783	1980	295,763
1968	90,112	1981	310,965
1969	99,381	1982	325,136
1970	103,905	1983	373,048
1971	116,434	1984	446,183
1972	131,258	1985	522,805

Source: Business Conditions Digest, May 1987, p. 97.

   a. Plot the data over time.

   b. Use a linear time trend to forecast *CICO* for 1986. (*Note*: The actual 1986 value was 577,789. How close were you?)

   c. Add the forecast values to your plot from part (a).

3. Based on the same data as in Exercise 2, use the simple exponential smoothing model to prepare a forecast for 1986. Let $w = 0.4$. Then prepare a second forecast with $w = 0.8$. Which works the best based on the root mean squared error? Based on the percent error for 1986 (knowing that the actual value was 577,789), which weighting factor was best?

4. Use a bivariate linear regression model to forecast personal consumption expenditures (*PCE*) as a function of gross national product (*GNP*) using quarterly

data from 1982 through 1984 to forecast *PCE* for 1985. The 1982.1 through 1985.4 data are

Period	PCE ($Billions)	GNP ($Billions)
1982.1	480.3	749.2
1982.2	502.8	792.1
1982.3	513.8	796.7
1982.4	553.8	828.0
1983.1	515.7	785.9
1983.2	546.7	840.0
1983.3	559.4	859.6
1983.4	607.6	916.0
1984.1	571.1	888.4
1984.2	599.9	941.4
1984.3	601.9	950.4
1984.4	650.2	994.5

Source: Survey of Current Business, March 1986, p. 121.

Use a linear time trend with $GNP = f(T)$, where $T = 1$ for 1982.1, to first project *GNP* through 1985. Then use those values to forecast *PCE*.

5. Use the time-series decomposition method to develop a forecast of sales for each quarter of 1989 based on the following sales data (sales are in thousands of units):

Period	Sales
1984.1	7
1984.2	6
1984.3	4
1984.4	6
1985.1	8
1985.2	7
1985.3	6
1985.4	7
1986.1	10
1986.2	9
1986.3	6
1986.4	9
1987.1	12
1987.2	10
1987.3	9
1987.4	12
1988.1	13
1988.2	10
1988.3	8
1988.4	11

Based on the seasonal indices, which quarter of sales lies closest to the long-term trend line? Show a graph of your actual and predicted values for each quarter as well as the forecast values for 1989.

6. Pick an industry in which you have some particular interest, and research the outlook for that industry by referring to the latest edition of *U.S. Industrial Outlook* in the library. Write a one-paragraph overview of the outlook for your industry. Then prepare your own forecast for that industry for the next four time periods (four quarters if you use quarterly data or four years if you use annual data).

7. Look up data for the population of the state in which you live for the 20 most recent years available. Use this information to prepare a linear time-trend forecast of the state's population for the next 5 years. How accurate do you think this forecast will be? On what do you base this judgment? Suggest how some two departments of state government might be able to use such a forecast. Be as specific as possible.

8. Refer to the most recent *Economic Report of the President* for data on U.S. merchandise exports of nonagricultural products. Record annual data for the most recent 16 years. Then use the first 15 of those years as the basis of a linear time-trend forecast of the sixteenth year's exports. Plot the original data along with the line representing your linear trend. Based on the coefficient of determination (R^2), how well do you think your trend line fits the data?

15.8   REFERENCES

David Ahlers and Josef Lakonishok, ''A Study of Economists' Consensus Forecasts,'' *Management Science*, 29(10), October 1983, pp. 1113 – 1125.

William C. Dunkelberg, ''The Use of Survey Data in Forecasting,'' *Business Economics*, January 1986, pp. 44 – 49.

Everette S. Gardner, Jr., and E. D. McKenzie, ''Forecasting Trends in Time Series,'' *Management Science*, 31(10), October 1985, pp. 1237 – 1346.

Barry Keating and J. Holton Wilson, ''Forecasting: Practices and Teachings,'' *Journal of Business Forecasting*, Winter 1987 – 1988, pp. 10 – 13.

Spyros Makridakis, Steven C. Wheelwright, and Victor E. McGee, *Forecasting: Methods and Applications*, 2d Ed. New York: Wiley, 1983.

John J. McAuley, *Economic Forecasting for Business: Concepts and Applications.* Englewood Cliffs, N.J.: Prentice-Hall, 1986.

Lloyd M. Valentine, *Business Cycles and Forecasting*, 7th Ed. Cincinnati, Ohio: South-Western Publishing, 1987.

J. Holton Wilson and Barry Keating, *Business Forecasting*. Homewood, Ill.: Irwin, 1990.

Victor Zarnowitz, ''The Accuracy of Individual and Group Forecasts from Business Outlook Surveys,'' *Journal of Forecasting*, 3, 1984, pp. 11 – 26.

_____ *MANAGERIAL CASE* _____

A VIEW FROM A BUSINESS ECONOMIST

The manager's role in the forecast process is to bring a broad perspective to decision making. It is necessary to insure that the process does not become isolated from users and that it is used to the fullest potential for helping management adapt to change.

Many conversations with users of forecasts start with the phrase "if only we could get accurate forecasts. . . ." These users normally then explain the difficulties faced by their respective function due to poor forecasts. What is the real problem? Are forecasters not doing their jobs well? Have the theoreticians let us down? Perhaps, the forecasters are doing as well as can be expected, but the users of the forecasts have unrealistic expectations.

Managers of forecasting groups are often placed in a difficult position of wanting to improve the process but not being sure what needs fixing. How can they decide what changes are necessary when users are dissatisfied and the forecasters respond that they are using the latest techniques and demonstrate this by displaying extremely complex mathematics? In this article I will suggest some general principles for managers to help them work through this predicament.

Forecasting—A Component of the Decision-Making Process

The first principle is that the forecasting process must be viewed as only one function within the overall decision-making process. It is not possible to view forecasting in isolation. For example, in telecommunications, forecasting is one stage in the total process of deciding upon the amount and deployment of equipment and manpower to provide service. An experience we had in GTE Midwestern Telephone Operations was that when we viewed the entire decision-making process for capital and manpower deployment, some problems which initially had been attributed to "bad forecasts" really had other causes. One instance involved a problem with central office switching equipment where additional line cards had to be ordered during the installation of a new digital switch. Without these line cards, the office could not be cut into service. These last-minute activities resulted in wasted effort and increased cost. The problem had been attributed to forecast inaccuracy since the engineers said they followed the forecast in calculating the equipment needed. However, in digging a little deeper, the problem really resulted from engineering decisions specifying the amount of test and administrative lines needed in a central office. Only customer lines had been included in the forecast and therefore additional capacity for admin-

This case represents some observations about forecasting made by Dr. Gary F. Wilkinson, manager of Network Product Management and Forecasting at GTE, Midwestern Telephone Operations. Adapted from Gary F. Wilkinson, "If Only We Could Get Accurate Forecasts," *The Journal of Business Forecasting*, Winter 1986–1987, pp. 2–4. Used with permission.

istrative and test lines needed to be added to the forecast to provide adequate equipment. Numerous other examples from other industries are available. The key lesson is that the manager must bring a broad perspective and understanding of how decisions are made in the company to assure the forecasting process is satisfying the information needs.

Dialogue Improves Forecasts

The second general principle is that it is necessary to insure considerable dialogue between users and the developers of the forecast. If managers find that forecast users have little idea of how the forecast was developed and the forecasters cannot explain in some detail how the forecasts are used, then fundamental discussions between these groups are necessary. All participants in the decision-making process should understand the purpose of the forecasts, data and techniques used to develop the forecast, expected accuracy, and the way the forecast is used.

Understand Limitations

A third principle is to understand the inherent limitations of the forecasting process. Although forecasters are generally optimistic about their ability to provide accurate forecasts, managers need to probe deeper. Graphs of older forecasts compared with actuals provide three indicators for the manager on forecast limitations. The first is simply the comparison of the various forecasts with the actuals. Naturally, large deviations indicate that a great deal of uncertainty exists in the forecasting process, and unless there is some major flaw in technique, this uncertainty can generally be expected to continue. A second indicator is the spread of forecasts made at different points in time. Ideally, the forecasts made at different points should be fairly consistent. If they vary greatly, probably the process is not well understood, either because of its complexity or because it has such a large random component. A final test in understanding forecast limitations is to inspect whether the forecasts have picked up turning points. No forecasting process is perfect at predicting turning points, but greater confidence can be placed in the forecasting process if it has demonstrated that it can predict changes in trend.

What is the value of understanding forecast limitations? In many cases, users want a single number without equivocations. However, the key to building an adequate decision-making process is to understand the risk in the forecast and build greater flexibility into the system as risk increases. A highly flexible system which can react quickly requires less accurate forecasts. In circumstances where forecasts have a great deal of uncertainty, the manager must attempt to build as much flexibility as practical into the system.

Simple Models

A fourth principle is to force the forecasters to simplify the process. Too many forecasting processes have become so complex that even those who built the models are not sure how they behave. Simple models are preferred to complex. Complexity, which adds little to expected accuracy, should be eliminated and managers should constantly question the need for complexity. Also, presentation of the forecasts to management should use simple illustrations and explanations. Forecasters tend to enjoy complex mathematics, but all forecasting processes should be able to be explained in laymen's terms. If the process cannot be explained to management without resorting to complex jargon, it should probably be discarded.

Fall in Love with Data, Not Models

A fifth principle is to guard against the tendency for forecasters to become enamored with technique. Clearly, technical expertise in building forecasting models is extremely important. However, applying a particular forecasting method follows the hard work of understanding the requirements of the decision-making process and the data used in developing the forecast. Gwilym Jenkins often said in his lectures that analysts should fall in love with their data not their forecasting models. In fact, forecasting models should never be trusted and should constantly be tested, and, if found inadequate, easily discarded. It is unfortunate that a number of forecasters keep using a particular technique because they have become comfortable with it.

Simulate Possible Outcomes

A final principle is to fully use the forecasting process to simulate a number of possible outcomes. This forces managers to consider a range of possible conditions in their planning. Clearly, businesses which have planned for a number of potential conditions are better able to adapt and profit from change than those companies who are unprepared for conditions other than those of a single forecast.

16

Business Cycles and Economic Forecasting

16.1 INTRODUCTION

Economic fluctuations, periods of expansion and decline, are well-recognized features of the landscape that makes up the economic history of the United States. Many people have devoted their professional lifetimes to the study of these patterns of boom and bust, but to date no one has successfully mastered the ability to predict them correctly and consistently. In this chapter we describe the general nature of the *business cycle*, the term used to identify these fluctuations in economic activity, including an overview of some theories about the cause of such widespread fluctuations. In addition, we look at three different forecasts of GNP based on models presented in Chapter 15 and at three alternative forecasts of two important sectors of the economy, automotive sales and housing starts.

16.2 THE BUSINESS CYCLE

Business cycles are fluctuations in economic activity that include expansion and subsequent contraction across a broad range of economic activities. Expansion leads to contraction, which, in turn, leads to the next expansion in a repetitive but not periodic sequence. Business cycles can be measured from peak to peak or from trough to trough. The latter is illustrated in Figure 16.1. The *expansion phase* runs from the beginning trough to the peak, while the *contraction phase* (also commonly called the recession phase) runs from the peak to the ending trough. The cycle illustrated in Figure 16.1 has a 6-

year, or 72-month, duration that is equally split between expansion and recession. A typical business cycle would not be so symmetrical, and there is no consistent relationship between the lengths of the two phases. The height of the expansion is measured from the beginning trough to the peak (A to B), while the depth of the recession is measured from the peak to the ending trough (C to D). These distances may be similar or very different. In Figure 16.1, the recession depth is slightly less than the height of the expansion. Thus the ending trough is higher than the beginning trough. This is common in a growing economy.

Table 16.1 provides the official reference dates and duration for business cycles in the United States starting with the trough of December 1854 and extending through the beginning of the expansion that officially started with the trough of November 1982. That expansion was still in process as of this writing, making it one of the longest peacetime expansions in history. You should consult a current issue of *Business Conditions Digest* to see if the peak for that expansion has yet been dated. In dating the end of expansions or recessions, a 3-month rule is used. That is, there must be 3 consecutive months of downturn before a peak is officially dated. In addition, revised data are evaluated before a signal of the change in the business cycle is provided. This means that we only have official dates for changes in the business cycle well after the change has occurred. Notice that the average

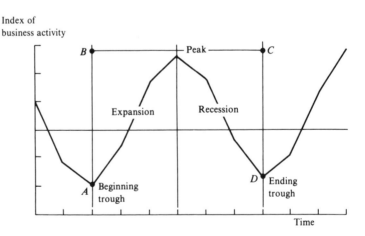

FIGURE 16.1   A Typical Business Cycle.
The business cycle includes a period of expansion and then a period of contraction followed by the next expansion. The cycle shown runs 6 years from trough to trough.

Duration in Months

Business Cycle Reference Dates

Trough	Peak	Contraction (Trough from Previous Peak)	Expansion (Trough to Peak)	Cycle Trough from Previous Trough	Cycle Peak from Previous Peak
December 1854	June 1857	—	30	—	—
December 1858	October 1860	18	22	48	40
June 1861	April 1865	8	46	30	54
December 1867	June 1869	32	18	78	50
December 1870	October 1873	18	34	36	52
March 1879	March 1882	65	36	99	101
May 1885	March 1887	38	22	74	60
April 1888	July 1890	13	27	35	40
May 1891	January 1893	10	20	37	30
June 1894	December 1895	17	18	37	35
June 1897	June 1899	18	24	36	42
December 1900	September 1902	18	21	42	39
August 1904	May 1907	23	33	44	56
June 1908	January 1910	13	19	46	32
January 1912	January 1913	24	12	43	36
December 1914	August 1918	23	44	35	67
March 1919	January 1920	7	10	51	17
July 1921	May 1923	18	22	28	40
July 1924	October 1926	14	27	36	41
November 1927	August 1929	13	21	40	34
March 1933	May 1937	43	50	64	93
June 1938	February 1945	13	80	63	93

(continued)

TABLE 16.1 Continued

	Business Cycle Reference Dates		Duration in Months			
					Cycle	
Trough	Peak		Contraction (Trough from Previous Peak)	Expansion (Trough to Peak)	Trough from Previous Trough	Peak from Previous Peak
October 1945	November 1948		8	37	88	45
October 1949	July 1953		11	45	48	56
May 1954	August 1957		10	39	55	49
April 1958	April 1960		8	24	47	32
February 1961	December 1969		10	106	34	116
November 1970	November 1973		11	36	117	47
March 1975	January 1980		16	58	52	74
July 1980	July 1981		6	12	64	18
November 1982			16	—	28	—
Average, all cycles:						
1854–1982 (30 cycles)			18	33	51	51
1854–1919 (16 cycles)			22	27	48	49
1919–1945 (6 cycles)			18	35	53	53
1945–1982 (8 cycles)			11	45	56	55
Average, peacetime cycles:						
1854–1982 (25 cycles)			19	27	46	46
1854–1919 (14 cycles)			22	24	46	47
1919–1945 (5 cycles)			20	26	46	45
1945–1982 (6 cycles)			11	34	46	44

Source: The Handbook of Cyclical Indicators: A Supplement to the Business Conditions Digest, U.S. Department of Commerce, Bureau of Economic Analysis, 1984, p. 178.

... time expansions, the postwar contractions, and the full cycles that include the wartime expansions (Civil War, World Wars I and II, peacetime expansion has been only 34 months in recent times (1945 to 1982), so the expansion that began in November 1982 stands out as a quite extended period of economic growth. You might want to consider why this expansion became so extended. How important were various economic policies developed by the Reagan administration in determining the length of the expansion?

Your search for reasons for the extended period of economic expansion that began in November 1982 may cause you to think about factors that have been considered by other cycle theorists. A comprehensive review of cycle theories goes beyond the scope of this text, but we will briefly consider some of the more prominent and/or interesting of these.[1] Monetary theories of business cycles hold that variations in the money supply represent the main causal factor in the broad economic swings we call *business cycles*. One monetary version of the business cycle is that during the recession, excess reserves accumulate in the banking system as firms cut back on borrowing. As these excess reserves build, bankers become increasingly anxious to make loans and thus lower interest rates. At lower interest rates, firms are more likely to borrow to finance long-term capital improvements and/or to finance inventory holdings. This increases aggregate demand, and the economy turns around, moving into an expansionary phase. New and higher incomes are generated, causing increased consumer spending, rising prices, still more incentive for retailers to increase inventories, and on and on the economy builds. However, this puts pressure on the banking system's excess reserves, interest rates rise, and businesses are inclined to cut back on investments in new plant and equipment as well as on inventory financing. Thus the stage becomes set for economic contraction.

Friedman and Schwartz are noted for their version of a monetary-based business cycle in which changes in the money stock initiate broad swings in the overall level of economic activity. Their theory has generated considerable attention in the last several decades. The concept of rational expectations has recently been applied to business cycles by Robert Lucas, Robert Barro, and others, who argue that it is unexpected changes in the money stock that bring about such long-term fluctuations in business activity.

An early investigation of the causes of business cycles by William Stanley Jevons (*circa* 1884) focused on a meteorologic basis for changes in economic activity. Jevons studied the relationship between sunspot activity and

[1]A more comprehensive overview is found in Lloyd M. Valentine, *Business Cycles and Forecasting*, 7th Ed. (Cincinnati, Ohio: South-Western Publishing, 1987), Chaps. 13 and 14, on which this discussion is based.

agricultural yields and attempted to relate the latter to levels of overall economic activity. Subsequent research ultimately showed that the connections he sought to make were far weaker than he had thought, if not absolutely wrong. However, the work of Jevons remains a classic example of the many attempts that have been made to establish a link between business cycles and some exogenous force.

Other cycle theories include those based on the effect of wars and resulting population changes, those based on ''underconsumption'' and the propensity for wealthier people to consume a smaller (save a larger) fraction of income, various psychological theories, Schumpeter's theory involving the role of innovations, and the more broad-based theories of Wesley Clair Mitchell, who studied a wide array of economic time series. It was Mitchell who founded the National Bureau of Economic Research (in the early 1920s), which today remains the agency that officially dates business-cycle activity in the United States.

16.3 ECONOMIC INDICATORS

Anyone involved in economic planning, budgeting, or forecasting would like to have an accurate and consistent indicator of what to expect some number of months into the future. No perfect indicator has been found, but ongoing research at the National Bureau of Economic Research (NBER) and elsewhere has provided some indices that correlate well with the general level of economic activity. Nearly everyone can recall hearing, on an evening newscast, a report concerning the ''index of leading economic indicators.'' Such reports usually include some economic/journalistic appraisal about what the news about the indicator means for the course of the U.S. economy in the months to follow. In this section we provide an introduction to the leading, lagging, and coincident indictors published each month in *Business Conditions Digest*.[2]

The cycle indicator's approach to analyzing and forecasting economic conditions has been widely used in both the private and public sectors of the economy. This approach identifies certain economic series as tending to lead, coincide with, or lag behind the general level of economic activity. All cyclical indicators are evaluated according to six major characteristics:

---

[2]See monthly issues of *Business Conditions Digest*, U.S. Department of Commerce, Bureau of Economic Analysis. Much of this section of the text is adapted from the discussion of cyclical indicators in the May 1987 issue (pp. 1 – 3).

Economic significance
Statistical adequacy
Consistency of timing at peaks and troughs
Conformity to business expansions and contractions
Smoothness
Prompt availability

The Bureau of Economic Analysis and the National Bureau of Economic Research developed a detailed weighting scheme to assess each series according to the preceding criteria. As a result, a list of indicators classified by economic process and typical timing at business-cycle peaks and troughs has been developed.

From this list of indicators, a set of composite indices has been established. These indices incorporate the best scoring series from many different economic process groups and combine those with similar timing, using their overall performance scores as weights. Because they include series of tested usefulness and timing, with varied economic coverage, composite indices give more reliable signals than do individual series. In addition, the development of composite indices smooths out measurement errors and other "noise" in the data.

The main composite indices are the index of leading indicators, the index of coincident indicators, and the index of lagging indicators. The *index of leading indicators* includes series that have historically reached their peaks and troughs earlier than the corresponding general business-cycle turns. The *index of coincident indicators* includes series that turn at about the same time as general economic activity, and the *index of lagging indicators* is composed of series that typically reach their peaks and troughs after the corresponding turns in general business. For the purpose of constructing composite indices, each component series is standardized so that more volatile series are prevented from dominating the index. The indices are constructed so that their long-term trends are similar to the long-term movement in aggregate economic activity (i.e., similar to the trend of GNP in constant dollars).

Figure 16.2 shows these three composite indices for the period from 1950 through the third quarter of 1988. Notice that the periods of official recessions, as dated by NBER, run from peak to trough as defined in Figure 16.1. You should compare the reference dates in Table 16.1 with these periods (note that the month for each peak and trough is shown along the top of the graph in Figure 16.2).

Along each series you see numbers that represent the number of months by which turning points for each index led ($-$) or lagged ($+$) the turning point in general economic activity, as judged by NBER. For example, above the index of eleven leading indicators just to the left of the shading for the July 1953 to May 1954 recession you see a -4 with a small right arrow beneath. This indicates that the index of leading indicators peaked 4 months prior to the July 1953 peak in overall economic activity. In that shaded region just below the index of leading indicators you see a -6, indicating that this index reached its trough 6 months before the trough in overall economic activity in May 1954.

In Figure 16.2 you also see that each of these composite indexes has its own series number: 910 for the index of leading indicators, 920 for the index of coincident indicators, and 930 for the index of lagging indicators. The numeric values upon which these graphs are based are also published in *Business Conditions Digest*. You see that the leading index is composed of 11 series (it used to be 12, but beginning with January 1984, series number 12—the index of net business formation—was suspended from the index), the coincident index includes four series, and the lagging index incorporates seven series. Identification of all these individual components and their classifications by economic process are given in Table 16.2.

16.4 FORECASTS OF GNP

Major econometric consulting firms such as the WEFA Group, Data Resources Incorporated, the Kent Economic and Development Institute, and others spend vast resources to model and forecast GNP and other economic series. It is not the purpose of this text to explain their models or forecasts, although the economic models you have studied earlier in the text provide the type of framework upon which such comprehensive models are constructed. Rather, our purpose is to illustrate in this section and the following two sections how some relatively simple forecasting methods can be applied to three important economic series: GNP, domestic car sales, and housing starts. (The methods used were discussed in Chapter 15. A knowledge of the computational procedures is not necessary, however, for your review of the applications in this chapter.) We begin with GNP.

Data for real GNP, in billions of 1982 dollars, are given in Table 16.3 and Figure 16.3. These data show the growth in overall economic activity in the United States through this period. While the general movement has been upward, you can probably pick out the dips or slower growth in periods that correspond to the recessions shown by the shaded areas in Figure 16.2. Note that 1987 values are withheld, since those are to be forecast. You might want to check a recent issue of *Business Conditions Digest* to see how well these models predicted GNP.

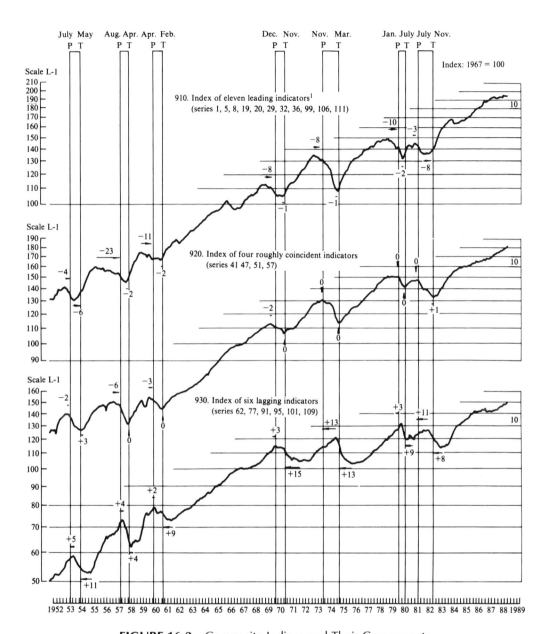

FIGURE 16.2   Composite Indices and Their Components.
This figure shows how the composite leading, coincident, and lagging indicators have behaved since 1950. The vertical strips represent recessions for which beginning (*P*) and ending (*T*) dates are
shown at the top.
Source: Business Conditions Digest, November 1988, p.10.

TABLE 16.2 Classification of Composite Index Components by Economic Process

				Economic Process			
Index	I. Employment and Unemployment	II. Production and Income	III. Consumption, Trade, Orders, and Deliveries	IV. Fixed Capital Investment	V. Inventories and Inventory Investment	VI. Prices, Costs, and Profits	VII. Money and Trade
Leading indicators	1. Average weekly hours of production or nonsupervisory workers, manufacturing 5. Average weekly initial claims for unemployment insurance, state programs		8. Manufacturers' new orders in 1972 dollars, consumer goods and materials industries 32. Vendor performance, percent of companies receiving slower deliveries 83. Index of consumer expectations	20. Contracts and orders for plant and equipment in 1972 dollars 29. Index of new private housing units authorized by local building permits	92. Change in manufacturers unfilled orders in 1982 dollars, durable goods, smoothed	99. Change in sensitive materials prices, smoothed 19. Index of stock prices, 500 common stocks	106. Money supply M2 in 1972 dollars
Coincident indicators	41. Employees on nonagricultural payrolls	51. Personal income less transfer payments in 1972 dollars 47. Index of industrial production	57. Manufacturing and trade sales in 1972 dollars				

Lagging indicators	91. Average duration of unemployment in weeks	77. Ratio, manufacturing and trade inventories to sales in 1972 dollars	62. Index of labor cost per unit of output, manufacturing — actual data as a percent of trade	109. Average prime rate charged by banks
			120. Change in consumer price index for services, smoothed	101. Commercial and industrial loans outstanding in 1972 dollars
				95. Ratio, consumer installment credit outstanding to personal income

Source: The Handbook of Cyclical Indicators: A Supplement to the Business Conditions Digest, U.S. Department of Commerce, Bureau of Economic Analysis, 1984, p. 66.

TABLE 16.3 Gross National Product in Billions of 1982 Dollars

Observation	First Quarter	Second Quarter	Third Quarter	Fourth Quarter
1960	1671.6	1666.8	1668.4	1654.1
1961	1671.3	1692.1	1716.3	1754.9
1962	1777.9	1796.4	1813.1	1810.1
1963	1834.6	1860.0	1892.5	1906.1
1964	1948.7	1965.4	1985.2	1993.7
1965	2036.9	2066.4	2099.3	2147.6
1966	2190.1	2195.8	2218.3	2229.2
1967	2241.8	2255.2	2287.7	2300.6
1968	2327.3	2366.9	2385.3	2383.0
1969	2416.5	2419.8	2433.2	2423.5
1970	2408.6	2406.5	2435.8	2413.8
1971	2478.6	2478.4	2491.1	2491.0
1972	2545.6	2595.1	2622.1	2671.3
1973	2734.0	2741.0	2738.3	2762.8
1974	2747.4	2755.2	2719.3	2695.4
1975	2642.7	2669.6	2714.9	2752.7
1976	2804.4	2816.9	2828.6	2856.8
1977	2896.0	2942.7	3001.8	2994.1
1978	3020.5	3115.9	3142.6	3181.6
1979	3181.7	3178.7	3207.4	3201.3
1980	3233.4	3157.0	3159.1	3199.2
1981	3261.1	3250.2	3264.6	3219.0
1982	3170.4	3179.9	3154.5	3159.3
1983	3186.6	3258.3	3306.4	3365.1
1984	3444.7	3487.1	3507.4	3520.4
1985	3547.0	3567.6	3603.8	3622.3
1986	3655.9	3661.4	3686.4	3696.1
1987	NA	NA	NA	NA

Source: Citibase: Citibank economic database (New York: Citibank, N.A., 1986).

16.4.1 A Trend Forecast of GNP

The first method we will use to forecast real GNP for 1987 is a simple linear time trend. Using data from 1960.1 (first quarter of 1960) through 1986.4 (fourth quarter of 1986), the following regression line was estimated:

Real GNP = 1649.05 + 18.52(time)

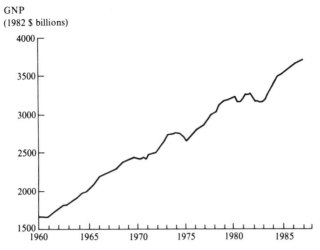

FIGURE 16.3   Real GNP in Billions of 1982 Dollars.
This graph shows the overall growth of the U.S. economy beginning
in 1960. However, the general upward trend has been interrupted
by occasional short periods of decline.

where

  time = 1 for 1960.1

The coefficient of determination was 0.986, and the coefficient for the time was significant at a 0.05 significance level. Figure 16.4 shows this trend line and the actual real GNP series for 1980.1 through 1987.4. A shorter time frame is used in this graph to allow for a better comparison of the two series in more recent years. In the figure, the recession from July 1981 through November 1982 is quite noticeable, as is the expansion period back toward the long-term trend and the continued stable growth through 1986. The values from the trend forecast for 1987 (in billions of 1982 dollars) are

  1987.1:   3715.1
  1987.2:   3734.2
  1987.3:   3753.2
  1987.4:   3772.3

16.4.2 A Simple Exponential Smoothing Forecast of GNP

The second forecasting technique applied to real GNP was an exponential smoothing model that incorporates a trend component. This is necessary

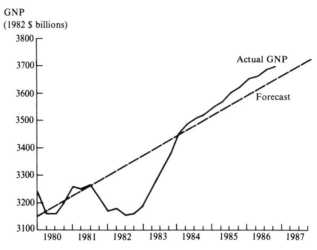

FIGURE 16.4   Real GNP and Linear Trend Forecast.
The forecast equation is real GNP = 1649.05 + 18.52 (time), where
time = 1 for 1960.1. The 1981 − 1982 recession and the following
recovery are seen by the substantial dip below the long-run growth
trend.

because real GNP has such a pronounced upward trend. The actual values
of real GNP along with the exponential smoothing forecast are shown in
Figure 16.5. You can see that this model does a reasonably good job of
forecasting real GNP by looking at the plot in Figure 16.5. The extension of
the simple exponential smoothing model used in this example is known as
Holt's exponential smoothing. The forecasts for the four quarters of 1987,
in billions of 1982 dollars, are

        1987.1:   3715.1
        1987.2:   3734.2
        1987.3:   3753.2
        1987.4:   3772.3

These are not all the same, as they would be for simple exponential smoothing, because the Holt's model incorporates a trend component. Other exponential smoothing models not discussed in this text also include a trend as
well as adjustments for seasonality where appropriate.[3]

---

[3]See, for example, Robert S. Pindyck and Daniel L. Rubinfeld, *Econometric Models and Economic
Forecasts*, 2d Ed. (New York: McGraw-Hill, 1981), especially Chap. 15, "Smoothing and Extrapolation
of Time Series."

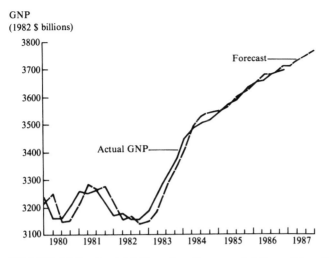

FIGURE 16.5   Real GNP and an Exponential Smoothing Forecast. Since there is such a strong trend in GNP, a type of exponential smoothing that incorporates the trend was used to provide this forecast of GNP. The method is called *Holt's exponential smoothing.*

16.4.3 A Bivariate Regression Forecast of GNP

The final forecast of GNP was made using a regression model with the change in real GNP (*CGNP*) as a function of the change in the level of employment (*CEMP*). This represents a simple supply-side view of the determination of GNP. The regression equation is

$$CGNP = 3.49 + 0.037CEMP$$

The coefficient of determination was 0.38, and the coefficient for employment was significant at a 0.001 significance level. Changes in the variables were used to avoid an autocorrelation problem. (The Durbin-Watson statistic is 0.097 if the original data are used, but it is 2.05 for the preceding model.)

   The forecast of real GNP based on this regression model is illustrated in Figure 16.6, where both the actual and forecast values are plotted over time from 1980.1 on. For use in the regression forecast model, the change in employment was first forecast using a simple exponential smoothing model. The resulting regression forecast for the four quarters of 1987, in billions of 1982 dollars, are

   1987.1:   3741.95
   1987.2:   3764.88

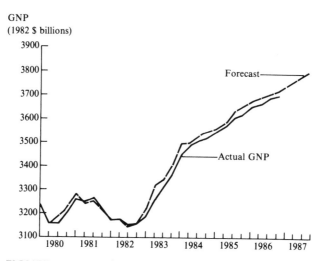

FIGURE 16.6   Real GNP and Regression Forecast.
The forecast equation is $CGNP = 3.49 + 0.037CEMP$, where $CGNP$ is the quarterly change in GNP, and $CEMP$ is the quarterly change in employment. The change in employment was forecast for 1987 using a simple exponential smoothing model, and those values were substituted into the regression model to derive the changes in GNP for each quarter of 1987. These in turn were added to GNP for 1986.4 to derive the forecast values of real GNP for 1987.

1987.3:   3787.81
1987.4:   3810.73

16.5 FORECASTING DOMESTIC CAR SALES

The automotive sector of the economy, and especially the domestic automobile sector, is very important in determining the overall health of the U.S. economy. Increases in domestic car sales bring about greater income to people employed in local dealerships, in automobile company corporate offices, in manufacturing plants, and in the distribution of new cars throughout the country. As these people earn more income, we know, from our knowledge about the marginal propensity to consume, that they will spend a substantial portion of it on a wide array of goods and services. This creates higher sales and thus higher incomes in those sectors of the economy. In addition, as new cars are produced, new tires, steel, plastics, batteries, and other inputs are demanded from a variety of suppliers. Employment in these related industries is bolstered, generating more dollars of income, more spending, still more employment, and so on. The multiplier process ripples its way through the economy with such force that many people seemingly far removed from domestic car sales (even a foreign car dealer) are affected. Of course, downturns in domestic car sales have comparable, but negative repercussions throughout the economy. A reasonably accurate forecast of the domestic automobile industry is therefore important for firms that supply the automobile industry, for financial institutions that deal with those supplying firms as well as with the automobile companies themselves, for government agencies that must plan for social programs, and so forth.

Data for domestic car sales (*DCS*) per quarter in thousands of units are shown in Table 16.4 and in Figure 16.7. Both forms reflect a good deal of seasonal variation and possibly some cyclical behavior, as well as a slight upward trend. These aspects of the data are, for most people, more easily recognized in the graphic form of Figure 16.7 than in tabular form. Three forecasting methods will be applied to this series:

> Simple exponential smoothing
>
> Time-series decomposition
>
> Multiple regression

The forecasts will be presented in the following pages.

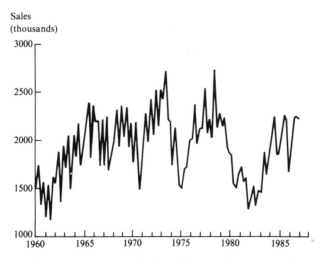

FIGURE 16.7   Domestic Car Sales per Quarter in Thousands. Domestic car sales are seen to exhibit a reasonably consistent seasonal pattern, a slight upward trend, and some cyclical behavior.

TABLE 16.4   Domestic Car Sales by Quarter in Thousands of Units

Observation	First Quarter	Second Quarter	Third Quarter	Fourth Quarter
1960	1514	1739	1330	1559
1961	1212	1539	1181	1624
1962	1559	1887	1360	1947
1963	1721	2055	1500	2059
1964	1844	2172	1742	1860
1965	2196	2380	1821	2365
1966	2206	2208	1744	2218
1967	1743	2235	1691	1898
1968	2021	2321	1935	2349
1969	2029	2347	1926	2162
1970	1783	2190	1656	1491
1971	1974	2276	1987	2425
1972	2064	2517	2147	2524
1973	2451	2718	2229	2190
1974	1752	2138	1927	1546
1975	1506	1709	1734	2002
1976	2025	2376	1970	2122
1977	2128	2538	2081	2223
1978	2027	2727	2140	2270
1979	2155	2231	1971	1875
1980	1850	1551	1515	1666
1981	1733	1576	1618	1282
1982	1401	1535	1327	1494
1983	1456	1876	1646	1813
1984	1994	2251	1855	1852
1985	2042	2273	2218	1672
1986	1898	2242	2247	2231
1987	NA	NA	NA	NA

Source: Citibase: Citibank economic database (New York: Citibank, N.A., 1986).

16.5.1 A Simple Exponential Smoothing Forecast of Domestic Car Sales

The first forecasting technique to be used for the domestic car sales data is a simple exponential smoothing model. The weighting factor used was $w = 0.44$. The entire data series, starting with the first quarter of 1960 (1960.1) and extending through the last quarter of 1986 (1986.4), has been used to prepare a quarterly forecast for 1987. The results of this forecasting model are shown in Figure 16.8. Only the period from 1980.1 is shown in this figure, so that the relation between the actual data and the forecast series is seen more clearly. You should notice that the forecast series reacts less than fully to movements in the raw data with a lag of one quarter. The exponential smoothing forecasts for the four quarters of 1987, in thousands of units, are

    1987.1:   2182.2
    1987.2:   2182.2
    1987.3:   2182.2
    1987.4:   2182.2

As with all simple exponential smoothing forecasts, the predicted value is the same throughout the forecast period. This is so because the method relies on the actual value of the previous quarter for each forecast and no such value is available for 1987.1. Thus we assume that the forecast of 2182.2 will be correct and use it as the actual value in forecasting 1987.2. Using this procedure for the entire forecast period yields the flat forecast shown previously and in Figure 16.8.

FIGURE 16.8   Domestic Car Sales and Exponential Smoothing Forecast. For the 1980 through 1986 period, the forecast series reacts partially to changes in the raw data with a one quarter lag. In the forecast period (1987), the exponential smoothing forecast is flat.

16.5.2 A Time-Series Decomposition Forecast of Domestic Car Sales

The next method applied to the problem of forecasting domestic car sales is time-series decomposition. From the original data series (see Fig. 16.7), we should expect that this model might work well, since seasonality appeared to exist and some cyclical behavior seemed likely. Further, any analyst familiar with the industry would anticipate these components to be important. Quarterly data from 1960.1 through 1986.4 were used to develop the forecast for the four quarters of 1987. The data were first deseasonalized using centered moving averages, and then the long-term trend was estimated based on the deseasonalized data. The long-term trend is only slightly positive, showing an average quarterly increase of 492 cars (i.e., the slope of the time-trend regression was 0.429, where the data were in thousands).

Seasonal factors for each quarter from 1960.3 through 1986.2 were calculated by dividing the original domestic car sales data by the deseasonalized data (the centered moving averages). These were then averaged and normalized to sum to 4 (since quarterly data are used) to determine seasonal indices for domestic car sales. The resulting seasonal indices are

    First quarter: 0.968
    Second quarter: 1.103
    Third quarter: 0.924
    Fourth quarter: 1.003

From these we see that (ignoring cyclical movements), on average, fourth quarter sales fall very close to the long-term trend, while first and third quarter sales are typically below the trend, by 3.2 and 7.6 percent, respectively. These percentages are based on the seasonal indices. For example, the first quarter seasonal index indicates that first quarter sales are on average 96.8 percent (0.968) of the long-term trend, or 3.2 percent below trend. The strong sales quarter is thus seen to be the second quarter, since its seasonal index is 1.103. This suggests that second quarter sales are typically 10.3 percent above the long-term trend, ignoring cyclical movements.

The cycle component of domestic car sales is evaluated by looking at the wavelike movements of the deseasonalized data relative to the long-term trend. The cyclical factor for each quarter is calculated by dividing each centered moving average (the deseasonalized value of car sales) by the trend value for each quarter. The values for the cyclical factor are shown graphically in Figure 16.9. From Figure 16.9 you can see that domestic car sales have moved through a series of cyclical fluctuations during this period. Values for 1987 and the last two quarters of 1986 were found using Holt's exponential smoothing.

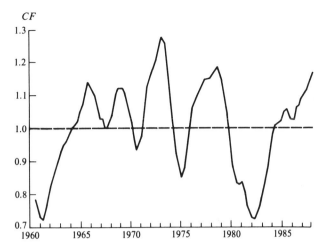

FIGURE 16.9   Cycle Factor for Time-Series Decomposition Forecast of Domestic Car Sales.

The cycle factor shows extended nonseasonal movement in domestic car sales around the long-term trend. Note the most recent trough, which corresponds to the national recessions of 1980 and 1981 – 1982.

Once the trend, seasonal, and cyclical components have been isolated in a time-series decomposition model, they can be combined in a multiplicative manner to provide estimates, or forecasts, of the original series. For 1987, this process is as follows:

Quarter	Trend	Seasonal Index	Cycle Factor	Forecast
1987.1	1964.997	0.968	1.10	2092.329
1987.2	1965.490	1.103	1.12	2428.088
1987.3	1965.982	0.924	1.14	2070.887
1987.4	1966.475	1.003	1.16	2287.954

These forecast values are shown in Figure 16.10 along with the actual data for domestic car sales. You will notice that the seasonality in the data is picked up by this forecasting method. It is most apparent in the 1987.2 peak in Figure 16.10. Figure 16.10 only shows the original and forecast series from 1980 on to make the correspondence of the two easier to see. If they are plotted for the entire period, starting with 1960.1, they fall so closely together that it would be hard to tell them apart.

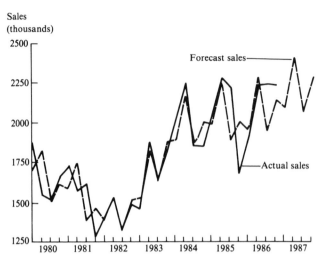

FIGURE 16.10   Time-Series Decomposition Forecast of Domestic Car Sales.
The forecast series shown here by the dotted line does follow the pattern of car sales through the historical period shown reasonably well. In the forecast period (1987), the second quarter seasonality is shown by a sharp peak.

16.5.3 A Multiple Regression Forecast of Domestic Car Sales

The final forecasting technique to be applied to domestic car sales is multiple regression. Based on economic reasoning, the following economic variables might be hypothesized to affect domestic car sales: some measure of price (*P*), income (*INC*), interest rates (*I*), and general consumer confidence (*CC*).[4] In addition, the plot of domestic automobile sales shown in Figure 16.7 suggests seasonality, so one or more seasonal dummy variables may be appropriate. The resulting single-equation multiple linear regression model, based on data from the first quarter of 1978 through the fourth quarter of 1986, is as follows:

$$DCS = -1474.04 - 19.25P + 0.47INC - 16.72I + 7.09CC$$
$$+ 201.82Q2$$

where *DCS* represents domestic car sales and *Q2* is a second quarter dummy variable.

---

[4]For the purpose of this illustrative model, the durable goods price index was used for *P*, real disposable personal income per capita (1982 dollars) was used for *INC*, the prime interest rate was used for *I*, and the Conference Board's index of consumer sentiment was used for *CC*. These are all variables that are readily available to students should you wish to verify or update this regression model.

Before using this model to forecast domestic car sales, let us evaluate the model to see if it makes sense. First, we should ask whether the signs of each of the coefficients make sense. The signs that economic theory would suggest for the causal variables would be

Variable	Direction of Causality	Expected Sign
P	Inverse	−
INC	Direct	+
I	Inverse	−
CC	Direct	+

The empirical model is thus consistent with our theoretical expectations for these independent variables. In addition, industry knowledge and our review of the time-series plot in Figure 16.7 suggest that the positive sign for the second quarter dummy variable is reasonable. Since we had on an a priori basis to suppose a particular sign for each independent variable, one-tailed t tests are appropriate. At a 5 percent level of significance and 30 degrees of freedom $[df = 36 - (5 + 1)]$, all five independent variables are found to be statistically significant. The adjusted R^2 value for the model was 0.819. (The Durbin-Watson statistic was 2.2.)

To use the preceding model to forecast domestic car sales for the four quarters of 1987, the four causal variables had to be forecast as well. In each case, a Holt's exponential smoothing model was used for this purpose. Once forecast values for the causal variables were obtained, the multiple linear regression model was used to prepare the 1987 forecast. The dummy variable ($Q2$) was equal to 1 for the second quarter and 0 otherwise. The resulting forecasts, in thousands, are

    1987.1:   2053.313
    1987.2:   2248.144
    1987.3:   2048.953
    1987.4:   2052.385

These results are shown in Figure 16.11. Again, only the period from 1980 on is shown to facilitate comparison of forecast with actual values. Based on a review of the two series in Figure 16.11, the multiple linear regression model appears to predict domestic car sales reasonably well in the historical period.[5] Note that the seasonality of the second quarter shows up clearly at 1987.2.

---

[5] You may want to check a recent issue of the *Survey of Current Business* to see how well all these models worked for the 1987 forecast period.

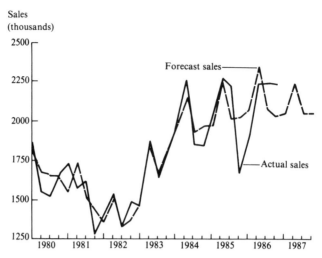

FIGURE 16.11   Domestic Car Sales with Multiple Regression Forecast. The multiple linear regression forecast of domestic car sales, shown here by the dotted line, follows the actual data series well through the historical period. The second quarter seasonality accounted for by the dummy variable shows up clearly, especially in the forecast period for 1987.2.

16.6 FORECASTING HOUSING STARTS

Like the automobile sector, the housing sector of the economy is extremely important in determining the overall health of the U.S. economy. The construction of new housing units suggests that new appliance, carpet, drapery, and furniture purchases are likely to follow. In addition, industries such as the wood products industry that supply materials used in housing construction are also affected strongly by housing starts. Thus many other sectors of our economy are affected quite directly by the rate of housing starts. Considering what you know about the multiplier process, you can see that changes in this sector will have a heavy impact on the overall health of the economy.

Data on housing starts in thousands of units are shown in Table 16.5 and Figure 16.12 for the period from the first quarter of 1973 (1973.1) through the fourth quarter of 1986 (1986.4). No data are given for 1987, since forecasts for that year will be made in the following sections using three different techniques. The forecasting methods applied to the housing starts data are, as they were for domestic car sales, simple exponential smoothing, time-series decomposition, and multiple linear regression.

TABLE 16.5   Housing Starts in Thousands of Units

Observation	First Quarter	Second Quarter	Third Quarter	Fourth Quarter
1973	484.6	641.6	548.2	370.8
1974	318.7	456.1	336.0	226.9
1975	191.0	324.3	348.5	296.6
1976	280.8	439.3	434.3	382.9
1977	367.4	581.1	561.5	477.1
1978	362.0	624.5	563.6	470.2
1979	325.6	541.9	498.2	379.3
1980	238.1	304.3	388.3	361.5
1981	264.2	338.7	270.3	210.9
1982	176.7	274.0	309.2	302.3
1983	322.2	483.9	493.3	403.6
1984	376.6	537.4	458.0	377.4
1985	345.8	509.2	469.1	417.6
1986	373.8	558.4	489.8	383.4
1987	NA	NA	NA	NA

Source: Citibase: Citibank economic database (New York: Citibank, N.A., 1986).

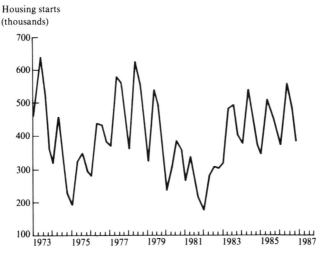

FIGURE 16.12   Housing Starts in Thousands of Units.
This time-series plot of housing starts shows seasonality and some cyclical movement but not much of a trend. The recessions of 1974, 1980, and 1981 – 1982 are evident.

16.6.1 A Simple Exponential Smoothing Forecast of Housing Starts

The first forecasting technique we apply to the housing starts data is a simple exponential smoothing model. For the model illustrated in Figure 16.13, a weighting factor of 0.47 was used. In this figure, two things are clear:

1. The forecast, as shown by the dotted line, reacts to movements in the actual data with a one quarter lag.
2. The forecast reacts less than fully to changes in actual housing starts.

Thus the forecast series falls within the extremes of the original data and does not reflect seasonal patterns in a timely manner. As with all simple exponential smoothing forecasts, the predicted values are constant throughout the forecast period. In this example, the 1987 forecast for housing starts is

1987.1: 436.63
1987.2: 436.63
1987.3: 436.63
1987.4: 436.63

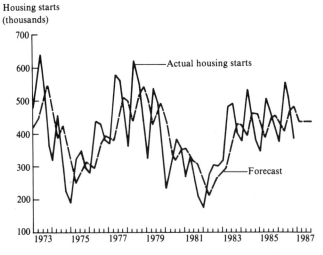

FIGURE 16.13   A Simple Exponential Smoothing Forecast of Housing Starts.
The simple exponential smoothing forecast of housing starts is shown by the dotted line. A weighting factor of 0.47 was used in developing this forecast. Notice that seasonality in the data is not reflected in a timely manner by the forecast series.

16.6.2 A Time-Series Decomposition Forecast of Housing Starts

The second forecasting technique applied to the problem of forecasting housing starts for each quarter of 1987 was the time-series decomposition method. Because housing starts appear to follow a definite seasonal pattern, as almost anyone would expect, and because the data in Table 16.5 and especially Figure 16.12 seem to indicate some cyclical behavior, this method would appear to be a likely candidate for the purpose of forecasting housing starts.

The time-series decomposition method begins by deseasonalizing the data by constructing centered moving averages of the original series. The centered moving averages represent the deseasonalized value of housing starts. By comparing the actual values for each quarter with the deseasonalized values, we find out the extent to which a seasonal pattern exists. Seasonal factors are calculated as the ratio of the original observation in each quarter to the centered moving average in each quarter. These seasonal factors are then averaged by quarter over the length of the data series, and the quarterly means are then normalized (to sum to 4) to form seasonal indices. For housing starts, these seasonal indices are

    First quarter: 0.781
    Second quarter: 1.179
    Third quarter: 1.117
    Fourth quarter: 0.924

Thus we see that housing starts tend to be quite low during the first quarter (January – March), strongest in the second quarter (April – June), still strong in the third quarter (July – September), and beginning to slow in the final quarter of the year (October – December).

The deseasonalized data (centered moving averages) are used as the basis for establishing the long-term trend in housing starts. As with the domestic car sales series discussed earlier, the long-term trend for housing starts is relatively flat, averaging about 467 additional units per quarter. The cycle factor for housing starts is found by measuring the movement of the deseasonalized data series around the long-term trend. The way this is done is to find the ratio of the deseasonalized data to the long-term trend value for each quarter. If this ratio is greater than 1, there is an up period for the cycle, and if it is less than 1, there is a down period. For housing starts, the cycle is shown in Figure 16.14. Since cycle factors could only be estimated through 1986.2, projections were made for 1986.3 to 1987.4 using a Holt's exponential smoothing model. This cycle factor has had considerable movement, reaching 30 percent above the long-term trend (1978.1) and falling to 60 percent of the trend (1982.1).

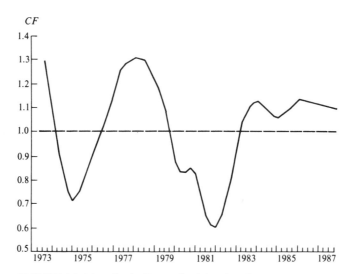

FIGURE 16.14 Cycle Factor for Housing Starts.
The housing start cycle factor has moved above and below the long-term trend by quite a lot during the period from 1973 through 1986. The projection starting with 1986.3 is based on a Holt's exponential smoothing model.

The time-series decomposition model is used to estimate housing starts in the historical and forecast periods by multiplying the trend component (*CMAT*) by the seasonal index (*SI*) and cycle factor (*CF*) for each quarter. That is, the forecast values are found as follows:

$$\text{Forecast} = CMAT \times SI \times CF$$

These values along with the original data are plotted in Figure 16.15. Note how well the model appears to follow the actual data and how clearly the seasonal pattern is reflected, even in the forecast period (1987). The actual values forecast for the four quarters of 1987 (in thousands) are

    1987.1:   351.865
    1987.2:   529.162
    1987.3:   499.421
    1987.4:   411.541

16.6.3 A Multiple Regression Forecast of Housing Starts

The third forecasting technique applied to housing starts is the multiple regression method. For purposes of illustration, the following economic vari-

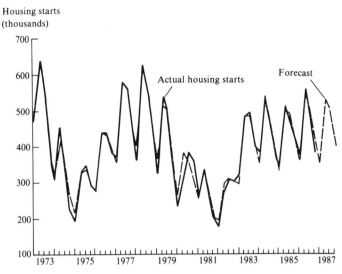

FIGURE 16.15 A Time-Series Decomposition Forecast of Housing Starts. The time-series decomposition model is seen to fit the data very well in the historical period. The seasonality in housing starts is well represented by this model even in the forecast period.

ables are hypothesized to have an impact on housing starts (the sign after each variable represents the a priori expectation of the direction of causation):

Mortgate rate, MR ($-$)

Real disposable personal income, DPI ($+$)

Unemployment rate, UR ($-$)

Change in housing price index, DP ($-$)

In addition, dummy variables were included for the second, third, and fourth quarters ($Q2$, $Q3$, and $Q4$, respectively). The statistical results are as follows:

Term	Coefficient	t-Ratio
Intercept	253.918	2.35
MR	-20.137	-2.74
DPI	0.213	4.27
UR	-21.587	-2.15
DP	-8.218	-1.66
Q2	166.017	6.80
Q3	132.970	5.45
Q4	50.242	2.06

Data for 1973.1 through 1986.4 were used in estimating these values. All the signs are as we would expect, and the *t* ratios indicate significance at a 5 percent level for a one-tailed test. The adjusted R^2 value is 0.685. The quarterly dummy variables indicate that quarters 2, 3, and 4 are all typically higher than the first quarter (the signs for *Q2*, *Q3*, and *Q4* are significantly positive), and it is clear that the second and third quarters are the strong periods for housing starts (these two quarters include April through September).

Before this model could be used in forecasting, each of the nondummy independent variables was forecast using a Holt's exponential smoothing model. Values of all the independent variables for the four quarters of 1987 were then substituted into the multiple linear regression equation given earlier to generate the following forecast (in thousands of units):

    1987.1:   458.41
    1987.2:   636.55
    1987.3:   615.27
    1987.4:   544.23

These results can be seen graphically in Figure 16.16. Notice that the regression model's predictions for each quarter follow the general pattern of the historical series reasonably well. This is due in large part to the inclusion of the quarterly dummy variables in the model.

16.7 SUMMARY

1. The United States and other market-driven economies have had a history of wide fluctuations in economic activity that are often described as business cycles. If the word *cycles* is interpreted strictly, it does not convey the true movement of economic activity, since the periodicity and amplitude are not regular. Therefore, the phrase *business fluctuations* may be more appropriate. Regardless of the term that is used, there are clear periods of economic expansion until a peak is reached, then economic decline (recession) follows until a trough is reached that is once more followed by expansion. Business-cycle reference dates dating back to 1854 were shown in Table 16.1. More recent recessions are highlighted in Figure 16.2.

2. The National Bureau of Economic Research (NBER) is the agency that officially dates recessions in the United States. The most convenient source of these dates is *Business Conditions Digest*, which is published monthly by the U.S. Department of Commerce.

3. *Business Conditions Digest* also publishes about 300 economic time series that are of significant value for macroeconomic research and economic

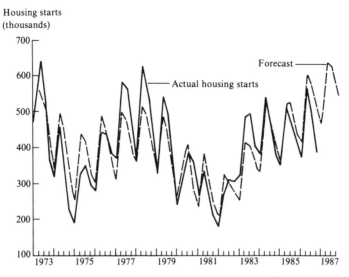

FIGURE 16.16   A Multiple Regression Forecast of Housing Starts. The multiple regression model follows the original data well and reflects the seasonality into the forecast period. Seasonality was accounted for by using dummy variables for the second, third, and fourth quarters. Other independent variables included the mortgage rate, real disposable personal income, the unemployment rate, and the change in the housing price index.

forecasting. Among those series are the index of leading economic indicators, the index of coincident economic indicators, and the index of lagging indicators. These are shown in graphic form in Figure 16.2 for the years starting with 1950.

4. An understanding of the macro economy and economic interrelationships is important in developing economic forecasts. Macroeconomic varibles such as GNP, personal income, the unemployment rate, and various interest rates are important in forecasting economic activity in various sectors of the economy.

5. When developing economic forecasts, it is wise to look at several different forecasts based on different forecasting techniques. Judgments based on expert experience are important in making a final determination of the most likely future values of any economic series.

16.8 EXERCISES

1. Look up data for real gross national product (in 1982 dollars) for each quarter of 1987 and use that data to evaluate the accuracy of the three real GNP forecasts presented in this chapter. If the data you find are monthly, use the average of each quarter's 3 months as the quarterly value. Calculate the root mean squared error (*RMSE*) for each model. $RMSE = [\Sigma(A - F)/n]^{0.5}$, where A is the actual value, F is the forecast value, and $n = 4$, since there are four quarters in this problem. (Raising anything to the 0.5 power is the same as taking the square root.)

2. Explain what is meant by the term *business cycle*. Include in your explanation the meaning of the following terms: *expansion*, *recession*, *peak*, and *trough*.

3. Suppose that you work for a major oil company that wants to forecast gasoline sales using multiple regression. Suggest three independent variables that you think would have an effect on gasoline sales, and explain the sign you would expect for each variable. In addition, explain why you would or would not expect gasoline sales to have a seasonal component.

4. Pick an industry and develop two separate forecasts for sales or production in that industry. Consult the most recent *U.S. Industrial Outlook*, and write a paragraph that summarizes what that source says about the future for your industry.

5. Data on the female labor force participation rate (*FLFPR*) from 1961 through 1980 follow:

Year	FLFPR (%)	Year	FLFPR (%)
1961	38.1	1971	43.4
1962	37.9	1972	43.9
1963	38.3	1973	44.7
1964	38.7	1974	45.7
1965	39.3	1975	46.3
1966	40.3	1976	47.3
1967	41.1	1977	48.4
1968	41.6	1978	50.0
1969	42.7	1979	50.9
1970	43.3	1980	51.5

Source: Economic Report of the President,
1987, p. 284.

Use these data to prepare a linear time-trend forecast of the female labor force participation rate for 1981 through 1986. Do you see any problem in using such a linear trend forecast for this series? Prepare a time-series plot in which you show both actual and predicted values for 1961 − 1980 along with the forecast values for 1981 − 1986.

6. Go to the library and find the most recent issue of *Business Conditions Digest*. Look up the index of leading economic indicators (series 910), and see how those values relate to the most recent official recession (as dated by the NBER). Also, compare the recent values to the series found in Figure 16.2.

7. Gather 5 years of data to prepare a simple exponential smoothing forecast of business failures for the following year. Use the series for total failures under the heading "Industrial and Commercial Failures" on page S-5 of the *Survey of Current Business*. Let $w = 0.7$ in preparing your forecast.

8. Data on gross private domestic investment (I) for 1961 through 1980 are provided below. Use these data to develop a forecast of I for 1981 through 1986. Look up the actual data for the forecast period, and write a paragraph in which you explain how successful you think you were in making the forecast. Include a time-series plot for 1961 through 1986 as part of your discussion.

Year	Investment ($ Billions)	Year	Investment ($ Billions)
1961	77.1	1971	172.5
1962	87.6	1972	202.0
1963	93.1	1973	238.8
1964	99.6	1974	240.8
1965	116.2	1975	219.6
1966	128.6	1976	277.7
1967	125.7	1977	344.1
1968	137.0	1978	416.8
1969	153.2	1979	454.8
1970	148.8	1980	437.0

Source: Economic Report of the President, 1987, p. 244.

16.9 REFERENCES

American Economic Association, *Readings in Business Cycle Theory*, Vol. 3. Homewood, Ill.: Irwin, 1965.

A. S. Blinder and S. Fischer, "Inventories, Rational Expectations, and the Business Cycle," *Journal of Monetary Economics*, November 1981, pp. 227–304.

Milton Friedman and Anna J. Schwartz, "Money and Business Cycles," *The Review of Economics and Statistics*, February 1963, pp. 32–64.

Nicholas Kaldor, *Essays on Economic Stability and Growth*, 2d Ed. New York: Holmes and Meier, 1980.

Wesley Claire Mitchell and Arthur F. Burns, *Statistical Indicators of Cyclical Revivals*, Bulletin No. 69. New York: National Bureau of Economic Research, 1938.

Wesley Claire Mitchell and Arthur F. Burns, *Measuring Business Cycles*. New York: National Bureau of Economic Research, 1947.

Joseph Schumpeter, *Theory of Economic Development*. Cambridge, Mass.: Harvard University Press, 1934.

Joseph Schumpeter, *Business Cycles*. New York: McGraw-Hill, 1939.

Albert T. Somers, *The U.S. Economy Demystified*. Lexington Mass.: D. C. Heath, 1985, especially Chap. 3, "How to Watch the Business Cycle," and Chap. 4, "The Influences of Economic Policy."

——— *MANAGERIAL CASE* ———————————————

INVESTMENT PLANS AS FORECASTS

The opening season of each new year sees an overwhelming number of economic forecasts. These economic forecasts differ not only by the individuals or institutions making them but also by the methodologies used. Some forecasts are primarily judgmental, others are based mainly on survey information, and still others employ econometric modeling techniques.

Important examples of the use of survey information in forecasting are the surveys of planned capital spending by business compiled by both the Commerce Department's Bureau of Economic Analysis (BEA) and the McGraw-Hill Publishing Company. The fall surveys recently released by BEA and McGraw-Hill indicate an increase of 0.2 percent and a decline of 3.1 percent, respectively, in real capital spending (nominal spending adjusted for anticipated changes in the prices of capital goods) from 1986 to 1987. Weak capital spending, in turn, is a key element in the moderate economic growth that most forecasters picture for 1987.

But just how useful is such survey information on capital spending compared to other available forecasts? This *Letter* examines whether the BEA and McGraw-Hill surveys provide very much useful information by comparing their forecasts with those from a standard econometric model.

SURVEYS VS. AN ECONOMETRIC MODEL

The BEA takes surveys of capital spending plans four times a year, while McGraw-Hill conducts its surveys every spring and fall. We will focus on the fall surveys, which give the outlook for a full year ahead. Respondents are asked how much their companies will spend on plant and equipment in the year ahead and also how much they expect the prices they pay for plant and equipment to rise. (Recently, BEA substituted an extrapolation of price increases in the previous year for the answer to the latter question.) By subtracting the expected percentage change in prices from the anticipated percentage increase in nominal spending, the surveys arrive at the percentage increase in real (or adjusted for prices) spending anticipated by the respondents.

Economic forecasters are generally most interested in the outlook for nonresidential fixed investment as measured by the national income accounts, which is not quite the same concept as the spending on plant and equipment used in the surveys. For example, investment in the farm sector is included in nonresidential fixed in-

The Federal Reserve Bank of San Francisco publishes a weekly letter that helps to keep business leaders informed about new events or ideas related to business functions. This article by Adrian W. Throop appeared in *FRBSF Weekly Letter*, February 13, 1987.

vestment but not in the plant and equipment series. Also, the nonresidential fixed investment series reflects the value of new construction put in place and shipments of equipment whereas the plant and equipment series reflects expenditures, which on balance tend to come later. Nevertheless, the value of nonresidential fixed investment is within 2 percent of total plant and equipment expenditures, and the two generally tend to move quite closely together.

The econometric model that we use to forecast nonresidential fixed investment follows the neoclassical approach elaborated by Professors Robert Hall and Dale Jorgenson. In neoclassical theory, capital is viewed as a substitute for other factors of production. Firms in neoclassical theory therefore respond to the relative prices of capital goods (their prices relative to that of other factors of production) in making their decisions to invest in plant and equipment. The relative prices of capital goods, in turn, depend importantly upon real (or inflation-adjusted) interest rates, taxes, and physical rates of depreciation. The higher the relative prices of capital goods, the lower will be the amount of capital per unit of output that firms will desire to hold, and the greater will be the amount of other factors, such as labor, that they will wish to employ.

Firms adjust to the difference between their desired and actual capital stocks gradually. As a result, the amount of new planned investment, equal to the amount of capital appropriations, is some fraction of the difference between the desired and actual capital stock plus the amount of investment for replacing existing stock. Actual spending or gross investment then occurs as a lagged amount of planned investment distributed over time. Empirically, there is about a two-quarter lag between the investment decision and appropriations, followed by a 7-quarter distributed lag between appropriations and expenditures.

Investment plans for the years 1967 through 1985, as indicated by the fall surveys conducted by BEA and McGraw-Hill, were compared with forecasts of nonresidential fixed investment generated by this standard econometric model. Forecasts with the econometric model were made outside the data sample used to estimate the model, with the estimate being updated each year. However, the forecasts were based on actually realized data for final sales, taxes, and interest rates within the year being forecast. Thus, they assume more information than would be available with certainty at the time of a forecast.

In actuality, not very much more information was assumed because of the long lags in the investment process. The assumptions with respect to the values of the above variables within the forecasting period actually made very little difference. Only 20 percent of the change in nonresidential investment was determined by the values of final sales, taxes, and real interest rates within the year being forecast, with the remaining 80 percent determined by already available information.

ACCURACY OF THE FORECASTS

The accuracy of alternative forecasts of the rate of change in real nonresidential fixed investment is measured by the root mean squared error of the forecast, which is calculated simply as the square root of the average of the squared errors. For an unbiased forecast (in which the errors tend to cancel out over time), we can expect that 70 percent of the time the true value of the change in nonresidential fixed investment will fall within an interval around the forecast equal to plus or minus the root mean squared error, and 95 percent of the time it will fall within an interval equal to plus or minus twice the root mean squared error.

As a benchmark of minimum acceptable accuracy, we use a "naive" forecast of no change in the percentage rate of expansion in investment from one year to the next. The naive forecast has errors that tend to cancel out over time, as indicated by an average error of only −0.4 percentage points. But its root mean squared error is 9.6 percentage points. This means that the naive forecast of no change in the rate of expansion of investment is correct within plus or minus 9.6 percentage points 70 percent of the time, and plus or minus 19.2 percentage points 95 percent of the time.

Errors from the naive forecast are so large that they make the forecast virtually useless, but fortunately the errors from alternative forecasts are much smaller. The errors in forecasts made from the BEA and McGraw-Hill surveys are very similar to one another. Although the average error is slightly positive in both, statistical tests reveal that it is not large enough in either case to be significantly different from zero. In other words, it is possible that errors from both surveys would cancel out in a larger sample. Most importantly, the root mean squared error of a forecast from either survey is about 3.5 percentage points less than that for the naive forecast. In addition, statistical tests reveal that this improvement over the naive forecast is not simply attributable to chance.

The BEA and McGraw-Hill surveys therefore contain useful information on the outlook for nonresidential fixed investment. Nevertheless, the size of their forecast errors is still rather high. The BEA survey predicts the true value of the growth in nonresidential fixed investment within plus or minus 6.0 percentage points 70 percent of the time, and within plus or minus 12.0 percentage points 95 percent of the time; forecast errors for the McGraw-Hill survey are slightly larger.

One might conceivably reduce these forecast errors by combining the two surveys. But we do not find that any combination of the BEA and McGraw-Hill surveys does, in fact, reduce the root mean squared error of the forecast to less than that using the BEA survey alone. Although the BEA survey appears to be slightly more accurate, the McGraw-Hill survey contains essentially the same information, so nothing is gained by combining the two.

As it turns out, the forecast errors generated by the econometric model are considerably lower than those from these two surveys. The econometric model's forecast errors average to nearly zero and give a root mean squared error of 3.3 percentage points—about half that for the surveys. Thus, the econometric model forecasts the actual rate of expansion in real nonresidential fixed investment within 3.3 percentage points 70 percent of the time, and within 6.6 percentage points 95 percent of the time.

Moreover, neither the BEA nor the McGraw-Hill survey, either singly or in combination, can be used together with the econometric forecast to produce significantly lower forecast errors. Thus, in recent years, forecasts from a standard econometric model of business fixed investment have been characterized by relatively low errors, and surveys of planned capital spending have not added any significant amount of information to those forecasts.

FORECASTS FOR 1987

As mentioned earlier, the BEA survey forecasts a 0.2 percent improvement in real nonresidential fixed investment in 1987, while the McGraw-Hill survey indicates a 3.1 percent decline. Our analysis of the historical forecast errors indicates that each of these surveys contain useful information, and that nothing is gained by combining them. It also indicates, however, that an econometric model can do even better and that the smallest forecast errors would have been obtained simply by using an econometric model alone.

The econometric model gives a forecast of 4.9 percent real growth in nonresidential fixed investment for 1987—a more optimistic forecast than that provided by the surveys. This forecast is based upon the growth rate of real GNP (about 3.0 percent), and hence final sales, and the path for interest rates (relatively constant) predicted by the sample of forecasters polled by the American Statistical Association and the National Bureau of Economic Research. The greatest source of the strength in the forecast comes from the lagged effects of recent declines in interest rates adjusted for inflation. However, the forecast is not very sensitive to the exact assumptions made about the course of interest rates and GNP during 1987.

Although our analysis suggests that the econometric forecast alone should be relied upon, there is at least one special factor this year about which the surveys may contain some useful information and which may not be captured by the standard neoclassical model. That factor is the 50 percent decline in the price of oil that occurred in 1986. The decline in the price of oil already appears to have depressed the structures component of nonresidential fixed investment substantially through its impact on the expected profitability of oil drilling, and it is likely to continue to hold down investment in structures into 1987.

To capture the effect of oil prices on business fixed investment, we reestimated the neoclassical model to include the influence of the real price of oil on the desired amount of capital in structures. We find that a fall in the real price of oil has the expected negative effect on investment, and significantly so. Moreover, this modified neoclassical investment equation predicts only a 2.8 percent rate of growth in real nonresidential fixed investment from 1986 to 1987.

Taking into account the mild tendency of the surveys of planned investment to underestimate actual investment, this final econometric forecast is about the same as the BEA survey and somewhat more optimistic than the McGraw-Hill survey. However, the historical record indicates that the two surveys do not really add any significant information to that already contained in the econometric forecast. The most reliable forecast is the econometric one, and there is no evidence to suggest that forecast errors can be reduced any further by combining it with the others.

APPENDIX 16A

INPUT/OUTPUT FORECASTING

Economic forecasts based on input/output analysis can be generated through the use of an input/output table. An *input/output table* is a matrix with each row showing how the output of a particular sector of the economy is distributed among all the sectors of the economy, including final demand. In the same manner, each column indicates all the inputs used by a particular sector of the economy. All figures are in dollars. As a very simple illustration, if we have an economy that is composed of three industries, A, B, and C, an input/output table for this economy might look like Table 16A.1.

In this example, note that the output of any sector of the economy can be purchased by the same sector, purchased by other producing sectors, or consumed as a final good by individuals, government, or businesses. When the output of a supplying sector is consumed as a final good (i.e., it is not an input for further processing), the transaction is listed under "Final Demand" in the input/output table. Thus the input/output table records all transactions, including both interindustry and intraindustry activity in the economy (whereas in order to avoid double counting, the national income and product accounts deal only with transactions of final goods and services). Therefore, the input/output table affords the forecaster an opportunity to discern the markets in which the outputs of the industry involved are being purchased.

The "Value added" row shows the resource cost of the labor and capital used and the profit earned by the sector listed in the column heading. As you can see, the row total for each sector equals the column total for the respective sector. The reason for this equality is that the rows and columns of an input/output table are accounting identities; i.e., the sum of revenues for an industry equals the sum of costs incurred plus the profits earned.

Although several input/output studies have been developed (many econometric forecasting services provide industry forecasts generated by input/output analysis) at various levels of disaggregation for commercial and academic use, the most widely used are the input/output tables produced by

TABLE 16A.1   Input/Output Total Transactions Table

| Selling Industries | Purchasing Industries | | | Final Demand | Total |
	A	B	C		
A	10	50	20	100	180
B	5	10	60	30	105
C	70	5	0	45	120
Value added	95	40	40		
Total	180	105	120	175	

the U.S. Department of Commerce. Three different tables are available, with the most detailed tables containing four-digit SIC[1] data: the transaction table, the direct requirements table, and the total requirements table.

The *transaction table*, which most economists refer to as an input/ output table (as shown in Table 16A.1), indicates in each row how the output of goods and services of a given industry is distributed to all industries and final users in the economy. According to our example, industry A produces $180 of total output, of which $80 constitutes intermediate goods sold to other industries (including industry A) for use in producing products, while the remaining $100 of output constitutes finished goods that are sold to final consumers. Each column, in turn, shows the consumption of goods and services from all industries and the value added for a given industry.

The *direct requirements table*, which is derived from the input/output table, presents in each column the dollar amount of input each industry listed down the left side of the table must supply for the industry named in the column heading to produce one dollar of output. Table 16A.2 is the direct requirements table generated from our simple transaction table. The short-coming of the direct requirements table is that, as its name suggests, only direct requirements are shown. In other words, looking at Table 16A.2, you see that in order for industry C to produce $1.00 of output, $0.50 of input from industry B would be required, along with $0.167 of output from industry A. However, for industry B to produce $0.50 of output, it would in turn require inputs from industries A and C and also from its own industry, and so on ad infinitum. The direct requirements table does not take into account these "second round" effects of an increased output in one industry.

The *total requirements table*, often called the *Leontief inverse matrix*,

TABLE 16A.2   Direct Requirement Table for Input/Output Analysis

Selling Industries	Purchasing Industries		
	A	B	C
A	0.056	0.476	0.167
B	0.028	0.476	0.500
C	0.389	0.048	—

[1] SIC refers to standard industrial classifications, according to which business activities are arranged by type of product or service produced. See *Standard Industrial Classification Manual* (Washington, D.C.: Statistical Policy Division, Office of Management and Budget, U.S. Government Printing Office, 1972).

which is generated from data contained in the direct requirements table, shows in each column the amount of total input, both direct and indirect, that each industry listed down the left side of the table must supply for the industry named in the column heading to produce one dollar of output for final demand. For our example, these data are given in Table 16A.3.[2] Such a table can be used in conjunction with the econometric models in deriving industry forecasts.

The following relationship is fundamental to the input/output model. The total requirements matrix can be multiplied by the final demand vector [which is an $(n \times 1)$ matrix] to determine the total output for each industry. In the present example,

$$
\begin{array}{ccc}
\textit{Total} & \textit{Final} & \textit{Total} \\
\textit{Requirements} & \textit{Demand} & \textit{Demand} \\
\textit{Matrix} & \textit{Vector} & \textit{Vector}
\end{array}
$$

$$
\begin{bmatrix} 1.321 & 0.726 & 0.584 \\ 0.335 & 1.319 & 0.716 \\ 0.530 & 0.345 & 1.262 \end{bmatrix} \times \begin{bmatrix} 100 \\ 30 \\ 45 \end{bmatrix} = \begin{bmatrix} 180 \\ 105 \\ 120 \end{bmatrix}
$$

Note that this product corresponds to the total demand or total output for industries A, B, and C, respectively. While this result is trivial, consider its ramifications: (1) we can now find the total demand vector for any composite of industry final demand, and (2) given the total demand for each industry's production, we can further calculate the new transaction matrix, i.e., how much industry B will have to purchase from industries A and C and how much industry B will use of its output. The latter is determined by

TABLE 16A.3   Total Requirements Table for Input/Output Analysis

Selling Industries	Purchasing Industries		
	A	B	C
A	1.321	0.726	0.584
B	0.335	1.319	0.716
C	0.530	0.345	1.262

[2]The calculation of the values in the total requirements matrix is performed by solving for the elements of the $(I - A)^{-1}$ matrix, where I is an identity matrix and A is the $(n \times n)$ matrix of direct requirements. In our sample, $n = 3$, since we have three interrelated industry sectors.

multiplying each element in any column of the direct requirements matrix by the total demand for the corresponding industry. Recall that the direct requirements table shows in each column the amount of input each industry listed down the left side of the table must supply to enable the industry named in the column heading to produce a dollar of output. For example, multiplying each element of column B in the direct requirements matrix by 105 gives us 50, 10, and 5, the elements of the transaction matrix in column B $(105 \times 0.476 = 50; \ 105 \times 0.095 = 10; \ \text{and} \ 105 \times 0.048 = 5)$. This means, of course, that in order for industry B to produce \$105 of total output, industry B requires \$50 of output from industry A, \$10 of its own output, and \$5 of output from industry C.

Econometric models are used to generate final demand, with the large econometric models providing very detailed consumption forecasts. These forecasts of final demand are then "driven" through the total requirements table to arrive at total industry forecasts. One of the greatest benefits of working with the input/output table is that the forecasts thus derived are internally consistent. This type of analysis also quickly points out bottlenecks and supply problems in the economy.

For example, suppose we have a reliable econometric forecast of the final demand for industry C. If the final demand for industry C is expected to increase to 60, what will be the total outputs of industries A, B, and C? The answer is found by multiplying the total requirements matrix by the new final demand vector:

$$\begin{bmatrix} 1.321 & 0.726 & 0.584 \\ 0.335 & 1.319 & 0.716 \\ 0.530 & 0.345 & 1.262 \end{bmatrix} \times \begin{bmatrix} 100 \\ 30 \\ 60 \end{bmatrix} = \begin{bmatrix} 189 \\ 116 \\ 139 \end{bmatrix}$$

Therefore, the new total outputs for industries A, B, and C are 189, 116, and 139, respectively. These new output levels give the new total demand for each industry, including all "second round" effects. We can use these values, as indicated earlier, to construct a new transactions table showing how much each industry will demand from each of the industries. The revised transactions matrix is given in Table 16A.4.

Another benefit of input/output analysis and forecasts is that the forecaster is able to specify and analyze changes in technology by changing the direct requirement coefficients a_{ij}. These are the values given in the body of Table 16A.2. The a_{ij} values show the dollar amount of product from the industry in row i that is used by the industry in column j to produce a dollar worth of industry j's output. Estimating these direct requirement coefficients can be accomplished by using engineering studies and/or from historical data.

In summary, input/output analysis is a valuable tool for the forecaster because it gives a total picture of the markets for any group of commodities. In addition, forecasts generated by input/output analysis are internally consistent, making it possible for the forecaster to determine what effect changes in demand will have on various industries.

TABLE 16A.4 Input/Output Total Transactions Table for Revised Final Demand for Industry C

Selling Industries	Purchasing Industries			Final Demand	Total
	A	*B*	*C*		
A	11	55	23	100	180
B	5	11	70	30	116
C	73	6	0	60	139

Index